Eric and Robert's Principles for Success

by Eric Tyson and Robert S. Griswald

- **Real estate is a proven wealth-building vehicle.** Investing in rental properties can generate current income and significant tax benefits as well as build equity from appreciation over the years and decades.

- **Although many people can succeed investing in real estate, rental property investing isn't for everyone.** Consider your investment preferences and personal temperament before buying property. Do you have the time to devote to real estate investing? Are you comfortable troubleshooting problems or hiring a property manager?

- **Make sure you're financially fit before investing in rental properties.** Pay particular attention to your monthly budget and make sure that you have adequate insurance coverage. Most successful real estate investors build their real estate investment portfolio through saving money and then gradually buying properties over the years.

- **Don't underestimate the importance of establishing good credit.** The best returns on real estate rely upon the use of credit to obtain the leverage of using OPM (other people's money).

- **Your first (and often one of the best) real estate investment is buying a home to live in.** Real estate is the only investment that we know of that you can live in or rent to produce income. You can also derive large tax-free profits when you sell your principal residence at a higher price than you paid for it.

- **Focus on residential properties in the beginning.** Residential property is an attractive investment and is easier to understand, purchase, and manage than most other types of property. If you're a homeowner, you already have experience locating, purchasing, and maintaining residential property.

- **Among residential property options, our top recommendations are small apartment buildings and single-family homes.** Attached housing makes more sense for investors who don't want to deal with building maintenance and security issues. Attached-housing prices tend to perform best in developed urban environments.

- **Have your real estate team in place before you begin your serious property searching.** Line up a real estate agent, loan officer, tax advisor, lawyer, and so on early because the real estate investor with the best resources can identify the properties to ignore and those worthy of careful consideration. Move quickly — the speed at which you can close a transaction is an advantage in any type of market.

- **Look for properties in the path of progress.** Areas where new development or redevelopment is heading are where you want to be. The best real estate investment properties are ones that are well located and physically sound but cosmetically challenged and poorly managed.

- ✔ **You don't get rich trying to find no-money-down real estate investment deals.** Don't believe infomercials hucksters. Don't expect to buy top-notch rental properties that way.

- ✔ **Making at least a 20 to 25 percent down payment provides access to the best financing terms.** You can make smaller down payments — even as low as 10 percent or less — but you often pay a much higher interest rate, loan fees, and private mortgage insurance. Leverage, or the use of the lenders' money to cover the majority of your acquisition costs, can boost your rates of return. But too much leverage can be dangerous if the rental market turns and your debt expenses are high.

- ✔ **As the size and complexity of the deal increases, financing options become less attractive.** The financing options for larger apartment buildings (five or more units), commercial, retail, industrial, and raw land generally require more money down and/or higher interest rates and loan fees. But more advanced real estate investors can enjoy higher overall returns plus the benefits of easier management and stability from long-term tenants.

- ✔ **For low entry costs, consider real estate investment trusts (REITs) and lease options.** You can buy these exchange–traded securities (which can also be bought through REIT focused mutual funds) for a thousand dollars or less. With lease options, you begin by renting a property you may be interested in purchasing later, and a portion of your monthly rent goes towards the future purchase. If you can find a seller willing to provide financing, you can keep your down payment to a minimum.

- ✔ **We prefer the adage of "Location, location, value."** It clearly emphasizes location but also the importance of finding good value for your investment dollar. Owning real estate in up and coming areas with new development or renovated properties enhances finding and keeping good tenants and leads to greater returns. Properties in great locations with extensive deferred maintenance, especially aesthetic issues that can be inexpensively addressed are another great opportunity.

- ✔ **Make real estate investments close by.** Buy property within two hours away by your favorite mode of transportation. Venture further only when you really know another real estate market and regularly find yourself there for other reasons or you've found an excellent property manager.

- ✔ **Any decision about where to invest starts with an evaluation of the overall region's economic trends.** If the area isn't economically sound, then the likelihood for successful real estate investments are diminished.

- ✔ **You're purchasing a future income stream or cash flow when you buy an investment property.** What you pay for a property and the cash flow it generates makes a significant difference in the success of your investment. The key is identifying which properties sellers have under-priced.

- ✔ **Don't rely on the seller's numbers when evaluating a property's potential.** Speak directly with the seller to determine the history of the property and their motivation for selling. But, don't rely on historic operating results offered by the seller or broker. Develop your own numbers through evaluating the property with a team of qualified professionals who are specialists in the physical and fiscal management of real estate.

✔ **The buy-and-flip real estate investment strategy can work, but it also has a downside.** Buying and flipping can be a way to make quick money in real estate if you time your investments correctly in a rapidly rising real estate market. However, flipping can cause your profits to be taxed as ordinary income and you could lose during a market downturn.

✔ *Bottom line:* **Real estate professionals, and you, should value a property based on the projected Net Operating Income (NOI).** Project the NOI preferably for next few years. Projecting the NOI is time consuming and requires a lot of experience, especially if you plan property changes to increase income and/or reduce expenses.

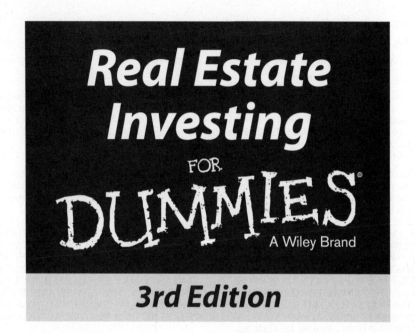

Real Estate Investing

FOR DUMMIES®

A Wiley Brand

3rd Edition

by Eric Tyson, MBA, and
Robert S. Griswold, MSBA

Real Estate Investing For Dummies®, 3rd Edition

Published by: **John Wiley & Sons, Inc.,** 111 River Street, Hoboken, NJ 07030-5774, www.wiley.com

Copyright © 2015 by John Wiley & Sons, Inc., Hoboken, New Jersey

Published simultaneously in Canada

For general information on our other products and services, please contact our Customer Care Department within the U.S. at 877-762-2974, outside the U.S. at 317-572-3993, or fax 317-572-4002. For technical support, please visit www.wiley.com/techsupport.

Wiley publishes in a variety of print and electronic formats and by print-on-demand. Some material included with standard print versions of this book may not be included in e-books or in print-on-demand. If this book refers to media such as a CD or DVD that is not included in the version you purchased, you may download this material at http://booksupport.wiley.com. For more information about Wiley products, visit www.wiley.com.

Library of Congress Control Number: 2014951023

ISBN 978-1-118-94821-7 (pbk); ISBN 978-1-118-94822-4 (ebk); ISBN 978-1-118-94823-1 (ebk)

Manufactured in the United States of America

10 9 8 7 6

Contents at a Glance

Table of Contents

Introduction

Welcome to *Real Estate Investing For Dummies, 3rd Edition!* We're delighted to be your tour guides. Throughout this book, we emphasize three fundamental cornerstones that we believe to be true:

- ✔ Real estate is one of the three time-tested ways for people of varied economic means to build wealth (the others are stocks and small business). Over the long-term (decades), you should be able to make an annualized return of at least 8 to 10 percent per year investing in real estate.

- ✔ Investing in real estate isn't rocket science but does require doing your homework. If you're sloppy doing your legwork, you're more likely to end up with inferior properties or to overpay. Our book clearly explains how to buy the best properties at a fair (or even below market value!) price. (Although we cover all types of properties, this book concentrates more on residential investment opportunities, which are more accessible and appropriate for nonexperts.)

- ✔ Although you should make money over the long-term investing in good real estate properties, you *can* lose money, especially in the short-term. Don't unrealistically expect real estate values to increase every year. Downturns in the local real estate prices may create temporary buying opportunities, but we aren't real estate day traders. When you invest in real estate for the long-term, which is what we advocate and practice, the occasional price declines should be merely bumps on an otherwise fruitful journey.

About This Book

Real Estate Investing For Dummies, 3rd Edition, covers tried and proven real estate investing strategies that real people, just like you, use to build wealth. Specifically, this book explains how to invest in single-family homes; detached and attached condominiums; small apartments including duplexes, triplexes, and multiple-family residential properties up to 20 to 30 units; commercial properties, including office, industrial, and retail; and raw (undeveloped) land. We also cover *indirect* real estate investments such as real estate investment trusts (REITs) that you can purchase through the major stock exchanges or a real estate mutual fund.

We've always relied on tried-and-true methods of real estate investing and our core advice is as true today as it was before the real estate downturn in the late 2000s. Our book is an especially solid reference in a down economy and will help you position yourself for the rebound.

If you expect us (in infomercial-like fashion) to tell you how to become an overnight multimillionaire, this is definitely *not* the book for you. And please allow us to save you money, disappointment, and heartache by telling you that such hucksters are only enriching themselves through their grossly overpriced tapes and seminars.

Unlike so many real estate book authors, we don't have an alternative agenda in writing this book. Many real estate investing books are nothing more than infomercials for high priced DVDs or seminars the author is selling. The objective of our book is to give you the best crash course in real estate investing so that if you choose to make investments in income-producing properties, you may do so wisely and confidently.

Here are some good reasons why we — Eric Tyson and Robert Griswold — are a dynamic duo on your side:

Robert Griswold has extensive hands-on experience as a real estate investor who has worked with properties of all types and sizes. He is also the author of *Property Management Kit For Dummies* (Wiley) and was the author of two popular syndicated real estate newspaper columns for more than 20 years. He has appeared for more than 15 years as the NBC-TV on-air real estate expert for Southern California. And for nearly 15 years, he was the host of the most popular and longest running real estate radio show in the country — *Real Estate Today! with Robert Griswold* on Clear Channel Communications.

Robert also holds the Counselor of Real Estate (CRE), Certified Commercial Investment Member (CCIM), Professional Community Association Manager (PCAM), and Certified Property Manager (CPM) designations. He earned a bachelor's degree and two master's degrees in real estate and related fields from the University of Southern California's Marshall School of Business.

Eric Tyson is a former financial counselor, lecturer, and coauthor of the national bestseller *Home Buying For Dummies* (John Wiley & Sons, Inc.), as well as the author or coauthor of numerous other bestselling books in the *For Dummies* series, such as *Personal Finance, Investing, Mutual Funds,* and *Small Business.*

Eric has counseled thousands of clients on a variety of personal finance, investment, and real estate quandaries and questions. A former management consultant to Fortune 500 financial service firms, Eric is dedicated to teaching people to better manage their personal finances. For more than

25 years, he has successfully invested in real estate and securities and started and managed several businesses. He earned an MBA at the Stanford Graduate School of Business and a bachelor's degree in economics at Yale.

Foolish Assumptions

Whenever an author sits down to write a book, he has a particular audience in mind. Because of this, he must make some assumptions about who his reader is and what that reader is looking for. Here are a few assumptions we've made about you:

- ✔ You're looking for a way to invest in real estate but don't know what types of properties and strategies are best.

- ✔ You're considering buying an investment property, be it a single-family home, a small apartment complex, or an office building, but your real estate experience is largely limited to renting an apartment or owning your own home.

- ✔ You may have a small amount of money already invested in real estate, but you're ready to go after bigger, better properties.

- ✔ You're looking for a way to diversify your investment portfolio.

If any of these descriptions hit home for you, you've come to the right place.

Icons Used in This Book

Throughout this book, you can find friendly and useful icons to enhance your reading pleasure and to note specific types of information. Here's what each icon means:

This icon points out something that can save you time, headaches, money, or all of the above!

Here we're trying to direct you away from blunders and boo-boos that others have made when investing in real estate.

This icon alerts you to hucksters, biased advice, and other things that can really cost you big bucks.

Here we point out potentially interesting but nonessential (skippable) stuff.

We use this icon to highlight when you should look into something on your own or with the assistance of a local professional.

This icon flags concepts and facts that we want to ensure you remember as you make your real estate investments.

Beyond This Book

In addition to the content of this book, you can access some related material online. We have posted the Cheat Sheet at www.dummies.com/cheatsheet/realestateinvesting that contains tips for investing. (You can also find the Cheat Sheet in the book, so feel free to share the online version with your friends and family and encourage them to read the book.)

We also share some additional bits of information and pointers at www.dummies.com/extras/realestateinvesting that can help you take your real estate investing to the next level. We also include a sample purchase agreement there.

Where to Go from Here

If you have the time and desire, we encourage you to read this book in its entirety. It provides you with a detailed picture of how to maximize your returns while minimizing your risks in the real estate market. But you may also choose to read selected portions. That's one of the great things (among many) about *For Dummies* books. You can readily pick and choose the information you read based on your individual needs. Just scan the table of contents or index for the topics that interest you the most.

Part I
Getting Started with Real Estate Investing

Head to www.dummies.com/cheatsheet/realestateinvesting for the online cheat sheet that includes Eric and Robert's principles of success.

In this part . . .

- ✔ Understand that real estate is just one of many available investment options for you and grasp why you may want to consider it in your investment portfolio.

- ✔ Identify the pros and cons of managing rental properties and how you can fit real estate into your overall personal financial plans.

- ✔ Examine the gamut of real estate options so that you know which ones may be better choices for you, depending on your circumstances.

- ✔ Separate fact from fiction when it comes to passive real estate investments (for example, real estate investment trusts) and riskier approaches like no money down and property flipping.

- ✔ Begin to assemble a team of competent professionals who can assist you with investing in real estate.

Chapter 1

Evaluating Real Estate as an Investment

. . . .

. . . .

*W*hen Robert first entered the real estate field while attending college decades ago, his father, a retired real estate attorney, advised that he use his monthly income primarily to pay day-to-day living expenses and allocate money each month into long-term financial investments like real estate. This solid advice has served Robert well over the years.

It's never too early or too late to formulate your own plan into a comprehensive wealth-building strategy. For many, such a strategy can help with the challenges of funding future education for children and ensuring a comfortable retirement.

The challenge involved with real estate is that it takes some real planning to get started. Contacting an investment company and purchasing some shares of your favorite mutual fund or stock is a lot easier than acquiring your first rental property. Buying property isn't that difficult, though. You just need a financial and real estate investment plan, a lot of patience, and the willingness to do some hard work, and you're on your way to building your own real estate empire!

In this chapter, we give you some information that can help you decide whether you have what it takes to make money *and* be comfortable with investing in real estate. We compare real estate investments to other investments. We provide some questions you need to ask yourself before making any decisions. And finally, we offer guidance on how real estate investments can fit into your overall personal financial plans. Along the way, we share our experience, insights, and thoughts on a long-term strategy for building wealth through real estate that virtually everyone can understand and actually achieve.

Understanding Real Estate's Income- and Wealth-Producing Potential

Compared with most other investments, good real estate can excel at producing periodic or monthly cash flow for property owners. So in addition to the longer-term appreciation potential, you can also earn investment income year in and year out. Real estate is a true growth *and* income investment.

The vast majority of people who don't make money in real estate make easily avoidable mistakes, which we help you avoid.

The following list highlights the major benefits of investing in real estate:

- ✔ **Tax-deferred compounding of value:** In real estate investing, the appreciation of your properties compounds *tax-deferred* during your years of ownership. You don't pay tax on this profit until you sell your property — and even then you can roll over your gain into another investment property and avoid paying taxes. (See the "Being aware of the tax advantages" section later in this chapter.)

- ✔ **Regular cash flow:** If you have property that you rent out, you have money coming in every month in the form of rents. Some properties, particularly larger multiunit complexes, may have some additional sources, such as from coin-operated washers and dryers.

When you own investment real estate, you should also expect to incur expenses that include your mortgage payment, property taxes, insurance, and maintenance. The interaction of the revenues coming in and the expenses going out is what tells you whether you realize positive operating profit each month.

- ✔ **Reduced income tax bills:** For income tax purposes, you also get to claim an expense that isn't really an out-of-pocket cost — depreciation. Depreciation enables you to reduce your current income tax bill and hence increase your cash flow from a property. (We explain this tax advantage and others later in the "Being aware of the tax advantages" section.)

✔ **Rate of increase of rental income versus overall expenses:** Over time, your operating profit, which is subject to ordinary income tax, should rise as you increase your rental prices faster than the rate of increase for your property's overall expenses. What follows is a simple example to show why even modest rental increases are magnified into larger operating profits and healthy returns on investment over time.

Suppose that you're in the market to purchase a single-family home that you want to rent out and that such properties are selling for about $200,000 in the area you've deemed to be a good investment. (*Note:* Housing prices vary widely across different areas but the following example should give you a relative sense of how a rental property's expenses and revenue change over time.) You expect to make a 20 percent down payment and take out a 30-year fixed rate mortgage at 6 percent for the remainder of the purchase price — $160,000. Here are the details:

[handwritten annotation: 20% = 40,000]

Monthly mortgage payment	$960
Monthly property tax	$200
Other monthly expenses (maintenance, insurance)	$200
Monthly rent	$1,400

In Table 1-1, we show you what happens with your investment over time. We assume that your rent and expenses (except for your mortgage payment, which is fixed) increase 3 percent annually and that your property appreciates a conservative 4 percent per year. (For simplification purposes, we ignore depreciation in this example. If we had included the benefit of depreciation, it would further enhance the calculated returns.)

Table 1-1	How a Rental Property's Income and Wealth Build Over Time			

Year	Monthly Rent	Monthly Expenses	Property Value	Mortgage Balance
0	$1,400	$1,360	$200,000	$160,000
5	$1,623	$1,424	$243,330	$148,960
10	$1,881	$1,498	$296,050	$133,920
20	$2,529	$1,682	$438,225	$86,400
30	$3,398	$1,931	$648,680	$0
31	$3,500	$1,000	$674,625	$0

Now, notice what happens over time. When you first buy the property, the monthly rent and the monthly expenses are about equal. By year five, the monthly income exceeds the expenses by about $200 per month. Consider why this happens — your largest monthly expense, the mortgage payment, doesn't increase. So, even though we assume that the rent increases just 3 percent per year, which is the same rate of increase assumed for your nonmortgage expenses, the compounding of rental inflation begins to produce larger and larger cash flow to you, the property owner. Cash flow of $200 per month may not sound like much, but consider that this $2,400 annual income is from an original $40,000 investment. Thus, by year five, your rental property is producing a 6 percent return on your down payment investment. (And remember, if you factor in the tax deduction for depreciation, your cash flow and return are even higher.)

In addition to the monthly cash flow from the amount that the rent exceeds the property's expenses, also look at the last two columns in Table 1-1 to see what has happened by year five to your *equity* (the difference between market value and mortgage balance owed) in the property. With just a 4 percent annual increase in market value, your $40,000 in equity (the down payment) has more than doubled to $94,370 ($243,330 – 148,960).

By years 10 and 20, you can see the further increases in your monthly cash flow and significant expansion in your property's equity. By year 30, the property is producing more than $1,400 per month cash flow and you're now the proud owner of a mortgage-free property worth more than triple what you paid for it!

After you get the mortgage paid off in year 30, take a look at what happens in year 31 and beyond to your monthly expenses (big drop) and therefore your cash flow (big increase).

Recognizing the Caveats of Real-Estate Investing

Despite all its potential, real estate investing isn't lucrative at all times and for all people — here's a quick outline of the biggest caveats that accompany investing in real estate:

- ✔ **Few home runs:** Your likely returns from real estate won't approach the home runs that the most accomplished entrepreneurs achieve in the business world.

- ✔ **Upfront operating profit challenges:** Unless you make a large down payment, your monthly operating profit may be small, nonexistent, or negative in the early years of rental property ownership. During soft periods in the local economy, rents may rise more slowly than your expenses or they may even fall. That's why you must ensure that you can weather financially tough times. In the worst cases, we've seen rental property owners lose both their investment property and their homes. See the section "Fitting Real Estate into Your Plans" later in this chapter.

✓ **Ups and downs:** You're not going to earn an 8 to 10 percent return every year. Although you have the potential for significant profits, owning real estate isn't like owning a printing press at the U.S. Treasury. Like stocks and other types of ownership investments, real estate goes through down as well as up periods. Most people who make money investing in real estate do so because they invest and hold property over many years.

✓ **Relatively high transaction costs:** If you buy a property and then want out a year or two later, you may find that even though it has appreciated in value, much (if not all) of your profit has been wiped away by the high transaction costs. Typically, the costs of buying and selling — which include real estate agent commissions, loan fees, title insurance, and other closing costs — amount to about 10 to 15 percent of the purchase price of a property. So, although you may be elated if your property appreciates 15 percent in value in short order, you may not be so thrilled to realize that if you sell the property, you may not have any greater return than if you had stashed your money in a lowly bank account.

✓ **Tax implications:** Last, but not least, when you make a positive net return or profit on your real estate investment, the federal and state governments are waiting with open hands for their share. Throughout this book, we highlight ways to improve your after-tax returns. As we stress more than once, the profit you have left after Uncle Sam takes his bite (not your pretax income) is all that really matters.

These drawbacks shouldn't keep you from exploring real estate investing as an option; rather, they simply reinforce the need to really know what you're getting into with this type of investing and whether it's a good match for you. The rest of this chapter takes you deeper into an assessment of real estate as an investment as well as introspection about your goals, interests, and abilities.

Comparing Real Estate to Other Investments

Surely you've considered or heard about many different investments over the years. To help you grasp and understand the unique characteristics of real estate, we compare and contrast real estate's attributes with those of other wealth-building investments like stocks and small business.

Returns

Clearly, a major reason that many people invest in real estate is for the healthy total *returns* (which include ongoing cash flow and the appreciation of the property). Real estate often generates robust long-term returns because, like stocks and small business, it's an *ownership investment.* By that, we mean that real estate is an asset that has the ability to produce periodic income *and* gain or profits upon refinancing or sale.

Our research and experience suggest that total real estate investment returns are comparable to those from stocks — about 8 to 10 percent annually. Over recent decades, the average annual return on real estate investment trusts (REITs), publicly traded companies that invest in income-producing real estate such as apartment buildings, office complexes, and shopping centers have appreciated at about this pace as well. See our discussion of REITs in Chapter 4.

And you can earn long-term returns better than 10 percent per year if you select excellent properties in the best areas, hold them for several years, and manage them well.

How leverage affects your real estate returns

Real estate is different from most other investments in that you can typically borrow (finance) up to 70 to 80 percent or more of the value of the property. Thus, you can use your small down payment of 20 to 30 percent of the purchase price to buy, own, and control a much larger investment. (During market downturns, lenders tighten requirements and may require larger down payments than they do during good times.) So when your real estate increases in value (which is what you hope and expect), you make money on your investment as well as on the money that you borrowed. That's what we mean when we say that the investment returns from real estate are enhanced due to *leverage.*

Take a look at this simple example. Suppose you purchase a property for $150,000 and make a $30,000 down payment. Over the next three years, imagine that the property appreciates 10 percent to $165,000. Thus, you have a profit (on paper) of $15,000 ($165,000 – $150,000) on an investment of just $30,000. In other words, you've made a 50 percent return on your investment. (**Note**: We ignore *cash flow* — whether your rental income that you collect from the property exceeds the expenses that you pay or vice versa, and the tax benefits associated with rental real estate.)

Remember, leverage magnifies all of your returns, and those returns aren't always positive! If your $150,000 property decreases in value to $135,000, even though it has only dropped 10 percent in value, you actually lose (on paper) 50 percent of your original $30,000 investment. (In case you care, and it's okay if you don't, some wonks apply the terms *positive leverage* and *negative leverage.*) Please see the "Understanding Real Estate's Income- and Wealth-Producing Potential" section earlier in this chapter for a more detailed example of investment property profit and return.

Risk

Real estate doesn't always rise in value — witness the decline occurring in most parts of the U.S. during the late 2000s. That said, market values for real estate generally don't suffer from as much volatility as stock prices do. You may recall how the excitement surrounding the rapid sustained increase of technology and Internet stock prices in the late 1990s turned into the dismay and agony of those same sectors' stock prices crashing in the early 2000s. Many stocks in this industry, including those of leaders in their niches, saw their stock prices plummet by 80 percent, 90 percent, or more. Generally, you don't see that kind of dramatic rollercoaster shifts in values over the short run with the residential income property real estate market.

However, keep in mind (especially if you tend to be concerned about shorter-term risks) that real estate can suffer from declines of 10 percent, 20 percent, or more. If you make a down payment of say, 20 percent, and want to sell your property after a 10 to 15 percent price decline, you may find that all (as in 100 percent) of your invested dollars (down payment) are wiped out after you factor in transaction costs. So you can lose everything.

You can greatly reduce and minimize your risk investing in real estate through buying and holding property for many years (seven to ten or more).

Liquidity

Liquidity — the ease and cost with which you can sell and get your money out of an investment — is one of real estate's shortcomings. Real estate is relatively *illiquid:* You can't sell a piece of property with the same speed with which you whip out your ATM card and withdraw money from your bank account or sell a stock or an exchange-traded fund with a phone call or click of your computer's mouse.

We actually view real estate's relative illiquidity as a strength, certainly compared with stocks that people often trade in and out of because doing so is so easy and seemingly cheap. As a result, many stock market investors tend to lose sight of the long term and miss out on the bigger gains that accrue to patient buy-and-stick-with-it investors. Because you can't track the value of investment real estate daily on your computer, and because real estate takes considerable time, energy, and money to sell, you're far more likely to buy and hold onto your properties for the longer term.

Although real estate investments are generally less liquid than stocks, they're generally more liquid than investments made in your own or someone else's small business. People need a place to live and businesses need a place to operate, so there's always demand for real estate (although the supply of such available properties can greatly exceed the demand in some areas during certain time periods).

Capital requirements

Although you can easily get started with traditional investments such as stocks and mutual funds with a few hundred or thousand dollars, the vast majority of quality real estate investments require far greater investments — usually on the order of tens of thousands of dollars. (We devote an entire part of this book — Part II, to be precise — to showing you how to raise capital and secure financing.)

If you're one of the many people who don't have that kind of money burning a hole in your pocket, don't despair. We present you with lower cost real estate investment options. Among the simplest low-cost real estate investment options are real estate investment trusts (REITs). You can buy these as exchange-traded stocks or invest in a portfolio of REITs through an REIT mutual fund (see Chapter 4).

Diversification value

An advantage of holding investment real estate is that its value doesn't necessarily move in tandem with other investments, such as stocks or small-business investments that you hold. You may recall, for example, the massive stock market decline in the early 2000s. In most communities around America, real estate values were either steady or actually rising during this horrendous period for stock prices.

However, real estate prices and stock prices, for example, *can* move down together in value (witness the severe recession and stock market drop that took hold in 2008). Sluggish business conditions and lower corporate profits can depress stock *and* real estate prices.

Opportunities to add value

Although you may not know much about investing in the stock market, you may have some good ideas about how to improve a property and make it more valuable. You can fix up a property or develop it further and raise the rental income accordingly. Perhaps through legwork, persistence, and good negotiating skills, you can purchase a property below its fair market value.

Relative to investing in the stock market, tenacious and savvy real estate investors can more easily buy property in the private real estate market at below fair market value because the real estate market is somewhat less efficient and some owners don't realize the value of their income property or they need to sell quickly. Theoretically, you can do the same in the stock market, but the scores of professional, full-time money managers who analyze the public market for stocks make finding bargains more difficult. We help you identify properties that you can add value to in Part III.

Being aware of the tax advantages

Real estate investment offers numerous tax advantages. In this section, we compare and contrast investment property tax issues with those of other investments.

Deductible expenses (including depreciation)

Owning a property has much in common with owning your own small business. Every year, you account for your income and expenses on a tax return. (We cover all the taxing points about investment properties in Chapter 18.) For now, we want to remind you to keep good records of your expenses in purchasing and operating rental real estate. (Check out Chapter 17 for more information on all things accounting.) One expense that you get to deduct for rental real estate on your tax return — depreciation — doesn't actually involve spending or outlaying money. *Depreciation* is an allowable tax deduction for buildings, because structures wear out over time. Under current tax laws, residential real estate is depreciated over 27½ years (commercial buildings are less favored in the tax code and can be depreciated over 39 years). Residential real estate is depreciated over shorter time periods because it has traditionally been a favored investment in our nation's tax laws.

Tax-free rollovers of rental property profits

When you sell a stock, mutual fund, or exchange-traded investment that you hold outside a retirement account, you must pay tax on your profits. By contrast, you can avoid paying tax on your profit when you sell a rental property if you roll over your gain into another like-kind investment real estate property.

The rules for properly making one of these 1031 exchanges are complex and involve third parties. We cover 1031 exchanges in Chapter 18. Make sure that you find an attorney and/or tax advisor who is an expert at these transactions to ensure that you meet the technical and strict timing requirements so everything goes smoothly (and legally).

If you don't roll over your gain, you may owe significant taxes because of how the IRS defines your gain. For example, if you buy a property for $200,000 and sell it for $550,000, you not only owe tax on the gain from the increased property value, but you also owe tax on an additional amount, the property's depreciation you used during your ownership. The amount of depreciation that you deduct on your tax returns reduces the original $200,000 purchase price, making the taxable difference that much larger. For example, if you deducted $125,000 for depreciation over the years that you owned the property, you owe tax on the difference between the sale price of $550,000 and $75,000 ($200,000 purchase price – $125,000 depreciation).

Deferred taxes with installment sales

Installment sales are a complex method that can be used to defer your tax bill when you sell an investment property at a profit and you don't buy another rental property. With such a sale, you play the role of banker and provide financing to the buyer. In addition to often collecting a competitive interest rate from the seller, you only have to pay capital gains tax as you receive proceeds over time from the sale. For details, please see Chapter 18.

Special tax credits for low-income housing and old buildings

If you invest in and upgrade low-income housing or certified historic buildings, you can gain special tax credits. The credits represent a direct reduction in your tax bill from expenditures to rehabilitate and improve such properties. These tax credits exist to encourage investors to invest in and fix up old or run-down buildings that likely would continue to deteriorate otherwise. The IRS has strict rules governing what types of properties qualify. See IRS Form 3468 to discover more about these credits.

Determining Whether You Should Invest in Real Estate

We believe that most people can succeed at investing in real estate if they're willing to do their homework, which includes selecting top real estate professionals. In the sections that follow, we ask several important questions to help you decide whether you have what it takes to succeed and be happy with real estate investments that involve managing property. Income-producing real estate isn't a passive investment.

Do you have sufficient time?

Purchasing and owning investment real estate and being a landlord is time consuming. The same way an uninformed owner can sell his property for less than it's worth, if you fail to do your homework before purchasing property, you can end up overpaying or buying real estate with a slew of problems. Finding competent and ethical real estate professionals takes time. (We guide you through the process in Chapter 6.) Investigating communities, neighborhoods, and zoning also soaks up plenty of hours (information on performing this research is located in Chapter 10), as does examining tenant issues with potential properties (see Chapter 11).

As for managing a property, you can hire a property manager to interview tenants, collect the rent, and solve problems such as leaky faucets and broken appliances, but doing so costs money and still requires some of your time.

If you're stretched too thin due to work and family responsibilities, real estate investing may not be for you. You may want to look into the less time-intensive real estate investments discussed in Chapters 3 and 4.

Can you deal with problems?

Challenges and problems inevitably occur when you try to buy a property. Purchase negotiations can be stressful and frustrating. You can also count on some problems coming up when you own and manage investment real estate. Most tenants won't care for a property the way property owners do.

If every little problem (especially those that you think may have been caused by your tenants) causes you distress, at a minimum, you should only own rental property with the assistance of a property manager. You should also question whether you're really going to be happy owning investment property. The financial rewards come well down the road, but you live the day-to-day ownership headaches immediately.

Does real estate interest you?

In our experience, some of the best real estate investors have a curiosity and interest in real estate. If you don't already possess it, such an interest and curiosity *can* be cultivated — and this book may just do the trick.

On the other hand, some people simply aren't comfortable investing in rental property. For example, if you've had experience and success with stock market investing, you may be uncomfortable venturing into real estate investments. Some people we know are on a mission to start their own business and may prefer to channel the time and money into that outlet.

Can you handle market downturns?

Real estate investing isn't for the faint of heart. Buying and holding real estate is a whole lot of fun when prices and rents are rising. But market downturns happen, and they test you emotionally as well as financially.

Consider the real estate market price declines that happened in most communities and types of property in the late 2000s. Such drops can present attractive buying opportunities for those with courage and cash.

None of us has a crystal ball though so don't expect to be able to buy at the precise bottom of prices and sell at the exact peak of your local market. Even if you make a smart buy now, you'll inevitably end up holding some of your investment property during a difficult market (recessions where you have trouble finding and retaining quality tenants, where rents and property values may fall rather than rise). Do you have the financial wherewithal to handle such a downturn? How have you handled other investments when their values have fallen?

Fitting Real Estate into Your Plans

For most nonwealthy people, purchasing investment real estate has a major impact on their overall personal financial situation. So, before you go out to buy property, you should inventory your money life and be sure your fiscal house is in order. This section explains how you can do just that.

Ensure your best personal financial health

If you're trying to improve your physical fitness by exercising, you may find that eating lots of junk food and smoking are barriers to your goal. Likewise, investing in real estate or other growth investments such as stocks while you're carrying high-cost consumer debt (credit cards, auto loans, and so on) and spending more than you earn impedes your financial goals.

Before you set out to invest in real estate, pay off all your consumer debt. Not only will you be financially healthier for doing so, but you'll also enhance your future mortgage applications.

Eliminate wasteful and unnecessary spending; analyze your monthly spending to identify target areas for reduction. This practice enables you to save more and better afford making investments including real estate. Robert's and Eric's parents also taught the importance of living below your means. As Charles Dickens said, "Annual income twenty pounds; annual expenditures nineteen pounds; result, happiness. Annual income twenty pounds; annual expenditure twenty pounds; result, misery."

Protect yourself with insurance

Regardless of your real estate investment desires and decisions, you absolutely must have comprehensive insurance for yourself and your major assets, including

- **Health insurance:** Major medical coverage protects you from financial ruin if you have a major accident or illness that requires significant hospital and other medical care.

- **Disability insurance:** For most working people, their biggest asset is their future income-earning ability. Disability insurance replaces a portion of your employment earnings if you're unable to work for an extended period of time due to an incapacitating illness or injury.

- **Life insurance:** If loved ones are financially dependent upon you, term life insurance, which provides a lump sum death benefit, can help to replace your employment earnings if you pass away.

- **Homeowner's insurance:** Not only do you want homeowner's insurance to protect you against the financial cost due to a fire or other home-damaging catastrophe, but such coverage also provides you with liability protection. (After you buy and operate a rental property with tenants, you should obtain rental owner's insurance. See Chapter 16 for more information).

- **Auto insurance:** This coverage is similar to homeowner's coverage in that it insures a valuable asset and also provides liability insurance should you be involved in an accident.

- **Excess liability (umbrella) insurance:** This relatively inexpensive coverage, available in million dollar increments, adds on to the modest liability protection offered on your basic home and auto policies, which is inadequate for more-affluent people.

Nobody enjoys spending hard-earned money on insurance. However, having proper protection gives you peace of mind and financial security, so don't put off reviewing and securing needed policies. For assistance, see the latest edition of Eric's *Personal Finance For Dummies* (John Wiley & Sons, Inc.).

Consider retirement account funding

If you're not taking advantage of your retirement accounts (such as 401(k)s, 403(b)s, SEP-IRAs, and Keoghs), you may be missing out on some terrific tax benefits. Funding retirement accounts gives you an immediate tax deduction when you contribute to them. And some employer accounts offer "free" matching money — but you've got to contribute to earn the matching money.

In comparison, you derive no tax benefits while you accumulate your down payment for an investment real estate purchase (or other investment such as for a small business). Furthermore, the operating positive cash flow or income from your real estate investment is subject to ordinary income taxes as you earn it. To be fair and balanced, we must mention here that investment real estate offers numerous tax benefits, which we detail in the "Being aware of the tax advantages" section earlier in this chapter.

Think about asset allocation

With money that you invest for the longer term, you should have an overall game plan in mind. Fancy-talking financial advisors like to use buzzwords such as *asset allocation,* a term that indicates what portion of your money you have invested in different types of investment vehicles, such as stocks and real estate (for appreciation or growth) versus lending vehicles, such as bonds and CDs (which produce current income).

Here's a simple way to calculate asset allocation for long-term investments: Subtract your age from 110. The result is the percentage of your long-term money that you should invest in ownership investments for appreciation. So, for example, a 40-year-old would take 110 minus 40 equals 70 percent in growth investments such as stocks and real estate. If you want to be more aggressive, subtract your age from 120; a 40-year-old would then have 80 percent in growth investments.

As you gain more knowledge, assets, and diversification of growth assets, you're in a better position to take on more risk. Just be sure you're properly covered with insurance as discussed earlier in the section "Protect yourself with insurance."

These are simply guidelines, not hard-and-fast rules or mandates. If you want to be more aggressive and are comfortable taking on greater risk, you can invest higher portions in ownership investments.

As you consider asset allocation, when classifying your investments, determine and use your *equity* in your real estate holdings, which is the market value of property less outstanding mortgages. For example, suppose that prior to buying an investment property, your long-term investments consist of the following:

Stocks	$150,000
Bonds	$50,000
CDs	$50,000
Total	$250,000

So, you have 60 percent in ownership investments ($150,000) and 40 percent in lending investments ($50,000 + $50,000). Now, suppose you plan to purchase a $300,000 income property making a $75,000 down payment. Because you've decided to bump up your ownership investment portion to make your money grow more over the years, you plan to use your maturing CD balance and sell some of your bonds for the down payment. After your real estate purchase, here's how your investment portfolio looks:

Stocks	$150,000
Real estate	$75,000 ($300,000 property – $225,000 mortgage)
Bonds	$25,000
Total	$250,000

Thus, after the real estate purchase, you've got 90 percent in ownership investments ($150,000 + $75,000) and just 10 percent in lending investments ($25,000). Such a mix may be appropriate for someone under the age of 50 who desires an aggressive investment portfolio positioned for long-term growth potential.

Become your own landlord

Many real estate investors are actually involved in other activities as their primary source of income. Ironically, many of these business owners come to realize the benefits of real estate investing but miss the single greatest opportunity that is right before their eyes — the prospect of being their own landlord. Robert has advised many business owners that they should purchase the buildings occupied by their own businesses and essentially pay the rent to themselves. If you own a business that rents, do yourself a favor — consider becoming your own landlord! Refer to Chapter 15 for more information.

Chapter 2

Covering Common Real Estate Investments

*I*f you lack substantial experience investing in real estate, you should avoid more esoteric and complicated properties and strategies. In this chapter, we discuss the more accessible and easy-to-master income-producing property options. In particular, *residential income property,* which we discuss in the next section, can be an attractive real estate investment for many people. Residential housing is easier to understand, purchase, and manage than most other types of property, such as office, industrial, and retail property. If you're a homeowner, you already have experience locating, purchasing, and maintaining residential property.

In addition to discussing the pros and cons of investing in residential income property, we add insights as to which may be the most appropriate and profitable for you and touch on the topics of investing in commercial property as well as undeveloped land.

Identifying the Various Ways to Invest in Residential Income Property

The first (and one of the best) real estate investments for many people is a home in which to live. In this section, we cover the investment possibilities inherent in buying a home for your own use, including potential profit to be had from converting your home to a rental or fixing it up and selling it. We also give you some pointers on how to profit from owning your own vacation home.

Buying a place of your own

During your adult life, you're going to need a roof over your head for many decades. And real estate is the only investment that you can live in or rent out to produce income. A stock, bond, or mutual fund doesn't work too well as a roof over your head!

Unless you expect to move within the next few years, buying a place may make good long-term financial sense. (Even if you need to relocate, you may decide to continue owning the property and use it as a rental property.) Owning usually costs less than renting over the long haul and allows you to build *equity* (the difference between market value and the current balance of the mortgage loans against the property) in an asset.

Under current tax law, you can also pocket substantial tax-free profits when you sell your home for more than you originally paid plus the money you sunk into improvements during your ownership. Specifically, single taxpayers can realize up to a $250,000 tax-free capital gain; married couples filing jointly get up to $500,000. In order to qualify for this homeowner's *gains tax exemption,* you (or your spouse if you're married) must have owned the home and used it as your primary residence for a minimum of 24 months out of the past 60 months. The 24 months doesn't have to be continuous. Additionally, the IRS now provides for pro-rata (proportionate) credit based on hardship or change of employment. Also note that the full exemption amounts are reduced proportionately for the length of time you rented out your home over the five-year period referenced above.

Some commentators have stated that your home isn't an investment, because you're not renting it out. We respectfully disagree: Consider the fact that many people move to a less costly home when they retire (because it's smaller and/or because it's in a lower cost area). Trading down to a lower priced property in retirement frees up equity that has built up over many years of homeownership. This money can be used to supplement your retirement income and for any other purpose your heart desires. Your home is an investment because it can appreciate in value over the years, and you can use that money toward your financial or personal goals. The most recent version of *Home Buying For Dummies* (John Wiley & Sons, Inc.), which Eric cowrote with residential real estate expert Ray Brown, can help you make terrific home buying decisions.

Converting your home to a rental

Turning your current home into a rental property when you move is a simple way to buy and own more properties. You can do this multiple times (as you move out of homes you own over the years), and you can do this strategy of acquiring rental properties not only with a house, but also with a duplex or other small rental property where you reside in one of the units. This approach is an option if you're already considering investing in real estate (either now or in the future), and you can afford to own two or more properties. Holding onto your current home when you're buying a new one is more advisable if you're moving within the same area so that you're close by to manage the property. This approach presents a number of positives:

- ✔ You save the time and cost of finding a separate rental property, not to mention the associated transaction costs.

- ✔ You know the property and have probably taken good care of it and perhaps made some improvements.

- ✔ You know the target market because the home appealed to you.

Some people unfortunately make the mistake of holding onto their current home for the wrong reasons when they buy another. This situation often happens when a homeowner must sell their home in a depressed market. Nobody likes to lose money and sell their home for less than they paid for it. Thus, some owners hold onto their homes until prices recover. If you plan to move and want to keep your current home as a long-term investment (rental) property, you can. If you fully convert your home to rental property and use it that way for years before selling it, after you do sell you can either take advantage of the lower long-term capital gains rates or do a tax deferred exchange. For tax purposes, you get to deduct depreciation and all of the write-offs during the ownership and you can shelter up to $25,000 in income from active sources subject to income eligibility requirements. (Please see Chapter 18 for more details.)

Turning your home into a *short-term* rental, however, is usually a bad move because:

- ✔ You may not want the responsibilities of being a landlord, yet you force yourself into the landlord business when you convert your home into a rental.

- ✔ You owe tax on the sales' profit if your property is classified for tax purposes as a rental when you sell it and don't buy another rental property. (You can purchase another rental property through a 1031 exchange to defer paying taxes on your profit. See the discussion in Chapter 18.)

Effective tax year 2009, you lose some of the capital gains tax exclusion if you sell your home and you had rented it out for a portion of the five-year period prior to selling it. For example, if you rented your home for two of the last five years, you may only exclude 60 percent of your gain (up to the maximums of $250,000 for single taxpayers and $500,000 for married couples filing jointly), whereas the other 40 percent is taxed as a long-term capital gain. Also be aware that when you sell a home previously rented and are accounting for the sale on your tax return, you have to recapture the depreciation taken during the rental period.

Investing and living in well-situated fixer-uppers

Serial home selling is a variation on the tried-and-true real estate investment strategy of investing in well-located fixer-upper homes where you can invest your time, sweat equity, and materials to make improvements that add more value than they cost. The only catch is that you must actually move into the fixer-upper for at least 24 months to earn the full homeowner's capital gains exemption of up to $250,000 for single taxpayers and $500,000 for married couples filing jointly (as we cover in the "Buying a place of your own" section earlier in this chapter).

Be sure to buy a home in need of that special TLC in a great neighborhood where you're willing to live for 24 months or more! But if you're a savvy investor, you would've invested in a great neighborhood anyway.

Here's a simple example to illustrate the potentially significant benefits of this strategy. You purchase a fixer-upper for $275,000 that becomes your principal residence, and then over the next 24 months you invest $25,000 in improvements (paint, repairs, landscaping, appliances, decorator items, and so on) and you also invest the amount of sweat equity that suits your skills and wallet. You now have one of the nicer homes in the neighborhood, and you can sell this home for a net price of $400,000 after your transaction costs. With your total investment of $300,000 ($275,000 plus $25,000), your efforts have earned you a $100,000 profit completely tax-free. Thus, you've earned an average of $50,000 per year, which isn't bad for a tax-exempt second income without strict office hours. (Note that many states also allow you to avoid state income taxes on the sale of your personal residence, using many of the same requirements as the federal tax laws.)

Now, some cautions are in order here. This strategy is clearly not for everyone interested in making money from real estate investments. We recommend that you bypass this strategy if any of the following apply:

- ✔ You're unwilling or reluctant to live through redecorating, minor remodeling, or major construction.

- ✔ You dislike having to move every few years.

- ✔ You're not experienced or comfortable with identifying undervalued property and improving it.

- ✔ You lack a financial cushion to withstand a significant downturn in your local real estate market as happened in numerous parts of the country during the mid-to-late 2000s.

- ✔ You don't have the budget to hire a professional contractor to do the work, and you don't have the free time or the home improvement skills needed to enhance the value of a home.

One final caution: Beware of transaction costs. The expenses involved with buying and selling property — such as real estate agent commissions, loan fees, title insurance, and so forth — can gobble up a large portion of your profits. With most properties, the long-term appreciation is what drives your returns. Consider keeping homes you buy and improve as long-term investment properties.

Purchasing a vacation home

Many people of means expand their real estate holdings by purchasing a *vacation home* — a home in an area where they enjoy taking pleasure trips. For most people, buying a vacation home is more of a consumption decision than it is an investment decision. That's not to say that you can't make a profit from owning a second home. However, potential investment returns shouldn't be the main reason you buy a second home.

For example, we know a family that lived in Pennsylvania and didn't particularly like the hot and humid summer weather. They enjoyed taking trips and staying in various spots in northern New England and eventually bought a small home in New Hampshire. Their situation highlights the pros and cons that many people face with vacation or second homes. The obvious advantage this family enjoyed in having a vacation home is that they no longer had the hassle of securing accommodations when they wanted to enjoy some downtime. Also, after they arrived at their home away from home, they were, well, home! Things were just as they expected — with no surprises, unless squirrels had taken up residence on their porch.

The downsides to vacation homes can be numerous, as our Pennsylvania friends found, including

- ✔ **Expenses:** With a second home, you have the range of nearly all of the costs of a primary home — mortgage interest, property taxes, insurance, repairs and maintenance, utilities, and so on.

- ✔ **Property management:** When you're not at your vacation home, things can go wrong. A pipe can burst, for example, and the mess may not be found for days or weeks. Unless the property is close to a good neighbor or other kind person willing to keep an eye on it for you, you may incur the additional expense of paying a property manager to watch the property for you.

- ✔ **Lack of rental income:** Most people don't rent out their vacation homes, thus negating the investment property income stream that contributes to the returns real estate investors enjoy (see Chapter 1). If your second home is in a vacation area where you have access to plenty of short-term renters, you or your designated property manager can rent out the property. However, this entails all of the headaches and hassles of having many short-term renters. (But you do gain the tax advantages of depreciation and all expenses as with other rental properties.)

✔ **Obligation to use:** Some second homeowners we know complain about feeling forced to use their vacation homes. Oftentimes in marriages, one spouse likes the vacation home much more than the other spouse (or one spouse enjoys working on the second home rather than enjoying the home itself).

Before we close out this section on vacation homes, we want to share a few tax tips, as found in the current tax code:

✔ If you retain your vacation home or secondary home as personal property, forgoing the large income streams and tax write-offs for depreciation and operating expenses associated with rental properties, you can still make a nice little chunk of tax-free cash on the side. The current tax code permits you to rent the property for up to 14 days a year — and that income is *tax-free!* You don't have to claim it. Yes, you read that right. And you can still deduct the costs of ownership, including mortgage interest and property taxes, as you do for all other personal properties.

✔ If you decide to maintain the property as a rental (you rent it out for more than 14 days a year), you, as the property owner, can still use the rental property as a vacation home for up to 14 days a year, or a maximum of 10 percent of the days gainfully rented, whichever is greater, and the property still qualifies as a rental. Also, all days spent cleaning or repairing the rental home don't count as personal use days — so that's why you paint for a couple of hours every afternoon and spend the morning fishing!

Before you buy a second home, weigh all the pros and cons. If you have a spouse or partner with whom you're buying the property, have a candid discussion. Also consult with your tax advisor for other tax-saving strategies for your second home or vacation home. And please see Chapter 18 for more tax related information on rental properties.

Paying for condo hotels and timeshares

Timeshares, a concept created in the 1960s, are a form of ownership or right to use a property. A more recent trend in real estate investing is condo hotels, which in many ways are simply a new angle on the old concept of timeshares. A condo hotel looks and operates just like any other first-class hotel, with the difference that each room is separately owned. The guests (renters) have no idea who owns their room.

Both timeshares and condo hotels typically involve luxury resort locations with amenities such as golf or spas. The difference between the traditional timeshare and condo hotel is the interval that the unit is available — condo hotels are operated on a day-to-day availability, and timeshares typically rent in fixed intervals such as weeks.

Some of the most popular projects have been the branded condo hotels such as Ritz Carlton, Four Seasons, Trump, W, Westin, and Hilton located in the high profile vacation destinations like Hawaii, Las Vegas, New York, Chicago, and Miami. You can also find many foreign condo hotel properties in the Caribbean and Mexico, and the concept is expanding to Europe, the Middle East, and Asia.

Two types of individuals are attracted to investing in condo hotels and time-shares. One group is investors who believe that the property will appreciate like any other investment. The other group is people who use the condo hotel or timeshare for personal use and offset some of their costs.

From an investment standpoint, the fundamental problem with timeshares is that they're overpriced, and like a condominium, you own no land (which is what generally appreciates well over time). For example, suppose that a particular unit would cost $150,000 to buy. When this unit is carved up into weekly ownership units, the total cost of all those units can easily approach four to five times that amount!

To add insult to injury, investors find that another problem with timeshares is the high maintenance or annual service fees. Is it worth buying a slice of real estate at a 400 to 500 percent premium to its fair market value and pay high fees on top of that? We don't think so.

Many owners of timeshares find that they want to vacation at a different location or time of year than what they originally purchased. To meet this need, several companies offer to broker or sell timeshare slots. However, timeshare availability and desirability have so many variables — including location, time of year, and quality of the particular resort — that it has been difficult to fairly value and trade timeshares. As a result, resort rating systems have been developed (Resorts Condominiums International and Interval International are two of the most well known) to compare resort location, amenities, and quality.

The developers and operators of condo hotels love the concept because one of the most consistently successful principles of real estate is increasing value by fractionalizing interests in real estate. As with timeshares, the developers are able to sell each individual hotel room for much more than they could get for the entire project.

Condo hotel operators are able to generate additional revenue from service and maintenance fees to cover their costs of operations. Often the owners' use of their own rooms doesn't negatively impact the overall revenues of the property because the rooms would have sometimes been vacant anyway. Condo hotels allow their owners to stay in their units but often impose limits on the amount of personal usage.

The purchaser of the condo hotel unit sees this type of investment as an option to direct ownership of a second home and likes the ability to generate income. The professional management is another one of the attractions to investors. The owners don't pay a management fee to the hotel operator unless their room is rented, and then the collected revenue is split.

These properties are often hyped, and the expectations of the condo hotel investor are often much greater than the reality. Investors are lured to condo hotels by the potential for appreciation and cash flow as well as professional management. Many investors find themselves being pressured into pre-sale offering presentations even before the units are built. These events can be tempting, but savvy investors need to do their own due diligence. So when you hear a sales pitch indicating that your proposed investment in a condo hotel unit will provide significant income from hotel rentals and cover most or all of your mortgage and carrying costs, that's the time to grab your wallet and find the nearest exit.

Many investors' first experiences with timeshares are tempting offers of a free meal, a great discount offer to a theme park, or even a free one or two night stay at the resort, with the catch that they have to spend some time listening to an informational presentation. These offers usually come from individuals contacting you in known tourist locations or when you check into a hotel that just happens to offer condos as well. Robert remembers his first exposure to timeshares was as a child in the early '70s on a family vacation to Florida, when his parents got a free camera just for attending a seminar on timeshares near Orlando. Even as a teenager, Robert didn't like the obvious pressure sales tactics he observed.

However, timeshares may make sense for you if you like to vacation at the same resort around the same time every year and if the annual service or maintenance fees compare favorably to the cost of simply staying in a comparable resort. Remember, though, that if the deal seems too good to be true, it *is* too good to be true. As with timeshares, the only folks who generally make money with condo hotels are the developers, not the folks who buy specific days of ownership.

Still interested in a timeshare? Read on.

Timeshares are packaged in a multitude of ways — some resorts offer fixed units where you vacation at the exact same unit every year either on set dates or set numbered weeks (though the actual calendar date may vary. Other timeshares are available as *biennial* (every other year) so you can have some variety. Some offer fixed weeks, where you have the same week every year but may be in a different unit.

Timeshares aren't just a one-time purchase; they also have monthly or annual service or maintenance fees. These funds are established each year by the homeowner's association or resort management company. There are different types of ownership for timeshare interests, with fee simple, right of use, and leasehold being the primary options:

✔ **Fee simple** ownership is an estate in real estate that provides the absolute ownership subject to state and local laws and government powers such as taxation, eminent domain, police power, and so on.

✔ **Right-to-use** are occupancy rights for a given number of years but no actual ownership interest in the property. Some states and many foreign countries don't allow the fee simple ownership of timeshares so they offer long-term lease or right-to-use agreements that can be from 20 to 99 years. The actual fee simple title of the real estate remains with the resort developer or management company. A homeowner's association or a resort management company typically handles the day-to-day operations of timeshares.

✔ **Leasehold** is an agreement between the lessee (tenant) and lessor (owner or landlord) specifying the lessee's right to use the leased property for a given purpose and given time at a specified rental payment.

If you're interested in buying a timeshare, know that timeshare owners are required by law to disclose their full, audited financials. Read them carefully. You can talk with the developer directly; this method may make sense if you're looking for a particular time of the year in the high season. The timeshare industry typically uses a color-coded pricing system to denote the seasonal demand for a particular timeshare property. Although the concept is pretty consistent, the designation of particular colors can vary from one resort to another. In general, the demand is broken down into three categories:

✔ Red for the prime or high demand

✔ Yellow or white for intermediate or medium season

✔ Green or blue for off-season or low demand

If you're looking for a week in the green or blue season, you can often find much better pricing from reputable resellers. The *reputable* is a key and elusive term here. Among companies to consider for reselling timeshares are RCI, Interval International, and Trading Places International.

Surveying the Types of Residential Properties You Can Buy

If you've been in the market for a home, you know that in addition to single-family homes, you can choose from numerous types of attached or shared housing including duplexes, triplexes, apartment buildings, condominiums, townhomes, and co-operatives. In this section, we provide an overview of each of these properties and show how they may make an attractive real estate investment for you.

From an investment perspective, our top recommendations are apartment buildings and single-family homes. We generally don't recommend attached-housing units. If you can afford a smaller single-family home or apartment building rather than a shared-housing unit, buy the single-family home or apartments.

Unless you can afford a large down payment (25 percent or more), the early years of rental property ownership may financially challenge you: With all properties, as time goes on, generating a positive cash flow gets easier because your mortgage expense stays fixed (if you use fixed rate financing) while your rents increase faster than your expenses. Regardless of what you choose to buy, make sure that you run the numbers on your rental income and expenses (see Chapter 12) to see if you can afford the negative cash flow that often occurs in the early years of ownership.

Single-family homes

As an investment, single-family detached homes generally perform better in the long run than attached or shared housing. In a good real estate market, most housing appreciates, but single-family homes tend to outperform other housing types for the following reasons:

- Single-family homes tend to attract more potential buyers — most people, when they can afford it, prefer a detached or stand-alone home, especially for the increased privacy.

- Attached or shared housing is less expensive and easier to build *and to overbuild;* because of this surplus potential, such property tends to appreciate more moderately in price.

Because so many people prefer to live in detached, single-family homes, market prices for such dwellings can often become inflated beyond what's justified by the rental income these homes can produce. That's exactly what happened in some parts of the United States in the mid-2000s and led in part to a significant price correction in the subsequent years. To discover whether you're buying in such a market, compare the monthly cost (after tax) of owning a home to monthly rent for that same property. Focus on markets where the rent exceeds or comes close to equaling the cost of owning and shun areas where the ownership costs exceed rents.

Single-family homes that require just one tenant are simpler to deal with than a multiunit apartment building that requires the management and maintenance of multiple renters and units. The downside, though, is that a vacancy means you have no income coming in. Look at the effect of 0 percent occupancy for a couple of months on your projected income and expense statement! By contrast, one vacancy in a four-unit apartment building (each with the same rents) means that you're still taking in 75 percent of the gross potential (maximum total) rent.

With a single-family home, you're responsible for all repairs and maintenance. You can hire someone to do the work, but you still have to find the contractors and coordinate and oversee the work. Also recognize that if you purchase a single-family home with many fine features and amenities, you may find it more stressful and difficult to have tenants living in your property who don't treat it with the same tender loving care that you may yourself.

The first rule of being a successful landlord is to let go of any emotional attachment to a home. But that sort of attachment on the tenant's part is favorable: The more they make your rental property their home, the more likely they are to stay and return it to you in good condition — except for the expected normal wear and tear of day-to-day living. (We discuss the proper screening and selection of tenants in Chapter 15.)

Making a profit in the early years of ownership from the monthly cash flow with a single-family home is generally the hardest stage. The reason: Such properties usually sell at a premium price relative to the rent that they can command (you pay extra for the land, which you can't rent). Also remember that with just one tenant, you have no rental income when you have a vacancy.

Attached housing

As the cost of land has climbed over the decades in many areas, packing more housing units that are attached into a given plot of land keeps housing somewhat more affordable. Shared housing makes more sense for investors who don't want to deal with building maintenance and security issues.

In this section, we discuss the investment merits of three forms of attached housing: condominiums, townhomes, and co-ops.

Condos

Condominiums are typically apartment-style units stacked on top of and/ or beside one another and sold to individual owners. When you purchase a condominium, you're actually purchasing the interior of a specific unit as well as a proportionate interest in the common areas — the pool, tennis courts, grounds, hallways, laundry room, and so on. Although you (and your tenants) have full use and enjoyment of the common areas, remember that the home-owner's association actually owns and maintains the common areas as well as the building structures themselves (which typically include the foundation, exterior walls, roof, plumbing, electrical, and other major building systems).

One advantage to a condo as an investment property is that of all the attached housing options, condos are generally the lowest-maintenance properties because most condominium or homeowner associations deal with issues such as roofing, landscaping, and so on for the entire building and receive the benefits of quantity purchasing. Note that you're still responsible for necessary maintenance inside your unit, such as servicing appliances, floor and window coverings, interior painting, and so on.

Although condos may be somewhat easier to keep up, they tend to appreciate less than single-family homes or apartment buildings unless the condo is located in a desirable urban area.

Condominium buildings may start out in life as condos or as apartment complexes that are then converted into condominiums.

Be wary of apartments that have been converted to condominiums. Although they're often the most affordable housing options in many areas of the country and may also be blessed with an excellent urban location that can't easily be re-created, you may be buying into some not so obvious problems. Our experience is that these converted apartments are typically older properties with a cosmetic makeover (new floors, new appliances, new landscaping, and a fresh coat of paint). However, be forewarned: The cosmetic makeover may look good at first glance, but the property probably still boasts 40-year-old plumbing and electrical systems, poor soundproofing, and a host of economic and functional obsolescence.

Within a few years, most of the owner-occupants move on to the traditional single-family home and rent out their condos. You may then find the property is predominantly renter-occupied and has a volunteer board of directors unwilling to levy the monthly assessments necessary to properly maintain the aging structure. Within 10 to 15 years of the conversion, these properties may well be the worst in the neighborhood.

Townhomes

Townhomes are essentially attached or row homes — a hybrid between a typical airspace-only condominium and a single-family house. Like condominiums, townhomes are generally attached, typically sharing walls and a continuous roof. But townhomes are often two-story buildings that come with a small yard and offer more privacy than a condominium because you don't have someone living on top of your unit.

As with condominiums, you absolutely must review the governing documents before you purchase the property to see exactly what you legally own. Generally, townhomes are organized as *planned unit developments* (PUDs) in which each owner has a *fee simple* ownership (no limitations as to transferability of ownership — the most complete ownership rights one can have) of his individual lot that encompasses his dwelling unit and often a small area of immediately adjacent land for a patio or balcony. The common areas are all part of a larger single lot, and each owner holds title to a proportionate share of the common area.

Co-ops

Co-operatives are a type of shared housing that has elements in common with apartments and condos. When you buy a cooperative, you own a stock certificate that represents your share of the entire building, including usage rights to a specific living space per a separate written occupancy agreement. Unlike a condo, you generally need to get approval from the co-operative association if you want to remodel or rent your unit to a tenant. In some co-ops, you must even gain approval from the association for the sale of your unit to a proposed buyer.

Turning a co-op into a rental unit is often severely restricted or even forbidden and, if allowed, is usually a major headache because you must satisfy not only your tenant but also the other owners in the building. Co-ops are also generally much harder to finance, and a sale requires the approval of the typically finicky association board. Therefore, we highly recommend that you avoid co-ops for investment purposes.

Apartments

Not only do apartment buildings generally enjoy healthy long-term appreciation potential, but they also often produce positive *cash flow* (rental income – expenses) in the early years of ownership. But as with a single-family home, the buck stops with you for maintenance of an apartment building. You may hire a property manager to assist you, but you still have oversight responsibilities (and additional expenses).

In the real-estate financing world, apartment buildings are divided into two groups based on the number of units:

- **Four or fewer units:** You can obtain more favorable financing options and terms for apartment buildings that have four or fewer units because they're treated as residential property.

- **Five or more units:** Complexes with five or more units are treated as commercial property and don't enjoy the extremely favorable loan terms of the one- to four-unit properties.

Apartment buildings, particularly those with more units, generally produce a small positive cash flow, even in the early years of rental ownership (unless you're in an overpriced market where it may take two to four years before you break even on a before-tax basis).

One way to add value, if zoning allows, is to convert an apartment building into condominiums. Keep in mind, however, that this metamorphosis requires significant research on the zoning front and with estimating remodeling and construction costs.

Easy fixes can yield big bucks

Avoid shared housing units in suburban areas with substantial undeveloped land that enables building many more units. Attached housing prices tend to perform best in fully developed or built-out urban environments.

For higher returns, look for property where relatively simple cosmetic and other fixes may allow you to increase rents and, therefore, the market value of the property. Examples of such improvements may include but not be limited to

- Adding fresh paint and flooring

- Improving the landscaping

- Upgrading the kitchen with new appliances and new cabinet/drawer hardware that can totally change the look

- Converting five-unit apartment buildings into four-unit buildings to qualify for more favorable mortgage terms (see the "Apartments" section earlier in this chapter)

Look for property with a great location and good physical condition but some minor deferred maintenance. Then you can develop the punch list of items with maximum results for minimum dollars — for example, a property with a large yard but dead grass, a two- or three-car garage but peeling paint or a broken garage door. You can also add a garage door opener to jazz up the property for minimum cost. You can also really add value to a property with a burnt-out, absentee, or totally disinterested owner who is tired of the property.

Considering Commercial Real Estate

Commercial real estate is a generic term that includes properties used for office, retail, and industrial purposes. You can also include self-storage and hospitality (hotels and motels) properties in this category. If you're a knowledgeable real estate investor and you like a challenge, you need to know two good reasons to invest in commercial real estate:

- ✔ You can use some of the space if you own your own small business. Just as it's generally more cost-effective to own your home rather than rent over the years, so it is with commercial real estate if — and this is a big *if* — you buy at a reasonably good time and hold the property for many years.

- ✔ You're a more sophisticated investor who understands the more complicated aspects of commercial leases and has a higher tolerance for risk because these properties can have longer intervals of vacancy or increased tenant improvement costs plus rent concessions. Of course, just like with residential income property, only invest when your analysis of your local market suggests that it's a good time to buy. We discuss more on this point in a moment.

We want to be clear, though, that commercial real estate isn't our first recommendation, especially for inexperienced investors. Residential real estate is generally easier to understand and also usually carries lower investment and tenant risks.

With commercial real estate, when tenants move out, new tenants nearly always require extensive and costly improvements to customize the space to meet their planned usage of the property. And you usually have to pay for the majority of the associated costs in order to compete with other building owners. Fortunes can quickly change — small companies can go under, get too big for a space, and so on. Change is the order of the day in commercial real estate, and especially in the small business world where you're most likely to find your tenants.

So how do you evaluate the state of your local commercial real estate market? You must check out, over a number of years, the supply and demand statistics. How much total space (sublease and vacant space) is available for rent, and how has that changed in recent months or years? What's the vacancy rate for comparable space, and how has that changed over time? Also, examine the rental rates, usually quoted as a price per square foot. We help you cover this ground in Chapter 12.

One danger sign that purchasing a commercial property in an area is likely to produce disappointing investment returns is a market where the supply of available space has increased faster than demand, leading to higher vacancies and falling rental rates. (This is called *negative absorption*. What you want instead is a track record and projections showing *positive absorption* — when the supply of space isn't keeping up with the demand.) A slowing local economy and a higher unemployment rate also spell trouble for commercial real estate prices. You not only have to consider vacant space, but also space available for subleasing (the current tenant isn't using the space and will rent it to someone else often at favorable terms) when evaluating the overall supply and demand for commercial income properties. Each market is different, so make sure you check out the details of your area.

Buying Undeveloped Land

For prospective real estate investors who feel tenants and building maintenance are ongoing headaches, buying undeveloped land may appear attractive. If you buy land in an area that's expected to experience expanding demand in the years ahead, you should be able to make a tidy return on your investment. This is called *buying in the path of progress,* but of course the trick is to buy before everybody realizes that new development is moving in your direction. (Check out Chapter 10 for a full discussion on the path of progress.)

You may even hit a home run if you can identify land that others don't currently see the future value in holding. However, identifying many years in advance which communities will experience rapid population and job growth isn't easy. Land prices in areas that people believe will be the next hot spot likely already sell at a premium price. That's what happened in most major cities with new sports facilities (especially because these decisions often are disclosed well in advance of the municipality leadership vote or the ballot initiative). You don't have much opportunity to get ahead of the curve — or if you guess wrong, you may own some costly land for a long time!

Investing in land certainly has other drawbacks and risks:

- ✔ **Care and feeding:** Land requires ongoing cash to pay the property taxes and liability insurance, and to keep the land clear and free of debris while it most likely produces little or no income. Although land doesn't require much upkeep compared with tenant-occupied property, it almost always does require financial feeding.

- ✔ **Opportunity costs:** Investing in land is a cash drain, and of course, purchasing the land in the first place costs money. If you buy the land with cash, you have the opportunity cost of tying up your valuable capital (which could be invested elsewhere), but most likely you will put down 30 to 40 percent in cash and finance the balance of the purchase price instead. Although you can often buy residential income property with much lower down payments, the fact that there is typically no periodic rental income with vacant undeveloped land means down payments are higher. Many times you can only acquire these properties with cash.

✔ **Costly mortgages:** Mortgage lenders require much higher down payments and charge higher loan fees and interest rates on loans to purchase land because they see it as a more speculative investment. Obtaining a loan for development of land is challenging and more expensive than obtaining a loan for a developed property.

✔ **Lack of depreciation:** You don't get depreciation tax write-offs because land isn't depreciable.

On the income side, some properties may be able to be used for parking, storage income, or maybe even growing Christmas trees in the Northwest or grain in the Midwest! (After you make sure you've complied with local zoning restrictions and have the proper insurance in place.)

Although large-scale land investment isn't for the entry-level real estate investor, savvy real estate investors have made fortunes taking raw land and getting the proper entitlements and then selling (or better yet, subdividing and then selling) the parcels to developers of commercial and residential properties (primarily home builders). If you decide to invest in land, be sure that you:

✔ **Do your homework.** Ideally, you want to buy land in an area that's attracting rapidly expanding companies and that has a shortage of housing and developable land. Take your time to really know the area. This isn't a situation in which you should take a hot tip from someone to invest in faraway property in another state. Nor should you buy raw land just because you heard that irresistible opening bid price advertised on the radio for the government excess land auction down at the convention center this Saturday.

✔ **Know all the costs.** Tally up your annual *carrying* costs (ongoing ownership expenses such as property taxes) so that you can see what your annual cash drain may be. What are the financial consequences of this cash outflow — for example, will you be able to fully fund your tax-advantaged retirement accounts? If you can't, count the lost tax benefits as another cost of owning land.

✔ **Determine what improvements the land may need.** Engineering fees; subdivision map and permit costs; running utility, water, and sewer lines; building roads; curbs and gutters; landscaping; and so on all cost money. If you plan to develop and build on the land that you purchase, research these costs. Make sure you don't make these estimates with your rose-tinted sunglasses on — improvements almost always cost more than you expect them to. (You need to check with the planning or building department for their list of requirements.)

Also make sure that you have access to the land or the right to enter and leave through a public right-of-way or another's property (known as *ingress* and *egress*). Some people foolishly invest in landlocked properties. When they discover the fact later, they think that they can easily get an *easement* (legal permission to use someone else's property). Wrong!

✔ **Understand the zoning and environmental issues.** The value of land is heavily dependent on what you can develop on it. Never purchase land without thoroughly understanding its zoning status and what you can and can't build on it. This advice also applies to environmental limitations that may be in place or that may come into effect without warning, diminishing the potential of your property (with no compensation).

This potential for surprise is why you must research the disposition of the planning department and nearby communities. Attend the meetings of local planning groups, if any, because some areas that are antigrowth and antidevelopment are less likely to be good places for you to buy land, especially if you need permission to do the type of project that you have in mind. Through the empowerment of local residents who sit on community boards and can influence local government officials, zoning can suddenly change for the worse — sometimes you may find that your property has been *downzoned* — a zoning alteration that can significantly reduce what you can develop on a property and therefore the property's value.

The dangers of downzoning

Robert owned raw land for many years in an area where a recent government action effectively downzoned his property from 4 acres to 2 acres. The multi-species conservation act designated huge swaths of undeveloped land as mitigation habitat for "endangered plant and animal species." This ordinance mandated that every parcel that wasn't already fully developed was subject to a development limitation of 2 acres.

Luckily for Robert, he had subdivided the original 20 acres into 4 smaller parcels of 4 to 5 acres each or the entire 20 acres would've only been allowed usage of 2 acres. Still, Robert's 4- to 5-acre parcels are now limited to 2 acres of development unless Robert pays a "mitigation fee" which is currently over $50,000 per acre! This story illustrates the dangers of buying and owning vacant real estate in areas where conservation activists are prevalent.

Chapter 3

Considering Foreclosures, REOs, Probate Sales, and More

. . . .

In This Chapter

▶ Mastering foreclosures and REOs

▶ Considering short sales

▶ Utilizing lease options

▶ Understanding probate sales and auctions

. . . .

Many real estate investors actually start their real estate portfolio conventionally by buying a home for their own use for a number of years and then purchasing a new home and renting out their first home. Other folks have found that the best way to quickly become a real estate investor is to purchase income-producing properties in a more unconventional manner.

In this chapter, we examine some of the most common of these methods of acquiring real estate investment properties or participating in the real estate market, and we tell you what we think about whether you should pursue these options. We start off with foreclosures, REOs, and lease options. We also cover some other, even more unusual ways to acquire real estate at below-market prices, such as probate sales and auctions. And besides REITs (discussed in Chapter 4), other avenues allow you to passively invest in real estate, including triple net properties, notes and trust deeds, and limited partnerships, which we also discuss.

Finding Foreclosures and REOs

Would you rather buy real estate at retail or at wholesale prices? Obviously the answer is "wholesale!" Just like in the stock market, the concept of *buy low, sell high* also applies to real estate.

One of the best ways to maximize your chances of earning a good return on your investment is to buy a property at foreclosure or as an REO. Such investments are generally a better value than a conventional purchase (but not without some increased risk)!

And of course, other real estate investors are also scouring your local real estate market for great deals. Clearly, real estate investors flush with cash aren't going to miss this opportunity. As an individual looking to buy just one or two foreclosure homes in your local market, you may be surprised to find that you're competing with very large and sophisticated Wall Street venture funds with tens of millions of dollars that are buying pools of bad loans or foreclosed properties.

Foreclosures are simply properties for which the owner has failed to meet his loan payment or other loan term obligations, forcing the lender, if they want to get some of their money back, to take over legal ownership and control of the property (or foreclose and *take title*). Although more formal in a legal sense and more time consuming, a real estate foreclosure is similar to a lender repossessing the car from an owner who fails to make her monthly car payments.

After completing the foreclosure process, the lender takes title, at which point it owns the property. The lender has to maintain and manage the property, so it turns the property over to asset managers in the lender's in-house real estate–owned (REO) department. The asset managers may keep the day-to-day property management in-house as well, but most lenders hire local property management firms to inspect the property, repair any emergency items, and essentially operate the property until the lender can sell it — usually within a few months unless the borrower has redemption rights (see the "Redemption period" section later in the chapter). Many major lenders call the department holding their repossessed properties Other Real Estate Owned (OREOs). No matter what the name, the savvy real estate investor willing to do the extensive due diligence required to find the rare diamonds in the rough will be rewarded.

When considering foreclosures and REOs, be sure to perform the necessary research:

- ✔ Inspect the property and determine the physical condition and the cost of any needed work. Be careful to rule out major structural issues or environmental concerns.

- ✔ Review a preliminary title report to see whether the property has any unpaid tax liens or encumbrances.

- ✔ Appraise the property and establish your target price and a firm maximum bid so that the emotions of bidding don't lead you to overpay.

Taking a closer look at foreclosures

The term *foreclosure* actually describes a process by which a lender takes title to a property on which a loan is in default. The two most common high-risk mistakes homeowners make that lead to foreclosure are

✔ **Failing to make the mortgage payments as required:** For example, homeowners who overstretched and bought their homes using up to 100 percent financing (they made little or even no down payment towards the home's purchase price) and were, in effect, living on the edge.

✔ **Borrowing too much when refinancing:** Low interest rates combined with the tremendous increase in real estate values in most parts of the country in the early- to mid-2000s led many homeowners to refinance their properties. Although there's nothing wrong with refinancing, as long as you don't borrow too much, some lenders promoted 110 to 120 percent loans that tempted homeowners to pull all of their equity — and more — out of their homes. The recent trend toward no-documentation or stated-income loans also greatly contributed to the real estate mess of this period.

The flawed theory was that real estate values only increased, so these folks were simply tapping their future equity. However, one slight stumble with a loss of a job or a drop in income, a serious illness, death, or divorce can lead to a missed mortgage payment or two and ultimately, foreclosure. That's what happened to millions of property owners who were overextended with mortgage debt when the real estate market turned against them in the late 2000s. Although some folks couldn't afford to keep up with their payments, others chose to walk away from properties worth less than their outstanding mortgage balance.

But properties can also be subject to foreclosure for other reasons:

✔ **Owners fail to meet other loan requirements.** Examples include not maintaining proper insurance coverage or not keeping the property in good physical condition.

✔ **Absentee owners are unable to effectively manage the property.** Good property managers regularly visit and inspect their properties. This level of involvement isn't practical from a distance.

This category of foreclosures is extremely prevalent in many of the most popular real estate investment markets for out-of-town speculators such as Las Vegas and Phoenix. If you're in these markets you may be able to pick up some great bargains, but don't make the same mistake that the earlier investors made when they purchased properties out of their comfort zone.

✔ **Owners walk away from serious problems.** Some properties fall into foreclosure because the property has serious and irreversible problems that are so bad that the current owner chooses to walk away rather than deal with them. Environmental hazards and serious physical problems where the cost of repair can exceed the value of the property (such as cracked slabs or landslides) often top the list. (In Chapter 14, we cover research you can perform to help avoid these types of problems.)

Many foreclosure properties also fall into this category because some real estate investors felt that the market was so strong that literally any property they bought would increase in value. Although this may have been true to a certain extent in some markets for a couple of years, the reality is that investors who bought properties without conducting proper due diligence often found that they had purchased white elephants, or properties that they can't sell for what they paid for them (or even rent out to cover their carrying costs).

Before you pursue foreclosure properties, determine the type of foreclosure process commonly used in your state. Check with your favorite lender, real estate agent, real estate attorney, or title company representative to find this information. Your state falls under one of two categories:

✔ **Deed of trust state:** When a loan is placed in a deed of trust state, the property title is held in the name of a third party or trustee. If the loan payments aren't made as promised or the loan is in default for another reason, the trustee can foreclose or take back the property. No court action is necessary, so a foreclosure in a deed of trust state can happen in 60 to 120 days. This process is referred to as *nonjudicial foreclosure*.

Be sure to check that you have the latest information on federal, state, and even local efforts by legislators and courts that have been quite aggressive in extending the timelines to give borrowers more time to avoid foreclosure.

✔ **Mortgage state:** In a mortgage state, no trustee or third party is named. When a mortgage goes into default for nonpayment or other breach, the holder of the mortgage must go to court and seek legal remedies including *judicial foreclosure*, which can take much longer than a nonjudicial foreclosure.

Foreclosure properties aren't that hard to find. Whether you're in a deed of trust state or a mortgage state, the filing of a Notice of Default (NOD) or a judicial foreclosure lawsuit are matters of public record. An additional public notice announcing a pending foreclosure sale must be published in a local legal newspaper. The timing of the publication prior to the sale varies by state. Many title companies and real estate firms track the Notices of Default and all the steps right through to the actual foreclosure. This information is public record and filed with the county recorder or equivalent, but subscribe to one of the local services offering this information via daily or weekly e-mails or faxes, because gathering this information on your own is time consuming.

Technically, there are four steps, and thus four buying opportunities, for a property subject to the typical foreclosure process. Knowing these steps, which we outline in the following sections, and the techniques or negotiating points necessary at each step to motivate the owner or lender is essential to mastering one of the best strategies of buying real estate at below market or wholesale prices.

Preforeclosure

Every potential foreclosure begins when the owner misses a payment on her debt service or is notified in writing by the lender that a condition or term of her loan isn't being met. The *preforeclosure* stage is the period of time before the lender formally files the Notice of Default, which triggers the legal foreclosure process.

The period of time before the formal foreclosure begins is an important buying opportunity: You can get in ahead of competing investors to identify properties on which the owner is delinquent on mortgage payments or violating other conditions of his loan. The key is to track and locate these defaulting owners.

This is the time when you want to offer a solution to the owner that'll get her out of the property and preserve her credit status so she can purchase property in the future. Also, every owner facing a mortgage delinquency needs some cash to pay for moving and relocation costs. Understanding the motivation of the owner and lender can allow you to formulate an investment strategy that meets everyone's needs and allows you to own a property before it becomes heavily exposed on the local multiple listing service!

Notice of Default

The first formal legal action in the foreclosure process is the filing of a Notice of Default. If the owner wasn't concerned when he first began missing loan payments, the filing of the Notice of Default should be a real wake-up call.

An owner who has received the Notice of Default is likely to be motivated to sell because she knows that the lender has begun the formal steps toward repossessing her property. But not all owners facing foreclosure are aware that the late charges, penalties, and hefty legal fees further erode their shaky financial position. They may not understand the logic that if they can't make their regular monthly payments, they're unlikely to catch up and pay all of the additional costs, which can literally double the delinquent amount.

The 60 to 90 days following the filing of the NOD are a great time to offer solutions to an owner facing a foreclosure. Most owners truly believe that their financial problems are temporary, so make your offer sensitive to the fact that preserving the owner's credit record is a key consideration: If you can buy the property quickly at a discount and then cure the default or pay off the delinquent mortgage, the seller only has the slow payments on his credit report rather than a foreclosure (or possibly a bankruptcy, which is often the only alternative for owners who are unwilling to voluntarily resolve their cash flow problems). Preserving credit has always been a key motivator to owners who are delinquent on their mortgage payments. However, legislative efforts in 2008 to forgive defaults have changed the dynamics significantly, and many homeowners are simply walking away with little concern that their credit will be an obstacle to entering the homeownership ranks at a future date.

Determine the loan balance and the value of the property to ensure that the owner has equity. Generally, the more equity the better, because this equity allows you to provide the owner with some quick cash so he can cover the costs of vacating the property and finding a new place to live. It's also this equity in the property that provides you with a profit potential after all of your costs of acquisition plus the required repairs and upgrades to maximize the resale value of the property.

Some real estate gurus recommend that you simply offer a nominal amount of cash to the owner facing a default and then begin making the payments on the existing loans or, in other words, purchase the property *subject to* the current loans. Be wary that the lender may not allow you to just step into the shoes of the original borrower and may still declare the loan to be in default. Have your legal advisor (see Chapter 6) look for an *assumption clause* in the loan documents that would allow you to properly assume the loan. Usually this process requires a loan application and a fee. You may also want to watch out for a *due on sale clause* that accelerates the entire loan and makes it due immediately upon the transfer of the property to a new owner. Foreclosure transactions aren't risk free; your legal advisor can tell you the potential downside of your proposed transaction with a defaulting buyer.

Many of the problems that occur in buying foreclosures can be avoided by structuring the purchase offer to require the owner to vacate the property immediately. It's difficult for an owner to lose her home, and it's often even more difficult for her to accept the fact that she's no longer the owner when she's still living in the property.

Foreclosure sale

Although the foreclosure process varies from state to state, the main difference is whether the loan is secured with a mortgage that requires a judicial foreclosure or by a deed of trust, in which case the nonjudicial process is used (for an introduction to these two types of states, see the beginning of this section).

- ✔ **Judicial foreclosure:** In a judicial foreclosure, the lender files a lawsuit against the borrower to get the property. Like any other lawsuit, it begins with the serving of a summons and complaint upon the borrower (along with any other parties with junior liens or encumbrances against the property). If the borrower responds, the court holds a hearing and rules that either the borrower has presented a legitimate issue (and alternate payment terms are arranged) or the lender is permitted to foreclose.

  The most common scenario is that the borrower doesn't respond and the lender receives a judgment by default and can proceed to have a referee appointed by the court. The lender then advertises the sale for four to six weeks and then, if full payment hasn't been made, a public sale is held, typically on the courthouse or town/city hall steps. The time frame for this entire judicial foreclosure process is usually between 4 and 6 months, although the process can take from as little as 3 months to as long as 12 months.

- ✔ **Nonjudicial foreclosure:** In a nonjudicial foreclosure state, lenders are allowed to foreclose without a lawsuit, using the power of sale provisions of the deed of trust. The deed of trust actually has three parties to the original loan agreement — the borrower (grantor), the lender (beneficiary), and the trustee who actually holds title during the term of the loan. In the event the borrower defaults, the trustee files a Notice of Default and a Notice of Sale in a legal newspaper.

  As with the judicial foreclosure, if the loan in a nonjudicial foreclosure isn't fully reinstated prior to the date and time of the trustee's sale, the public auction or sheriff's sale occurs on the steps of a prominent public location in town such as a courthouse. If no one bids, the lender bids the amount of its loan plus accrued penalties and fees and takes title to the property. This is the most common scenario unless the property is desirable and has equity, in which case many interested bidders may compete in a free-for-all.

Bidding on and purchasing properties at the foreclosure sale can be exciting and even profitable if you do your homework and know everything about a property before you bid. But getting a little lazy or going with your gut feeling can lead to a disaster, and it often takes quite a few home runs to offset even one disaster. Something as simple as an unrecorded tax lien or latent physical problems like a cracked slab or expansive soil can turn your lemonade back into a lemon! Be sure to get a title report showing clear title and an owner's title insurance policy.

Redemption period

Some states allow the borrower the right to redeem her property after the sale during a *redemption period* in which she can pay the full amount owed, including the loan balance, late charges, legal fees incurred by the lender, and all of the costs of sale, and get title to the property back. The length of the redemption period varies from state to state. This period is also an opportunity to reach an agreement with the borrower for her deed. If successful, the purchaser then essentially obtains the borrower's redemption rights and has the right to redeem the property.

Even if you're the successful purchaser at the foreclosure sale, you still have to give the borrower the opportunity to redeem the property per the state-required redemption period. Don't make significant improvements only to have the borrower redeem the property and then thank you for renovating his distressed property from the worst on the block to the model home!

Because the majority of properties at a foreclosure sale end up with the lender (because most properties aren't desirable investment properties at this time due to foreclosure risks and limited due diligence, as we discuss in this section), you have a great opportunity to make a deal with the lender just after the foreclosure sale and before they've incurred the expense of hiring an agent to market and sell the property.

You may also be able to make a better deal if the property has significant deferred maintenance or code violations, because the local building inspector or code enforcement departments know when a deep-pocketed lender has title to the property, and they expect all citations for substandard conditions or code violations to be corrected immediately. You may be able to relieve the lender of this liability while allowing yourself to negotiate a favorable transaction.

The ethics of foreclosures

One of the most difficult moral dilemmas facing real estate investors is the ethics of negotiating with an owner facing a foreclosure. Are you helping her or are you a vulture seeking to profit upon the misfortune of another? You walk a fine line in some of these situations.

Although there's some value to a distressed seller in a quick transaction that provides needed cash, pushing too hard for a bargain can be unethical. Robert uses the "pillow test" to guide his conscience: Can you fall asleep at night and not feel guilty about your moral and ethical conduct?

Examining lender REOs (Real Estate Owned)

Because titles to the majority of foreclosed properties end up with the lender, you may find that your next opportunity to purchase the property is from the lender's real estate–owned (REO) department that specializes in handling foreclosed properties. Some investors have found that this is one of the best times to buy a property because they're not dealing with an emotional or unreliable owner. Discovering the ins and outs of the lenders' policies and procedures of disposing of these foreclosed properties can be invaluable to your goal of buying real estate at below market prices.

The days of stealing prime REO properties from the Resolution Trust Corporation (RTC) are gone. The RTC was a quasi-federal government entity established by Congress to dispose of the tremendous number of foreclosed assets of the major lenders during the real estate market downturn in the early '90s. Due to the numbers of properties and the relative inexperience of and limited due diligence by the RTC in some areas of the country, a once-in-a-lifetime real estate investment opportunity did fall into the lap of savvy real estate investors who had large amounts of cash, could act quickly, and then had the financial horsepower to ride out the market downturn.

Lender REOs remain one of the favorite strategies for the late-night infomercial gurus, but the reality is that today's lenders are neither foolish nor benevolent. Although these nonperforming loans are a negative on their balance sheet, they're not going to sell a property below its market value just to get it off their books.

The disposition specialists in the REO department are professionals who understand the real estate markets well and are usually wired into the best real estate brokers in the market. These real estate brokers are often compensated as a percentage of the sales price and thus also motivated to achieve the highest value as is reasonably possible.

The only angle a real estate investor usually has with an REO is financing and the continued operating losses that often occur because the lender is merely holding the property and isn't willing to invest the time and money necessary to enhance the property physically and reposition it to perform better in the market.

Sales are as-is, and lenders are often exempt from the standard disclosure rules.

When lenders have an excessive number of REOs, they become more flexible, but they're often limited by the Office of Thrift Supervision (OTS), a government agency that oversees many savings banks and savings and loan associations and routinely audits their loan portfolio and their REOs.

An option for first-time buyers: FHA/VA repos

Government agencies such as the Federal Housing Administration (FHA) and the Department of Veterans Affairs (VA) guarantee loans made by lenders to qualified individuals. When these home buyers fail to make their payments, the lender goes through the foreclosure process and ultimately repossesses the house. The government pays the lender the guaranteed loan amount and then takes possession of the property.

These FHA and VA repos are then listed for sale through real estate agents approved by the Department of Housing and Urban Development (HUD). Typically, real estate investors don't find these properties as attractive as some other real estate investment opportunities, because they're usually offered at or just a shade under market prices. Qualified first-time home buyers should look for these FHA/VA repos, because they're often available with favorable financing, including low, or no, down payments.

Getting a Jump On Foreclosure and REO Competition with Short Sales

Savvy real estate investors know that some of the best properties are the ones that aren't exposed to the open market where the competition has a chance to drive up the price. They also know that the best deals can be made with motivated sellers — and there's not much stronger motivation for a house seller than to know that they'll soon lose their property to foreclosure and find their credit ruined.

These homeowners don't have any equity, and the existing debt on the property exceeds the current loan balance. If the owners were to sell the property, they would owe the lender more money than they'd receive from the sale. In the late-2000s real estate market downturn, this was true for increasing numbers of properties. This is the concept and strategy behind short sales. A *short sale* occurs when you buy a property from the owner and have an agreement with the lender or lien holder that it will accept an amount that is less than its loan balance as payment in full.

Recognizing seller benefits

With the advent of subprime and zero-down-payment loans in the mid-2000s, combined with the decline in home values, many owners found that they had negative equity in their homes in the late 2000s; they literally couldn't afford to sell the properties because the sale proceeds wouldn't cover the loan balance (a situation known as being *upside down*).

Some of these owners had other financial challenges and little savings to fall back on, so they were unlikely to be able or willing to continue making their debt service payments on the upside down property. An owner in this situation is a prime candidate for a short sale.

The current owner or seller receives no proceeds from a short sale but will find it a quick exit strategy from a troubling situation, with the goal of minimizing damage to his credit (because he will likely want to be a homeowner again someday). Another benefit to the current owner is that the real estate investor is likely looking for a great tenant, and who would be a better tenant than the current occupant of the property? The current owner may no longer own the property, but he can at least continue to live there and not disrupt his life completely. Being able to remain in the property also avoids some of the stigma of losing the house. Plus, immediately having a tenant can help you get a loan for the property.

Comparing short sales to other properties

Many real estate investors find that buying foreclosures or REO properties can be challenging. With foreclosures, the public sale is published and readily known to all interested real estate investors, but there is limited information and rarely an adequate opportunity to conduct proper due diligence. For example, buyers usually can't go inside the property to do inspections. Foreclosure properties can be full of surprises!

You often find that the best properties at the foreclosure auction attract the attention of other (often sophisticated) buyers who are prepared to pay more for the property than you are if they know they can make a good profit down the road. You also need to have 10 percent of the purchase price in cash and immediately have to find a loan for the balance within 30 days, whereas with the short sale you can usually negotiate for a sale closing date that gives you more time to find financing. A short sale also helps you avoid the complications of a borrower redemption possible with a judicial foreclosure.

Tracking down the property information for REO properties can be challenging, and the lenders or their agents may not be cooperative with requests for inspections or details about the condition of the property. Though the reputation for REOs is that lenders are anxious to sell these properties at any price, the reality is that they often go for close to the full market value when discounted for the condition and quick sale terms that they require.

Find properties that are in preforeclosure — that is, properties where the owner is delinquent on her debt service payments — and make a deal to buy the property from the owner before she loses it anyway and ruins her credit. These situations became more common with the excessive use of highly leveraged financing where borrowers had loans that were equal to (or even greater than) the full value of the property when it was acquired. Some borrowers took out second loans, and the combined debt exceeded the value of the property.

Finding short-sale opportunities

The concept sounds much easier than it is to actually execute. The main problem is trying to identify the properties where the owner of the property is behind on payments but the lender hasn't filed a Notice of Default.

With foreclosures, you can generally find lists available from real estate agents and even the lenders themselves, or you can drive through the neighborhoods that appeal to you and find signs that say *bank owned*. But with preforeclosure properties that are still owner-occupied and candidates for a short sale, there may not be an indication that anything is wrong. This is particularly true with many lenders now being asked to be extra patient with borrowers who are a little behind on their mortgage payments.

If you're looking for these opportunities, you can find them in many ways. Some companies specialize in assisting homeowners who know they'll have difficulty in making their mortgage payments; they work with the owners and the lenders to try and make loan modifications or alternative payment plans. These attempts may be successful, but many times they aren't, and they provide one source for identifying owners who are short-sale candidates.

Another way to identify potential short sale properties is when the mortgage holder sends a Notice of Default. But this document is public information, so many other real estate investors may be in contact with the owner seeking to arrange a short sale.

Just like in a regular foreclosure, you can find this information, and in the early days of the preforeclosure period many buyers may be willing to consider a short sale. Of course, you need to convince the lender and not just the current owner.

Note that lien holders may have purchased the underlying loan at a discount, and they may be more willing to negotiate with you to accept less money, which will enhance the prospects of a sale of the property. Your research will often reveal whether the loan that is in default has recently been sold; this is important information that can assist you with your negotiating strategy.

The concept of short sales often comes up if you have foreclosures in your area, but be careful: You need to check out the property just as thoroughly. You actually should have a better opportunity and better access to the property. It's not as bad as with foreclosure properties, but it has been our experience that short sale properties can also be properties that the owner is willing to walk away from for a reason. So be very careful because what may seem like the deal of the century may actually be a money pit.

Convincing a lender to a short sale

In addition to the difficulty inherent in finding an opportunity for a short sale, you may also have a difficult time convincing the lender to agree to a short sale. The recent trend by the federal government has been to require lenders to work with borrowers at an unprecedented level of patience and cooperation. Some lenders become overwhelmed with the large numbers of negative equity loans and the thousands of requests they receive to restructure financing. On one hand, lenders are motivated to consider short sales, but they're also under pressure to formulate a workout strategy with the current borrower. This trend may actually reduce the motivation for lenders to cooperate with short sales.

The viability of short sales is really a function of the lenders and their business strategies to minimize their losses. The lenders know that the payments aren't being made and it's inevitable that they'll complete the foreclosure, have to hold the property for some period, and incur costs before they ultimately sell it.

If they have a large number of nonperforming loans on their books, they may be motivated to quickly make a few short-sale deals. However, our experience has been that some lenders with few delinquent loans are actually more willing to agree to a buyer proposing a short sale because they want to cut their losses quickly and not risk government intervention or negative publicity. Lenders that participate in short sales are always secretive about it too.

A legislative change that has really helped owners of properties who want to work out a short sale is the Mortgage Forgiveness Act of 2007. Previously, mortgage debt that was forgiven or canceled by a lender had to be included on the borrower's tax return as taxable income. Under this new law, any loan that was used to buy, build, or substantially improve the borrower's principal residence (not second homes or investment properties) qualifies for the exemption from taxation as ordinary income. A refinance loan for the same purposes also qualifies. The lender is required to report the debt cancellation to the IRS on Form 1099-C, and the borrower must file Form 982. This law is expired at the end of 2013, but may be extended. Be sure to seek the advice of your tax professional before agreeing to any short sale.

You need to send the lender a short sale package with the following information:

- ✔ A hardship letter or proof from the borrower that he is unable to continue to make mortgage payments.
- ✔ Copies of the borrower's income tax returns.
- ✔ Information on the current condition of the property with contractor estimates or proposals to make any needed repairs.
- ✔ The estimated value of the property and your offer for the property.

The lender will want to verify current market conditions where the loan balance is greater than the current value of the property. They'll obtain a Broker's Price Opinion (BPO) of the property. This figure acts as the basis for their negotiations with you, with the goal of achieving as close as possible to the BPO.

The one common denominator to short sales with all lenders is that short sales require a lot of phone calls and investigative legwork to even find out whether the lender is open to receiving an offer for less than the current loan balance. Each lender has a different organizational structure for various individuals or departments that handle non-performing loans. Some lenders have automated phone systems that can be helpful and allow you to get right through to people you need; others are best described as "voice mail jail." Live operators are probably already familiar with what you're looking for, and you just need to describe that the purpose of your call is to find someone in charge of loss mitigation or foreclosures. If all else fails, you should contact the customer service department and ask to speak to someone who is authorized to make sales on preforeclosure properties. Have the property address and the borrower name and loan number (if available).

These transactions aren't likely, and are a sure bet to take at least 30 to 90 days (or even more) because most lenders are now much more inclined to work with the current borrower if at all possible. Our advice is that short sales can be effective in limited circumstances and only if you have the ability to reach a decision-maker at a lender that is inclined to participate. The real estate investor looking for just one property may find that the effort exceeds the return and that there are better ways to locate and purchase rental properties.

Don't forget that with short sales, you need to have some cash as well as be preapproved for loans so that you can make deals quickly. Lenders that are willing to agree to short sales are going to require all cash and won't be willing to offer any sort of financing. Lenders that are likely to be sources of funds for your loan on a short sale are going to be selective about making loans on non-owner-occupied rental properties. Your credit worthiness and having an established banking relationship is helpful if you're going to be successful with buying short sales.

Short sales in Hollywood

The short-sale concept has received a lot of notoriety, and late-night gurus promote seminars touting that they can teach you everything you need to know about short sales. Even Donald Trump has gotten into the game. Trump made the headlines when he proposed a short sale to help retired TV host Ed McMahon and his wife from losing their home in Beverly Hills. The McMahons were apparently $643,597 behind in payments on their $4.8 million loan. The Donald offered to buy the house, with Countrywide Home Loans taking a discounted payoff, and allow the McMahons to continue to live in the property as renters. Ultimately, the parties reached another solution, but this was a well-known example of how the short sale process works.

Contemplating Lease Options

A *lease option* is an excellent way to control and eventually purchase a property without the significant cash investment in a down payment. A lease option is essentially two different types of contracts combined into a single agreement. You have a lease (rental agreement), which has all of the usual terms, but the tenant also has the unilateral right to buy the property under certain terms and conditions in the future.

A lease option obligates the owner to sell the property but doesn't obligate the tenant to buy. This is a unilateral contract until the tenant exercises the option and a bilateral contract is created. One of the key issues with lease options is the *option price* (purchase price) that the buyer must pay. This figure can be a fixed price based on current market value, but often it's a future projected value based on anticipated appreciation with set time limits for exercising the option. For example, a home valued at $200,000 today may be offered as a lease option with an option price of $210,000 that can be exercised anytime in the next 12 months in a market where the seller expects appreciation of 5 percent per year. Of course, a savvy buyer doesn't exercise the option if the option price exceeds the market value of the property.

Lease options are much easier to find, and much more favorable deals can be made, when there are limited buyers, and sellers are anxious to sell. Lease options are most commonly used with single-family homes and condos, but the concept can be used with any type of property. Overall, in virtually all areas of the country, the demand for lease options is greater than the supply.

Remember that lease options aren't just a great way for real estate investors to buy property; they're also an opportunity for many first-time home buyers to ease into home owning. They're often in high demand relative to their supply, so lease options are rarely advertised; you may even need to run your own ad seeking lease options. Another way to track down a possible lease option is to respond to ads for "house for rent." When you own a property that you want to use a lease option to sell, a small ad often brings a large response. Check out Chapter 18 for more information on using a lease option as an exit strategy.

Probing Probate Sales and Auctions

A discussion of the more unusual real estate investments must include probate or sales of properties in estates. Also, auctions are becoming a more popular way to dispose of real estate, particularly because of the continued expansion of the Internet. Keep reading for more in-depth information.

Examining probate sales

Even more reliable than taxes, death creates opportunities for the purchase of good real estate at attractive prices. Every day someone in your area dies and leaves behind real estate that his heirs may not have any desire to retain. These properties are sold in *probate sales* by executors of the estate with the assistance of probate attorneys (or by the public administrator if the owner dies without a trust or will).

Know the laws and rules regarding probate sales in your area, because waiting periods and even court confirmation may be required before the sale is finalized. Also, these sales are often subject to *overbids*. A potential buyer can use the overbid process to appeal directly to the court (before the court issues the order approving the probate sale) to outbid you and purchase the property for more than the current offer under consideration. Generally, the right to overbid requires an offer that exceeds the existing offer by at least 5 percent. Be aware that this possibility exists, and be prepared to raise your bid. Just be careful not to get caught up in a bidding war and overpay for a property. Set a maximum price for yourself before you begin bidding.

Robert has a friend who bought a one-of-a-kind beachfront property in San Diego at significantly below market value from the estate of an elderly gentleman who died and left the property to his son. Apparently, the son had no interest in living near the ocean because of the noise and traffic that accompanies beachfront properties. So, the son contacted a real estate broker. He was anxious to sell the property, including the house and two rental units, for not much more than the value of the land alone. The real estate broker and Robert's friend were surfing buddies and because the broker owed Robert's friend a favor, the broker was glad to give him the first shot at this once-in-a-lifetime opportunity!

Trying real estate auctions

Real estate auctions, in which companies claim to be selling prime real estate at below-market prices, have become one of the most popular ways for builders and investors to market their excessive inventory of properties in some areas. Don't confuse these auctions with the foreclosure sales that are referred to as auctions in some regions. We're talking about public auctions where antiques or collectibles may also be sold on the same afternoon. In strong real estate markets, even new home builders have turned to private auctions to sell their new homes in an attempt to generate interest and excitement in areas where demand is low.

Private individuals, government entities, and companies that specialize in auctions all use this method of selling real estate to the public. You can often find real estate auctioneers listed in your local yellow pages. Like any auction, the goal is to generate interest and competition among potential purchasers in order to drive up the sales price. Often a minimum or reserve price is set to protect the seller from giving the property away too cheaply.

These real estate auctions are promoted heavily in newspapers, on radio and television, and on the Internet with sample prices that sound enticing. They claim to have all types of properties and usually promote a few irresistible-sounding properties — like 10 acres of pristine land for only $5,000. Of course, who knows how far out into the boonies the property is located?

Our experience is that auctions are rarely great opportunities for investors, because too many people compete for the unusual, quality property. Plus, the reserve or minimum prices are set so close to the actual market value of the property that the buyer essentially pays retail under the illusion that she's buying at wholesale. But some good opportunities do arise now and then, so check out these auctions to see if you can find anything worth pursuing.

If you do find a property of interest in an auction, follow the same thorough due diligence process that applies to foreclosures and REOs (see "Finding Foreclosures and REOs" earlier in this chapter).

Unfortunately, proper due diligence isn't always possible due to the short time frame available before the sale or because the auctioneer doesn't provide enough information. For example, the best way to minimize the possibility that the property contains some costly environmental hazards is to have a professional firm prepare a Phase I environmental report (see Chapter 14). But you're unlikely to be able to afford one for every property that interests you at an auction. This is just one example of the dangers in buying properties without a thorough and exhaustive due diligence investigation, so don't be rushed. Real estate is one investment that you can't easily get out of if you make a mistake. Remember — you don't want any surprises!

If you're the lucky buyer, you must immediately produce a certified funds check for at least 10 percent of the purchase price. Your final closing date usually falls within the next 30 days.

The Internet is the preferred method of promoting real estate auctions. As with many Internet opportunities, great care should be taken to ensure that you're dealing with a reputable firm. *Never* even consider buying *any* real estate sight unseen no matter how good the deal seems!

Chapter 4

Taking the Passive Approach

● ●

● ●

*M*any investors want the diversification and solid returns offered by real estate but aren't qualified for or interested in actively managing their real estate holdings. These real estate investors often look for investment opportunities that require no management or even minimal interaction with a property manager. Real estate investment trusts (REITs) are probably the easiest to understand and access, but other avenues allow you to passively invest in real estate, including tenants in common, triple net properties, notes and trust deeds, tax lien certificate sales, and limited partnerships.

Current federal tax laws favor real estate investments in which the real estate investors qualify as active investors, and this book focuses on real estate investment strategies that qualify as active activities in order to garner the full tax benefits. If you're seeking a passive investment, though, this chapter is for you.

Using Real Estate Investment Trusts

Real estate investment trusts (*REITs*) are for-profit companies that own and generally operate different types of property, such as shopping centers, apartments, office buildings, warehouses, hotels, self-storage, medical facilities, student housing, cell towers, and other rental buildings (see Figure 4-1). These property-holding REITs are known as *equity REITs*. Some REITs, known as *mortgage REITs,* focus on the financing end of the business; they lend

Figure 4-1:
Property
types
invested in
by REITs.

to real estate property owners and operators or provide credit indirectly
through buying loans (mortgage-backed securities).

Equity REIT managers typically identify and negotiate the purchase of properties that they believe are good investments and manage these properties
directly or through an affiliated advisory and management company, including all tenant relations. Thus, REITs can be a good way to invest in real estate
for people who don't want the hassles and headaches that come with directly
owning and managing rental property.

Distinguishing between public and private REITs

We recommend that investors not be shy about asking for full disclosure of
the relationship between the REIT, its advisors, and the management companies. REITs often involve conflicts of interest that aren't clearly disclosed
or pay significant above-market fees that ultimately lower the cash flow and
return on investment available for distribution.

Public REITs are traded on the major stock exchanges and thus must meet
strict SEC reporting requirements:

✔ **Liquidity:** Public REITs trade every business day on a stock exchange and
thus offer investors the ability to buy and sell as they please. Of course,
as with other similarly liquid investments (like stock in companies in a
variety of industries), liquidity can have its downside. More-liquid real
estate investments like REITs may inspire frequent trades caused by
making emotional decisions or trying to time market movements.

✔ **Independent board of directors:** A public company must have directors, the majority of whom are independent of its management. Shareholders vote upon and elect these directors.

✔ **Financial reporting:** Public REITs, like other public companies, must file comprehensive financial reports quarterly.

We recommend that you stay away from private REITs unless you're a sophisticated, experienced real estate investor willing to do plenty of extra research and digging. Because they're not publicly traded, private REITs don't have the same disclosure requirements as public REITs. This difference means an investor in a private REIT had better carefully scrutinize the prospectus and realize that the private REIT has the ability to make changes that may not be in the investor's best interests but that reward the private REIT sponsors or their affiliates.

Taking a look at performance

So what about performance? Over the long term, REITs have produced total returns comparable to stocks in general. In fact, REIT returns historically have been as good or better than stock returns, whereas REITs have also generally been less volatile than stocks. In the context of an overall investment portfolio, REITs add diversification because their values don't always move in tandem with other investments.

One final attribute of REITs we want to highlight is the fairly substantial dividends that REITs usually pay. Because these dividends are generally fully taxable (and thus not subject to the lower stock dividend tax rate), you should generally avoid holding REITs outside of retirement accounts if you're in a high tax bracket (for instance, during your working years).

In case you care, and you may well not, the reason for the high dividends is the legal requirement in REIT charters that they have to distribute 95 percent of their income. In other words, REITs can legally only retain a maximum of 5 percent of their net income; they must distribute everything else to the shareholders.

Investing in REIT funds

You can research and purchase shares in individual REITs, which trade as securities on the major stock exchanges. An even better approach is to buy a mutual fund or exchange-traded fund that invests in a diversified mixture of REITs. Some of the best REIT mutual funds charge 1 percent per year or less in management fees. Vanguard's REIT index fund charges just 0.20 percent per year in fees and has produced average annual returns of about 11 percent since its inception in 1996.

Want still lower fees? You can buy Vanguard REIT ETF (exchange-traded fund) through most discount brokers; it boasts a low management fee of 0.10 percent. (You can buy it without any brokerage fees through Vanguard.) Larger balance investors can buy into the Admiral share class of the Vanguard REIT index fund with a minimum of $10,000 and enjoy an annual operating expense ratio of just 0.10 percent.

In addition to providing you with a diversified, low-hassle real estate investment, REITs offer an additional advantage that traditional rental real estate doesn't. You can easily invest in REITs through a retirement account such as an IRA or Keogh. As with traditional real estate investments, you can even buy REITs and mutual fund REITs with borrowed money (in nonretirement accounts). Although risky, you can buy with 50 percent down, known as *buying on margin,* when you purchase such investments through a brokerage account.

Table 4-1 contains a short list of the best REIT mutual funds and ETFs currently available.

Table 4-1	The Best REIT Funds	
Fund	*Toll-Free Number*	*Web Site*
American Century Real Estate Investments	800-345-3533	www.americancentury.com
Cohen & Steers Realty Shares	800-437-9912	www.cohenandsteers.com
Fidelity Real Estate Investment	800-544-8888	www.fidelity.com
Third Avenue Real Estate Fund	800-443-1021	www.thirdavenuefunds.com
TIAA-CREF Real Estate	800-223-1200	www.tiaa-cref.org
T. Rowe Price Real Estate	800-638-5660	www.troweprice.com
Vanguard REIT ETF	800-662-7447	www.vanguard.com
Vanguard REIT Index	800-662-7447	www.vanguard.com

If you really have your heart set on becoming the next Warren Buffett and you enjoy the challenge of selecting your own stocks, you can research and choose your own REITs to invest in. Both of the investment research publications *Morningstar* and *Value Line,* which can be found at many local libraries as well as online (www.morningstar.com and www.valueline.com), produce individual stock page summaries on various REITs. In addition to having a professional manager deciding what REITs to buy and when, the mutual fund REITs listed in Table 4-1 also provide consolidated financial reporting. If you purchase individual REITs, you have to deal with tax statements for each and every REIT you're invested in.

Understanding Tenants in Common

Tenants in common (TIC) real estate investments have been heavily promoted as the *common man's opportunity* to own a piece of institutional-grade (commonly known as *trophy*) properties that the average investor could never acquire on her own. Due to a March 2002 IRS real estate tax ruling, tenants in common real estate ownership gained momentum.

Tenants in common ownership is arranged by sponsors that form a TIC investment group for each property; each individual investor actually receives a title deed for an undivided fractional share in a large institutional-grade property. The TIC sponsors either already have purchased or at least control these properties. TIC sponsored properties available for investment include regional shopping malls, large luxury apartment buildings, or even *class A* (with the best-quality locations, construction, and finishes) high-rise office buildings in major metropolitan areas.

These TIC investments do have some limitations: For instance, there are often limits on the number of investors (usually 35, and married couples count as a single investor) and their financial strength; each investor is proportionately responsible for the debt on the property, if any; and each owner must actually hold a specific fractional deeded interest in the property. All owners must share and pay all profits and losses proportionately, and the TIC sponsor can't advance funds to cover any expenses. The IRS also requires each owner to have a vote equal to his percentage of ownership.

Don't feel too confident about your voting rights, because you probably own only a small percentage (sometimes as little as 1 or 2 percent of the total property); you may find that the majority make decisions about management and leasing. Plus, the IRS requires unanimous approval of all co-owners to borrow against the property or sell — which may or may not coincide with your goals and needs.

Our advice is that although TICs provide some advantages for real estate investors seeking passive tax-sheltered income, new real estate investors and those with modest assets who may need to liquidate or sell their interest should avoid this investment now because the current TIC offerings are typically overpriced investments at full-market or *retail* pricing with extremely high sales commissions and costs. TICs aren't right for many investors, and the number of sponsors offering these products has greatly diminished whereas the number of TICs in expensive and exasperating litigation has increased dramatically. We question whether there will ever be a large market for these investments and believe that investors should look to invest in real estate with more traditional investment methods or sell their real estate and invest in REITs.

Paying for 1031 availability and "hassle free" management

Although we prefer REITs, tenants in common (TIC) can be right for certain investors with significant net worth and no desire to directly own real estate — as long as they fully understand the benefits and drawbacks. The minimum investment for most TICs is measured in the hundreds of thousands of dollars, although some TIC sponsors offer fractionalized ownership for as little as $50,000.

Traditionally, owners with significant equity can use a *tax-deferred exchange* (also known as a *1031 exchange*) to either sell or exchange into a larger property, or simply continue to hold and refinance the highly appreciated property to generate cash for additional real estate investments, which also offer additional tax benefits. But TIC candidates are usually real estate owners currently in or contemplating a tax-deferred exchange that are facing the strict time limits and haven't been able to find a suitable property on their own. (See Chapter 18 for a discussion of the tax-deferred exchange.)

If you're considering a TIC as an alternative for your tax-deferred exchange, verify in advance with your tax advisor that your transaction qualifies. Doing so is critical. Don't overlook this important step. A tax-deferred exchange is limited to like-kind property with specific rules about how you hold title of both the relinquished and replacement properties. If the property being sold is directly owned, the transaction most likely meets the requirements and isn't taxable at the time of sale as long as the TIC property is a direct ownership of real estate and *not* a security. But many investors may find that the property they're selling is a partnership interest in real estate and doesn't qualify for the tax-deferred treatment because the two investments aren't like-kind. It's also true if the IRS deems the replacement property ownership interest to be a security or anything other than direct ownership of real estate. Obtaining competent legal and tax advice in advance is essential, or you may have a very unpleasant surprise when the IRS declares that your transaction is fully taxable.

However, the TIC sponsors have targeted these owners of highly appreciated properties who are considering a tax-deferred exchange but are at a stage in their lives in which they're not interested in expanding their real estate empire. Or they may have used all of the tax benefits of depreciation (see Chapter 18) and really should sell their property and simply pay the capital gains.

A downside of these TIC investments is that they're often extremely expensive. Because the majority of the potential purchasers for these real estate investments are coming out of a tax-deferred exchange, they're subject to tight time limits. The IRS requires 1031 exchanges to identify the replacement property within 45 days of the close of escrow of the property being sold. And the replacement property transaction must be completed within 180 days. Please see Chapter 18 for more details.

Thus, the syndicators of the tenants in common product are always standing by with a pending real estate acquisition for those buyers whose time limits are running short and who need to identify and close on a property within the time limits imposed by the IRS. If the owner is unable to meet the deadlines, they lose all of the tax deferral benefits, so they're often willing to overpay. The TIC sponsors know that many real estate investors panic and commit to real estate investments that aren't prudent or suited to them just to avoid paying the capital gains tax.

In exchange for this flexibility and readily available product, the syndicators have prepurchased these properties and rolled them over to the tenants in common investors at *full market value*, which is a higher price than the properties would sell in an arm's-length transaction in a competitive free market. (An *arm's-length transaction* simply means between an independent buyer and seller — for example, not related parties like relatives.) Further, the syndicators usually associate with financial advisors who receive hefty sales commissions of 3 to 5 percent and even as high as 10 percent of the investors' initial investment, plus a spread to the TIC sponsor to cover their internal marketing and administration costs. Then many TIC sponsors have separate advisory firms that are closely held by the principals of the sponsor, and they commonly charge upfront, plus ongoing, consulting fees. Thus, the purchaser of a tenants in common real estate investment is paying top dollar for the property and is only receiving the benefit of as little as 90 percent of her gross investment because of commissions and fees paid upfront.

The TIC sales pitch also places a heavy emphasis on the desirability of eliminating the trials and tribulations often associated with an owner trying to manage his own property. TIC sponsored properties are professionally managed by the sponsor or a property manager of their choice.

Asking whether TICs are right for you

Be aware that TIC sponsors often provide attractive teaser rates of return that are guaranteed only for the first couple of years. For example, a review of the private placement offering may indicate that investors will receive a 7 percent cash distribution per year for the first two years only. This rate may potentially entice investors who have built up significant equity in their real estate holdings but haven't seen their cash flow increase as fast.

Also, like many other financial products, a lot of effort goes into the promotion and sales of TICs, often through independent investment advisors, which translates to a lot of overhead to cover. You typically get slick marketing materials and are referred to fancy Web sites or supposedly free seminars reminiscent of the late-night infomercial gurus. These promotional efforts are high on fluff and scarce on details.

You need to determine whether TICs are right for you by asking your investment advisor and the TIC sponsor for written answers to some basic questions before sending them your money:

- ✔ **Who's receiving commissions and how much?** The TIC sponsor receives a commission or spread right off the top, plus the investment advisors (broker) who refer their clients get a piece of the action, too.

- ✔ **Was the offered property recently acquired and at what price?** Many TIC investors purchase the properties and then resell them within days or months at full retail or top of the market pricing, so it may be informative to know how much the TIC sponsor has made on the investment in addition to the commissions.

- ✔ **How much of my net investment is actually invested in the property?** At the end of the day, after everyone has been paid, how much of my investment actually is invested into the property?

- ✔ **How solid is the tenant(s) occupying the property and what are the terms and length of their lease?** The property may be a Class "A" building with a Fortune 500 tenant today, but how long is the tenant committed to the space? Are there out clauses in case of a merger or the tenant relocates? (*Out clauses* are any language in the lease that would allow the tenant to legally and unilaterally break the lease with only limited or no further financial obligation.) What is the likely demand for this property should the unexpected happen and the Class "A" anchor tenant leaves? What are the rent increases and do they keep up with expected inflation?

✔ **What's the amount and timing of the cash distributions?** If based on a certain percentage rather than actual operating results, are the distributions guaranteed, and if so, for how long and by whom? Many TIC sponsors use an above-average cash distribution as a hook to entice new investors, but property performance may not generate enough cash to cover the distributions, and investors may actually be required to cover operating losses. Where's that fact in the fancy brochure?

✔ **What are the charges for property and asset management?** Most TIC sponsors have affiliated property management firms that handle the day-to-day management — but at fees toward the high end of reasonable. Also, there may be another layer for an asset manager or advisory firm that supervises the property management company, and they're also often controlled by or associated with the TIC sponsor. You have no guarantee that the asset or property management is qualified or competent, so be sure to ask questions about their experience and credentials; excellent management is extremely important. Remember that this is a passive investment, so you have little say in making any changes if they don't meet your expectations.

✔ **How liquid is my investment, and does the sponsor offer a buyback or loan program?** Currently, there's no viable secondary market for TIC investments, so you're at the mercy of the TIC sponsor or possibly another investor who'd be willing to buy you out. Anyone buying a fractional ownership is going to expect and receive a significant discount from the actual asset value. Have you ever tried to sell a timeshare interest at the price you paid originally from the developer?

Of course, many investors are attracted to the fact that someone else (all TIC sponsors claim to be experts) is tracking down the properties and doing all of the due diligence, and you definitely pay a price for these benefits. So follow the money and make sure you're comfortable with this investment, because it isn't easy to sell should your needs change.

Our advice for investors considering TIC: Buyer beware. Do your due diligence and speak to your independent real estate, legal, and tax advisors before making any investment. Also, explore the alternatives of other forms of real estate investments or simply sell the real estate and pay your capital gains taxes and taxes on any recapture of depreciation.

Comprehending Triple Net Properties

Triple net property is a common term for a type of net lease where the tenant pays some or all of the property operating and repair and maintenance expenses in addition to the rent. Many investors are attracted to the minimal property management and maintenance requirements of triple net properties because the tenant is responsible for the majority of all operating costs and maintenance.

Triple net properties are often promoted as another real estate option for investors looking to avoid the headaches of day-to-day management. These investments may seem like real estate investments, but they're primarily an investment in the net cash flow (after debt service) from a lease to a credit tenant, and they're promoted based on the cash-on-cash rate of return or cap rate (see Chapter 12 for information on these measures of investment return).

For years, these properties have been the favorites of real estate investors who like the steady income stream and safety usually associated with bonds. But net leases come in all varieties, and though all net leases are often referred to generically as triple net leases, the reality is that there is no standardization of terms or definitions. So the challenge is always to determine exactly which responsibilities belong to the landlord and which are the tenant's, and it's those vagaries that often make it difficult to precisely evaluate these investments.

Thinking ahead about landlord/tenant division of duties

There are several different types of triple net properties. All net leases have some aspect of the tenant paying for operating expenses, taxes, insurance, maintenance, repairs, and even capital improvements. These investments (sometimes referred to as *bond leases*) include net leases where the total responsibility rests with the tenant. In a bond lease, the tenant is fully responsible for the repairs, maintenance, and operating expenses (including taxes and insurance) of the entire property without any limitations.

The *net net net leases (or NNN leases)* are similar to the bond lease, with the tenant being responsible for all operating and fixed costs of the property, but often come with limitations on capital improvements or upgrades that the landlord can pass on to the tenant.

Another type of net lease is the *net net lease* (or *NN lease*), which is an investment where the tenant pays most operating expenses but the landlord retains responsibility for the structural components such as the foundation, bearing walls, and roof. Sometimes a net net lease also includes a property where the owner is also responsible for major building systems such as HVAC equipment, electrical, plumbing, and driveways and parking areas.

If you're considering an investment in any type of net lease, you must carefully review the lease to determine exactly who is responsible for each of the components of the building. You should also be very specific on your requirements or expectations about the quality of the maintenance of the property as well as the details of the insurance coverage, including making sure you're named on all polices as an additional insured. If you're a novice, be sure to use the services of a real estate attorney or lease expert to prepare a *lease abstract,* which is a summary of the pertinent information from the lease.

A triple net lease typically involves a fast-food franchise, restaurant chain, local chain drugstore, or similar retail outlet. The owner buys the building, which is built precisely to the tenant's specifications, and the tenant then enters a long-term fixed-rent lease in which she pays for almost everything, including the property taxes, insurance, utilities, and most of the maintenance. Many companies rely heavily on the sale/leaseback of their newly built locations. The advantage to the tenant is that they free up capital to expand and grow their primary business, which isn't real estate.

Originally, these investments were offered by developers who worked exclusively with such companies, but now many brokers specialize in the marketing and sale of triple net properties.

The owner should regularly inspect the property under any type of net lease that isn't a bond lease because she retains ultimate control — and thus the liability — if the tenant fails to properly maintain the building. Robert has seen a litany of litigation between the owner and tenant over issues of exactly what type of net lease exists, with the key dispute being an interpretation of who is responsible for the repair and maintenance of building components. These lawsuits often result from third-party injuries, with the landlord and the tenant each accusing the other of failing to properly inspect, maintain, and/or repair the property.

Minimizing the risks of triple net investments

Lately, the returns available on these triple net properties have been low due to the perception that they're essentially a risk-free investment. However, should the tenant find that the location isn't profitable, you may find yourself owning a customized taco stand that requires a lot of modifications to be a viable location for another business.

Triple net real estate investments are suitable for some, but stay away from them unless you're really comfortable with the tenant and the location and are willing to accept relatively low rates of return. Also, look closely at the rent structure because most leases have many years of flat, fixed rental income with an occasional upward adjustment that's likely to be lower than the future market rent. Triple nets may make some sense if you can consistently earn a return that's higher than a comparable bond investment. But you always run a risk with any single-tenant investment property, and fast-food and drugstore chains can (and do) go out of business. We advise investors interested in this type of investment to consider the diversification and lower risk associated with purchasing REITs (discussed earlier in this chapter) that hold triple net properties (among others) rather than a direct purchase of a triple net property.

Robert is aware of many triple net properties that probably seemed like great deals at the time buyers purchased them with a *national credit tenant* (an expanding company that has a very solid financial balance sheet) on a long-term lease. What could go wrong? A lot. With leases as long as 50 years and set rents that are modestly adjusted over time, you run a serious inflation risk unless the rents can adjust to fair market rent at least every 5 to 10 years. The more specialized the use of the building by the tenant, the more challenging your life can be if the tenant vacates, so consider whether the tenant improvements are suitable or can be modified at a reasonable cost to suit the needs of a replacement tenant.

Eyeing Notes and Trust Deeds

Although the vast majority of real estate loans for purchasing or renovating properties comes from conventional lenders, some private sources of money make loans backed by notes or trust deeds. Real estate investors have found that they can benefit from the strong demand for real estate in their area by acting as a lender. They purchase notes and trust deeds that are backed by pledged real estate. *Pledged real estate* is the collateral or security interest provided to the investors to protect them from nonpayment by giving them the ability to foreclose on the real estate. Besides the interest earned on the investment, the note or trust deed holder has the collateral of the underlying real property if the borrower defaults on the loan.

Real estate investors who buy and sell trust deeds are also often interested in making private *hard money loans* (loans on top of the first mortgage made by a traditional lender) to property owners or other real estate investors. These hard money loans are secured by the owner's equity in the property and offer potentially favorable returns for the lender willing to make loans to borrowers that often have poor credit. Although your risk increases when the borrower has credit issues, the terms can be quite attractive — typically above-market interest rates ranging from 10 to 15 percent, plus loan fees of 3 to 5 points (a *point* is 1 percent of the loan amount and is essentially prepaid interest), plus prepayment penalties that lock in the high interest rates or require a hefty payment for the privilege of refinancing.

Your loan is secured by a mortgage or deed of trust against the property, so it's extremely important to be conservative with the loan-to-value ratio or the amount of money you actually lend the borrower versus the fair market value of the property. At times, borrowers damage or neglect the property if they fall behind on the payments, so we advise real estate investors to limit their exposure to no more than 50 to 60 percent of the value of the property.

Although making and purchasing real estate notes and trust deeds can be a lucrative investment vehicle, acting as a real estate lender can be risky for the novice. Properties with latent problems or unrecorded tax liens are just some of the potential pitfalls. Should you decide that lending money on real estate offers you the high returns you're looking for without the headaches of ownership, proceed with caution. Also be sure that you have an experienced real estate advisor and/or your real estate attorney review the documents before making an agreement or advancing any funds (see Chapter 6).

The safest approach to making secured loans on property is to thoroughly evaluate the pledged collateral to protect your investment and determine the fair market value if you had to foreclose. Never make a loan on a property that you wouldn't be willing to own if that becomes your best way to protect your investment. Some lenders actually hope that the borrower does default so they can obtain the property for a fraction of its market value.

However, don't forget that you're responsible for legal fees and foreclosure costs in addition to the unpaid balance of your loan and accrued interest in the event that the borrower defaults.

Looking At Tax Lien Certificate Sales

Real estate owners who fail to pay their property taxes in a timely manner find that the local county files a lien on their property. A *lien* is any legal claim or charge against real or personal property for the satisfaction of a debt or duty that includes the right to take the property if the obligation isn't discharged. The county ultimately sells the property in a tax lien certificate sale auction to generate the funds necessary to satisfy the unpaid real estate property taxes, along with the accrued penalties and fees.

But local municipalities don't want to foreclose or wait for payment because they need the funds today to pay the costs of government, so they auction off these tax lien certificates to investors.

Tax lien certificates can be a good investment regardless of the economic cycle, because some property owners will always be unable to pay their property taxes. When you buy a real estate tax lien, you're simply providing the government entity with the funds for the delinquent taxes and buying the rights to collect those taxes from the property owner (plus penalties and a fixed rate of interest that can range from 12 to 24 percent per year).

The property owner can't sell or pledge her real estate without paying the outstanding tax liens, so over 90 percent of the tax lien certificates are redeemed within 24 months (or the maximum allowable redemption period set by each state or county). Look for tax lien certificates in certain types of real estate, such as owner-occupied properties, because these tend to have nearly a 100 percent redemption rate. You may ultimately have to give the required legal notices and foreclose on the underlying real estate to achieve your return of capital and realize your return on investment, so always limit your purchase of tax lien certificates to properties that you're willing to own.

Tax lien certificates aren't available in every state, and you don't have any way to control the timing of the redemption. Savvy real estate investors that have done quite well with tax lien certificate sales generally buy multiple liens to spread out their anticipated payoffs. Also, they read the fine print of the government rules and regulations concerning these sales, because the rules vary greatly from state to state — and each county within a state may have different rules. Contact your county tax collector to see whether real estate tax lien certificates are a viable investment alternative in your area.

You have to devote the time necessary to really find out about the underlying properties even though finding information is difficult. The conventional sources of local real estate knowledge — brokers and agents — don't work in this market because they offer no opportunities for them to earn commissions.

Considering Limited Partnerships

Unlike a *general partnership,* in which every partner has full management authority and accountability, a real estate *limited partnership* is an investment program in which general partners manage property and accept unlimited liability, and the limited partners don't participate in management decisions and their liability for losses is limited to their investment. A limited partnership offers advantages to real estate investors who want to participate in the market while limiting their day-to-day involvement and liability.

The disadvantage of limited partnerships is that limited partners don't have any authority, so limited partnerships are passive investments.

In a limited partnership, the general partner makes all the decisions of management and even decides when to sell the property. Upon disposition, many limited partnerships provide for the general partner to receive a portion of the appreciation (usually from 10 to 25 percent) right off the top — prior to distributions to the limited partners who get a share of the remaining realized appreciation based on their ownership percentage. This equity kicker for the general partner is typically in addition to brokerage fees upon acquisition and disposition, plus market rate or higher fees for property management and asset management.

Although some limited partnerships are formed by general partners who treat each partner as an equal, the majority is structured by general partners with the perspective of "Heads: I win! Tails: You lose!" Some limited partnerships are nothing more than a pure profit play for the general partner in which they get their money upfront — often while the limited partners are held captive and can only hope to see the return of their capital and some appreciation in the distant future.

Limiting the scope of limited partnerships

Limited partnerships have been available for many years. Prior to the extensive overhaul of the federal taxation of real estate investments in the 1980s, they were a common method of real estate investing. Up until that time, all losses from real estate were fully deductible, and these loopholes created opportunities for aggressive tax management to avoid legal tax liabilities.

In 1986, Congress passed new tax regulations that eliminated the favorable tax treatment of most losses unless the real estate investor was an active participant. To qualify as an active participant, an individual must be involved in direct management decisions of the property, although the day-to-day rental activities of collecting rent, overseeing repairs, and paying bills can be delegated to a property manager.

Further, the federal tax code limits the deductibility of your passive losses against your earned income (salary, dividends, and interest) to a maximum of $25,000, as long as your adjusted gross income doesn't exceed $100,000. The maximum $25,000 passive loss deduction phases out at a ratio of $1 for every $2 in adjusted gross income between $100,000 and $150,000. For real estate owners with adjusted gross income exceeding $150,000, any passive losses are carried forward to future years or until the property is sold.

However, we discuss an extremely valuable exception for real estate investors who qualify as real estate professionals in Chapter 18.

Chapter 5

Fast Money: Small Down Payments and Property Flips

*T*he only thing better for a small-time investor than getting rich is getting rich quickly. Entire books have been written about hitting the real estate big time with little money to invest through buying and flipping properties to turn quick profits.

Does this scenario sound too good to be true? Of course it does! In rare cases, these strategies have proven profitable — but those success stories are few and far between. That's why we warn you about the realities and truths of the get-rich-quick-and-with-little-money sales pitches in this chapter, and we offer our best advice to guide you in case you choose to walk these dangerous paths despite our persistent warnings!

Purchasing with No Money Down

If you've ever had insomnia and turned on the television in the middle of the night, you've likely seen the late-night infomercial real estate gurus who claim to possess the true secrets of buying real estate significantly below market value — and they don't even use their own money! They tell viewers that anyone can buy real estate tomorrow using their no-money-down strategies. And it gets even better — they tell you that you can actually receive money from the seller to buy her property.

The birth of the no-money-down movement

The popularity of no-money-down investing peaked in the early-1980s when most real estate loans were *assumable* — the buyer of the property essentially took over or assumed the payments on the current loan from the seller. Properties weren't appreciating that quickly in that time frame, so many owners didn't have significant equity in their homes and were willing to take small down payments or carry seller financing as part of the transaction. The advent of the due on sale clause in many mortgages virtually eliminated the ability of buyers to assume the seller's current loan.

Although finding a buyer who is so motivated that she'll actually pay you to take a property off her hands is possible, the reality is that the vast majority of such properties don't prove to be profitable for you in the long run. Ask yourself — why would anyone give away a property unless it had some really serious problems?

Understanding why we recommend skipping these investments

The concept of buying real estate without using any of your own money is clearly dependent on finding an extremely motivated seller. A *motivated seller* is one who faces circumstances that don't allow him the flexibility to achieve full market value for his property. For sure, a certain number of motivated sellers exist in any market.

The late 2000s downturn in the real estate market may seem a perfect opportunity to explore the benefits of putting less money down to purchase a property. The reality is that most lenders are no longer in the creative financing business after being burned by the stated income or "no doc" and similar subprime loans in which the buyers have no vested interest and were counting on unsustainable appreciation to create equity.

There are also fewer sellers with significant equity in their properties so the margin for seller financing is diminished. Low money down and/or installment sales are much more likely and feasible when you have a seller with plenty of equity. However, many of the most motivated current sellers are owners of properties in which they owe as much or more than the property's current market value.

The stock market is a relatively liquid market where buyers and sellers can enter or leave the market quickly with broad knowledge of current pricing. In contrast, real estate assets are *illiquid* — it can take a relatively long time to enter or leave the real estate market. Real estate is also unique: A share of your favorite stock always represents the same investment; not so with real estate. This creates the opportunity to profit from pricing inefficiencies between one property and another. Also, the ability to complete a real estate transaction quickly provides an additional factor that can affect the price.

The following are examples of motivated sellers who may be willing to accept a no-money-down offer:

- ✔ **A seller who's relocating and needs to sell in a hurry:** An owner who's leaving the area may need to quickly sell his home so he can buy a replacement home in his new location. In order to complete the sale in a timely manner, he may be willing to lower the price to slightly below the *full market value* (the price he could have received if he were not in such a hurry).

  Finding a seller in a hurry is one of the most reliable ways to buy real estate with little or no money down.

- ✔ **A seller who's desperate to sell and exasperated by the effort:** The owner of a property that has been vacant for an extended time period or that requires extensive renovation may be eager to sell. The property may have a deadbeat tenant, or maybe it's vacant after being destroyed by the last tenant and the owner lacks the cash to make the significant investment in repairs. This type of seller may be willing to offer generous seller financing terms or even pay you to remove him from his liability.

- ✔ **The current owner may have challenges in his life with his health, relationships, or job.** Managing rental properties is time consuming and at times draining, both emotionally and financially, especially when something major — such as replacing a roof — needs to be done. Also, any reason that the current owner no longer has other sources of income that can support rental properties with negative cash flow can be an opening for you. Most owners have mortgages with payments due each month, and if the property isn't generating enough income to cover the mortgage and operating expenses, the owner has to come up with the additional cash from other sources.

But even when sellers find themselves in such positions, who will stamp "Desperate to Sell" on their forehead? Trying to determine a seller's motivation takes effort and investigation. Check out Chapter 13 for more on the subject.

Although, clearly, such real estate owners exist, they're not as common as some of the real estate investment gurus would have you believe. There are always anecdotal stories about an amazing success story, but there are many more untold stories of cocky novice real estate investors who found out the hard way that you get what you pay for.

Finding no-money-down opportunities (if you insist)

No-money-down sellers are in greater abundance in a weak real estate market (or *buyer's market*) because sellers have fewer options. The target market for no-money-down deals is a real estate market environment with highly motivated sellers facing dire consequences (including foreclosure, which we discuss in Chapter 3) unless they dispose of their property. Usually, sellers that need to sell quickly are in one of the following situations:

✔ **A seller who has had some unfortunate circumstances** such as an illness, a death in the family, a divorce, a job loss, or a significant loss of income such that she can no longer afford to make the payments and handle the ongoing expenses of the property — this situation is often the one that leads to a no-money-down offer. Because of her compromised situation, such a property seller may not readily qualify for new or additional loans that would allow her to handle the cash flow dilemma she faces. Although home equity loans may be available in these circumstances, the owner may be so financially overwhelmed that she prefers to sell her property and downsize her financial obligations to a more manageable level.

✔ **A seller with significant equity but limited options to tap that equity** is likely to have cash flow problems, but the overall equity in the property can allow her to act as a lender to you (see Chapter 8 for seller-financing strategies).

The two most common *good candidates* (as opposed to the classic definition of owners who would be flexible out of desperation) for no-money-down scenarios are

• Folks at or approaching retirement age who would prefer a steady income stream to a lump sum.

• Individuals who inherited the property and are looking for monthly income without the hassles of being a landlord.

In order to know whether the candidates you're considering fall into one of the preceding scenarios, you need to assess their motives. Chapter 13 helps you do that.

Buying, Fixing, and Flipping or Refinancing

In a solid real estate market, you often find properties appreciating at an annual rate of 3 to 5 percent — a solid and sustainable rate of appreciation that rewards investors with long-term investment horizons who take the buy-and-hold approach with their real estate assets. This buy-and-hold strategy works and should always be the foundation of your wealth building.

But in some areas, the demand for housing has been so great that the limited supply of new and existing properties available in the market is insufficient to meet the demand. It's in these markets of high demand and rapidly escalating prices that real estate speculators with a buy-and-flip strategy tend to appear.

There's nothing wrong with the buy-and-flip strategy, but we prefer the more conventional and lower-risk strategy of buy, fix, and hold.

The buy-and-flip strategy

The buy-and-flip strategy can also work with existing homes that the investor can purchase from a motivated seller at a wholesale price that is below the market value. The investor may not even have to close escrow before finding a buyer willing to pay a retail price. There may be some minor cosmetic work or simple improvements needed before reselling, but typically, buy-and-flip investors really make their money when they buy at a discount and then locate a buyer at full market value.

You generally can only do work on a property that you have closed upon and own. Even if a seller allowed you to do work on it before closing, you're taking a huge risk (loss of your money and time spent) doing it in the event that the deal ends up falling apart for some reason (such as you don't get financing, an inspection finds something concerning, and so on).

This high-risk strategy requires a rapidly rising real estate market with higher than normal appreciation rates to allow for profits on short-term investments. Not only do you have to have excessive demand driving up the prices of real estate, but you also have to cover all of the costs of real estate. With online stock trading firms, you can buy shares of your favorite company in minutes with relatively low transaction costs. But with real estate, the costs of buying, holding, and selling a property are much higher and unknown, and generally include

- ✔ **Acquisition costs:** Due diligence and inspection fees plus loan fees/costs and points

- ✔ **Transaction costs:** Closing and escrow fees

- ✔ **Repair or upgrade costs:** Costs and contingencies to renovate or fix property to make it more desirable and generate the highest resale price (unless the property is brand-new)

- ✔ **Holding costs:** Property taxes, insurance, and any negative cash flow while the property sits vacant or if the rental income doesn't cover the carrying costs

- ✔ **Sales costs:** Commissions and title insurance from the sale of the property

Even during the weak real estate market in the late 2000s, you saw late-night infomercials promoting the flipping strategy, but they often cited examples with just limited information. These ads featured an average Joe who invests his excess income in a fixer-upper down the street — he pays $150,000 for it and then sells it for $200,000 after replumbing the property and installing all new flooring, window coverings, and appliances. The infomercials implied that he just made a quick and effortless $50,000.

But what they don't say is that he has $3,000 in acquisition costs, $2,000 more in transaction costs, $15,000 in repairs and upgrades, and $10,000 in sales costs for a total of $30,000. That brings the theoretical profit down to $20,000 before factoring in holding costs. Even if everything works out well for Joe, his property likely sits empty for at least six months while he renovates it, puts it on the market, and shows it to prospective buyers. So by the time Joe has completed this investment cycle, he's quite possibly spent another $6,000 in mortgage interest payments, plus $2,000 in property taxes and insurance. His pre-tax profit is now $12,000 if everything goes well. But wait — there's more. Because he only held this investment for less than one year, he pays income tax at his nominal ordinary earned income tax rate of, say, 30 percent, which brings his amazing $50,000 profit down to a measly $8,400.

But what if there are some additional problems with the property when Joe opens up the walls to replumb his new investment gem? Maybe there are termites or roof leaks or problems with the foundation. What if the demand for this property diminishes and he has to hold the property for 12 months? (Some folks got burned in the late 2000s when the demand for housing suddenly evaporated.) Even in the best scenario, where Joe has accurately estimated the repair and upgrade costs and there are no surprises, he finds that just owning the property for six months longer than he expected doubles the holding costs from $8,000 to $16,000, reducing the pre-tax profit to $4,000. By the time he is done paying 30 percent of that in taxes, Joe has just $2,800 to show for his efforts.

You may be located in a market that has experienced rapid housing price increases, but be careful. If there is too much excess demand for new housing in the area, real estate speculators — not long-term investors or homeowners — can make up the majority of the purchasers. This tendency can be dangerous when the majority of buyers in the market are looking for the quick profit rather than a long-term, stable real estate investment. When enough of these speculators head for the exits (as happened in some areas in the late-2000s real estate market decline) and don't return, prices can quickly turn tail. The speculators are then forced to mitigate their losses by renting out their properties (sometimes for years) until the real estate market rebounds and they're able to sell the property to break even.

For example, the greater Las Vegas area in the early to mid-2000s became known as a place where investors could make quick cash. The large number of new home tracts and increased demand and rising new home prices over a relatively short timeframe created an opportunity for aggressive investors to place small cash deposits on new homes that were going to be built. Typically each new phase of a developer's project would see price increases (annualized at 10 to 20 percent in many cases) so these savvy investors would sell their holding at a profit to a buyer just about the time the new home was completed for a nice return on their investment. Las Vegas wasn't the only part of the country that experienced this real estate investment strategy, but it was the most prevalent with an estimated 40,000 to 60,000 of investor-owned homes (many of them vacant with no demand from buyers) after the financial and real estate markets collapsed starting in mid-to-late 2007.

But we're pragmatists — we know that lightning may strike and you may run into a property that turns out to be a buy-and-flip candidate. So in Chapter 13, we detail how to keep this possibility open by using an assignment clause when completing a purchase agreement. And we also cover possible tax drawbacks of losing the advantages of lower capital gains taxes in Chapter 18.

The buy, fix, and refinance strategy

With the *buy, fix, and refinance strategy,* you invest in properties where value can be added to the property through repairs, upgrades, and improvements that take a distressed property and turn it into a solid and well-maintained property with a good stable tenant. Over the years, with increased equity in the property and as long as interest rates are attractive, you could refinance the property if you so choose and use some of your equity towards other real estate investments.

We strongly prefer this method because it has proven throughout the years to be the lowest risk, highest probability way to make money in real estate. You can think of it as the tortoise in the old tortoise-and-the-hare story, where the hare is the fast-money, high-risk, high-return strategy. The tortoise may be slow and steady, but he ends up winning in the long run. As an example, Robert is a conservative person by nature, yet he has acquired a significant real estate portfolio by simply purchasing well-located but often distressed properties and renovating, filling them, and then refinancing and holding them for the long run.

Chapter 6

Building Your Team

There are some investments — called *passive investments* — where you can simply turn your money over to professional money managers or financial advisors who then act on your behalf and make the day-to-day investment decisions, buying and selling investment assets within the portfolio. Mutual funds are an example of this type of passive investment. You send your money to your favorite mutual fund firm and periodically evaluate how your fund's managers are doing.

Investments in real estate that you're directly involved in managing are the norm, because passive investments in real estate aren't readily available (except for REITs and TICs, which we discuss in Chapter 4). And for most real estate investors, real estate investing is hands-on and complicated enough to require the services and knowledge of a team of professionals. Although you may be skilled in your chosen field, it's unlikely that you possess all of the varied and detailed skills and knowledge necessary to initiate and close a good real estate transaction.

Evaluate proposed real estate investments carefully and methodically before you make the ultimate purchase decision. The uniqueness of each potential real estate opportunity requires the investor to patiently critique the pending investment. You should understand the economic climate and potential for growth, the current physical condition of the property, the tenants, and the value of the property in the marketplace. Then you should ensure that you've got a solid negotiating strategy to orchestrate a deal, that the financing comes through, and that the transfer of real estate is handled properly. This requires a team approach.

In this chapter, we discuss the different real estate professionals and service providers that you should consider teaming up with as you search for real estate investment opportunities and proceed with the purchase of property.

Knowing When to Establish Your Team

Some real estate investors make the mistake of looking for a property to buy without spending enough time upfront thinking about and identifying the pros whose help should be retained. We recommend that you have your team in place before you begin your serious property searching, for two reasons:

- ✔ **You can move quickly.** The speed at which you can close a transaction is an advantage in any type of market. In a soft or buyer's market, some sellers are desperate for cash and need to close quickly. In a rising or seller's market, sellers typically don't tolerate having their property tied up for a long time until closing with a buyer who doesn't understand the current market conditions or how to properly evaluate the property. Sellers may be missing out on a better deal with a buyer willing to close quicker and/or pay more. In a buyer's market, although less property may be selling overall, there is always demand for the most appealing properties that are priced right and well located. These properties often attract multiple offers, so being organized and efficient can make the difference between securing and losing a desirable property.

- ✔ **You can effectively research the property before making an offer.** Prudent investors conduct research and gather information before they even make an offer, so they know which property or properties are worth seriously pursuing. Typically, the real estate industry describes *due diligence* as the period of time after you place a property under contract (see Chapter 14). But you really need to perform due diligence even before making an offer. You don't want to waste time or money on a property that can't meet your goals.

Some real estate investors like to make an offer and get a property under contract before they begin due diligence. We believe that this is a mistake and can lead to a reputation with sellers (and agents) that you're not a serious buyer (see the "Working with Brokers and Agents" section later in the chapter). We recommend only making offers when you have done enough due diligence to feel comfortable that your further, thorough review of the property interiors and books probably won't reveal any surprises that will lead to canceling the purchase.

The most effective research is done with the assistance of real estate professionals to give you the advice and information you need to make an intelligent decision. This pre-offer period is critical; it's the one real opportunity for a prospective buyer to investigate a property while retaining the ability to terminate the transaction without a significant monetary loss. You may invest time and several hundred to several thousand dollars to perform the necessary due diligence, but this is a small amount compared to the potential losses from the purchase of a bad property. (We cover this prepurchase research in Chapters 10 through 12.)

Adding a Tax Advisor

A tax advisor may not be the first person that you think to consult before making a real estate transaction. However, our experience is that a good tax advisor can highlight potential benefits and pitfalls of different real estate investment strategies. Of course, make sure that your tax person has experience with real estate investing and understands your needs and specific goals in regard to your property investments. (We cover the ins and outs of real estate accounting and taxation in Chapters 17 and 18.)

Although you may pick up a lot of information about real estate and discover some of the advantages of property investing speaking with some tax people, don't rely on generic information ("investing in real estate offers a terrific tax shelter," for example). You need specific feedback and ideas from a tax expert regarding your unique financial situation and which types of real estate investments work best for you.

Based on your age, income, and other important factors, the benefits you seek from real estate may be entirely different from other investors. Many real estate investors are looking for immediate cash flow from their properties. But others have sufficient income currently from other sources and prefer to look at real estate as a wealth builder for their retirement years. And almost all real estate investors are looking for tax benefits.

The role of your accountant is to evaluate and recommend investments and tax strategies that maximize your financial position. Remember the old adage that says, "It's not what you make that matters but what you keep."

A good tax advisor with property investment experience can tell you whether your best real estate investment is the direct ownership of properties or perhaps owning triple net leased properties with lower returns but fewer management headaches. An accountant can inform his clients as to whether they can (or how to) meet the active participation required for certain tax benefits while hiring a property management company to handle the bulk of the day-to-day tenant/landlord issues.

You may also want to find out whether you qualify for the added tax benefits that are available for some investors who qualify as real estate professionals. Achieving such qualification isn't easy, and the IRS may someday audit you, so be sure to implement a reliable method to document to ensure that you meet the requirements. Meet with your tax advisor and get to know the benefits and pitfalls of your proposed real estate investments before you start making offers.

Finding a Financial Advisor

Over the years, Eric has written extensively about the financial planning profession and how individuals can best navigate important personal financial decisions with and without the help of planners. In theory, everyone entering into major investments like real estate should seek holistic financial advice from a financial advisor who charges an hourly fee.

In reality, many financial consultants sell investment and insurance products that provide them with commissions or manage money for an ongoing percentage in stocks, bonds, mutual, and exchange-traded funds, and the like. Such salespeople and money managers can't provide objective, holistic advice, especially on real estate transactions. When you buy property, you spend money these people want to manage. Check out the "Avoiding financial conflicts of interest" sidebar in this chapter for more information.

If you've worked with or can locate a financial advisor who sells her time and nothing else, just as a good tax advisor does, consider hiring her. A true financial advisor can help you understand how real estate investment property purchases fit with your overall financial situation and goals. (Chapter 1 discusses all the variables that affect the way your investments mesh with your situation and goals.)

Avoiding financial conflicts of interest

Here are a couple of stories that highlight the conflicts of interest you may be subjected to when working with a financial advisor.

✔ While serving as an expert real estate witness, Robert had a case where a retired couple was given some self-serving advice by their financial planner. This couple owned their principal residence plus three

other rental homes valued at $1 million. All of their real estate was owned free and clear, and the rentals were in great condition with good long-term tenants. The properties provided a nice monthly income stream that was mostly tax-free due to their depreciation deduction (see Chapter 18). Although the real estate was clearly their largest asset and completely debt-free, they also had nearly $500,000 in liquid assets such as stocks, bonds, and IRAs and seemed to be fairly set. That was, until their new financial advisor told them that their retirement was at risk because they had too much invested in real estate. The planner's recommendation was to keep their own home as their real estate investment, but sell the three highly appreciated rental properties and invest the proceeds in mutual funds and other financial products from companies affiliated with the planner.

The planner failed to disclose his relationship with the sponsors of the new investments and also failed to warn them about the significant capital gains taxes that would be due upon sale. By the time they met with their accountant, it was too late — two of the three rental properties had been sold and more than $200,000 in taxes was due. The accountant advised the couple to contact an attorney and file a lawsuit against the financial advisor. Although the couple prevailed, they recovered only a small portion of what they paid in taxes. Even worse — they lost the benefits of cash flow and appreciation on their real estate while now owning fully taxable investments.

✔ In Eric's previous work as an hourly-based financial advisor, he often had clients come to him who were disappointed with the biased and confusing advice they got from various so-called financial planners. In one typical case, a widow had been told by an advisor to sell her two investment properties because he believed that the stock market would produce better returns. She set the wheels in motion to unload the properties but put the brakes on at the last minute after deciding she needed a second opinion. She met with Eric. The first thing that she noticed working with him was that he was far more thorough in examining her overall financial situation, including *all* of her investments, insurance, and resources for retirement. She also realized that she was happy with her real estate holdings and really didn't have any motivation to sell them. Furthermore, she found out from Eric that over the long-term, the returns from stocks and real estate were quite comparable. She thus decided to keep her life simple and stable and hold onto her nicely performing rental properties.

Don't get us wrong, selling real estate can make sense at times. However, you must ask a lot of questions and run any proposed investment strategies by good independent advisors before you make the decision to liquidate your real estate and shift your investments to other opportunities.

Lining Up a Lender or Mortgage Broker

Before looking at specific real estate opportunities, you need a budget. And because your budget for real estate purchases is largely a function of how much you can borrow (in addition to your cash available for a down payment), you need to determine the limits on your borrowing power. If you can't afford a property, it doesn't matter what a great deal it is.

Postpone making an appointment to look at investment properties until after you examine the loans available. You have two resources to consult:

- ✔ **Lender** is a generic term for any firm, public or private, that directly loans you the cash you need to purchase your property. This type of lender is often referred to as a *direct lender*. Most often, your list of possible lenders includes banks, credit unions, and private lenders (including property sellers). Lenders tend to specialize in certain types of loans.

- ✔ A **mortgage broker** is a service provider that presents your request for a loan to a variety of different lenders in order to find the best financing for your particular needs. Just like real estate or insurance brokers, a good mortgage broker can be a real asset to your team (we cover mortgages in detail in Chapter 8, along with the advantages and disadvantages to working with mortgage brokers versus direct lenders in Chapter 9).

Understanding lending nuances

Lenders and mortgage brokers are in the business of making loans. That's how they make money. Their product is cash, and they make money by renting it to people and businesses that pay them the money back plus *interest,* which is the cost of renting the money. Money is a commodity just like anything else and its availability and pricing are subject to an assortment of variables.

Lenders and mortgage brokers want to find you money for your next real estate purchase, but they're not objective advisors to provide counsel for how much you should borrow. They're trained to calculate the maximum that you *may borrow.* Don't confuse this figure with the amount that you *can truly afford* or that fits best with your overall financial and personal situation. Because they only are paid when they make loans, many borrowers have learned the hard lesson that some lenders and mortgage brokers are willing to make any loan.

So why is getting a loan so difficult at times? Because lenders want to make loans to those investors who are a good credit risk and who they think have a high probability of repaying the loan in full plus the interest. This concern became more pronounced in the late 2000s as real estate prices fell and defaults and foreclosures escalated. The lender has costs of doing business and needs to make a profit. Because the money they lend often belongs to their depositors, lenders need to be careful and selective about the loans they make. (See Chapter 9 for more information on the necessity of a good credit rating when investing in real estate.)

On the upside, we've found that lenders can also serve a valuable role by preventing you from making serious mistakes. Particularly in overheated seller's markets where prices are irrationally climbing with little fundamental economic support, your lender and the required appraisal from a competent professional appraiser can keep you from getting caught up in a buy-at-any-price frenzy. (Of course, this isn't always the case; look no further than the subprime loan debacle that came to light in the late 2000s.) In these markets, lenders tend to be a little more conservative, limiting loan amounts and requiring larger down payments. These factors provide the lender with additional protection should market prices fall, but they're also a signal that the lender feels the loan exceeds the intrinsic value of the property that they'll be stuck with if you default. Smaller loan offers with higher down payments are a clue that you may be paying more than a property is worth or buying at the market's peak.

The lender requires collateral to protect them if the borrower doesn't make the debt service payments as required. *Collateral* is the real or personal property that's pledged to secure a loan or mortgage. If the debt isn't paid as agreed, the lender has the right to force the sale of the collateral to recover the outstanding principal and interest on the loan. Typically, the property being purchased is the pledged collateral for real estate loans or mortgages.

Building relationships with lenders

Relationships with lenders can take time to build, so begin looking for lenders that specialize in the types of properties within the geographic area that you have targeted. They can help you understand your financial qualifications or how much you can borrow before you begin your search for an investment property. Although lenders only make money by making loans and some lenders seem to be willing to lend money on any property at any price, the type of lender you should associate with is one who understands real estate cycles and your local real estate market. Not all lenders and mortgage brokers were hit by the subprime lending mess, and it does matter that you develop a relationship with a lender that's likely to be there when you want to acquire additional properties.

When you get together with your lender or mortgage broker, provide them with your latest personal financial statement, which includes your income and expenses as well as your assets and liabilities and net worth. The days of "no documentation" or "stated income" loans are hopefully over.

Always be truthful with your lender. One way to sabotage a relationship with a lender is to exaggerate or stretch the truth about your current financial situation or about the potential for your proposed property acquisition. Most lenders require supporting documents for your income and assets and will obtain a current credit report. When you don't oversell yourself or your proposed property, lenders are often more willing to work with you and even offer better terms.

Working with Brokers and Agents

Your investment team should include a sharp and energetic real estate broker or agent. All real estate brokers and agents are licensed by the state in which they perform their services. A real estate *broker* is the highest level of licensed real estate professional, and a licensed real estate sales *agent* is qualified to handle real estate listings and transactions under the supervision of a broker. The vast majority of real estate licensees are sales agents. Throughout this chapter, we refer to both real estate brokers and agents simply as agents.

A real estate agent must have his license placed under a supervising broker who's ultimately responsible for the actions of their sales agents. Real estate brokers often begin their careers as real estate agents, but it's possible to meet the more stringent qualifications and immediately qualify as a broker. Brokers and agents can perform the same functions; many real estate agents actually have more practical experience and hands-on market knowledge than the brokers they work for. Brokers that have many agents reporting to them often spend most of their time educating, supervising, and reviewing the transactions presented by their agents. So, if you have a problem with an agent, contact the broker — the buck stops with her!

Generally, you deal with real estate agents, but the added experience and dedication of a broker can be beneficial to you if you're involved in larger and/or more complicated transactions. Real estate agents are fine to handle the majority of real estate transactions, including the typical purchase or sale of an owner-occupied single-family home or condo. However, many owners of investment real estate don't want the disruption that can occur with openly listing the property. The management company and employees begin to worry about their jobs, and tenants become concerned that rents will be raised. These problems can be avoided by quietly talking to one or two top brokers in an area with the understanding that the potential transaction is to be kept confidential. This leads to some great opportunities for the top brokers and their clients.

Whether you use a broker or an agent, make sure that this person has a solid track record with investment property transactions in your area. And although having a real estate agent on your team is an excellent strategy that gives you a competitive edge, don't completely ignore the Multiple Listing Service or in-house listings of brokers. Such sources often include properties that other investors overlooked because they didn't have the vision or the right team members to see a potential opportunity.

Seeing the value of working with an agent

In many metropolitan areas, looking at the properties on a Multiple Listing Service (MLS) or in the newspaper or online listings isn't enough. The best deals are often the ones that don't make it into these sources. This is where the "insider information" from real estate sales agents can make you the bride and not the bridesmaid. (Of course, many brokers are themselves interested in investing in income producing properties, and they have the first chance at the best deals.)

You want to be the first one contacted about the best properties coming on the market rather than one of many when everyone knows about the property from the MLS. The *MLS* is a service created and maintained by real estate professionals per guidelines established by the National Association of Realtors (NAR). This service gathers all of the local property listings into a single place so that purchasers may review all available properties from one source. The MLS also deals with commission splitting and other relations between agents.

For many years the MLS dominated the markets, but the Department of Justice filed an antitrust lawsuit that was settled with NAR in 2008, agreeing that other listing services would be given access to the same listings. Now there are several investment real estate listing services that are gaining market share and offering instant access to an incredible database of information on all types of properties from single-family homes and condos to large commercial, industrial, and retail properties. Two of the most popular listing services for investment properties are Loopnet (`www.loopnet.com`) and CoStar (`www.costar.com`).

Grasping the implications of agency: Who the agent is working for

When you deal with a real estate agent, you need to know who she represents. Real estate investors need to understand the concepts of dual agency and single agency and the implications of each:

- ✔ **Single agency:** This is when an agent only represents the buyer or the seller. The other party either represents herself or is represented by an agent who doesn't work for the same broker as the other agent. For example, a buyer's agent only has a fiduciary relationship with the buyer. The buyer's agent has a duty to promote the interests of the buyer and keep all information confidential unless legally required to disclose. The buyer's interest should be first and foremost, and no information is passed to the seller without your knowledge other than that information that directly affects your ability to perform on the contract as written.

We strongly recommend that you work with an agent who operates as a single agency representative. A lot of money is involved in income property transactions, and you want to have someone looking out for your interests whether you're buying or selling an investment property.

🖙 **Dual agency:** A situation in which the same individual agent represents both the seller and the buyer *or* when two different agents representing the seller and buyer are from the same firm (with the same broker). With any transaction, each agent involved owes a fiduciary duty of loyalty to each client he represents, but this is nearly impossible for one agent who is representing both the buyer and seller in the same transaction (and difficult as well if two agents work for the same broker).

Avoid the inherent conflict of interest found with dual agency and establish a relationship with a single agency agent who represents only *your* interests. Dual agency makes it extremely challenging for one agent, or two agents working for the same broker, to be loyal to clients with opposing interests. For example, an agent may hear confidential information from sellers about what their minimum acceptable price is, and the same agent or another agent from the same firm hears from buyers that they're willing to pay more than what they first offered.

Agents, and especially their brokers, prefer dual agency — they generate more commissions by representing both sides of the transaction. That's why many agents start out showing their clients only properties that are listed by their firms. However, this desire to capture a bigger share of the real estate commission has led to some serious conflicts of interest. Now most states either prohibit dual agency or at least require the agent to disclose the exact nature of the agency relationship prior to commencing the representation of a client by taking a listing, showing a property, or making an offer.

Getting a feel for compensation

Real estate agents are generally motivated to see the transaction go through because they're compensated when a sale is made. Compensation for agents is typically calculated as a percentage of the sales price paid for a property. So the agents actually have an interest in the property going for a higher price. Commissions vary based on the property and the size of the transaction:

🖙 Individual residential properties, such as single-family homes and condos, have commissions of 5 to 6 percent of the sales price.

🖙 Small multifamily and commercial properties are often in the 3 to 5 percent range.

🖙 Larger investment properties have commissions of 1 to 3 percent.

✔ Raw land (in its natural state with no grading, construction, or improvements) is usually at 10 percent, unless the acreage is large. Subdivided or finished developable lots in suburban areas typically draw a lower commission.

These commissions are typically split between the firm listing the property for sale and working with the seller and the agent representing the buyer. The actual proportion of the split varies, with the listing agent sometimes taking a smaller percentage than the buyer's agent if the commissions aren't evenly split. The commission actually is paid to the broker, and the agent receives his share based on his employment or commission agreement, which also often calls for the agent to cover some of his own expenses and overhead.

Real estate commissions can be a significant cost factor for real estate investors. Most listing agreements acknowledge that commissions aren't fixed by law and are negotiable. Traditionally, the seller "pays" the commission to the real estate agents involved in the transaction, although because the buyer is the one paying for the property, we say that both the buyer and seller ultimately pay for the agent's commissions.

Real estate agents do add to the cost of purchasing property, but a good agent, like a good property manager, can justify the cost of her services by introducing you to properties that you would not otherwise have an opportunity to purchase. A good agent earns her commissions other ways as well — as a good negotiator and through her other marketplace knowledge.

Some real estate investors get a real estate license so that they can eliminate paying at least one-half of the real estate commission to agents. Be sure to disclose immediately to all parties prior to entering into any transaction that you're a licensed real estate agent. And at times you'll be able to use your sale's or broker's license to effectively reduce your transaction expenses and investment requirement by representing yourself in a transaction. This is particularly helpful when you're looking to sell a property in a strong seller's market.

But as a licensee you need to be very careful to follow all real estate disclosure laws about your licensing status to all parties in the transaction. Generally, a real estate agent is expected to have more knowledge in a real estate transaction than others without such credentials. Thus, you must be very careful when you act as an agent and a principal in a purchase or sale transaction.

Although you may often have superior knowledge of market values and opportunities in the marketplace, you need to make sure that you're not self-dealing or taking advantage of insider information that would have a material impact on the value of the property. A real estate agent who buys properties for the long-term for his own account is not likely to be challenged, but such an individual that uses his knowledge to flip properties for a quick profit may be subject to claims by the seller that he withheld information. For example, you may find yourself named in a lawsuit if you bought a property at a low price when you knew that a new road was going to be built that would greatly enhance the property value in the next year or so.

Robert has seen many allegations against licensed real estate professionals who have been accused of self-dealing or failing to act properly in real estate transactions when they buy the property for an entity that they have a financial interest in or have a straw man or secret partner. This situation can happen even if you disclose your real estate license status and your financial interest in the buyer entity, but it is illegal and likely to be considered more egregious if you conceal this information from the seller. Agents have also been accused of illegal activity when they sell their own property (for example, as a tenants in common or triple net investment opportunity) at a much higher than market value.

One example from Robert's litigation consulting practice involved a real estate agent who advised an elderly owner to sell a residential rental fourplex where the apartments were contiguous but each rental unit was on a separate lot. The agent advised this unsophisticated owner to sell all four units as a single property to a business associate of the agent. Then the new owner turned around and within less than 12 months had sold each of the four individual properties separately at a gross profit of over $1 million. The agent clearly knew that real estate sold in smaller increments generates a higher overall value. The aggrieved elderly owner filed suit against the agent.

Finding a good broker or agent

The key to finding a good broker or agent to assist you in the purchase of investment real estate is to narrow the field down to those individuals who are the best. Look for folks with the following qualifications:

- ✔ **Full-time professional:** Because the commissions earned on the sale of a large income property can be so great, you'll find that almost every broker or agent will claim that she can represent you. But you want to eliminate those brokers or agents who are greedy, incompetent, or simply mediocre. Although many part-time real estate professionals sell single-family homes and condos, you'll quickly find that the most qualified real estate investment property agents are full-time.

- ✔ **Expert in the geographic market and specific property type:** Find someone who knows your market and the specific property type you're seeking. This knowledge is especially important if you don't live nearby. Avoid brokers who aren't experts in your specific property type. For example, don't use a broker who specializes in single-family homes and condominiums unless that's your target market. Likewise, a commercial property broker is unlikely to have the best investment opportunities for your consideration with single-family investment property.

Some real estate investment books advise you to contact every broker or real estate agent who targets your preferred geographic area. Although casting a bigger net has some inherent attraction, our experience is that you should only work with one broker or agent at a time in a given market area.

Real estate agents can be a key source for new investment opportunities and general market information. This is where our advice about finding an experienced agent who specializes in the types of properties you're looking for and knows the local market pays off. These agents know buyers and sellers and also possess contacts for other services and products that you need as your real estate investment portfolio expands.

After narrowing down the candidates, you can apply many standard screening techniques to pinpoint the top three that you should interview:

- ✔ **Verify the professional's license status:** Nearly every state has an online broker and agent database, so this step is simple. Confirm that their real estate license is current with no citations or disciplinary action for past or pending violations. Note that not all states will post pending violations but only adjudicated or resolved matters, so ask your agent directly. If you're using a real estate agent, check both the license status of the agent and her supervising broker. If the broker or agent has been disciplined by the state, inquire further to understand the relevance to your transaction. A suspension or temporary revocation of a license can be a serious issue — even if it was reinstated. The facts of the case may be material to your choice of a real estate professional.

- ✔ **Check references:** Get the names and numbers for at least three clients (in the geographical area where you're seeking property) that the broker or agent has worked with in the past year. Investment real estate transactions tend to be fewer than owner-occupied property transactions, so speaking with three or more clients from the last year maximizes your chances of speaking with clients other than the agent's all-time favorites.

  Don't just ask for the references; call them. And don't just ask generic questions about whether the client was happy with the broker or agent. Dig deeper — find an agent who you can work with on investments that are critical to your long-term wealth-building goals. Ask questions about the types of properties and the geographic locations involved. Ask questions like, "Did the broker or agent assertively represent you and take charge of the transaction or did you have to initiate conversations?"

Consider these traits when investigating potential brokers and agents as well:

- ✔ **Willingness to communicate with you:** The number one complaint about real estate professionals is that they don't keep their clients informed during transactions. You're looking for someone with experience who isn't necessarily the top producer, because you want someone who can take the time to communicate regularly with you.

- ✔ **Interpersonal skills:** A broker or agent needs to get along with you and with a whole host of others involved in a typical real estate deal: other agents, property sellers, inspectors, lenders, and so on. An agent needs to know how to put your interests first without upsetting others.

- ✔ **Negotiation skills:** Putting a real estate deal together involves negotiation, so you want a broker or agent with negotiating skills and lots of experience in larger transactions. Is your agent going to exhaust all avenues to get you the best deal possible? Be sure to ask the agent's former clients how the agent negotiated for them.

- ✔ **Reputation for honesty, integrity, and patience:** When it comes to the brokering of investment properties, the reputation of your representative can be critical. Brokers or agents with a track record of dealing fairly with their clients and their peers can greatly assist in gaining the cooperation of an adversarial seller. And gaining such cooperation is often needed to close a complicated transaction. Some strife is almost guaranteed when buying investment real estate — there are several opportunities where the transaction can unravel and only the trustworthiness, perseverance, and patience of the real estate professionals involved can keep the transaction on course.

Making the most of your agent

To get the best deals, timing is critical. You want your broker or agent to think of you first. To do this, you need to build a solid rapport with your agent, which you can do by building a track record of not wasting the time of your professional team. Because agents only get paid for deals they close, they're not interested in investing time and energy with numerous potential buyers. They want serious buyers who will close the deal. Plus, if you garner a reputation of tying up properties and then renegotiating the deal or canceling the escrow, you'll find that your offers won't be accepted in the future. Sellers and their brokers don't want to waste time with phantom buyers.

If you're not interested in or not able to purchase a property at the time, let your agent know at once and explain your situation and thank him for thinking of you. A handwritten thank-you note or simple gift also lets him know that you appreciate his efforts — and keeps you at the top of his lists for the next opportunity.

Considering an Appraiser

Many real estate investors know appraisers solely in the role of providing the property valuation report required by lenders. And it's generally in this role that investors can find appraisers to be a source of aggravation rather than a potential resource. However, an appraiser can be an effective team member if your real estate investment strategy involves buying and selling properties with somewhat-hidden opportunities to add value. Appraisers see many properties over their career and thus often possess insight into real estate opportunities that others miss.

Appraisers can help you by telling you the current value of a property, but they bring real value as part of your real estate investment team by

- ✔ Providing insight into the factors that can lead to an increase in the market value of a property.

- ✔ Assisting you in maximizing the return on your investment by suggesting cost-effective and high demand upgrades to distressed or fixer-upper properties.

- ✔ Giving you useful information on the demographics of the area and helping to identify those properties that are distressed but have plenty of upside potential (properties requiring work in good neighborhoods).

One of Robert's partners, a highly successful real estate investor in foreclosure properties, has even hired an appraiser as an in-house member of his real estate investment team. Virtually every property that appears on the weekly Notice of Default list from the title company is reviewed first by the appraiser, who looks for properties that are located in the path of progress and with some real upside potential if brought to marketable condition physically and aesthetically. (For more on Notice of Default, see Chapter 3; for information on getting in front of the path of progress, see Chapter 10.)

The appraiser is also able to assist in determining the as-is value and the cost of making the necessary repairs and upgrades to the property. This information helps the investor establish the maximum price she should pay for the property, based on comparable sales in the market.

As many have learned from the debacles of the real estate collapse in the early-1990s and the late-2000s subprime disaster, appraisals are often an art and can be very subjective. You need to make sure you find an appraiser that has a comprehensive education and training in proper appraisal techniques and complies with the Uniform Standards of Professional Appraisal Practice (USPAP) set out by the Appraisal Foundation. The appraiser you use should have extensive product knowledge of your target property type (residential, commercial, and so on.) along with significant experience and market knowledge in your area. Contact the local American Society of Appraisers and the Appraisal Institute for referrals. Like many of the top professionals you seek for your team, you should not simply look for the lowest price, because you may end up with an inferior appraisal.

Finding an Attorney

You may think that adding an attorney to your real estate investment team seems like an expensive luxury that you can't afford. Indeed, you may be able to purchase properties when you're just starting out as a real estate investor without consulting an attorney, because buying a small rental property is often not much different from purchasing your own home. The process is relatively simple with preprinted forms that seem so easy to complete. And you usually have an experienced real estate agent to guide you through the process. (See Chapter 13 for information on locating forms.)

For simple transactions, the retention of an attorney is strictly a function of whether attorneys are traditionally involved as the intermediary or closing agent. If you live in an area where attorneys aren't usually involved in real estate transactions, an attorney may not be necessary. In some states, having an attorney is essential to handle the transaction and closing.

We strongly suggest that you consult with an experienced real estate attorney as your investments increase in size and complexity. With more complicated transactions, have the attorney review the documents — even in states where the title or escrow company handles the paperwork and serves as the independent intermediary or closing agent. A good real estate attorney can help you structure proposed transactions. Particularly if you're looking into a large transaction where you assume loans or you're attempting to secure special financing, a competent real estate attorney can be invaluable.

Robert's late father, a real estate attorney, taught him early in his real estate investment career that the best time to consult with an attorney is before you finalize the proposed transaction. There is nothing your attorney can do to avoid legal snafus and expensive litigation if he isn't hired to draft, review, and negotiate the terms of your proposed transaction in advance. Although such a review may cost you some money up front, it's definitely much more economical than having to hire an attorney to get you out of a bind.

Part II
How to Get the Money: Raising Capital and Financing

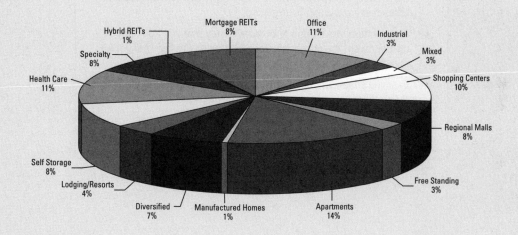

Hybrid REITs
1%

Mortgage REITs
8%

Office
11%

Industrial
3%

Mixed
3%

Specialty
8%

Shopping Centers
10%

Health Care
11%

Regional Malls
8%

Self Storage
8%

Free Standing
3%

Lodging/Resorts
4%

Diversified
7%

Manufactured Homes
1%

Apartments
14%

Go to www.dummies.com/extras/realestateinvesting for additional information that can help you when investing in real estate.

In this part . . .

- ✔ Understand the amount of money that you need to have in hand for various real estate investments so that you're well prepared when making a down payment.

- ✔ Know where you can go to borrow money that you don't have for the rest of the purchase price, because very few real estate investors buy property with 100 percent cash.

- ✔ Examine seller-financing options in case you don't want to go the traditional lending route to borrow money.

- ✔ Comprehend how you can save money and get the best mortgage rate for your loan.

Chapter 7

Identifying Sources of Capital

. . . .

In This Chapter

▶ Moving beyond the no-money-down myth

▶ Knowing what you need to get going in real estate

▶ Locating cash when starting out and for experienced investors

. . . .

For many people, the trouble with real estate investing is that they lack the access to cash for the down payment. The old adage that "it takes money to make money" is generally true in our experience. Most real estate investing books make one of two assumptions. Some assume that you have plenty of money and just need to figure out how to buy, add value to a property, and then sell. Of course, it would be great if that were true, but not everyone is flush with cash. The other common assumption is that you have no money and must resort to scouring the real estate market in search of sellers so desperate to sell that they or their lenders don't require any down payment. We assume neither.

So how do you get started in real estate if you don't want to own distressed properties in the worst neighborhoods, and you don't have a six-figure balance in your bank account to pay top dollar in the best neighborhoods? You muster all the patience you can and embrace a long-term vision. You don't have to be wealthy or have great savings to begin making attractive real estate investments. In this book, we present a wide range of investment options, so there's something for virtually everyone's budget and personal situation. Our method of building real estate wealth over time is to create investment returns that are sustainable and provide generous returns on your investments.

Calculating the Costs of Admission

At some point in your life, you've surely had the experience of wanting to do something and then realizing that you don't have sufficient money to accomplish your goal. Perhaps it was as simple as lacking the pocket change to buy a chocolate bar as a child. Or maybe it happened on a vacation when you ran low on funds and tried to do business with a merchant who only took Visa when you only carried American Express. No matter — the world of real estate investing is no different. You can't play if you can't pay.

In the following sections, we discuss the realities of the cash requirements to be a successful real estate investor.

Forgetting the myth of no money down

The title of this chapter says it all: To invest in real estate, you need capital, and likewise you need a source from which to gather said capital. On late-night infomercials, at seminars, on audiotapes, and in some books, you may hear many self-appointed real estate experts tell you that you can invest in real estate with literally no money. And if that's not enticing enough, you may hear that you can buy properties where the seller will put cash in your hands.

Have such no-money-down situations ever existed among the billions of completed real estate transactions in the history of the modern world? Why, yes they have. Realistically, can you find such opportunities among the best real estate investing options available to you? Why, no you can't.

Think of the people you know who still haven't found the perfect mate after decades of searching. Mr. and Ms. Perfect don't exist. Ditto the ideal real estate investment. If you use our sensible criteria when seeking out properties that'll be good real estate investments and then add the requirement that you can only make such investments with no money down, you'll probably waste years searching to no avail. We've never made a no-money-down real estate investment because the best properties simply aren't available on that basis.

Our experience is that the no-money-down properties we have seen aren't properties we want to own. And if you receive cash out of escrow upon closing on a property, you're either buying a severely distressed property that will soon require major cash infusions or you've overleveraged the property. If it sounds too good to be true, it *is* too good to be true! For a more complete discussion of no money down, please see Chapter 5.

Determining what you need to get started

Most of the time, real estate investors make a down payment and borrow the majority of the money needed to complete a purchase. That is the conventional way to purchase real estate investment properties and will be the most successful method for you in the long run (as it has been for us).

In order to qualify for the most attractive financing, lenders typically require that your down payment be at least 20 percent of the property's purchase price. The best investment property loans sometimes require 25 to 30 percent down for the most favorable terms. Lenders tend to be more conservative and require larger down payments during periods of falling real estate prices such as most areas experienced in the late 2000s.

For most residential investment properties, such as single-family homes, attached housing such as condos and townhomes, and small apartment buildings of up to four units, you can get access to the best financing terms by making at least a 20 to 25 percent down payment. (Mortgages on non-owner-occupied property tend to be ¼ to ½ percent higher). You may be able to make smaller down payments (as low as 10 percent or less), but you'll pay much higher interest rates and loan fees, including private mortgage insurance. (We cover the topic of financing in Chapter 8.)

You won't find such wonderful financing options for larger apartment buildings (five or more units), commercial real estate, and raw land. Compared with residential properties of up to four units, such investment property generally requires more money down and/or higher interest rates and loan fees. See Chapter 8 for more details.

Determining how much cash you need to close on a purchase is largely a function of the negotiated purchase price, including all closing costs and fees. Suppose you're looking to buy some modest residential housing for $100,000. For a 25 percent down payment you need $25,000, and adding in another 5 percent for closing costs brings you to $30,000. If you have your heart set on buying a property that costs three times as much ($300,000 sticker price), you need to triple these amounts to a total of about $90,000 for the best financing options.

Getting in the door with good credit

Don't underestimate the importance of establishing good credit because the best returns on real estate rely upon the use of credit to obtain the leverage of using OPM (other people's money). Lenders, property sellers, potential partners, and so on all prefer to deal with you if you've established a reputation for paying your bills. Good to great credit is essential. Why pay more for money when you can show the ability to handle it properly and be rewarded with a lower price?

Both of us began building our credit through the responsible use of credit cards in our 20s (paying monthly bills in full), and to this day, our high FICO scores have allowed us to borrow at favorable rates and terms and save tens of thousands of dollars per year in financing costs. And that difference will sometimes enable us to make a deal work that otherwise won't. We cover the importance of good credit and ways to establish a reputation of responsible debt payments and how to remove unsightly blemishes on your credit history that may keep you from getting solid interest rates in Chapter 9.

Rounding Up the Required Cash by Saving

Most successful real estate investors that we know, including us, got started building their real estate investment portfolio the old-fashioned way — through saving money and then gradually buying properties over the years. Many people have difficulty saving money because they don't know how to or are simply unwilling to limit their spending. Easy access to consumer debt (through credit cards and auto loans) creates huge obstacles to saving more and spending less.

Investing in real estate requires self-control, sacrifice, and discipline. Like most good things in life, you must be patient and plan ahead to be able to invest in real estate.

As young adults, some (but not most) people are good savers out of the gate. Those who save regularly are often folks who acquired sound financial habits from their parents. Other good savers have a high level of motivation to accomplish goals such as retiring young, starting a business, buying a home, having the flexibility to spend time with their kids, and so on. Achieving such goals is much harder (if not impossible) when you're living paycheck-to-paycheck and worried about next month's pile of bills.

If you're not satisfied with how much of your monthly earnings you're able to save, you have two options (and you can take advantage of both):

✔ **Boost your income:** To increase your take-home pay, working more may be a possibility, or you may be able to take a more lucrative career path. Our main advice on this topic is to keep your priorities in order. You shouldn't put your personal health and relationships on the back burner for a workaholic schedule. We also believe in investing in your education. A solid education is the path to greater financial rewards and leads to all of the great goals we discuss here. Education is key not only for your chosen profession but also for real estate investing. Consider getting a real estate license or learn to be an appraiser or property manager — skills that not only help you with your property investing but that also may allow you to take on part-time work to supplement your income.

✔ **Reduce your spending:** For most people, this is the path to increased savings. We have both routinely generated cash flow for investments by living well beneath our means. Start by analyzing how much you expend on different areas (for instance, food, clothing, transportation, insurance, and entertainment) each month. After you've got the data, decide where and how you want to cut back. Would you rather eat out less or have a maid come less often? How about driving a less expensive (but not less safe) car versus taking lower cost vacations? Although the possibilities to reduce your spending are many, you and only you can decide which options you're willing and able to implement. If you need more help with this vital financial topic, consult the latest edition of Eric's bestseller *Personal Finance For Dummies* (John Wiley & Sons, Inc.).

Overcoming Down Payment Limitations

Most people, especially when they make their first real estate purchase, are strapped for cash. If you don't have 20-plus percent of the purchase price, don't panic and don't get depressed — you can still own real estate. We've got some solutions — you can either change your approach, allowing you more time to save or lowering your entry fees, or you can seek other sources of funding. In the following sections, we lay out your options.

Changing your approach

Some ways you can alter your approach without having to find money elsewhere are as follows:

- ✔ **Seek low-money-down loans with private mortgage insurance:** Some lenders may offer you a mortgage even though you may be able to put down only 10 percent of the purchase price. These lenders will likely require you to purchase *private mortgage insurance* (PMI) for your loan. This insurance generally costs several hundred dollars per year and protects the lender if you default on your loan. (When you do have at least 20 percent or higher equity in the property, you can generally eliminate the PMI.)

- ✔ **Delay your gratification:** If you don't want the cost and strain of extra fees and bad mortgage terms, postpone your purchase. Boost your savings rate. Examine your current spending habits and plan to build up a nest egg to use to invest in your first rental. Often real estate investors get started by actually buying a new home and simply keeping their old home as a rental. Robert did this when he and his wife bought a new single-family home in anticipation of the birth of their first child while retaining the condo they had purchased and lived in when they were first married.

- ✔ **Think smaller:** Consider lower-priced properties. Smaller properties and ones that need some major work can help keep down the purchase price and the required down payment. For example, a duplex where you live in one unit and rent out the other is also a cost-effective way to get started. We know many people who have used this entry strategy into rental property ownerships to achieve two goals: an owner-occupied place to live and a rental property that is convenient to manage.

✔ **Turn to low entry cost options:** For the ultimate in low entry costs while adding real estate to your investment allocation strategy, *real estate investment trusts* (REITs) are best. These stock exchange traded securities (which can also be bought through REIT-focused mutual funds and EFTs [exchange-traded funds]) can be bought into for several thousand dollars or less (you can invest even less in ETFs). REIT mutual funds can often be purchased for $1000 or less inside retirement accounts. (See Chapter 4 for more on investing in REITs.)

Lease options represent another low cost (although more complicated) opportunity. With these, you begin by renting a property you may be interested in purchasing down the road. In the interim, a portion of your monthly rental payment goes toward the future purchase price. If you can find a seller willing to provide financing, you can keep your down payment to a minimum. Turn to Chapter 3 for more on lease options.

Tapping into other common cash sources

Saving money from your monthly earnings will probably be the foundation for your real estate investing program. However, you may have access to other financial resources for down payments. Before we jump into these, we offer a friendly little reminder: Monitor how much of your overall investment portfolio you place into real estate and how diversified and appropriate your holdings are given your overall goals. (Refer to Chapter 1.)

Dipping into your retirement savings

Some employers allow you to borrow against your retirement account balance, under the condition that you repay the loan within a set number of years. Subject to eligibility requirements, first-time homebuyers can make penalty-free withdrawals of up to $10,000 from IRA accounts. (*Note:* You still must pay regular income tax on the withdrawal, which can significantly reduce the cash available.)

Borrowing against home equity

Most real estate investors that we know began building their real estate portfolio after they bought their own home. Conservatively tapping into your home's equity may be a good down payment source for your property investments.

You can generally obtain mortgage money at a lower interest rate on your home than you can on investment property. The smaller the risk to the lender, the lower its required return, and thus, the better rates for you as the borrower. Lenders view rental property as a higher risk proposition and for good reason: They know that when finances go downhill and the going gets really tough, people pay their home mortgage to avoid losing the roof over their heads before they pay debts on a rental property.

Unless your current mortgage was locked in at lower rates than are available today, we generally recommend refinancing the first trust deed loan and freeing up equity that way versus taking out a home equity loan or line of credit.

A variation on the borrowing-against-home-equity idea uses the keep-your-original-home-as-a-rental strategy. You build up significant equity in your owner-occupied home and then need or want a new home. Refinance the existing home (while you still live there, for the best owner-occupied rates) and then convert it into a rental. Take the tax-free proceeds from the refinance and use that as the down payment on your new owner-occupied home.

Before you go running out to borrow to the maximum against your home, be sure that you

✔ **Can handle the larger payments:** In the first edition of this book, we said,

> *"We don't recommend borrowing more than the value of your home, as you may be enticed to do with some of the loan programs that pitch borrowing upwards of 125 percent of the value of your home. We hear these programs being routinely touted as not only a way to free up equity and pay down consumer debt, but also encouraging people to borrow in excess of the current value of their home so they can invest in more real estate. This excessive leveraging is dangerous and could come back to haunt you!"*

We're proud to have provided this sage advice well before the real estate crisis hit home in the late 2000s. Please see Chapter 1 for the big picture on personal financial considerations.

✔ **Understand the tax ramifications of all your alternatives:** Borrowing more against your home at what appears to be a slightly lower rate may end up costing you more after taxes if some of the borrowing isn't tax deductible. Under current tax laws, interest paid on home mortgages (first and second homes) of up to $1 million is tax deductible. You may also deduct the interest on home equity loans of up to $100,000.

Be careful to understand the tax-deductibility issue when you refinance a home mortgage and borrow more than you originally had outstanding on the prior loan. If any of the extra amount borrowed isn't used to buy, build, or improve your primary or secondary residence, the deductibility of the interest on the excess amount borrowed is limited. Specifically, you may not deduct the interest on the extra amount borrowed that exceeds the $100,000 home equity limit.

✓ **Fully comprehend the risks of losing your home to foreclosure:** The more you borrow against your home, the greater the risk that you may lose the roof over your head to foreclosure should you not be able to make your mortgage payments. That's exactly what happened to too many folks during the late-2000s real estate market decline. Although you need to use your cash for investing in and improving real estate, our advice always includes keeping some cash in a checking or money market rainy day account (for example for a new roof, painting, and so on) and not cutting things so close that you could lose it all.

Moving financial investments into property investments

As you gain more comfort and confidence as a real estate investor, you may want to redirect some of your dollars from other investments like stocks, bonds, mutual, and ETFs into property. If you do, be mindful of the following:

✓ **Diversification:** Real estate is one of the prime investments (the others being stocks and small business) for long-term appreciation potential. Be sure that you understand your portfolio's overall asset allocation and risk when making changes. Please see Chapter 1 for more details.

✓ **Tax issues:** If you've held other investments for more than one year, you can take advantage of the low long-term capital gains tax rates if you now want to sell. The maximum federal tax rate for so-called long-term capital gains (investments sold for more than they were purchased for after more than 12 months) is now 20 percent. If your modified adjusted gross income exceeds $200,000 for single taxpayers or $250,000 for married taxpayers filing jointly, you have to pony up an extra 3.8 percent to help pay for the Affordable Care Act (also known as Obamacare). Investors in the two lowest federal income tax brackets of 10 and 15 percent enjoy a 0 percent long-term capital gains tax rate. Try to avoid selling appreciated investments within the first year of ownership. Be sure to check on the latest tax laws because there's no guarantee these rates will continue in the future.

Separating investments from cash value life insurance

You may own a *cash value* life insurance policy — one that combines a life insurance death benefit with a savings type account in which some money accumulates and on which interest is paid. In addition to being a costly cash drain with its relatively high premiums, cash value life insurance investment returns tend to be mediocre to dismal.

You're best off separating your life insurance purchases from your investing. If you need life insurance (because others are dependent on your income), buy a *term life* policy, which is pure, unadulterated life insurance. But don't cancel your current cash value policies before replacing them with term if you do indeed need life insurance protection.

Robert had a $500,000 whole life policy that he was sold when he was much younger and more naive — and before he knew of Eric and his financial advice! He ultimately decided to cash out the policy, the proceeds from which he used to invest in an apartment deal. So rather than earning a meager few percent per year in a cash value life policy, Robert has since enjoyed double-digit annualized returns in a good real estate investment.

Capitalizing on advanced funding strategies

Sophisticated investors who develop an extensive real estate investment portfolio can employ more complicated strategies. In this section, we outline those along with our advice for how to make them work.

Leveraging existing real estate investments

Over time, if the initial properties you buy do what they're supposed to do, they'll appreciate in value. Thus, you may be able to take extra tax-free cash from your successful investments to make more purchases. This tactic is called *hypothecating* your real estate. As we discuss in the section "Borrowing against home equity" earlier in this chapter, many investors begin by employing this strategy with their owner-occupied home. They buy a home, it appreciates over the years, and then they tap that equity to fund other real estate purchases. By the same token, as you acquire more properties and they then appreciate, you can tap their equity for other purchases.

As you build a real estate empire, exercise care not to overextend yourself. The downside to continually pulling equity out of appreciated properties is that your fortunes may change. If the local real estate market or economy hit difficult times as happened in some areas in the late 2000s, you may find yourself with vacancies and falling rents. In the worst cases, excessively leveraged real estate investors have ended up losing some properties or even going bankrupt.

Bringing in partners or other investors

If smaller, lower-priced properties don't satisfy your desires, you may be able to find a partner. For example, find a duplex and get a partner where you both initially occupy the property and make the payments, because duplexes are typically more cost-effective per unit than unattached properties.

Especially to accomplish larger deals, you may need or want to invest with a partner or other investors for the sake of diversification and risk reduction. Bringing in a partner can also provide additional financial resources for down payments and capital improvements as well as greater borrowing capability.

Partners can be either the best thing or the worst thing that ever happened to you. Although the additional financial resources are essential when you're starting out in real estate, attempt to find partners with complementary skills to really take advantage of the potential of real estate investment partnerships.

For example, Robert has focused on establishing partnerships where each partner brings a needed skill to the table. One partnership consisted of a top local real estate broker who identified properties along with a partner who was a real estate lender and knew the ins and outs of lending. Robert's company provided the property and asset management to reposition the property and create value. This team used their complementary skills to successfully purchase, renovate, and later resell a 48-unit apartment building while providing cash distributions to the partners during the holding period.

With the assistance of a good attorney, prepare a legal contract to specify (among other issues) what happens if a partner wants out. A *buy/sell agreement* makes a lot of sense because it outlines the terms and conditions in advance for how partnership assets can be redistributed. With life events (death, divorces, new marriages, lawsuits, and business failures) constantly changing partnerships, having a buy/sell agreement in place at the time the partnership is initially established prevents bickering down the road. Partnership disputes often enrich attorneys and accountants, rather than the partners or their intended beneficiaries.

Family members sometimes make good partners. Parents, grandparents, and perhaps even siblings may have some extra cash they want to loan or invest. But some families aren't suited for partnering to buy and operate real estate. Disputes over management style, cash distributions versus reinvesting in the property, and how and when to sell are difficult in any partnership but particularly in families where there may be different goals based on the age or personal or professional desires of the family members. If you already don't get along well at family gatherings, throw in a real estate partnership to really get the fireworks going! To minimize the potential problems, we strongly suggest documenting any real estate investment or lending relationship in writing just as diligently as you would with a non–family member. When working with family, you may be better off borrowing money with a promissory note, a repayment plan, and interest payments. Always document any agreements in writing. Check out Chapter 14 for more on partnerships.

Seeking seller financing

You may be able to find some properties that your research suggests offer potentially attractive investment returns and for which the seller may be willing to extend financing. Some property owners or developers may finance your purchase with as little as 10 percent or even less down. This method can be an extremely beneficial way to buy real estate when your cash position is limited. You can often set up the transaction as an installment sale so that the seller has the added benefit of stretching the reporting of income over a period of time and thus reducing her tax liability. You conserve your cash; the seller reduces her taxable income.

The drawback with seller-financed properties is that you can't be as picky about what you get; a limited supply is available, and many properties offered with seller financing need work or haven't yet sold for other reasons. Often these are reasons that only become apparent after you're the owner!

Avoid properties that are *distressed* (have major problems and flaws). Don't get sucked in by great financing alone; only consider purchasing a property with seller financing that you would be willing to buy conventionally. The seller financing should just be an extra benefit, not the only benefit! Please see Chapter 8 for details.

Taking on margin debt

In the section "Moving financial investments into property investments" earlier in this chapter, we cover selling some of your non–real estate investments in order to raise capital for property purchases. If you own stocks and other securities in a brokerage account, you can actually borrow funds against those investments. For example, if you're the proud owner of $100,000 worth of so-called marginable securities in a brokerage account, you may be able to borrow up to $50,000 at attractive interest rates, typically a little lower than on fixed rate mortgages for a home.

In addition to providing you with a relatively low-cost source of funds, utilizing margin debt for real estate purchases also enables you to hold onto more securities, which can better diversify your real estate holdings.

Be careful when using margin debt. Stocks, bonds, and other investments can drop in value, sometimes sharply. When that happens as it did in 2008, you may face what is known as a *margin call,* where you have to increase the equity in your brokerage account, either by adding cash to it directly or by selling some of your securities. Having to sell during tough times can force you to liquidate shares at low prices. To add insult to injury, a significant stock market decline like the ones that occurred in 2008 or in the early 1990s, can coincide with a slumping real estate market.

Chapter 8

Financing Your Property Purchases

We know property investors who spent dozens to hundreds of hours finding the best locations and properties only to have their deals unravel when they were unable to gain approval for needed financing. You can't play if you can't pay.

This chapter covers the financing options you should consider (and highlights those that you should avoid). We explain how to select the mortgage that is most appropriate for the property you're buying and your overall personal and financial situation. In Chapter 9, we cover the actual process of applying for and locking up the specific loan you want.

Taking a Look at Mortgage Options

Although you can find thousands of different types of mortgages (thanks to all the various bells and whistles available), only two major categories of mortgages exist: fixed interest rate and adjustable rate. Technically speaking, some mortgages combine elements of both — they may remain fixed for a number of years and then have a variable interest rate after that. This section discusses these major loan types, what features they typically have, and how you can intelligently compare them with each other and select the one that best fits with your investment property purchases.

Fixed-rate mortgages

Fixed-rate mortgages, which are typically for a 15- or 30-year term for single-family properties, condos, and one- to four-unit apartments, have interest rates that remain constant over the life of the loan. Because the interest rate stays the same, your monthly mortgage payment stays the same.

Examining the pros and cons

For purposes of making future estimates of your property's cash flow, fixed-rate mortgages offer you certainty and some peace of mind because you know precisely the size of your mortgage payment next month, next year, and ten years from now. (Of course, the other costs of owning investment property — such as property taxes, insurance, maintenance, and so on — still escalate over the years.) But this piece of mind comes at a price:

- ✔ You generally pay a premium, in the form of a higher interest rate, compared with loans that have an adjustable interest rate over time. If you're buying a property and planning to improve it and sell it within five to ten years, you may be throwing money away by taking out a fixed-rate loan to lock in an interest rate for decades.

- ✔ If, like most investment property buyers, you're facing a tough time generating a healthy positive cash flow in the early years of owning a particular investment property, a fixed-rate mortgage is going to make it even more financially challenging. An adjustable-rate mortgage, by contrast, can lower your property's carrying costs in those early years. (We discuss adjustable-rate mortgages in the next section.)

- ✔ Fixed-rate loans carry the risk that if interest rates fall significantly after you obtain your mortgage and you're unable to refinance, you're stuck with a relatively higher-cost mortgage. For example, you may be unable to refinance if you lose your job, your employment income declines, the value of your property decreases, or the property's rental income slides. Also remember that even if you're able to refinance, you'll probably have to spend significant time and money to get it done.

Making a point of comparing fixed rates

In addition to the ongoing, constant interest rate charged on a fixed-rate mortgage, lenders also typically levy an upfront fee, called points, which can be considered prepaid interest. *Points* are generally a percentage of the amount borrowed. To illustrate, 1.5 points are equal to 1.5 percent of the loan amount. So, for example, on a $200,000 mortgage, 1.5 points translate into $3,000 upfront (also known as prepaid) interest. Points can add significantly to the cost of borrowing money, particularly if you don't plan to keep the loan for long.

Generally speaking, the more points you pay on a given loan, the lower the ongoing interest rate the lender charges on that loan. That's why you can't compare various lenders' fixed-rate loans to one another unless you know the exact points on each specific mortgage, in addition to that loan's ongoing interest rate.

The following are two approaches to dealing with points, given your financial situation and investment goals:

✔ **Minimize the points:** When you're running low on cash to close on a mortgage, or if you don't plan to hold the loan or property for long, you probably want to keep your points (and other loan fees discussed in the next section) to a minimum. You may want to take a higher interest rate on your mortgage.

✔ **Pay more points:** If you're more concerned with keeping your ongoing costs low, plan to hold the property for many years, and aren't cash-constrained to close on the loan now, consider paying more points to lower your interest rate. This is known as _buying down the loan rate_ and can be an excellent strategy to lower your overall costs of borrowing and increase the property's cash flow and equity buildup.

To make an easier apples-to-apples comparison of mortgages from different lenders, get interest rate quotes at the same point level. For example, ask each lender for the interest rate on a particular fixed-rate mortgage for which you pay one point or two points, for example. You may also compare the _annual percentage rate_ (APR), which is a summary loan cost measure that includes all of a loan's fees and costs. However, please remember that the APR assumes that you hold the mortgage for its entire term — such as 15 or 30 years. If you end up keeping the loan for a shorter time period, either because you refinance or pay off the mortgage early, the APR isn't valid and accurate (unless you recalculate based on the changed term and payoff).

Adjustable-rate mortgages (ARMs)

Adjustable-rate mortgages (ARMs) carry an interest rate that varies over time. An ARM starts with a particular interest rate, usually a good deal lower than the going rate on comparable length (15- or 30-year) fixed-rate mortgages, and then you pay different rates for every year, possibly even every month, during a 30-year mortgage. Because the interest rate on an ARM changes over time, so too does the size of the loan's monthly payment. ARMs are often attractive for a number of reasons:

✔ You can start paying your mortgage with a relatively low initial interest rate compared with fixed-rate loans. Given the economics of a typical investment property purchase, ARMs better enable an investor to achieve a positive cash flow in the early years of property ownership.

✔ Should interest rates decline, you can realize most, if not all, of the benefits of lower rates without the cost and hassle of refinancing. With a fixed-rate mortgage, the only way to benefit from an overall decline in the market level of interest rates is to refinance.

ARMs come with many more features and options than do fixed-rate mortgages, including caps, indexes, margins, and adjustment periods. The following sections help you to understand these important ARM features.

Start rate

The *start rate* on an ARM is the interest rate the mortgage begins with. Don't be fooled though: You don't pay this often tantalizingly low rate for too long. That is why it's often called a *teaser rate.* The start rate on most ARMs is set artificially low to entice you. In other words, even if the market level of interest rates doesn't change, your ARM is destined to increase as soon as the terms of the loan allow (more on this topic in a minute). An increase of one or two percentage points is common. The formula for determining the future interest rates on an ARM and rate caps is far more important in determining what a mortgage is going to cost you in the long run.

Future interest rate

The first important thing to ask a mortgage lender or broker about an ARM you're contemplating is the formula for determining the future interest rate on your loan. ARMs are based on the following formula:

Future Interest Rate = Index + Margin

The *index* is a designated measure of the market interest rate that the lender chooses to calculate the specific interest rate for your loan. Indexes are generally (but not always) widely quoted in the financial press. The *margin* is the amount added to the index to determine the interest rate that you pay on your mortgage.

For example, suppose that the loan you're considering uses a one-year Treasury bill index, which say is at about 2 percent, and the loan you're considering has a margin of 2.75 percent (also often referred to as 275 *basis points;* 100 basis points equals 1 percent). Thus, the following formula would drive the rate of this mortgage:

One-Year Treasury Bill Rate (2 percent) + Margin (2.75 percent)

Do the math and you get 4.75 percent. This figure is known as the *fully indexed rate* (the rate the loan has after the initial rate expires and if the index stays constant). If this loan starts out at just 2 percent, you know that if the one-year Treasury bill index remains at the same level, your loan can increase to 4.75 percent. If this index rises one percent to 3 percent during the period that you're covered by the ARM's start rate, that means the loan's fully indexed rate goes to 5.75 percent (3.00 + 2.75), which is nearly three percent higher than the loan's start rate.

Compare the fully indexed rate on an ARM you're considering to the current rate for a comparable term fixed-rate loan. You may see that the fixed-rate loan is at about the same interest rate, which may lead you to reconsider your choice of an ARM that carries the risk of rising to a higher future level.

Understanding ARM indexes

The different indexes used on ARMs vary mainly in how rapidly they respond to changes in interest rates. If you select an adjustable-rate mortgage tied to one of the faster-moving indexes, you take on more of a risk that the next adjustment may reflect interest rate increases. When you take on more of the risk that rates may increase, lenders cut you breaks in other ways, such as through lower *caps* (the maximum rate increase possible over a given time period; see "Future interest rate adjustments" later in the chapter), lower margins or lower points.

Should you want the security of an ARM tied to a slower-moving index, you pay for that security in one form or another, such as a higher start rate, caps, margin, or points. You may also pay in other, less-obvious ways. A slower-moving index, such as the 11th District Cost of Funds Index (COFI, discussed later), lags behind general changes in market interest rates, so it continues to rise after interest rates peak and goes down slower after rates have turned down. The following list covers some of these indexes.

- ✔ **Treasury bills (T-bills)** are IOUs that the U.S. government issues. Most ARMs are tied to the interest rate on 6-month or 12-month T-bills (also referred to as the one-year constant maturity Treasury index). This is a relatively rapidly moving index. Some investment property mortgages are tied to the rate on ten-year Treasury Notes. Being a somewhat longer-term bond, a ten-year index doesn't generally move as rapidly as the shorter-term indexes.

- ✔ **Certificates of deposit (CDs)** are interest-bearing bank deposits that lock the depositor in at a set interest rate for a specific period of time. ARMs are usually tied to the average interest rate that banks are paying on six-month CDs. Like T-bills, CDs tend to respond quickly to changes in the market's level of interest rates.

- ✔ **London Interbank Offered Rate Index (LIBOR)** is an average of the rate of interest that major international banks charge each other to borrow large sums of U.S. dollars, which is commonly referred to by real estate lenders as an index for their adjustable loans. LIBOR tends to move and adjust quite rapidly to changes in interest rates and is at times even more volatile than the U.S. Treasury or CD index rates.

✔ **Eleventh District Cost of Funds Index (COFI)** is a relatively slow-moving index. Adjustable-rate mortgages tied to the 11th District Cost of Funds Index tend to start out at a higher interest rate. A slower-moving index has the advantage of moving up less quickly when rates are on the rise. On the other hand, you have to be patient to benefit from falling interest rates.

In a relatively low-interest rate environment, fewer lenders tend to offer COFI loans. This illustrates the point that lenders don't always offer the same choice of indexes. Rather, each lender offers one or typically no more than two indexes, and borrowers should specifically look at the index as part of their overall decision on choosing a lender.

Future interest rate adjustments

After the initial interest rate ends, the interest rate on an ARM fluctuates based on the loan formula. Typically, ARM interest rates change every 6 or 12 months, but some adjust every month. In advance of each adjustment, the lender sends you a notice telling you your new rate. Be sure to check these notices because on rare occasions, lenders make mistakes.

Almost all ARMs come with a rate cap, which limits the maximum rate change (up or down) allowed at each adjustment. This limit is usually referred to as the *adjustment cap.* On most loans that adjust every six months, the adjustment cap is 1 percent; the interest rate charged on the mortgage can move up or down no more than one percentage point in an adjustment period.

Loans that adjust more than once per year usually limit the maximum rate change that's allowed over the entire year as well — known as the *annual rate cap.* On the vast majority of such loans, 2 percent is the annual rate cap. Likewise, almost all ARMs come with *lifetime caps,* which represent the highest rate allowed over the entire life of the loan. Lifetime caps of 5 to 6 percent higher than the initial start rate are common for adjustables.

Many ARMs also have a *rate floor* that is the minimum interest rate that will apply to the loan. Often the *rate floor* is equal to the *start rate,* which means that your loan can adjust up or down over the life of the loan, but never lower than the *start rate.* Robert has an ARM loan that adjusts annually up or down based on the COFI index. During the low interest rate years, this loan has actually adjusted down, but it can go no lower than the *rate floor,* which was specified in the loan documents.

Taking an ARM without rate caps is like heading out for a weeklong outdoor trek without appropriate rain gear and clothing for varying temperatures. When you consider an adjustable-rate mortgage, you must identify the maximum payment that you can handle. If you can't handle the payment that comes with a 10 or 11 percent interest rate, for example, don't look at ARMs that may go that high. As you crunch the numbers to see what your property's cash flow looks like under different circumstances (see Chapter 12), consider calculating how your mortgage payment changes based on various higher interest rates.

Avoiding negative amortization ARMs

As you make mortgage payments over time, the loan balance you still owe is gradually reduced or *amortized. Negative amortization* (when your loan balance increases) is the reverse of this process. It occurs when the monthly loan payments are less than the amount of interest that is accruing during that time. Some ARMs allow negative amortization. How can your outstanding loan balance grow when you continue to make mortgage payments? This phenomenon occurs when your mortgage payment is less than it really should be.

Some loans cap the increase of your monthly payment amount but don't cap the interest rate. Thus, the size of your mortgage payment may not reflect all the interest that you currently owe on your loan. So, rather than paying the interest that you owe and paying off some of your loan balance (or *principal*) every month, you end up paying off some, but not all, of the interest that you owe. Thus, lenders add the extra, unpaid interest that you still owe to your outstanding debt.

Negative amortization is similar to paying only the minimum payment that your credit card bill requires. You continue to rack up finance charges (in this case, greater interest) on the unpaid balance as long as you only make the artificially low payment. Taking a mortgage with negative amortization defeats the whole purpose of borrowing an amount that fits your overall financial goals.

Avoid ARMs with negative amortization. The only way to know whether a loan includes negative amortization is to ask explicitly. Some lenders and mortgage brokers aren't forthcoming about telling you. If you have trouble finding lenders that will deal with your financial situation, make sure that you're especially careful — you find negative amortization more frequently on loans that lenders consider risky, which should be taken as a sign that maybe you're overreaching for a property that isn't an ideal investment. You're likely only to be considering such a mortgage because your cash flow won't allow you to have a fully amortized loan. Therefore you would need to achieve significant appreciation in the property to cover this negative cash flow plus your desired rate of return in order for this investment to make sense.

Reviewing Other Common Fees

Whether the loan is fixed or adjustable, mortgage lenders typically assess other upfront fees and charges. The lender must disclose these ancillary fees. You may have to search carefully to find them in the paperwork, so make sure that you do because they can significantly add up to quite a bundle with some lenders. Here's our take on the typical extra charges you're likely to encounter and what's reasonable and what's not:

- ✔ **Application fee:** Most lenders charge several hundred dollars to work with you to complete your paperwork and see it through their loan evaluation process. Should your loan be rejected, or if it's approved and you decide not to take it, the lender needs to cover its costs. Some lenders credit or return this fee to you upon closing with their loan, but you need to verify it up-front in writing.

- ✔ **Credit report charge:** Most lenders charge you for the cost of obtaining your credit report, which tells the lender whether you've filed bankruptcy in the last seven years, plus repaid other loans, including *consumer debt* (such as credit cards, auto loans, and so on), on time. A credit report also allows the lender to verify your employment and personal residence and business addresses. Your credit report should cost about $50 for each individual or entity that will be a borrower.

- ✔ **Appraisal fee:** The property for which you borrow money needs to be valued. If you default on your mortgage, a lender doesn't want to get stuck with a property that's worth less than you owe. The cost for standard form appraisal typically ranges from several hundred dollars for most residential properties of one to four units to as much as $1,000 or more for larger investment properties. (On particularly large properties, this fee can be more significant — on a 30,000-square-foot office building, an appraisal may run around $5,000; on a 300-plus-unit apartment building, it is more in the $10,000 range.) You may be able to save some money if the property has been appraised recently and you contact the appraiser and he's willing and able to provide you with an updated appraisal.

- ✔ **Environmental assessment or phase I:** Virtually all lenders making loans on residential properties with five or more units or, especially, commercial property, require a qualified engineering company to perform a site assessment and overview of the entire area in which the property is located to identify possible environmental issues. This type of report is commonly referred to as a *phase I environmental report,* and the cost directly correlates to the location, type of property, size, and even the prior use of the property and the surrounding area. Phase I reports can run from $300 to as much as tens of thousands of dollars. (We include more details in Chapter 14.)

- ✔ **Third-party physical inspection:** Depending on the property being financed, lenders often require third-party inspections by competent professionals. For example, an inspection report from a licensed pest control firm documenting the property condition and specifically the presence of termites and/or wood-destroying organisms is required in virtually all transactions, including single-family homes and commercial properties. Again, the cost of these reports varies depending on the property. (More details to come in Chapter 14.)

Request a detailing of other fees and charges in writing from all lenders that you're seriously considering. You need to know the total of all lender fees so that you can accurately compare different lenders' loans and determine how much closing on your loan will cost you. For residential and commercial income properties, the lender usually asks for a deposit that the lender uses to cover the types of fees and charges outlined here.

To reduce the possibility of wasting your time and money applying for a mortgage that you may not qualify for, ask the lender for any reasons it may not approve you. Disclose any problems on your credit report or with the property. Don't expect the lender to provide you with a list of credit or property problems that may conceivably put the kibosh on a mortgage.

No-point mortgages aren't no-brainers

Some property buyers are attracted to *no-point* or *zero-cost mortgages* (which also sometimes have no other loan fees or costs either). Remember that if a loan has no points, it's sure to have a higher interest rate. That's not to say that no-point loans are better or worse than comparable loans from other lenders, but don't get duped into a loan because of a no-points sales pitch. The lenders who heavily promote these types of loans rarely have the best mortgage terms.

Consider a no-point/no-fee mortgage if you can't afford more out-of-pocket expenditures now or if you think that you'll only keep the loan a few years. But if you're that cash constrained, you may want to consider whether you can truly afford to buy investment property (see Chapter 1). This same advice applies to the *no-document* or *stated income loans* that are currently out of favor due to their poor track record of having a very high default rate.

Making Some Mortgage Decisions

You can't (or at least shouldn't) spend months deciding which mortgage may be right for your situation. So, in this section, we help you zero in on which type is best for you.

Choosing between fixed and adjustable

Choosing between a fixed-rate or adjustable-rate loan is an important decision in the real estate investment process. Consider the advantages and disadvantages of each mortgage type and decide what's best for your situation prior to going out to refinance or purchase real estate. This section covers the key factors to consider.

Your ability and desire to accept financial risk

How much risk can you handle in regard to the size of your property's monthly mortgage payment? If you can take the financial risks that come with an ARM, you have a better chance of saving money and maximizing your property's cash flow with an adjustable-rate rather than a fixed-rate loan. Your interest rate starts lower and stays lower with an ARM, if the overall level of interest rates stays unchanged. Even if rates go up, they'll likely come back down over the life of your loan. If you can stick with your ARM for better and for worse, you should come out ahead in the long run.

ARMs make more sense if you borrow less than you're qualified for. If your income (and applicable investment property cash flow) significantly exceeds your spending, you may feel less anxiety about the fluctuating interest rate on an ARM. If you do choose an adjustable loan, you may feel more financially secure if you have a hefty financial cushion (at least six months' to as much as a year's worth of expenses reserved) that you can access if rates go up.

Some people take ARMs when they can't really afford them. When rates rise, property owners who can't afford higher payments face a financial crisis. If you don't have emergency savings that you can tap into to make the higher payments, how can you afford the monthly payments and the other expenses of your property?

If you can't afford the highest-allowed payment on an ARM, don't take one. You shouldn't take the chance that the rate may not rise that high — it can, and you can lose the property.

Ask your lender to calculate the highest possible monthly payment that your loan allows. The number the lender comes up with is the payment that you face if the interest rate on your loan goes to the highest level allowed, or the *lifetime cap.* (For more on caps, see the "Future interest rate adjustments" section earlier in the chapter.)

Don't take an adjustable mortgage because the lower initial interest rate allows you to afford the property that you want to buy (unless you're absolutely certain that your income and property cash flow will enable you to meet future payment increases). Try setting your sights on a property that you can afford to buy with a fixed-rate mortgage.

Length of time you expect to keep the mortgage

Saving interest on most ARMs is usually a certainty in the first two or three years. An adjustable-rate mortgage starts at a lower interest rate than a fixed one. But, if rates rise, you can end up repaying the savings that you achieve in the early years of the mortgage.

If you aren't going to keep your mortgage for more than five to seven years, you pay more interest to carry a fixed-rate mortgage. A mortgage lender takes extra risk in committing to a fixed-interest rate for 15 to 30 years. Lenders don't know what may happen in the intervening years, so they charge you a premium in case interest rates move significantly higher in future years.

You may also consider a hybrid loan, which combines features of fixed- and adjustable-rate mortgages. For example, the initial rate may hold constant for three, five, seven, or ten years and then adjust once a year or every six months thereafter. Such loans may make sense for you if you foresee a high probability of keeping your loan seven to ten years or less but want some stability in your future monthly payments. The longer the initial rate stays locked in, the higher the interest rate. Don't confuse these loans with the often-unadvisable balloon mortgage (which we discuss in the "Mortgages That Should Make You Think Twice" section later in the chapter).

Selecting short-term or long-term

Most mortgage lenders offer you the option of 15-year or 30-year mortgages. You can also find 10-year, 20-year, and 40-year options, but they're unusual. Some lenders are even allowing you to select *customized* or *other length amortization terms* that allow you to personalize the number of years of your mortgage. Personalizing your mortgage may make sense if you have a specific goal in mind such as completing your mortgage payments before tackling college tuition bills or a retirement date. So how do you decide whether a shorter- or longer-term mortgage is best for your investment property purchase?

To afford the monthly payments and have a positive cash flow, many investment property buyers need to spread their mortgage loan payments over a longer period of time, and a 30-year mortgage is the way to do it. A 15-year mortgage has higher monthly payments because you pay it off quicker. At a fixed-rate mortgage interest rate of 7 percent, for example, a 15-year mortgage comes with payments that are about 35 percent higher than those for a 30-year mortgage.

Locking yourself into higher monthly payments with a 15-year mortgage may actually put you at greater financial risk. If your finances worsen or your property declines in value, odds are you'll have trouble qualifying for a refinance. You *may* be able to refinance your way out of the predicament, but you can't count on it.

Don't consider a 15-year mortgage unless you're sure that you can afford the higher payments that come with it. Even if you can afford these higher payments, taking the 15-year option isn't necessarily better. You may be able to find better uses for the money. If you can earn a higher rate of return investing your extra cash versus paying the interest on your mortgage, for instance, you may come out ahead investing your money rather than paying down your mortgage faster. Some real estate investors, including Robert, are attracted to 15-year mortgages to get their loans paid off by or even before retirement age.

If you decide on a 30-year mortgage, you still maintain the flexibility to pay the mortgage off faster if you choose to. You can choose to make larger-than-necessary payments and create your own 15-year mortgage. However, you can fall back to making only the payments required on your 30-year schedule when the need arises. The only situation in which you can't pay off your 30-year mortgage faster is if the loan has a *prepayment penalty* (a penalty for paying off your loan before you're supposed to), which we dislike. Normally, prepayment penalties don't apply if you pay off a loan because you sell the property, but when you refinance a loan with prepayment penalties, you typically have to pay the penalty.

Typically the interest rate will be lower for a 15-year loan than a 30-year loan, but if they're the same or very close, then you gain the flexibility with a 30-year loan with no prepayment penalty at zero cost. You can then adjust your payments over the life of the loan to customize your loan to exactly the term you desire. (Robert did so years ago when he decided that he and his wife should pay off their primary residence mortgage in full within nine years because their oldest daughter was scheduled to graduate high school and had upcoming costly college tuition payments.)

Borrowing Against Home Equity

Home equity loans (or a derivative called a *HELOC* — home equity line of credit) enable you to borrow against the equity in your home. Because such loans are in addition to the mortgage that you already have (known as the *first mortgage*), home equity loans are also known as *second mortgages*.

A home equity loan may provide a relatively low-cost source of funds for an investment property purchase, especially if you're seeking money for just a few years. You can refinance your first mortgage and pull cash out for an investment property purchase, but we don't advise doing that if your first mortgage is at a lower interest rate than you can obtain on a refinance.

Home equity loans generally have higher interest rates than comparable first mortgages because they're riskier to a lender. The reason: In the event that you default on the first mortgage or file for bankruptcy protection, the first mortgage lender gets first claim on your home.

Interest paid of up to $1 million on home mortgages for primary or secondary residences is tax deductible (on loans taken out after October 13, 1987). The tax deduction for home equity loans is limited to the interest paid on up to $100,000 of home equity debt. See Chapter 7 for a discussion of borrowing against home equity in the context of finding down payment money.

Getting a Seller-Financed Loan

Not every seller needs or even wants to receive all cash as payment for his property, so you may be able to finance part or even all of an investment property purchase thanks to the property seller's financing. The use of seller financing is the cornerstone of most no-money-down strategies.

Seller financing is a transaction in which the seller accepts anything less than all cash at closing. One form of an all-cash transaction to the seller is the buyer literally paying all cash, but typically it's a transaction in which the buyer uses a *conventional loan* (money to purchase the property from a lender other than the seller) so that the seller effectively receives all cash at closing.

Some sellers are financially well off enough that they don't need all of the sales proceeds immediately for their next purchase or are buying a property for less money — or maybe not buying a replacement property at all — and prefer to receive payments over time. They may be looking for the payments to replace their income in retirement or they may prefer to receive the funds over time so they can reduce their taxable income.

 Any seller with equity can offer seller financing, but usually private individuals are the best sources. The best candidates for seller financing are sellers with significant equity or, best of all, folks who own their property free-and-clear (without any debt on the property at all). Many seniors have owned their properties for years and may be more willing to extend a loan.

Sometimes sellers offer this option, but in other cases, you need to pop the question. We can think of two good reasons to ask for the seller to help finance an investment property purchase:

  ✔ **Better terms:** Mortgage lenders, which are typically banks or large monolithic financial institutions, aren't the most flexible businesses in the world. You may well be able to obtain a lower interest rate, lower or waived fees, and more flexible repayment conditions from a property seller. There are also many expenses with conventional loans that a property seller may not require: loan points, origination fees, and an appraisal. Some sellers may not even require a loan application or credit report, but they'd be wise to go through due diligence (including a personal financial statement) on the buyer.

- ✔ **Loan approval:** Perhaps you've had prior financial problems that have caused mortgage lenders to routinely deny your mortgage application. Some property sellers may be more flexible, especially in a slow real estate market or with a property that's challenging to sell. A seller can also make a decision in a few days, whereas a conventional lender often takes weeks.

Be careful when considering a property where a seller is offering financing as part of the deal; this act may be a sign of a hard-to-sell property. Investigate how long the property has been on the market and what specific flaws and problems it may have.

Some of the reasons why sellers may offer their own financing include

- ✔ **They're attracted to the potential returns of being a mortgage lender.** This reason shouldn't concern the buyer as long as the terms of the seller financing are reasonable and avoid the issues raised elsewhere in the chapter about balloon payment, and negative amortization or interest-only loans.

- ✔ **The seller has significant equity.** This situation creates another win-win opportunity for both the buyer and seller to use seller financing.

- ✔ **The current financing has prepayment issues.** This road can be a problem for the buyer; if the underlying financing has a due-on-sale clause and the lender becomes aware of the sale, it can demand the full payment of the outstanding loan balance on short notice. The seller is responsible for any prepayment penalties for their current financing when they pay it off.

- ✔ **They're seeking a price that exceeds the normal conventional loan parameters, or the property doesn't qualify for a conventional loan for some reason.** Examples of qualification issues include a cracked slab, environmental issues (including drug manufacturing like methamphetamine), improvements done without permits, and so on. This scenario is risky for the buyer and may be an indication that they're over-reaching or pursuing a property that's not a good investment.

Be sure that your seller financing agreement is nonrecourse (as discussed later in the chapter) and doesn't contain a *due-on-sale clause* prohibiting you from selling the property without paying off the loan in full. If the seller requires a due-on-sale clause, you have to pay off the full balance owed to the seller when you sell the property. Most sellers wisely ask for the due-on-sale clause so that the property can't be sold to another owner.

Mortgages That Should Make You Think Twice

You may come across other loans such as balloon loans and interest-only mortgages. We also want you to know the potential risks associated with recourse loans and loan guarantees. The following section presents our thoughts on these options.

Balloon loans

One type of loan that is sometimes confused with a hybrid loan is a balloon loan. *Balloon loans* start off just like traditional fixed-rate mortgages. You make level payments based on a long-term payment schedule, over 15 or 30 years, for example. But at a predetermined time, usually three to ten years after the loan's inception, the remaining loan balance becomes fully due.

Balloon loans may save you money because they have a lower interest rate than a longer-term fixed-rate mortgage. Sometimes, balloon loans may be the only option for the buyer (or so the buyer thinks). Buyers are more commonly backed into these loans during periods of high interest rates. When a buyer can't afford the payments on a conventional mortgage and really wants a particular property, a seller may offer a balloon loan.

Balloon loans are dangerous for the simple reason that your financial situation can change, and you may not be able to refinance when your balloon loan is due. What if you lose your job or your income drops? What if the value of your property drops and the appraisal comes in too low to qualify you for a new loan? What if interest rates rise and you can't qualify at the higher rate on a new loan? We recommend balloon loans only when the following conditions apply:

- ✔ Such a loan is your sole financing option.
- ✔ You've really done your homework to exhaust other financing options.
- ✔ You're certain that you can refinance when the balloon comes due.

If you take a balloon loan, get one with as much time as possible, preferably seven to ten years, before it becomes due.

Interest-only loans

In the early years of such mortgages, your monthly mortgage payment is used only to pay interest that is owed. Although this helps to keep your payments relatively low (because no money is going toward repaying principal), the downside is that you're not making any headway to pay down your loan balance.

Usually, after a preset time period, such as five or seven years, your mortgage payment jumps substantially so that you can begin to pay down or amortize your loan balance. Our experience and observation has been that many people don't really understand or investigate how this increased payment affects them, which is why we've long advised against taking these types of loans.

The main attraction that we see for interest-only mortgages for investment property purchases is that the low initial payments help you achieve more positive cash flow early on. Our concern, however, is seeing some property buyers attracted to interest-only loans to afford purchasing high-cost property that is difficult to realize positive cash flow from.

If the only way for you to invest in an income property is to use an interest-only loan, perhaps you shouldn't invest. Investing in rental real estate is risky, and you can lose your entire investment if the market turns and you don't have the staying power to ride through the real estate cycles. The margin of safety that you have with a decent down payment and an amortizing loan (where each payment reduces your loan balance) can be very positive if your rental property hits a rough patch.

If you consider an interest-only mortgage, be sure that you understand upfront exactly how high your payment will be after the loan moves out of the interest-only payment phase. And be sure that you've surveyed the mortgage marketplace and understand how the terms and conditions of interest-only loans stack up versus other types of mortgages.

Recourse financing

The goal of most real estate investors is to accumulate wealth over time while not taking any unreasonable risks. That's why we discourage using interest-only loans or loans with balloon payments. But there is another factor to explore before agreeing to any loan: Is the loan nonrecourse or recourse?

- ✔ **Nonrecourse financing:** In the event you fail to fulfill the terms of your loan, this type of loan limits the lender to only foreclosing on the underlying property. *Foreclosure* is the full and complete satisfaction of the loan, and the lender can't seek a deficiency judgment or go after your other assets. Agreeing only to loans with nonrecourse financing is extremely important because you increase your overall net worth through real estate investing. You don't want one bad investment to jeopardize your successful properties or, even worse, the equity in your primary residence or a business.

✔ **Recourse loans:** These loans lower the lender's risk because they offer additional protection. The lender has the legal right to seek a deficiency judgment against you personally or pursue other assets to cover any shortfall should the property value not fully cover the lender's outstanding debt balance. Remember that after a loan is in default, the interest penalties and legal fees can add up quickly. If you're already in default on the loan for your rental property, the last challenge you need is to have a lender looking to take your home or other viable rental properties to satisfy their deficiency judgment.

As long as you're not too aggressive and don't overleverage your rental properties, real estate investing can be relatively safe, and the chances are you won't be faced with losing your property by defaulting on your loan. But there are limits to your ability to control all of the diverse factors that can affect your property. For example, your cash flow will definitely suffer if the major employer in your area suddenly leaves.

Nonrecourse financing has more stringent qualification standards, such as higher debt coverage ratios, and generally results in a lower loan amount. But just as with borrowers who utilize interest-only loans so that they can borrow as much money as possible, the closer you live to the edge, the more likely you'll regret it.

Many of the loans you consider will be nonrecourse, but if you're seeking financing for an *unstabilized property* (a property whose cash flow is uncertain due to vacancy or unusually high expenses) or a property requiring major renovation, you may find that lenders are willing to provide the funds you need only with a full recourse loan.

Typically you're evaluating different loan proposals with either full recourse or full nonrecourse financing. But lenders can also offer a partial recourse loan. A *partial recourse loan* allows the lender to seek a deficiency judgment up to a certain limit if you default. Again, there may be great real estate investment options where such a loan makes sense, but be very careful before agreeing to such terms, and include the consequences to your overall financial status in a worst-case scenario in your overall analysis.

No matter what type of loan you use, we strongly recommend that you only use nonrecourse financing. You'll sleep better at night!

Loan guarantees

Another way that lenders reduce their risk of a loan defaulting is requiring a loan guarantee. A *loan guarantee* is a promise by the guarantor (the person or entity subject to the loan guarantee and legally responsible for repayment of any shortfall) to assume the debt obligation of the borrower if the borrower defaults on the loan. Investment real estate is often purchased in the name of a legal entity that may not have other assets than the real property subject to the loan. In these instances, a *personal loan guarantee* will be required from an individual, which is usually the person that is the owner or one of the owners of the legal entity that owns the real property.

Particularly if the loan is nonrecourse, the lender will want a loan guarantee to be included. The loan guarantee can be limited or unlimited, which controls if the guarantor is responsible for some or all of the debt. You may have seen or heard about guarantors for leases, such as a parent serving as the guarantor of their child's college apartment.

Chapter 9

Securing the Best Mortgage Terms

· ·

In This Chapter

▶ Understanding the best ways to shop for mortgages

▶ Solving common borrowing problems

· ·

*I*n Chapter 8, we discuss how to choose among the many loan options available to select the one that best suits your personal and financial situation. In the process of delving into the different types of real estate investment financing, you may have already begun the process of speaking with different lenders and surfing websites.

In this chapter, we provide our top tips and advice for shopping for and ultimately securing the best financing that you can for your real estate investment purchases and refinances. We also cover common loan problems that may derail your plans.

Shopping for Mortgages

Financing costs of your real estate investment purchases are generally the single biggest expense by far, so it pays to shop around and know how to unearth the best deals. You may find that many lenders would love to have your business, especially if you have a strong credit rating. Although having numerous lenders competing for your business can save you money, it can also make mortgage shopping and selection difficult. This section should help you simplify matters.

Relying on referrals

Many sources of real estate advice simply tell you to get referrals in your quest to find the best mortgage lenders. Sounds simple and straightforward — but it's not. For instance, loans for commercial investment properties and residential rental properties with five or more units have different lender underwriting requirements and terms compared with residential one- to four-unit loans (see Chapter 2 for explanations of these types of investments).

Good referrals can be a useful tool for locating the best lenders. Here are a few sources we recommend:

- ✔ Start with a bank or credit union that you have a relationship with currently and then seek referrals from it if it's not interested in making the specific loan you have in mind.

- ✔ Collect referrals from people who you know and trust and who have demonstrated some ability to select good service providers. Start with the best professional service providers (tax advisors, lawyers, financial planners, real estate agents, and so on) you know and respect, and ask them for their recommendations.

- ✔ Contact associations of real estate investors, especially those in your state. (You can find a comprehensive list organized by state at the website www.realestateassociations.com.) Networking with local investors is a great way to learn about the local real estate market and to benefit from other people's experiences.

Don't take anyone's referrals as gospel. Always be wary of business people who refer you to folks who have referred business to them over the years. You want to make sure that the referral is not just a payback or reciprocal arrangement with no justification, but actually someone that warrants consideration. Whenever you get a recommendation, ask the person doing the referring why they're making the referral and what they like and don't like about the service provider.

Mulling over mortgage brokers

You don't need to use a mortgage broker unless you're trying to get a loan for a property that has some challenges or you as the buyer have less than stellar credit or want to put the minimum down. Mortgage brokers also may not be justified when the market conditions are favorable and many lenders are aggressively seeking to make loans. Thus, in these instances, we recommend going directly to lenders for simple deals (a relatively small price tag, a property that's in good condition and enjoys a good location, and so on) and using mortgage brokers for bigger, more complicated, or more difficult deals and especially if the capital markets are tight and lenders aren't motivated to make deals.

But many property buyers get a headache trying to shop among the enormous universe of mortgages and lenders. Check out the following sections when deciding on whether you want to use a broker.

Counting a broker's contributions

A good mortgage broker can make the following contributions to your real estate investing team:

- **Advice:** If you're like most people, you may have a difficult time deciding which type of mortgage is best for your situation. A good mortgage broker can take the time to listen to your financial and personal situation and goals and offer suggestions for specific loans that match your situation. Brokers do work on commission, which unfortunately can temper the objectivity of their advice, so tread carefully. Don't blindly accept a mortgage broker's advice, which may be nothing more than a commission-driven sales pitch masquerading as counsel.

- **Shopping:** Even after you figure out the specific type of mortgage that you want, dozens (if not hundreds) of lenders may offer that type of loan. (You'll find fewer lender options for five-plus-unit residential properties and commercial properties.)

  Thoroughly shopping among the options to find the best mortgage takes time and knowledge you may well lack. A good mortgage broker can probably save you time and money by shopping for your best deal. Brokers can be especially helpful if you have a less than pristine credit report or you want to buy property with a low down payment — like 10 percent of the value of a property. Purchasing a multifamily residential property with five or more units or a commercial, industrial, or retail property is difficult with less than a 20- to 30-percent down payment.)

  Be careful when selecting a broker, because the worst among them get in the habit of repeatedly using the same lenders — perhaps because of the lofty commissions those lenders pay out. (More on understanding mortgage broker's commissions in the "Keeping up with commissions and other contingencies" section.)

- **Paperwork and presentation:** An organized and detail-oriented mortgage broker can assist you with completing the morass of forms most lenders demand. The paperwork can be truly overwhelming and tedious if you haven't been through the process before and your records aren't in order. Mortgage brokers and escrow officers can assist you with preparing your loan package so that you put your best foot forward with lenders. The mortgage broker only gets paid if the loan is funded so she can also be an advocate and lobby the lender on doing some more difficult deals that take some trust and creativity to complete.

  Have your personal financial statement prepared in advance so that it can be easily updated. Each time you seek a loan for an investment property, you have to provide a current financial statement to the broker (and, actually, all potential loan sources).

✔ **Closing the deal:** After you sign a purchase agreement to buy a real estate investment property, you still have a lot to do before you're the proud new property owner (see Chapter 14 for all the details). A competent mortgage broker makes sure that you meet the important deadlines for closing the deal.

Keeping up with commissions and other contingencies

A mortgage broker typically gets paid a percentage, usually between 0.5 and 1 percent, of the loan amount. This commission is completely negotiable, especially on larger loans that are more lucrative. (In case you're interested, the commission on larger deals — say, on a loan of $25 million or more — is 0.25 to 0.5 percent.) Don't confuse the mortgage broker commission with the lender-required points. When lenders have a lot of money to place, you may find that using a mortgage broker doesn't cost you the full amount of their quoted commission because lenders will reduce their points by enough to cover a portion or even all of the mortgage broker fees.

The mortgage broker may also be receiving compensation (or other financial incentives based on the volume of placed loans) from certain lenders that further complicates your analysis. It also means that you need to explore fully the fee structure with each proposed loan. Be sure to ask what the commission is on every alternative loan that a broker pitches. Some brokers may be indignant that you ask — that's their problem. You have every right to ask; after all, it's your money.

Even if you plan to shop on your own, talking to a mortgage broker may be worthwhile. At the very least, you can compare what you find with what brokers say they can get for you. Again, be careful. Some brokers tell you what you want to hear — that is, that they can beat your best find — and then aren't able to deliver when the time comes. Some mortgage brokers promise fantastic terms to get you in the door; then, when you're just about ready to close on your loan, they come up with a last minute problem with your credit report, appraisal or some other issue that prevents them from delivering on the loan as quoted. This bait-and-switch tactic often works because most borrowers have some blemish or negative on their loan application or credit report. So make sure you find a mortgage broker who doesn't overpromise and underdeliver.

If your loan broker quotes you a really good deal, ask who the lender is. Most brokers refuse to reveal this information until you pay the necessary fee to cover the appraisal, credit report, and required environmental reports. But after taking care of those fees, you can check with the lender to verify the interest rate, the points, the amortization term, and the prepayment penalties (if any) that the broker quotes you, and make sure that you're eligible for the loan.

Web surfing for mortgages

You can shop for just about anything and everything online, so why should mortgages be any different? Mortgage websites often claim that they save you lots of time and money.

In our experience, the Internet is better used for mortgage research than for securing a specific mortgage. That's not to say that some sites can't provide competitive loans in a timely fashion. However, we've seen some property purchases fall apart because the buyers relied upon a website that failed to deliver a loan in time.

Here's a short list of some of our favorite mortgage related websites that you may find helpful:

- **HSH Associates:** The folks at HSH Associates (www.hsh.com) collect mortgage information for most metropolitan areas. For $10, you can receive a list of dozens of lenders' rate quotes, but you need to be a real data junkie to wade through all the numbers on the multipage report that features lots of abbreviations in small print.

- **Government-related sites:** The websites of the U.S. Department of Housing and Urban Development (www.hud.gov) and the Veterans Administration (www.va.gov) provide information on government loan programs and feature foreclosed homes for sale.

  Fannie Mae, which stands for the Federal National Mortgage Association (www.fanniemae.com), and Freddie Mac, which is the Federal Home Loan Mortgage Corporation (www.freddiemac.com), have worked over the years with the federal government to support the mortgage marketplace.

- **Mortgage Bankers Association:** The trade association for mortgage lenders, the Mortgage Bankers Association (www.mbaa.org), has articles and data on the mortgage marketplace. Its Web resources page also includes links to state and local mortgage banker associations.

  This group is an excellent source of information on loans for residential properties with five or more units and commercial, industrial, and retail properties.

- **E-LOAN:** One of the first major online lenders, E-LOAN has stood the test of time and continues to offer competitive loans (www.eloan.com). This well-organized site can give you a quick overview of competitive mortgage pricing. Of course, you're under no obligation to use one of its mortgages just because you survey the options available.

✔ **Journalistic sites:** Numerous websites feature news and information about the real estate markets around the country. Several journalistic sites worth perusing include www.realtytimes.com, www.deadlinenews.com, www.inman.com, and www.erictyson.com.

✔ **Legal research sites:** Legal issues certainly raise their ugly heads on many a real estate deal. The website of self-help legal publisher Nolo Press (www.nolo.com) offers some free resources as well as details on all of the company's legal books.

Solving Potential Loan Predicaments

The best defense against loan rejection is avoiding it in the first place. To head off potential rejection, disclose anything that may cause a problem *before* you apply for the loan. For example, if you already know that your credit report indicates some late payments from when you were out of the country for an extended period or your family was in turmoil over a medical problem, write a letter to your lender that explains this situation. Or perhaps you're self-employed and your income from two years ago on your tax return was artificially much lower due to a special tax write-off. If that's the case, explain that in writing to the lender.

With the non-cash deduction of depreciation taken by most real estate investors, working with a lender that routinely makes real estate investment property loans is particularly important because she'll understand your tax return and how to calculate your actual net cash flow. These lenders will add back in the non-cash deduction whereas an inexperienced lender's underwriters will use only the taxable income line on your IRS Form 1040.

Even if you're the ideal mortgage borrower in the eyes of every lender, you may encounter financing problems with some properties. And of course, not all real estate buyers have a perfect credit history, lots of spare cash, and no debt. If you're one of those borrowers who must jump through more hoops than others to get a loan, don't give up hope. Few borrowers are perfect from a lender's perspective, and many problems aren't that difficult to fix.

Polishing your credit report

Late payments, missed payments, or debts that you never bothered to pay can tarnish your credit report and squelch a lender's desire to offer you a mortgage loan. If you've been turned down for a loan because of your less-than-stellar credit history, request a free copy of your credit report from the lender that turned you down.

Getting a report before you even apply for a loan is advisable and no longer costs you any money. Once a year, you're entitled to obtain a free copy of your credit report from each of the three credit bureaus. The contact information for the credit bureaus is

- ✔ **Equifax:** 800-685-1111; www.equifax.com
- ✔ **Experian:** 888-397-3742; www.experian.com
- ✔ **Transunion:** 800-916-8800; www.transunion.com

If problems are accurately documented on your credit report, try to explain them to your lender. Getting the bum's rush? Call other lenders and tell them your credit problems up front and see whether you can find one willing to offer you a loan. Mortgage brokers may also be able to help you shop for lenders in these cases.

Sometimes you may feel that you're not in control when you apply for a loan. In reality, you can fix a number of credit problems yourself. And you can often explain those that you can't fix. Some lenders are more lenient and flexible than others. Just because one mortgage lender rejects your loan application doesn't mean that all the others will.

As for erroneous information listed on your credit report, get on the phone to the credit bureaus. If specific creditors are the culprits, call them too. They're required to submit any new information or correct any errors at once. Keep notes from your conversations and make sure that you put your case in writing and add your comments to your credit report. If the customer service representatives you talk with are no help, send a letter to the president of each company. Getting mistakes cleaned up on your credit report can take the tenacity of a bulldog — be persistent.

Another common credit problem is having too much *consumer debt* at the time you apply for a mortgage. The more credit card, auto loan, and other consumer debt you rack up, the less mortgage you qualify for. If you're turned down for the mortgage, consider it a wake-up call to get rid of this high-cost debt. Hang on to the dream of buying real estate and work at paying off your debts before you make another foray into real estate. (See Chapter 8 for more information.)

Conquering insufficient income

If you're self-employed or have changed jobs, your income may not resemble your past income, or more importantly, your income may not be what a mortgage lender needs to see relative to the amount that you want to borrow. A simple (although not always feasible) way around this problem is to make a larger down payment.

If you can't make a large down payment, another option is to get a cosigner for the loan — your relatives may be willing. As long as they aren't overextended themselves, they may be able to help you qualify for a larger loan than you can get on your own. As with partnerships, make sure that you put your agreement in writing so that no misunderstandings occur.

Dealing with low property appraisals

Even if you have sufficient income, a clean credit report, and an adequate down payment, the lender may turn down your loan if the appraisal of the property that you want to buy comes in too low. This is a relatively rare situation that happens more in rapidly appreciating markets; it's unusual for a property not to appraise for what a buyer agrees to pay.

Many sellers have a distorted view and are unrealistic about the true value of their real estate and need a reality check. This is especially true during a period like the late 2000s when real estate values generally fell. Assuming that you still like the property, use the low appraisal to renegotiate a lower price from the seller. Or if you still really want the property, and because you won't likely be able to get the full amount of the loan you planned as part of your acquisition deal structure, you may be able to get the seller to carry back part of the purchase price as seller financing at favorable terms. The seller gets the price that she wants, but you'll need to get below-market financing to still make the deal work from your perspective.

You may be the owner of a property in need of refinancing because the loan is coming due or the terms are unfavorable and the appraisal is too low. In this case you obviously need to follow a different path. If you have the cash available, you can simply put more money down to get the loan balance to a level for which you qualify. If you don't have the cash, you may need to forgo the refinance until you save more money or until the property value rises.

Part III
Finding and Evaluating Properties

Property Knowledge Sheet

Property Information

Rental address _____ Unit # _____ City _____ Zip code _____
Office hours (if any) _____ Square footage of unit(s) _____
Unit mix—Studios ____ 1 Bedroom ____ 2 Bedroom/1 Bath ____ 2Bedroom/2 Bath ____ Other _____
Rent—Studios _____ 1 Bedroom _____ 2 Bedroom/1 Bath _____ 2Bedroom/2 Bath _____ Other _____
Application fee _____ Security deposit _____ Concessions _____
Age of rental _____ Type of construction _____ Parking _____
Recreational facilities _____ Laundry _____ Pets _____
Storage _____ Utilities (who pays?) _____ AC/Heat _____
Appliances _____ Floor coverings _____
Special features/comments _____
_____
_____

Community Information

School district _____ Grade school _____ Jr. high _____
High school _____ Jr. college _____ College _____
Trade school _____ Pre-school (s) _____
Childcare _____ Places of worship _____
Police station _____ Fire station _____ Ambulance _____
Electric _____ Natural gas _____ Telephone _____ Cable _____
Water _____ Sewer _____ Library _____ Post office _____
Hospital _____ Pharmacy _____ Vet _____
Other medical facilities _____
Nearby employment centers _____
Transportation _____
Groceries _____ Other shopping _____
Local services _____
Restaurants _____
Comments _____
_____

Rental Market Information

Rental competitors/rental rates/concessions _____
_____
Our competitive advantages _____
_____
Our disadvantages _____
_____

Check out www.dummies.com/extras/realestateinvesting for helpful advice on using standardized contracts when investing in real estate.

In this part ...

- ✔ Understand the what, where, and how to buy a rental property so that you have a solid plan in place as you shop around and purchase a property.

- ✔ Examine the differences between residential and commercial leases so that you know what to expect if the property you want to buy has an existing lease and tenants.

- ✔ Know how to value and evaluate real estate investment properties using a variety of financial tools and techniques.

- ✔ Make sure that when you consider purchasing any real estate that you understand the return on investment (ROI), which is really the purchase of a future income stream or cash flow.

- ✔ Grasp the ins and outs of negotiating a real estate contract, which is a legally binding written agreement between two people regarding an exchange of some sort.

- ✔ Get the lowdown and our advice about performing due diligence, doing the necessary inspections, and closing your property so that you're ready to take ownership.

Chapter 10

Location, Location, Value

. . . .

In This Chapter

▶ Choosing your investment area

▶ Looking at what makes a good investment location

▶ Discovering what's in your own backyard

▶ Comparing neighborhoods

▶ Getting to know seller's markets and buyer's markets

. . . .

*A*s the well-known real estate saying goes, "The three most important factors to success in real estate are location, location, and location!" There *is* a strong correlation between the location of your real estate investments and your financial success. And we firmly agree that the location of your real estate investment is critical in determining your success as a real estate investor. But we prefer the phrase coined by Eric: "Location, location, value." This revised adage clearly emphasizes location but also stresses the importance of finding good value for your investment dollar.

Merely owning real estate isn't the key to success in real estate investing; acquiring and owning the right real estate at the right price is how to build wealth! As you gain experience in real estate, you'll develop your own strategy, but to make any strategy succeed, you need to do your homework and diligently and fairly evaluate both the positive and negative aspects of your proposed real estate investment. That's where we come in.

In this chapter, we cover important aspects of regional and local demographics, how to analyze the economy, and which factors are most important to real estate investing. We also discuss barriers to entry and the supply/demand equation. Then we show you where to find this information and how to interpret the numbers to determine your local areas with the most potential. Finally, we discuss real estate cycles and timing.

Deciding Where to Invest

If you're going to invest in real estate, you need to decide on a location. Most real estate investors initially — and wisely — look in their local communities.

We give you the tools to evaluate properties anywhere, but you have an inherent advantage if you begin your search close to home. Unless you really know another real estate market and regularly find yourself there for other reasons anyway, we recommend that you stay close to home with your real estate investments — no more than one to two hours away by your favorite mode of transportation.

Robert has had success with a real estate investment strategy that limits his potential markets to cities where he had personal management experience when he worked for a large national real estate firm. He also limits himself to areas that are no farther than a one-hour, nonstop flight on Southwest Airlines.

Although we strongly advise that you cut your teeth on an income property or two in your local market, establish parameters that meet your specific needs. For example, maybe you have family responsibilities that limit the amount of time you can devote to overseeing and managing your real estate investments. The one-hour-flight rule that Robert uses would likely be too taxing in that situation, and could be replaced by something like a 30-minute-drive rule.

Although virtually everyone lives in an area with opportunities for real estate investing, not everyone lives in an area where the prospects are good for real estate in general. That's why it's important to broaden your geographic investment horizon as long as you don't compromise your ability to effectively manage and control your property.

Even if you decide to invest in real estate in your own locale, you still need to do tons of research to decide where and what to buy — extremely important decisions with long-term consequences. In the pages that follow, we explain what to look for in a region, a community, and even a neighborhood before you make that investment decision. Keep in mind, though, that you can spend the rest of your life looking for the *perfect* real estate investment, never find it, never invest, and miss out on lots of opportunities, profit, and even fun.

The dangers of investing out of your area

In many regions of the country, real estate prices escalated in the early- to mid-2000s to the point that it was difficult for entry-level real estate investors to buy. And in some areas it's starting to happen again (as this book goes to press in early 2015). If you live in such an area, you may be tempted to go far afield in search of reasonably priced property. The subsequent decline in prices after the market peaked in some areas was and in a few places still is equally enticing, but you need to exercise caution.

Regardless of whether prices are up or down, a proliferation of seminars always seems to promise real estate investment opportunities in other areas of the country. In California and other areas (where prices fell, but are now rebounding and are always relatively high-priced), seminar sponsors target owners and wannabe real estate investors, touting the great investments that can be found in other, often unnamed, parts of the country. They claim that you can buy rental real estate for a fraction of your local prices and achieve high returns on your investment. They even provide pictures of these properties — but there are always tiny little disclaimers somewhere on the page!

We strongly advise against investing blindly in areas that you don't know personally. And never consider these investments unless you have the proper local contacts such as a great property manager, contractors and suppliers, and competent legal and accounting advice. In the greater Las Vegas area alone, at the peak of the investor-led bubble in the mid-2000s, an estimated 40,000 non-owner occupied rental homes were primarily owned by out-of-state real estate speculators that bought new homes as investments to flip but got stuck with them when the market turned.

Falling property values in the Las Vegas area has led to a feeding frenzy among bottom-feeders looking to lowball and buy up virtually any property without doing proper due diligence when Las Vegas led the nation in home foreclosures. Of course, such investing isn't risk-free because even though these homes are being purchased for much less than what the original investor paid as a brand new home, it will be years before the demand from owner-occupants will absorb all the excess inventory. In the meantime, investors may have a lower cost basis (even after the costly repairs and renovation of these long-term vacant or neglected rental properties). However they'll continue to struggle to keep their rental home occupied with any decent cash flow while waiting for an opportunity to sell with anything more than modest appreciation after all the carrying costs are deducted.

Robert routinely serves as an expert witness and recently had a case where an out-of-state owner saw a great investment opportunity for an upscale four-bedroom executive home. Even though he worked more than 3,000 miles away, what could go wrong with such a beautiful rental in a dynamic and prosperous suburb of San Diego? It looked like a good investment in a great neighborhood, and the property manager found a respectable renter in just a few days.

Unfortunately, what seemed so good suddenly turned south when the initial check for the security deposit and first month's rent was returned, marked "account closed." Later that week, the owner got a long-distance call from a disgruntled neighbor complaining about the barking dog and that many more people were occupying the home than just one family. Six months later, after paying hefty legal bills for the eviction plus making several cross-country airline flights, the owner finally regained possession of his now-trashed executive home. Aside from the lost rent for six months, the damage to the home was in excess of $50,000. In the subsequent lawsuit against the broker, it came out that the broker had recommended an unlicensed property manager who never did any screening of the tenant.

One experience like this, and you may wish to forever shun real estate investment properties. So when you read about great real estate opportunities in faraway places, remember that it's better to be safe than sorry. Our experience indicates that if it sounds too good to be true, it *is* too good to be true! Risk and return are truly related. It's better to have a more solid and easy-to-manage property in your own community than to try and hit a home run in a different time zone.

Finding Properties to Add Value

So you're looking for properties that allow you to make physical and/or fiscal improvements that will ultimately lower the expected cap rate to a future investor, which is essentially lowering the required rate of return because you have taken out much of the risk. You want to buy when you determine that the property has a strong likelihood of producing future increases in NOI and cash flow. So you should look for properties where your analysis shows that the income for the property can be increased or the expenses reduced.

As you look for your next rental property, many sellers, and especially their real estate brokers, will assure you that the current rents are really too low, and that there is tremendous upside in the property to be tapped simply by buying the property and raising the rents. If it were only that easy, then why wouldn't the current owner raise the rent and then sell the property for a higher price?

However, if you thoroughly research the market, you'll know how to identify certain clues that indicate whether a property really has rents that are below market. Properties with no vacancies and a waiting list are prime candidates. Other telltale signs are properties that have low turnover and then have multiple applicants for those rare vacancies. Economics 101 says that if demand exceeds supply, the price is too low.

Some owners actually market their real estate investment properties at a below-market price. These are motivated sellers, probably with a variety of personal reasons for their need to sell more quickly and cheaply than they would if they had more time and patience. Health reasons, family dissolutions, financial issues, and so on are all likely reasons that a seller will agree to a quick sale at a below-market price.

However, some sellers don't achieve the top value in the market for other reasons. For example, some owners despise the whole process of selling their rental properties so much that they knowingly underprice the property to ensure a quick and clean transaction and retain the ability to reject any and all contingencies that a buyer would typically require in a *market deal*. The elimination of hassling and haggling is paramount to these sellers; they just want to get the sale done, so they're willing to give the buyer such a good deal that the buyer takes the property essentially as-is.

Some sellers are truly ignorant of the actual market value of the property they're selling. There really is no excuse (save laziness) for a seller in a major metropolitan area to not know the true value of the property he owns, because there are many real estate professionals who can inexpensively assist sellers in determining the estimated value of their property. Simply ask a real estate broker for a comparative market analysis (CMA) or hire an appraiser, and you'll get a detailed report determining the current as-is value of the investment property. Of course, a seller should always keep in mind that some real estate brokers may be overly optimistic on pricing with the hope that they can get a listing and then still close the sale at a price that is really the market value.

The most common question Robert hears from real estate investors is "How do I find these underpriced properties?" Our experience indicates that under-priced investment properties typically have older owners with no mortgage who have exhausted the possibility of taking depreciation deductions on their tax returns.

Look for properties where you can increase value. These *value-added proper-ties* are properties that allow you to either increase the NOI or decrease the rate and thus create value. As we point out in Chapter 12, the value of a prop-erty is increased with an increase in NOI or a decrease in the capitalization rate. The capitalization rate is directly correlated to the anticipated risk of the investment, so stabilizing properties through long-term leases and more financially viable tenants can reduce risk and lead to a lower cap rate and hence a higher value.

A simple example of how to increase the value of a building is to find a resi-dential rental property in a high demand area where all rental rates are the same for similar floor plans. In reality, the rents should reflect the fact that, say, not all two-bedroom units have the same location benefits. For example, a unit overlooking the pool is often more desirable than a unit on the main street or units on the upper floors are in greater demand, so raising the rents for the more desirable units increases rental income.

Evaluating a Region: The Big Picture

Though we advise you to think local, any decision about where to invest should start with an evaluation of the overall economic viability and trends of the surrounding region. If the region isn't economically sound, the likeli-hood for successful real estate investments within that area is diminished. Understand how to evaluate important economic data so that you can invest in the areas that are poised for growth.

We define a *region* as a concentrated population base (rather than an entire state or section of the country). Data for any larger geographic area would be difficult to use for the types of real estate investments you'll be making. For example, data for the state of Texas isn't as important as vital economic trends for your proposed investment in the Houston area.

Gathering and analyzing the relevant economic data has never been easier, thanks to the Internet. The most important data for population growth, job growth, and economic trends is available online, and there are numerous entities tracking this information. From the federal government, to state and local governments, to universities and business groups, information on regional economic trends is readily available.

In addition to the academic and governmental agencies that provide broader economic indicators, several private firms specialize in providing specific data on occupancy, availability, and rental rates for different types of real estate for many of the major cities throughout the country. These services offer limited information to non-subscribers. For example, two of our favorites with a national perspective are the CoStar Group (www.costar.com) and Real Estate Research Corporation (www.rerc.com). There are many smaller firms that specialize in specific geographic areas, like MarketPointe Realty Advisors, which focuses on Southern California (www.marketpointe.com), or Pierce-Eislen (www.pi-ei.com), which focuses on larger apartment communities of 50 or more units throughout most major metropolitan areas of the country. Check with real estate investment professionals that hold the Certified Commercial Investment Member (CCIM) designation in your area, because they have access to the excellent CCIM Institute's Site to Do Business (STDB) (www.stdbinc.com).

You can find the vital economic data you need for your evaluation through your local economic development department, chamber of commerce, or public library. Real estate lenders often have in-house economists that collect information concerning areas where they lend money, and these folks are often the first to detect weaknesses in the market. So if your lender isn't particularly enamored about the location for your proposed real estate investment, it probably knows something that you should heed. Also, contact a professional appraiser in your area, because they routinely collect this information for their appraisals.

These sources collect, record, analyze, and report information according to specific geographic boundaries as established by the federal government. The U.S. government divides urbanized areas of the country into *Standardized Metropolitan Statistical Areas* (SMSA). SMSA's are large areas that consist of one or more major cities. For example, the entire San Francisco Bay Area, the combined areas of Dallas and Fort Worth, Greater Los Angeles, and Greater New York City are each a single SMSA.

If your proposed investment isn't in an area tracked as part of an SMSA, much of the same information is available, but you have to do a little more digging.

You're looking for more than just numbers. Attitude and leadership are important as well. Many neighboring cities are working together with regional planning boards and economic development agencies. Their goal is job creation, and they possess great powers to make important economic decisions regarding regional airports, mass transportation, and the reuse of surplus military installations. Clearly, such regional governance can have a major impact for better or worse on your real estate investments.

You're looking for a region or area that is growing and has a diverse economic base with strong employment prospects. In the following sections, we cover some of the more significant factors that can impact real estate demand and values.

Population growth

Population growth is one of the cornerstones upon which demand for real estate is based. More people means more demand for housing, retail shopping, and offices and service providers. In other words, people use real estate, so the demand for real estate is enhanced as the population increases.

Increases or decreases in population are the result of three activities: births, mortality, and people moving into or out of the area. In most areas, births exceed deaths, and thus most areas experience moderate growth. So the real impact comes from a dynamic and mobile society. We've seen tremendous shifts in population from northern states to the more temperate climates of the Sunbelt. Immigration has also been a major factor in many parts of the country.

How does population growth affect your real estate decisions? Simply put, economists find that a new household is needed for every increase in population of three persons. Of course, these numbers can vary based on average household size, which is different in some parts of the country, especially in urban areas with population increases from immigration. So if you're considering investments in rental homes or small apartment buildings in a certain area, the overall net population growth can be a factor in determining current and future demand for rental housing.

But knowing the increase in population for the entire SMSA or region isn't enough because population growth isn't evenly spread and can vary. As you get down to the next level in your research (see the "Investigating Your Local Market" section later in the chapter), you need to determine the communities and even neighborhoods where the increased population will want to live, work, and shop. Real estate developers, and their lenders, look closely at net population growth in specific submarkets to forecast the demand for their proposed developments.

Job growth and income levels

Job growth is another fundamental element in determining demand for real estate. Economists generally predict that a new household is needed for every 1.5 jobs created. So if a new employer moves into the area and brings 150 new jobs, the local real estate housing market will need approximately 100 new dwelling units. Of course, these new jobs also positively impact the demand for commercial, industrial, and retail properties.

The U.S. Bureau of Labor Statistics compiles job growth and other economic data by SMSA as well as by county. This info is available at the Bureau's website (www.bls.gov). Other great sources for economic data are local colleges and universities and good local libraries.

But you need more information about the types of jobs before you can esti-mate their effect on the demand for each type of real estate. Although job growth is critical, so are the following factors:

- ✔ **Income levels:** Without stable, *well-paying* jobs, an area can stagnate. Even with positive growth in population and jobs, a lack of income can stifle the demand for additional residential and commercial properties.

- ✔ **Level of employment diversification:** If the local economy is heav-ily reliant on jobs in a small number of industries, that dependence increases the risk of your real estate investments. Some areas of the country have plenty of jobs, but they're lower- rather than higher-paying jobs. Ideally, look to invest in real estate in communities that maintain diverse job bases.

- ✔ **Industries represented:** Consider which industries are more heavily represented in the local economy. If most of the jobs come from slow-growing or shrinking employment sectors, such as farming, small retail, shoe and apparel manufacturing, and government, real estate prices are unlikely to rise quickly in the years ahead. On the other hand, areas with a greater preponderance of high-growth industries, such as technology and biotech, generally stand a greater chance of faster price appreciation.

- ✔ **Types of jobs:** The specific types of jobs available can be important depending on the target market for your income property. If you're buying a class A office building in an urban area, look for statistics on current and future employment levels for professional employment. For example, owning an office building across the street from the new regional courthouse gives you a real advantage in attracting law firms and legal support firms. Of course, you also want to make sure that the area boasts a good mix of nearby retail and food services to complement and support the tenants in your building.

In addition to job growth, other good signs to look for include the following:

- ✔ **Stable-to-increasing wages:** The demand for real estate clearly correlates to income levels, so local jobs with strong underlying demand are key. With many jobs being outsourced to other parts of the country and world, it's important that the local jobs aren't only secure but also unlikely to see an erosion in purchasing power.

- ✔ **A recession-resistant employment base:** Traditionally, jobs that enjoy stability are in the fields of education, government, and health care. Even areas renowned for strong demand and limited supply of real estate can slow down if the economy is hit hard, as shown by the collapse of some technology firms in the early 2000s and outsourcing or consolidations and mergers in the mid-2000s.

- ✔ **Employment that's highly unlikely to be outsourced:** Jobs can flow to another area of the country or overseas to the latest low-cost manufacturing base.

- ✔ **Declining unemployment:** Examine how the jobless rate has changed in recent years.

No one can precisely predict the future. And with due respect to our friendly economists, forecasts of population and job growth can go awry.

Investigating Your Local Market

Although everything starts at the regional level, you need to fine-tune your perspective and look at your local real estate market, too. All of the same types of economic data that you collect on a regional basis are important in evaluating your local real estate market.

With real estate investing, deciding where to invest is frequently more important than choosing the specific rental property. You can have a rental property that meets the needs of the market, but if it's located in a declining area where the demand is weak or an area with overbuilding and an excess of available properties, your investment won't perform financially. (These properties perform the worst over time, but are typically the types of properties highly touted by the infomercial gurus who love to brag about how much real estate they control but rarely tell you about their long-term investment returns.)

Likewise, you need to determine the areas that may be too richly priced, because your cash flow and future appreciation will be hurt if you overpay for a property. Often properties in the best neighborhoods in town are so overpriced that there is little appreciation potential and thus we advise you to seek other properties unless you're content with low returns similar to investing in safe and low yielding bonds.

In many local real estate markets, the demand for real estate is impacted more by the regional economy than by the local economy. For example, bedroom communities have high demand for rental homes and apartments even though they may only have service sector jobs in the immediate area, because the higher income professional and manufacturing jobs are concentrated in other areas of the region.

In the sections that follow, we help you research quantitative issues to consider when deciding where to invest in real estate. But you also must consider other factors, for instance, the weather or recreation and entertainment options — all key factors in the livability or quality of life for citizens. All of these criteria contribute to the overall desirability of a local market area and should be important considerations for the real estate investor. And don't underestimate the image or reputation of an area.

Supply and demand

The supply and demand for real estate in a given market has a direct impact on the financial performance of your income property. And although we firmly believe that the overall economic prospects for a region or community are vital, you must also find supply and demand information about the specific type of real estate that you plan to purchase.

Obviously, the best environment for investing in real estate is one with strong demand and limited supply. When the demand exceeds supply, shortages of available real estate push up prices.

Both sides of the equation — supply and demand — have indicators that you should evaluate in forming your consensus about the strength of the local real estate market. In the sections that follow, we take a close look at each indicator in detail. Supply-side indicators include building permits, the rate at which new properties have been rented or absorbed into the market, and the availability of alternatives for similar real estate. Demand indicators include occupancy and rent levels.

The overall relationship between supply and demand determines the market conditions for real estate. For example, a large number of pending or recently issued building permits, weak absorption or rental of new properties, and an excess of income property listings that have been on the market for an extended time are all indicators that the supply of a specific product type is greater than the demand. Such market conditions soon result in lower occupancy, lower rents, and often rental concessions like free rent or lower rental rates early in the lease, which mean lower cash flow and smaller appreciation potential. These aren't the markets you should be seeking.

When the demand for real estate is high, there are few vacancies, and property owners raise rents and eliminate or minimize any concessions. In commercial properties, landlords cut back on the tenant improvement (TI) allowance and require the tenants to take the space as-is and make any upgrades or changes to the space at their own expense.

Building permits and absorption

Building permits are often the first tangible step outlining the intent of a developer to build new real estate projects. Therefore, knowing about the issuance of building permits is an essential leading indicator to future supply of real estate.

The trend in the number of building permits tells you how the supply of real estate properties may soon change. A long and sustained rise in permits over several years can indicate that the supply of new property may dampen future price appreciation. Many areas experienced enormous increases in new building during the late 1980s, right before prices peaked due to excess inventory. Conversely, new building dried up in many areas in the late 1970s and early 1980s as onerous interest rates strangled builders and developers. In the late 1990s, despite the low-interest-rate environment, most parts of the country weren't overbuilding, but by the mid-to-late 2000s, there was nevertheless an excess of supply. The problem was that the demand was artificially inflated, which was the result of governmental pressure to increase home ownership by offering creative financing to individuals who were unqualified to borrow such large amounts, as well as speculation by some real estate investors. The crazy and irresponsible speculation was particularly pronounced in certain Sunbelt areas like Las Vegas, Phoenix, and many parts of Florida.

Absorption, the rate at which new buildings are rented and occupied, can be useful to determine the potential for the market to become *saturated,* or over-supplied with certain types of real estate. A healthy real estate market is one in which the available new properties have rented in a relatively short period of time — typically measured in months. Absorption is measured in housing units for residential properties and in square footage for all commercial types of properties.

Absorption can be either a positive or negative number and is usually tracked on a quarterly and annual basis:

- **Positive absorption:** More space is rented or occupied by owners/users during the measured time period than was built or taken out of the rental housing supply by demolition or even conversion to owner-occupied condominiums.

- **Negative absorption:** The new supply of a given type of real estate is being built faster than users can or want to use it.

You can obtain information on building permits from your local planning or building department. Absorption statistics aren't as easy to find, but local real estate appraisers and real estate brokers track absorption. For example, professional real estate brokers holding the CCIM (Certified Commercial Investment Member) designation specialize in the sale of income properties and often have that information. See Chapter 6 for many other reasons to have an appraiser on your real estate team.

Building permits and absorption are property-type specific, and an over-supply in industrial properties generally has no bearing on other types of commercial income properties such as retail or office. The only exception is when the use of a property can be changed. For example, many industrial properties have been upgraded to add office space for manufacturing firms so they can have their administrative functions and operations in the same facility. This type of hybrid usage is more difficult to track — but extremely important to note if it's occurring in your proposed investment market.

Another noteworthy trend for residential real estate investors is that new construction favors single-family homes rather than multifamily apartments. This discrepancy can have a significant impact on your decision whether to invest in single-family rental properties or multifamily properties, because multifamily properties benefit from the reduced competition. There are several reasons for this phenomenon, and we discuss some of them in the section "Considering barriers to entry" later in this chapter.

Availability of alternatives — renting versus buying

When the cost of buying is relatively low compared with the cost of renting, more renters can afford to purchase, thus increasing the number of home sales and lowering demand for rentals. A key indicator you can use to gauge the market is the number of property listings:

- ✔ **Increase in property listings:** Increasing numbers of property listings or a significant increase in the time the average property is unsold is an indication of future trouble for real estate price appreciation. However, as property prices reach high levels, some investors decide that they can make more money cashing in and investing elsewhere. When the market is flooded with listings, prospective buyers can be choosier, exerting downward pressure on prices.

- ✔ **Decrease in property listings:** A sign of a healthy real estate market is a decreasing and low level of property listings, which indicates that the demand from buyers meets or exceeds the supply of property for sale from sellers. At high prices (relative to the cost of renting), more prospective buyers elect to rent, and the number of sales relative to listings drops.

Occupancy levels

Before you invest your hard earned money, determine the current occupancy levels for your proposed type of income property.

The market occupancy rate is another way to gauge the supply and demand for a given property type in the local market. The *market occupancy* rate for a particular type of property is the percentage of that type of property available for occupancy that's currently rented. For example, you may find data telling you that there are 2,312 total residential rental units in apartment buildings in a local market, and the occupancy rate is 97 percent (or 2,242 are occupied), which would mean that 3 percent (or approximately 70) of the units are vacant. For commercial, industrial, and retail properties, the occupancy level is calculated based on square footage.

With commercial, industrial, and retail properties, determining the occupancy levels is relatively easy. A quick look at the directory or a walkthrough of the property can give you a lot of information.

The true occupancy rate is actually much more difficult to determine with apartment buildings. With apartments, the vacancies aren't as obvious, and obtaining accurate information can be challenging — most professionally managed properties don't advertise their occupancy levels or volunteer this info (nor do they post tenant directories anymore due to safety and privacy concerns). But fear not, we have some suggestions:

- ✓ **Trade organizations and industry service providers:** Some of these groups track this data. For example, the local affiliates of the National Apartment Association (www.naahq.org) and the Building Owners and Managers Association (www.boma.org) often publish vacancy and rent surveys for apartments and office buildings, respectively.

- ✓ **The do-it-yourself approach:** You can contact owners of comparable properties and offer to collect this data and give them a copy of the results.

After you acquire the info, here's how to use it:

- ✓ **Low vacancy rates:** When combined with a low number of building permits, low vacancy rates generally foretell future real estate price appreciation. If you find minimal vacancy in your market, it's a landlord's market with higher demand from tenants for existing units, which is a good sign for real estate owners. And it's good for real estate investors, if the market prices remain reasonable.

- ✓ **High vacancy rates:** High rates indicate an excess supply of real estate, which may put downward pressure on rental rates as many landlords compete to attract tenants.

Concessions, which typically include free rent, often indicate weakness in the rental market. However, some types of real estate and rental markets almost always have concessions, no matter how strong the rental market. This practice is very common in larger professionally managed apartment communities where a prospective tenant's first question when calling to inquire about a potential rental unit is inevitably "What's your special?" Apartments in Phoenix and many other areas of the Sunbelt may be able to raise their rents and maintain occupancies at or above 95 percent, but they can't eliminate the rental concessions or their rental traffic will diminish. In commercial properties, the TI or tenant improvement allowance is similar, with many markets requiring certain levels of dollars per square foot in custom build-outs or upgrades when the rental rate is actually less negotiable. (Check out Chapter 12 for more information on concessions.)

Rental levels

The trend in *rent levels,* or *rental rates,* that renters are willing and able to pay over the years also gives a good indication as to the supply/demand relationship for income properties. When the demand for real estate just keeps up with the supply of housing and the local economy continues to grow, rents generally increase. This increase is a positive sign for continued real estate price appreciation.

Of course, you need to be careful to make sure that you're getting the true and complete story on rents. Owners and their property managers are very smooth and savvy and don't allow their quoted rental rates to fall when the market shows some signs of softening. This strategy is logical because other tenants may have recently leased at a higher rate and would be upset to see the new tenants getting a better deal. So owners and property managers offer concessions or other perks to make sure that they're competitive in the current market while maintaining the perception of stable rents.

As a prospective rental property owner competing against these owners, you need to evaluate the current rent levels on a level playing field, so you want to calculate the *effective rental rate.* For example, if you see a comparable rental property available at $1,200 per month, but the owner is offering a concession of one month free rent on a 12-month lease, the effective rent is really $1,100 per month (the $1,200 loss of one month's rent spread out over the rest of the year).

An advantage of investing in commercial real estate is that there are few governmental regulations and controls, and the relationship between tenants and landlords is essentially a free market. However, residential *rent control* or *rent stabilization* (local laws regulating how much rents may increase) is an issue in some cities and towns. Investing in markets with rent control, or even with a pro-tenant environment where a landlord has difficulty terminating a lease, may not provide adequate returns on investment, and appreciation will be more limited. Although occupancy levels are usually strong in such areas, your overall cash flow may be threatened because the property's expenses may rise faster than you can legally raise the rents. In these communities, landlords who invest in major upgrades or capital improvements to a rental unit may not be able to raise rents or recover their costs because any rent increases must be approved by the local rent control board. Then, even if allowed at all, the approved capital improvements are amortized or spread over many years. Don't put your real estate future in the hands of others! If you're considering property in a rent-controlled area, you may find the recent edition of Robert's *Property Management Kit For Dummies* (John Wiley & Sons, Inc.) helpful.

Focusing on the path of progress

Buying real estate in up-and-coming areas with new development or renovated properties not only greatly enhances the ease of finding and keeping good tenants but also leads to higher occupancy, lower turnover, and higher rates of appreciation.

In virtually all major cities, some areas are experiencing new construction and growth — and have the reputation of being *the* area to live in. But by the time most folks feel this way, you've lost an opportunity to get in when prices have more appreciation potential. So, here are a few indicators to use to stay ahead of the game:

- ✔ **Follow the retailers:** You can often take a clue about where you should invest by looking for major retailers who do extensive research before making a decision to open in a given neighborhood. For instance, maybe a new Costco or Sam's Club is anchoring the new shopping center.

- ✔ **Follow the highways:** One of the best and most obvious indicators of where new development is headed is transportation. But make sure that the roads or mass transit projects actually get built. With so many funding and environmental challenges today, it can be extremely risky to invest in real estate based on proposed transportation projects. But after they're built, you're sure to find real estate investment opportunities.

But the path of progress isn't limited to new development. Many cities have areas that have seen better days and local leaders are doing their best to revitalize these tired and even blighted sections of town. A key component can be redevelopment districts that are formed with the property tax revenues being diverted to a special redevelopment agency that promotes new projects through a streamlined approval process and financial assistance. Often, the traditional downtown areas are being redeveloped with many incentives for developers and owners willing to be among the first ones in.

Stepping in the path of progress

One of Robert's best real estate investments was a 30,000-square-foot, two-story medical center complex on three acres in Santee, California, a suburban bedroom community of San Diego. The building had been a hub of activity before the large medical group that occupied the property disbanded. The building was foreclosed on by the lender and was virtually vacant for several years, because the area didn't easily attract new tenants due to the lack of nearby sit-down restaurants and shopping.

However, Robert found out that major redevelopment was planned around the new trolley and transportation center located within a half mile. Besides a proposed multiscreen cinema as the anchor tenant, the brand-new center would include everything from apparel and shoe stores to bookstores and a large fitness club, plus several new restaurants. Robert was confident that the new center would be a catalyst for the entire area, so he quickly purchased the rundown and neglected two-building center for less than the assessed value on the property

tax rolls. His investment plans included significant renovation — including complete exterior painting, parking lot repairs, installation of a large monument sign for tenant promotion, plus cleaning and upgrading the vacant suites. He also renamed the complex Santee Professional Center to improve its image, build identity in the community, and attract nonmedical tenants.

Lest you think that Robert made the perfect investment that had no snags, soon after his purchase the national cinema chain filed bankruptcy and the developer halted plans. But a new developer came in and signed the national department store Target as the anchor tenant, and within 18 months, they had built and fully leased the new 500,000-square-foot shopping center. Now there are several other new office buildings completed or planned, as well as major upgrades to the other buildings in the area. The Santee Professional Center has been running at high occupancy and was recently appraised at more than four times the acquisition price!

Although redevelopment areas can be great opportunities, significant risk is associated with investing in areas that are dynamic and changing. Like transportation projects, sometimes the best intentions of local leaders and redevelopment agencies can hit a snag.

Considering barriers to entry

Investing in real estate in an area that has strong demand and limited supply is likely to enhance your profits. One of the trends to follow is the creation of more roadblocks to new development and thus severe limitations on the construction of additional buildings to meet even the increasing demands for real estate from natural population growth.

For example, maybe your chosen area has inhabitants with strong anti-apartment sentiments or concerns about the environment. If you currently own or quickly invest in existing apartments in such areas, these factors can actually work to your benefit, because they make the addition of more housing units (competition) difficult.

We suggest that you look for markets where natural and even man-made barriers to entry exist.

The popular board game Monopoly taught most people from an early age about the importance of location and barriers to entry. When you control the playing field and prime properties, you dramatically improve your odds of successfully building wealth. (**Note:** The real world of real estate isn't like Monopoly where you're getting money at the other players' expense.) In the following sections, we cover some of the more prominent factors that limit the supply of real estate and enhance cash flow and future appreciation for those who already own existing properties.

But, in the long term, the lack of buildable land in an area can prove a problem. Real estate prices that are too high may cause employers and employees to relocate to less expensive areas. If you want to invest in real estate in an area with little buildable land and sky-high prices, run the numbers to see whether the deal makes economic sense. (We explain how to do this in Chapters 11 and 12.)

Environmental issues

Individuals and organizations concerned about the environment aren't a new trend. Environmental issues are now a key factor in the potential development of real estate projects in just about every area of the country.

Those concerned about the environment are expressing their disapproval of new and proposed projects with more authority and success because federal and state laws require excruciating investigative reports on all aspects of proposed land development. It's extremely difficult in most urban areas to find land suitable for development that doesn't have some limitations or require remediation, such as the relocation or preservation of endangered species or plants. (Remediation can also include the cleanup and removal of contaminants.)

Many of these laws or guidelines find universal support — no one wants to live in a concrete world or destroy our beautiful countryside. And nearly everyone wants clean air, clean water, and the highest quality of living possible.

But preserving and protecting our environment comes at a cost: A large portion of potential developable land is being taken out of production or even consideration for use. The land that isn't available for development is being broadened and now includes much of the government-owned lands and virtually all land that can be classified as a hillside, wetland, or *vernal pool* (seasonal or temporary wetland). In many areas, additional swaths of public and private land are being designated and set aside by governmental agencies to protect endangered plants and wildlife.

These man-made decisions to preserve land, combined with other factors, can lead to a shortage of buildable land.

Shortage of buildable land

Economics 101 teaches that strong demand and a limited supply lead to rationing through higher pricing. Well, that is exactly what's happening over the decades in many of America's major metropolitan areas as people exhaust the supply of buildable land (notwithstanding the general decline in real estate prices in the late 2000s).

Upward pressure on real estate prices tends to be greatest in areas with little buildable land. This characteristic was one of the things that attracted Eric to invest in real estate in the San Francisco Bay Area when he moved there in the mid-1980s. If you look at a map of this area, you can see that the city of San Francisco and the communities to the south are on a peninsula. The ocean, bay inlets, and mountains bound the rest of the Bay Area. More than 80 percent of the land in the greater Bay Area isn't available for development because state and federal government parks, preserves, and other areas protect the land from development, or the land is impossible to develop. Of the land available for development in San Francisco and the vast majority of it in nearby counties, virtually all of it had already been developed.

CANES: Citizens Against Nearly Everything

Many cities are now putting more authority into the hands of local and even neighborhood planning boards that exercise their influence and control over proposed new developments. Although many of the representatives on these local planning boards are just interested in maintaining the aesthetics or compatibility of proposed developments with the existing land uses, some are motivated by another agenda.

The term CANES — *Citizens Against Nearly Everything* — was coined by then-San Diego Padres President Larry Lucchino, whom Robert interviewed on his weekly radio show many times while the baseball team proposed and fought for the development of a new ballpark. Various groups claiming to represent taxpayers, citizens, and environmentalists objected at every opportunity. Ultimately, after years of delays and dozens of lawsuits, the ballpark finally opened in downtown San Diego and has been a tremendous catalyst for redevelopment just as new sports venues have done in many other cities.

This trend isn't unique to San Diego. Across the country, those opposed to growth seek to avoid increased traffic, congestion, and overcrowding of their schools and parks. In many communities and neighborhoods, homeowners are expressing their disapproval of new multifamily development.

(If you want a big turnout at city hall, just announce that 300 new low-income apartments are being built across the street from the new for-sale housing tract.)

Such resistance to new development or even redevelopment isn't new. But it does seem to be a trend that should be considered by even a real estate investor with a duplex or a couple of rental homes. Unbridled growth isn't the answer (nor are stagnation and decline), but our point is that you need to evaluate the impact of such attitudes on your income properties. Barriers to entry are a reality that you shouldn't overlook.

For example, increased demand in a community opposed to growth results in higher prices, so investing in these areas certainly enhances your prospects for appreciation. However, well-planned or *smart* growth can also lead to a higher quality of living and greater long-term returns on your investment.

Condo conversion and construction defect lawsuits

The real estate boom and bust cycles are often most pronounced in those cities that experience large numbers of apartment buildings being converted to condominiums. When the prices for new construction homes becomes too high, developers have a lucrative market to buy apartments and cosmetically upgrade the units and sell them to entry-level buyers who want to own rather than rent. The early projects often do well, but the developers who are late entries after the initial demand has been met and when the market becomes oversaturated aren't so fortunate.

Carefully evaluate the impact of the condominium market in your area because it can have a material effect on the overall supply of rental housing. Apartments converted to condos often result in fewer rental units because condo conversion units are typically purchased by owner-occupants that find such housing to be a financially viable entry-level opportunity.

But the reverse trend is also a concern because many areas have a significant number of failed condo conversion projects where only a portion of the units are sold; the remaining units are in foreclosure or bankruptcy and are being sold in bulk to owners who rent them until the market improves. Investors often purchase new condominiums to use as rentals that will compete for tenants. Some of these projects were financially unsuccessful and are in the hands of court-appointed receivers or lenders. These are supply and demand factors that can affect your real estate market and should be part of your real estate strategy.

Many apartment buildings in urban areas were originally built as condominiums, but market weakness or the threat of construction defect legislation (discussed later in this section) led to a business decision by the developers to operate these condos as rental units. There isn't much controversy about the ultimate conversion of these rental condos to owner-occupied units; it's just a function of market timing, with most remaining as rentals in the current market environment.

However, a dilemma faced by many cities is the excessive number of conversion projects of apartment rental communities into condominiums. On one hand, the severe shortage of affordable entry-level housing in many cities made the conversion of apartments to condominiums an excellent opportunity for first-time home buyers. The concern was that conversion of apartments to owner-occupied condos reduced the supply of rentals.

How are condo conversions typically handled? The most common game plan for a conversion of an existing apartment community to a condominium project almost always consists of extensive exterior renovation, including painting, landscaping, and other cosmetic items. Occasionally, local ordinances require some structural repairs or upgrades, but the exterior work is primarily limited to the cosmetic issues. In other words, rarely do developers spend a lot of money on a new roof!

The unit interiors also receive a complete overhaul and upgrade — new flooring, window treatments, new and often upgraded appliances, and solid countertops and other decorative touches to really make the unit shine. These converted condos can be quite attractive as reasonably priced investments that look great and are well located, many times in areas where new development is difficult because the area is completely built-out and the cost to acquire the land would be prohibitive. But you need to look deeper than the smoke and mirrors that create the attractive façade of quality construction.

The problem is that in most cases, the existing building systems, such as the roof, plumbing, electrical, and HVAC, haven't been upgraded or replaced. So you may have a brand-new interior that looks sharp, but the major structural systems are quite old. Also, properties built under the code requirements in effect at the time of original construction usually have lower standards for weatherproofing, insulation, and noise reduction. If you buy one of these converted apartments as a rental property, you may not know that your tenants can hear everything (and we mean everything) that goes on in the adjacent unit. That is, until they call to complain!

This conversion of apartments to condominiums can impact the rental market in one of two ways.

> ✔ Some of the condos are purchased by individuals who intend to live there personally. In this case, that reduces the rental housing stock, which means less competition for apartments.

Further, a good balance of owner-occupied housing units (with their inherent increased pride of ownership) can be healthy for the overall rental market. We strongly advise real estate investors to purchase rental homes in areas that are predominantly owner-occupied.

> ✔ Other converted condos aren't owner occupied, with many investors snapping up the reasonably priced units, speculating that they'll enjoy good returns. These units will be rented out, so there is no reduction in the rental housing stock.

In the long run, we believe that investing in condominiums that began life as apartments isn't wise. In the early years, when the appliances and surface interior and exterior cosmetic finishes are relatively new, not much can go wrong. But after the true age of the building begins to show through increased repairs and maintenance, the volunteer association board of directors will face challenges. Will it be willing and able to dramatically increase the monthly assessments to cover the increased costs and to accrue the funds necessary to handle major capital items? Robert has managed associations for 30+ years, and his experience is that the assessments stay artificially low and the property condition declines over time. You don't want to own a unit in an association with major physical problems and no reserves.

The construction of new, attached, for-sale housing (or condominiums) has been severely restricted since the 1990s in many parts of the country due to *construction defect lawsuits*. The building industry claims that such lawsuits are unnecessary and extremely wasteful, and the attorneys representing homeowners insist that litigation would be unwarranted if the builders simply didn't build such shoddy and poorly constructed housing units. Construction defect lawsuits are reducing the number of attached housing projects that are being built, because insurance is virtually nonexistent for developers and subcontractors.

Government's effect on real estate

This country offers many examples of the importance of state and local government on prospects for prosperity. The following are key governmental and quasi-governmental factors to consider when researching a prospective community in which to invest:

> ✔ **Tax considerations:** For decades, California had an unbeatable combination of great weather and job growth that attracted millions from around the world. Over the past decade and with no end in sight, California has suffered from a declining economy and what some real estate investors and business owners feel is excessive government regulation and taxation. After the recall of Governor Gray Davis in 2003 and the election of Arnold Schwarzenegger, there was a lot of reason for "Kali-fornians" to be optimistic. Unfortunately, the subsequent years, under Governor Jerry Brown and his super majority in the state legislature, has seen an ever-increasing litany of pro-tenant, anti-investment, job-killing

legislation policies that offset many of the natural attributes of California and are being exploited by other western states.

California real estate investors and others with means are establishing legal residency in Nevada, Texas, Washington, Florida, and other states without state income taxes in increasing numbers. Many states (such as Colorado, Illinois, Indiana, Massachusetts, and North Carolina) have established flat rate taxes whereas other states (like Kansas, Ohio, and Wisconsin) lowered their state income taxes. Of course, local taxes can be a factor for real estate investors as well.

So relocating your place of legal residence can make a significant improvement in a person's overall income tax liability, and it may not even be that much of a sacrifice. For example, a California real estate syndicator that attended one of Robert's property management courses found that living on the east side of beautiful Lake Tahoe (in the state of Nevada) was just as nice as the west (or California) side, where the top income tax rate can add up to another 13.3+ percent in addition to the federal income tax.

You should also have a detailed understanding of the property taxation system and appeals process. Be sure to determine whether a proposed income property acquisition is in a special assessment district where additional taxes are assessed against properties. Such special assessment districts may offer some advantages like better schools, parks, and fire and police services and may be well worth the additional annual investment. But you should know in advance how much the additional costs will be, how long you'll be required to participate, and exactly what you're getting in return so that you can properly evaluate whether you'll be able to generate a commensurate increase in your rental income.

✔ **Economic development incentives:** The economic development groups for many of these states are advertising in business publications and major newspapers and aggressively encouraging employers to relocate with incredible real estate incentives such as virtually free land or lower property and/or income taxation. Besides lucrative offers of real estate and tax incentives, as the global economy becomes ever more competitive, businesses are being lured to locations that can reduce their costs of labor, energy, and transportation.

✔ **Community's reputation:** Your local chamber of commerce, tourism bureau, and city hall all work very hard to establish the right reputation and attract the top employers. These organizations can have a real impact on the market environment for businesses and thus create more jobs in the long run, which leads to increased population and higher demand for all types of real estate.

✔ **Business-friendly environment:** You can't underestimate the importance of a probusiness attitude among state, regional, and local governments to help create a vibrant economy where your real estate investments can prosper.

Evaluating Neighborhoods

The reputation of particular neighborhoods can be based on many factors. Certain key or essential elements, which we discuss in these sections, differentiate the neighborhoods with good reputations and positive trends from the areas that are stagnant or trending the wrong direction.

Schools

If you don't have school-age children, you may not be concerned about the reputation and test scores of the local schools. But, whether you're investing in residential or commercial income properties, schools matter. The demand for residential and commercial property (and the subsequent value of the property) is highly correlated to the quality of local schools.

Ask any real estate agent about the impact of schools on the demand and sales price for a home in a great school district. Likewise, employers use the quality of local schools in recruiting their key personnel — and sometimes even relocate company facilities to be near areas known for their schools.

The Internet can be a very useful tool in determining the quality of local schools. Most school districts have websites that include information on the test scores of their students for mandatory state and federal testing. Unfortunately, many people make snap judgments about school quality without doing their homework. Visit the schools and don't blindly rely on test scores. Talk to parents and teachers, and discover what goes on at the school.

Crime rates

Crime can have a significant and sobering effect on the demand and desirability of all types of income properties. No one wants to live in a high crime area, and commercial tenants and their customers neither work at nor patronize unsafe businesses. No areas are going to be crime-free, but you don't want to find out after the close of escrow that you have purchased a rental property that is claimed by rival gangs. Before you make your investment decision, consult these sources:

- ✔ **Local law enforcement:** Contact local law enforcement and obtain the latest and historical crime statistics.

- ✔ **Local newspapers:** Newspapers (and their websites) often have a police-blotter section that provides information on major and even petty crimes in the community.

✔ **Sexual-offender databases:** Laws require certain convicted sexual offenders to register with local law enforcement. These databases allow you to identify the general locations of convicted sex offenders who have committed sexual offenses against minors and violent sexual offenses against anyone.

These databases aren't foolproof. A few states haven't been consistent in their efforts to maintain and make them available. Also, persons required to register don't always follow the requirements, but at least you can find out about the known ones.

Even if not legally required in your area, be sure to advise your tenants to check the database; this information is dynamic, and everyone needs to make his own decision about the safety of his family.

Pride of ownership

Pride of ownership is an intangible attitude that has tangible results. Pride of ownership also has no economic boundaries — even modest-income areas can really look sharp. Look for rental properties in neighborhoods that reflect pride of ownership — well-kept and litter-free grounds, trimmed plants, beautiful flowers, fresh paint, and so on. This curb appeal helps you attract and retain your tenants.

Although everyone may have a different perception of exactly what constitutes a well-maintained property, pride of ownership is readily apparent, and the effort made by business owners and homeowners to keep their properties looking sharp is important to real estate values.

You may find that some of the more aesthetically pleasing areas look that way for a reason. Homeowner's associations and business parks typically have a board of directors and architectural review committees that routinely inspect the properties under their jurisdiction, as well as review and restrict improvements to meet certain standards.

Other areas may have informal committees of neighbors who band together to keep their properties in tiptop condition. This tendency is also true of multifamily residential and commercial properties, and these properties usually must also submit to local laws and regulations enforced by the building or code enforcement departments.

You can control the appearance, condition, and maintenance of your own property, but your options are limited if the properties surrounding it fall into disrepair. Your purchase of a fixer-upper and the investment of time, money, and sweat equity won't be rewarded financially if the surrounding properties are in a state of disrepair and have owners who don't really care.

Property values, occupancy, and rental rates all sag when property owners no longer take pride in their property. Avoid declining neighborhoods that display the red flags of dispirited owners — poorly kept properties, junk-filled vacant lots, inoperative cars in the parking lot or street, graffiti, vandalism, and deferred maintenance. Neighborhood deterioration is a blight that spreads from one property to another.

Role play: What attracts you to the property?

One of the best ways to evaluate the prospects for a particular neighborhood is to play the role of a residential tenant looking for the best place to call home. Go back in time to when you made the decision to live in your neighborhood. What were the primary criteria you used to make that determination? You're probably typical of many of your potential tenants. They prefer rental properties in close proximity to various amenities, all of which can be captured in a property knowledge sheet.

Property knowledge sheets

One of the best ways to have the answers to the questions that may be raised by your rental prospect is to prepare a property knowledge sheet for each of your rental property locations. A *property knowledge sheet* contains all the basic information about your rental property, such as the size and type of the rental unit and the unit number (for multiple-unit properties), plus the age, type of construction, and other important details about the unit.

A thorough property knowledge sheet also contains important information about the local neighborhood and general area. Like the chamber of commerce or visitor's information bureau, you want to be able to answer questions accurately about the area. Rental prospects are generally interested in knowing about employment centers, transportation, local schools, child-care, places of worship, shopping, and medical facilities. You can really make a positive impression on your rental prospect if you can tell them where the nearest dry cleaners or Thai restaurants are located.

With all this vital information from your property knowledge sheet at your fingertips, you can be ready to answer your rental prospect's questions. The more you know about your property, the easier it is for you to offer important reasons for a prospect to select your rental over the competition.

Property knowledge sheets can definitely give you the edge over your competition. Because you're often competing with large multifamily rental properties, you need to be prepared to answer important questions about the area. Often, immediately knowing a detail such as whether a certain child-care center is in your area can make the difference between success and failure.

Check out Figure 10-1 for an example of a property knowledge sheet.

Property Knowledge Sheet

Property Information

Rental address _____Unit # _____ City _____ Zip code _____
Office hours (if any) _____ Square footage of unit(s) _____
Unit mix—Studios ____ 1 Bedroom ____ 2 Bedroom/1 Bath ____ 2Bedroom/2 Bath ____ Other _____
Rent—Studios ____ 1 Bedroom ____ 2 Bedroom/1 Bath ____ 2Bedroom/2 Bath ____ Other _____
Application fee _____ Security deposit _____ Concessions _____
Age of rental _____ Type of construction _____ Parking _____
Recreational facilities _____ Laundry _____ Pets _____
Storage _____ Utilities (who pays?) _____ AC/Heat _____
Appliances _____ Floor coverings _____
Special features/comments _____
_____
_____

Community Information

School district _____ Grade school _____ Jr. high _____
High school _____ Jr. college _____ College _____
Trade school _____ Pre-school (s) _____
Childcare _____ Places of worship _____
Police station _____ Fire station _____ Ambulance _____
Electric _____ Natural gas _____ Telephone _____ Cable _____
Water _____ Sewer _____ Library _____ Post office _____
Hospital _____ Pharmacy _____ Vet _____
Other medical facilities _____
Nearby employment centers _____
Transportation _____
Groceries _____ Other shopping _____
Local services _____
Restaurants _____
Comments _____
_____

Rental Market Information

Rental competitors/rental rates/concessions _____
_____

Our competitive advantages _____
_____

Our disadvantages _____
_____

Figure 10-1:
Property
knowledge
sheet.

Commercial property considerations

Looking at a property from a tenant's perspective is also useful if you're investing in commercial properties. Remember that your commercial tenants are in business to make money — and their location is often a key factor. Have you ever seen a small retail center that includes several vacant suites with butcher paper in the windows? That is the universal sign that a property is in financial trouble and in need of proactive ownership, management, and leasing — or the spiral toward foreclosure will continue.

Right down the street from a failing property, you may find another retail property with long-term leases and a waiting list, because successful retailers almost always flock together. That explains the success of many regional shopping malls that command high rents. Sometimes, just getting the right anchor or primary tenant in a commercial, industrial, or retail income property is all it takes to start the chain reaction toward the dream for any landlord — high occupancy, high rents, and low turnover!

Finding well-situated properties is easier when you're considering investing in an area where you've lived your entire life, but not as easy for investing in other locales. Nonetheless, every area has potential if you know what you're looking for and are willing to take the time to do the research.

Mastering Seller's and Buyer's Markets

Some real estate investors make the mistake of not continuing to research the economics of their real estate markets after they've made their investments. Even if you plan to buy and hold, you need to pay attention to the market conditions. As we have seen, the criteria we advise you to consider in making decisions about which markets are the best for investing are dynamic and can fluctuate.

Savvy real estate investors monitor their markets and look for the telltale signs of real estate cycles. These cycles present opportunities for expanding your real estate portfolio or repositioning from weakening markets to strengthening markets because not all areas experience peaks and troughs at the same time. That is why you need to know and track the timing of seller's and buyer's markets.

Understanding real estate cycles

Real estate markets are cyclical and successful real estate investors remain aware of the real estate cycles in their areas. First, we need to define what we mean by seller's or buyer's market:

- ✔ A **buyer's market** occurs when current property owners are unable to sell their properties quickly and must be more flexible on the price and terms. This is a great opportunity to seek seller financing.

- ✔ A **seller's market** is almost like the classic definition of inflation — "too much money chasing too few goods." In this case, the goods are real estate properties, which are in high demand. When sellers are receiving multiple offers within 24 to 48 hours of a listing or you see properties selling for more than the asking price, you're in a strong seller's market.

Real estate traditionally experiences cycles as the demand for real estate leads to a shortage of supply and higher rents and appreciation. That leads to the building of additional properties, which, along with changes in demand due to economic cycles, usually results in overbuilding and a decline in rents and property valuation.

However, not everyone agrees that real estate cycles are relevant to residential real estate investors. Some of the real estate infomercial gurus claim that real estate investing in homes and apartments is recession-proof because people always need a place to live. Although that is partly true, we think that the economic base of the community where you invest does have a direct impact on all aspects of your operations — occupancy, turnover, rental rates, and even quality of tenant.

For example, when times are tough, residential tenants are the first to improvise, with some finding that "doubling up" or even taking in roommates is palatable if it results in lower costs for housing. Some younger renters are even willing to move back in with Mom and Dad or another relative when their personal budgets don't allow them to have their own rental unit.

Robert has managed all types of income properties throughout the western states and has observed a broad cross-section of economic activity. He has seen how real estate cycles may be similar in a particular region but often vary from region to region. For example, when some areas of the country were setting records for rents in the mid-'80s, landlords couldn't give away their apartments in Texas. Even venerable California was a miserable place to own real estate in the early '90s. In the late 2000s, areas where real estate speculation and condo converters went crazy have suffered.

Can real estate investors who track these real estate cycles make investment decisions based on this information? Absolutely. That is where most successful and knowledgeable real estate investors see potential for increasing their real estate investment returns by timing the real estate market.

Timing the real estate market

Although the length and depth of the real estate cycles vary, there are clear highs and lows that real estate investors need to consider.

In some real estate markets, the double-digit appreciation over the first half of the 2000s brought record prices for homes and income properties. In the mid-2000s, the most common question for Robert on his live Southern California NBC call-in feature was "Should I buy income properties in Southern California at these seemingly high price levels, or should I invest elsewhere?" These callers didn't want to miss out on what they thought was almost guaranteed price appreciation. But what goes up must come down, so when the market corrected in the late 2000s with significant price declines in most areas of the country, the question Robert most heard was, "When will we reach the bottom of the market?"

No one-size-fits-all answer solves this critical question. A key factor is the *investment horizon,* or planned holding period for a particular investor and that specific investment. If the holding period is long enough, even purchasing income properties in today's seemingly overpriced markets will probably look good 15 to 20 years from now.

The alternatives are to identify those markets with excellent economic fundamentals where prices have remained low and invest there. The concept is similar to the "buy low, sell high" truism for stocks, except you sell in overpriced markets and reinvest in the lower priced markets. Such markets do exist, but the question is whether the properties in the lower priced markets are going to provide the same or better investment returns in the long run versus alternative markets.

Unlike the stock market, real estate transactions entail significant transaction costs (as a percentage of the market value of the property). That's why selling and buying property too frequently undermines your returns.

It's our contention that even in the few markets where such "bargains" exist, they aren't really great opportunities. We are reminded of the business concept that in the long run you usually get what you pay for! There is so much more than just the projected rent and the selling price. Without going into a detailed analysis of property condition, expenses, and other invaluable criteria, you should simply consider whether these areas pass muster after performing the economic analysis described earlier. Probably not.

Carleton Sheets, plus many other well-known infomercial gurus, have traditionally advised their followers that you should seek income properties where the projected gross monthly income is at least 1 percent of the purchase price. This strategy would mean that if you acquire a rental property with a projected monthly income of $2,000, your acquisition costs should not exceed $200,000. The advice is sound, but there are few markets where such properties exist. You may remember from your reading on investments that risk and return are generally related. That is, the lower the risk you take, the lower your expected return. (That is why short-term government-backed bonds and federally insured money market accounts offer nominal rates of interest or return on investment, and investments with higher risk, such as real estate, demand higher rates of return.)

So the real question is, what are the risk-adjusted returns like for investing in these areas of the country with record high prices versus the risk-adjusted returns available in other, lower-priced real estate markets? You may find a rural property where the monthly rent exceeds 1 percent of the purchase price, but what about rent growth and appreciation? At the end of the day, you may find that your lower priced market with all of those "bargains" provided you with minimal cash flow and marginal appreciation.

Knowing when to sell and when to buy real estate is easier said than done. But if you follow the fundamentals of economic analysis, and remember that "location, location, value" is the key to successful real estate investing, you can do well.

Chapter 11

Understanding Leases and Property Valuation

*W*hat you pay for the property and the cash flow it generates make a significant difference in the success of your investment. Leases generate the income stream you should base your real estate investment strategy on. All the quantitative analysis we guide you through in Chapter 12 is for naught if you don't have a handle on the leases. Therefore, in this chapter, you start your research, analysis, and evaluation of specific properties by analyzing the leases.

We then introduce you to the concepts behind evaluating potential investment properties and explain the key principles behind property valuation that you need to be familiar with. We also provide you with a few quantitative tools you can use to size up prospective properties and determine whether you should move on to other properties or investigate further.

The Importance of Evaluating a Lease

A *lease* is a contractual obligation between a *lessor* (landlord) and a *lessee* (tenant) to transfer the right to exclusive possession and use of certain real property for a defined time period for an agreed *consideration* (money). A verbal lease can be enforceable, but it's much better to have a written lease that defines the rights and responsibilities of the landlord and the tenant.

Owning a rental property with attractive and well-maintained buildings may give you a sense of pride of ownership, but what you're really investing in are the leases. Successful real estate investors know that an excellent opportunity is to find properties with leases that offer *upside potential* in the form of higher income and/or stability of tenancy.

Regardless of the type of property you're considering as an investment, make sure that the seller provides all of the leases. And don't accept just the first page or a summary of the salient points of the lease — insist on the full and complete lease document along with any addendums or guarantees or written modifications with the seller's written certification that the document is accurate and valid. (Verbal modifications to the written lease aren't generally enforceable.) Have your real estate legal advisor review the leases as well (see Chapter 6).

Existing leases almost always *run with the property* upon transfer of ownership and thus are enforceable. The new owner of the property can't simply renegotiate or void the current leases he doesn't like. Because you're legally obligated for all terms and conditions of current leases if you buy a property, be sure that you thoroughly understand all aspects of the property's current leases.

You may find that you're presented with the opportunity to purchase properties with leases that are detriments to the property and actually bring down its current and future value. The most common example is a long-term lease at below-market rental rates. But you could also have leases that are so far above the current market conditions that you should discount the likelihood that the leases will be in place and enforceable in the future.

Other common problems with leases include

- ✔ The leases are preprinted boilerplate forms (as opposed to a customized lease tailored to the specific tenant-landlord agreement) that may or may not comply with current laws or issues relevant for the specific tenant.

- ✔ The charges for late payments, returned checks, or other administrative fees may not be clearly defined or may be unenforceable.

- ✔ The rules and regulations may not be comprehensive or enforceable.

- ✔ There is no *rent escalation* clause, which spells out future rent increases, or it isn't clearly defined.

We're not saying to bypass purchasing any properties with leases with these problems. Just be aware and factor the effect, if any, into your purchasing decision, or just simply note that you need to change the onerous terms upon renewal.

Reviewing a Lease: What to Look For

A seller should be honest and disclose all material facts about the property he's selling, but most states don't have the same written disclosure requirements that are mandated for residential transactions. So even though your broker or sales agent and other members of your due diligence investigation team (see Chapter 6) may be assisting you with inspecting the property and reviewing the books provided during the transaction, remember that you need to be the one who cares the most about your best interests.

Note the expiration dates of the leases, because any lease that's about to expire should be evaluated based on current market conditions. Future leases may not be at the same rent level, plus you must consider the concessions or tenant improvements necessary to get the lease renewed:

- Residential lease renewals may require a monetary concession or possibly a perk for the tenants, such as cleaning their carpets or installing microwaves or ceiling fans.
- Commercial lease renewals can require significant tenant improvements or rent concessions.

Factor these costs into your analysis because renewing a tenant, even with the associated costs, is typically much more cost effective than losing the tenant. The higher expenses you incur for advertising, screening prospects, and preparing the rental property (cleaning, painting, maintenance, and repairs) plus the loss of income while your rental is vacant are certainly much more expensive than renewing the existing tenant even at a lower rental rate.

Comprehending a residential lease

The analysis of current leases for residential properties is usually fairly straightforward, but that doesn't mean you shouldn't do your homework! Review *each and every* residential lease to make sure that no hidden surprises are awaiting you, such as future free rent, limits to rent increases, or promises of new carpet or other expensive upgrades. Some sneaky sellers of residential properties know that some buyers don't thoroughly review each lease, so they load the leases with future rent concessions in exchange for higher rents up front, which they use to make the property's financial statements look more desirable. Be sure that you determine the *net effective rent* and base your offer for a property on those numbers. An apparent above-market lease isn't really above market if you're giving away free rent or promising to replace the carpet upon lease renewal.

Making sense of a commercial lease

Commercial leases are much more complicated than residential ones. Thus, the commercial real estate investor must have a thorough understanding of the contractual obligations and duties of the lessor (landlord) and lessee (tenant).

The analysis of commercial leases is typically called *lease abstraction.* A *lease abstract* is a written summary of all the significant terms and conditions contained in the lease and is much more than a rent roll. Although a good *rent roll* covers the lease basics — rent, square footage, length of lease, and renewal date or options — a good abstract covers other key tenant issues such as signage, rights of expansion and contraction, and even restrictions or limitations on leasing to other tenants that offer similar products and services. Have written lease abstracts prepared for any commercial property you're considering to ensure that you understand all the terms.

When obtaining financing for commercial properties, lenders typically require a certified or signed rent roll along with a written lease abstract for each tenant. However, because the income of the property is critical to the owner's ability to make the debt service obligations, most lenders don't simply rely on the buyer's numbers but independently derive their own income projections based on information they require the purchaser to obtain from the tenants. This information includes

- ✔ **Lease estoppel:** A *lease estoppel* certificate is a legal document completed by the tenant that outlines the basic terms of his lease agreement and certifies that the lease is valid without any breaches by either the tenant or the landlord at the time it's executed. These estoppel certificates also benefit the purchaser of the property; you should seriously consider requiring estoppels from all tenants when you purchase a commercial building — regardless of the requirements of any lender.

    Although tenant or lease estoppel certificates are rarely required by lenders or purchasers for residential transactions, there is a strong argument that the benefits of the estoppel certificate also apply in the residential setting. Residential tenants are more likely to dispute the amount of the security deposit or claim that they were entitled to unwritten promises by the previous owner — free rent, new carpet, new appliances, extra parking, or waived late charges.

- ✔ **Financial statements:** The rent provided in the lease is a concern, but the amount you actually collect determines the profitability of your real estate investment. Because of this, many leases require the commercial tenant to periodically provide (or present upon request) a recent financial statement and even personal tax returns if the lease is guaranteed.

✔ **Recent sales info:** Most retail leases have provisions for *percentage rents,* in which the tenant pays a base rent plus additional rent based on a percentage of sales. The percentage rent is often on a sliding scale: The percentage paid by the tenant increases as its sales increase. Be sure that you receive and review recent sales information and ensure that the tenant is current on its percentage rent payments.

Reviewing the financial strength or sales figures for your commercial and retail tenants can be an excellent indicator of the future results of your property. Many of your best tenants in the future will be your small tenants that have successful businesses and need to expand. Also, look at the personal guarantees provided to see whether they're backed by sufficient resources. The compatibility of the tenant mix is also important. You want your property to have a variety of goods and services that are complimentary and synergistic, which will help your tenants grow and expand their business.

One of the best ways to make money in real estate is to find commercial leases where the person in charge of the property isn't collecting the proper rent due under the terms of the lease. For example, you may find that the rent roll from the seller of a property you're considering for purchase hasn't implemented rent increases when due. Even more common is the failure of landlords and their property managers to correctly calculate and collect the common area maintenance charges or ancillary fees and reimbursements due from the tenant (see Chapter 12). Of course, you may also find that the landlords are actually overcharging the tenants or there was a one-time insurance reimbursement from a claim, and thus you never want to purchase a property relying on phantom income that you don't have the legal right to collect.

Understanding the Economic Principles of Property Valuation

Knowing certain economic principles can be useful when seeking to evaluate the current and future value of potential real estate investments. In this section, we supply you with some background information to help you determine which properties are likely to have strong demand.

Have you ever traveled to a foreign country and observed miles of beautiful coastline that you know would be worth a fortune at home? A few years ago, Robert returned from Costa Rica, where he saw dozens of faded "For Sale" signs on mile after mile of unimproved oceanfront property with spectacular water views. Local folks told him that these properties rarely sell and are available at low prices. The weather is humid but not much different than similar weather along the Florida coast, where property is expensive. So what are the factors behind such wide disparities in pricing and value?

Well, you need to consider several important economic principles when evaluating the potential value of a property. The basis of value for any piece of real estate is grounded in the following four concepts:

- **Demand:** The need or desire for possession or ownership backed by the financial means or purchasing power to satisfy that need. Having the desire to buy and the ability to buy is *effective demand*.

- **Utility:** The property's ability to meet a need or satisfy its intended purpose. Various influential factors are location, physical attributes, and governmental regulation, such as zoning or environmental limitations. For example, a very inaccessible location isn't suitable for a retail property. Amenities or special features of the property or even off-site but in the neighborhood can enhance the utility. This could be an onsite pool or fitness center while proximity to schools, parks, or public transportation in the area can add value.

- **Scarcity:** *Scarcity* refers to the relative demand versus the relative supply of a specific type of property. For example, there is high demand and relatively low supply of coastal land in California, yet there is low demand and abundant supply of California desert land between Los Angeles and Las Vegas. Hence, coastal land with limited supply and high demand is scarcer and has higher value. Properties are unique and finite, and the concept of substitution doesn't apply unless another property can meet the same needs. *Substitution* is the idea that an investor won't pay more for a property than the price of another, similar property.

- **Transferability:** This term refers to the relative ease with which ownership rights are transferred from one owner to another and the rights associated with the ownership and control of a given property. It also includes the ability for private parties to own and control real estate, which generally isn't a problem in the United States, but would be a major factor for real estate investors seeking to invest internationally.

  Value can also be affected when certain restrictions (such as the association conditions, covenants, and restrictions found in most homeowners associations) are elements of utility while also being part of transferability because they run with the land and limit the rights of future owners.

In the earlier example, the oceanfront land in Costa Rica wasn't in high demand, was relatively inaccessible (the closet major airport was in the capital city of San Jose — nearly 100 miles away), the availability of so many similar properties made the scarcity a nonissue, and the complications of the government requirements for foreign ownership may limit the ability to transfer the property to non–Costa Ricans.

An understanding of the current value and future potential of real estate investments is based on these four concepts. But three other important economic principles can affect the value of real estate now and in the future:

- ✔ **Regression:** A property's value is negatively impacted by surrounding properties that are inferior, of lower value, or in worse condition. In other words, don't buy the best property in a bad neighborhood.

- ✔ **Progression:** A property's value is positively impacted by surrounding properties that are superior, in better condition, and have a higher value.

This concept is one of the most important for the real estate investor looking for long-term success. Seek a well-built but neglected and poorly maintained property located in a good neighborhood. You then add significant value by repositioning the property up to the level of the surrounding properties through proper maintenance, repairs, and upgrades.

- ✔ **Conformity:** Property values are optimized when a property generally conforms to the surrounding properties, and negatively impacted when it doesn't. Higher or optimized value through conformity is what you're seeking when you purchase the distressed property and renovate it to enhance its appearance and utility. This is also the economic principle that cautions against overimproving the property.

Determining highest and best use

All of these economic principles are based on the premise that the maximum value of real estate is achieved when a property is being utilized in its highest and best use. *Highest and best use* is the fundamental concept that there is one single use that results in the maximum profitability by the best and most efficient use of the property. (This concept focuses solely on financial issues. For example, it says nothing about the impact that a significant, dense property development has on traffic and the local environment.)

The highest and best use of a specific property doesn't remain constant over time. Zoning of a property can eliminate certain possible uses of a property at the time of evaluation. However, particularly for properties in the path of progress, time can create new opportunities. For example, agricultural land in the middle of a rapidly expanding commercial and resort area isn't the highest and best use (financially speaking) of the property. (Check out Chapter 10 for more on zoning issues.)

This was the case for the strawberry fields that bordered the west side of Disneyland in Anaheim for several decades. The long-time owner of the property wasn't interested in selling at any price, so the property wasn't utilized to its highest and best use. However, after the owner passed away, his heirs quickly sold the property, and the Disney resort developed the property.

Comparing fair market value and investment value

When discussing real estate values, most people immediately think of fair market value — basically, the price that the buyer and seller can agree to for a real estate transaction. Determining the fair market value of real estate often seems like an elusive concept much like the old adage "Beauty is in the eye of the beholder."

A bit more specifically, the *fair market value* is the most likely price a buyer is willing to pay and a seller is willing to accept for a property at a given time. This definition is based on three assumptions:

- ✔ The market for similar real estate is open and competitive.
- ✔ The buyer and seller are both motivated, acting prudently and with knowledge.
- ✔ The buyer and seller aren't under any undue influence or affected by unusual circumstances.

However, real estate investors encounter another type of value — investment value. Although the market value is the value of a property to a typical investor, *investment value* is its value to a specific investor based on his particular requirements, such as the cost of capital, tax rate, or personal goals.

Someday, you may find yourself competing against another buyer for a prime investment property only to be surprised that she seems willing to pay much more. If you've carefully analyzed the property, and the seller provided the same information about the property to all potential purchasers, the other buyer is likely basing her offer on the property's investment value to her.

Maybe the other buyer needs a replacement property for a 1031 exchange and has the strong motivation of potentially losing the deferral of significant capital gains unless she buys property of equal or greater value within certain defined time periods (see Chapter 18). Such buyers are often willing to pay a premium for a property to avoid losing the tax deferral benefits available under federal and many state tax codes.

You don't want to get into a bidding war for a property and overpay, so remember that fair market value and investment value are two different concepts. Investment value can be higher or lower than market value. For example, an investor who can't use the tax benefits of depreciation would be willing to pay less for a property that would generate large annual depreciation than would an investor that has other passive income and can use the deferral of taxation to reduce his current income tax obligations.

Reviewing the Sources of Property-Valuing Information

As a prospective buyer, you may find that quite a few folks have an idea of what a piece of property is worth:

- **Professional appraisers:** Owners and lenders hire these property valuation specialists to formulate the value of a property at a given point in time. Sellers rarely consult appraisers unless the sale is the result of litigation or probate, or a government entity is the buyer or seller.

- **Brokers and agents:** A Competitive Market Analysis (CMA) or the similar but more in-depth Broker Price Opinion (BPO) is an estimate of market value that is generally available from brokers or agents active in the local area where the property is located. Some lenders also use the term Broker Opinion of Value (BOV). Because brokers and agents routinely track the listing and sale of comparable properties, they offer this information to owners with the goal of getting a listing on the property. Their valuation may be fair and reasonable; however, a buyer should remember that the real estate agent isn't a disinterested third party, but rather only paid if he's involved in a sales transaction — and then he's compensated more for a higher sales price.

- **Sellers:** Many sellers also do their own informal or anecdotal research by obtaining information about recent sales of properties they know in the area. Ultimately, the seller must make the final critical decision as to the asking price for a property. Because the valuation of real estate has many variables, inefficiencies in the pricing of income properties are common.

As a prospective buyer, the values these folks come up with are merely starting points for your analysis. Much more research is required. We spend the balance of this chapter, and Chapter 12, helping you do your research.

Many real estate investors find that becoming real estate appraisers can be helpful to their success in investing in real estate. You may want to get a certification in real estate appraisal while making your real estate investments. Another benefit of this choice is that you qualify for the favorable tax treatments offered to real estate professionals (as we describe more in Chapter 18). Or you may just want to have a better understanding of the techniques used by appraisers for evaluating your own properties. For more information on professional appraisers and their education and training, please refer to www.appraisalfoundation.org or www.appraisalinstitute.org.

Establishing Value Benchmarks

The proper analysis of real estate requires due diligence and research, which starts with evaluating the existing leases (see the "The Importance of Evaluating a Lease" section earlier in this chapter) and continues with crunching the numbers (refer to Chapter 12). However, almost more than any other investment, the real estate industry has relied for years on value benchmarks to set prices and evaluate potential purchases.

One of the reasons value benchmarks are so widely used is that they can easily be calculated by using basic information available on a property. Virtually all properties you encounter for sale include this information in the listing brochures or offering packages provided by sellers or their brokers or sales agents.

These value benchmarks are general guidelines only, and they can be misleading, especially to the novice real estate investor. When you first hear them, they sound impressive, but they're only quick and simple indicators of value. Don't make investment decisions without calculating the Net Operating Income (NOI), which we cover in detail in Chapter 12. The measures in this section shouldn't be *the* sole basis for the purchase of income-producing real estate.

Some professional appraisers may perform these calculations as a verification test to ensure that their results are in the ballpark and even include them in their appraisal. However, these numbers aren't as accurate at indicating value as the traditional methods of appraising the value of real estate (the cost approach, market data approach, and income capitalization approach discussed in Chapter 12). Neither are they formally recognized and mandated by the professional appraisal institutes or federal lending guidelines as approved methods of appraising real estate.

In the following sections, we cover the standard value benchmarks that apply to all types of real estate, as well as some that are unique to a specific sector.

Gross rent/income multiplier

Two important value benchmarks include

- ✓ **Gross Rent Multiplier (GRM):** GRM is most commonly used for residential income properties, such as single-family rental homes and small apartment buildings, because virtually all of their income is in the form of rent payments from tenants.

- ✓ **Gross Income Multiplier (GIM):** GIM includes rent plus all other sources of income and therefore is more widely used to quickly evaluate commercial or industrial real estate investments.

The monthly rent or income is used in some areas of the country, but typically the GRM and GIM are calculated by using annual numbers. Both the GRM and GIM are calculated by dividing the proposed acquisition price by the annual rent or total income. For example, the GRM for a rental home that can be acquired for $100,000 with a monthly rent of $750 ($9,000 annualized):

$$GRM = \frac{\text{Proposed acquisition price}}{\text{Annual rent}}$$

$$= \frac{\$100,000}{\$9,000}$$

$$= 11.1$$

Likewise, an industrial building that sells for $250,000 with an annual gross income of $20,000 has a GIM of 12.5.

These formulas require little information and are a simple way to quickly compare similar properties. Savvy real estate investors glance at the GRM or GIM on a listing sheet and may either eliminate some properties from or earmark them for further consideration, but they don't write an offer to purchase just because the ratio seems attractive. Experienced investors know that much more analysis is needed because these formulas don't consider future appreciation, financial leverage, the risk of the investment, or operating expenses. They focus on gross income only, which can be deceptive.

Here's how relying on these formulas can be tricky: If the GRM and GIM ratios seem high, you need to check further to see whether the price is too high — in which case you should pass on this property. Or maybe the rents are below market value and the price is reasonable. Conversely, you may see a low GRM and think that you found your next investment prospect only to discover that the property is really overpriced because the seller has projected unrealistic rents based on seasonal rentals for dilapidated furnished studio apartments in a beach community.

Because both GRM and GIM only consider the income side of the investment, these formulas don't differentiate between the operating and capital expense levels of each property. The income is important, but what you're left with after paying the expenses makes your mortgage payment and provides you with cash flow. As we discuss in Chapter 12, the operating and capital expense levels can make a tremendous difference in the overall cash flow and the value of the property.

For example, compare two small apartment communities — both available for $1 million and each with an annual gross income of $100,000. On each, the GRM is 10. But which is the better investment? The GRM doesn't give any indication, but further analysis gives you the answer because expenses for each property probably differ.

One apartment building is more than 40 years old and has only month-to-month rental agreements with a high turnover of tenants. The property has interior hallways, is poorly maintained, and has an elevator that has never been modernized. This property suffers from above-average annual operating expenses of $85,000. The other potential investment is also an older property but caters to seniors on long-term leases who rarely move and do little damage. The building is a two-story, garden-style walk-up with annual expenses of $45,000. Clearly, assuming you use the same financing for each property, the second property (with $40,000 less in expenses) should result in greater cash flow to the owner.

Price per unit and square foot

For apartment investors, the asking *price per unit* can provide a general feel for the reasonableness of the seller's pricing. Price per unit is calculated by simply dividing the asking price by the number of units. For example, a six-unit building priced at $240,000 works out to $40,000 per unit.

Like the GRM calculation, the price per unit does have its limitations. The calculation doesn't account for the location or age of the property, the quality of construction or amenities, or the size and condition of the units. You should only use it as a quick indicator of relative value when comparing similar properties in the same market area.

The *price per square foot* is a widely used yet simple calculation most often associated with commercial, industrial, and retail properties (and sometimes used for residential properties). To find this number, take the asking or sales price of a property and divide it by the square footage of the buildings. It's only a ballpark gauge of relative value and can be limited because it doesn't factor in the location or quality of the improvements or other important issues like the parking ratio or the occupancy level and rent collections.

For example, a 5,000-square-foot building going for $250,000 may seem like a good value at $50 per square foot in your market until you find that it hasn't been occupied for years and is in a distressed area of town. Or a 10,000-square-foot building for $1.25 million may seem overpriced at $125 per square foot until you discover that the U.S. Postal Service just signed a 20-year net lease at full market rent with generous annual cost-of-living increases.

Replacement cost

Replacement cost is another factor that real estate investors should consider prior to making a real estate investment. The *replacement cost* is the current cost to construct a comparable property that serves the same purpose or function as the original property. The calculation of replacement cost is usually done by comparing the price per square foot to an estimate of the cost per square foot to build a similar new property, including the cost of the land.

If you buy an investment property below its replacement cost, you can generally know that a prudent builder probably won't construct a similar new product. This fact minimizes the chance that overbuilding will result in excess supply. It isn't until resale value (minus depreciation) of existing properties equals the cost to construct new properties that a builder will find it financially feasible to build an additional product.

Especially when considering investing in a real estate market that seems overpriced, avoid buying investment properties where the cost for new construction is equal to or lower than the replacement cost of a similar building. When prices rise to the point that it's more economical to build a new product rather than buy existing investment properties, builders know that they can build an additional product and sell it at a profit. And you will then have additional properties to compete with.

Chapter 12

Valuing Property through Number Crunching

*W*ith the help of your real estate team, you should narrow your real estate investment opportunities down to just those properties that seem to have the best chance to produce financially in the long run. In Chapter 11, we cover the basics of property valuation and provide you with the information you need to examine the leases of prospective properties.

In this chapter, we get down to the business of running the numbers. We cover the essential elements of understanding and arriving at a property's income and expenses and Net Operating Income — and we explain what that is! We then take these important numbers a step further and show you the best valuation tools traditionally used by appraisers and commonly used by lenders to determine what a property is worth.

But after you've done all of your research and analysis, the reality is that you still need to establish whether a proposed property has the potential to be a good investment opportunity. Overpaying for a good property isn't any better than getting a deal on a bad property. Neither will meet your goals. So we close the chapter by putting it all together to help you decide how much you should consider paying for a particular property.

Understanding the Importance of Return on Investment

The purchase of an investment property is really the purchase of a future income stream or cash flow. Although pride of ownership or the satisfaction of being the owner of a rental property may be an important issue for some people, most real estate investors focus primarily on the investment returns that they can generate from a given property.

Four elements determine the return you see on your investment:

- ✔ **Net cash flow:** *Net cash flow* is money generated by the property after deducting all costs and debt service from the income. See the "Calculating Cash Flow" section later in this chapter.

- ✔ **Tax benefits of depreciation:** Many investors are able to use these tax benefits to shelter other sources of income which gives you in essence an interest-free loan by deferring taxes (we cover this subject in Chapter 18).

- ✔ **Buildup of equity:** If you acquired the property with debt, the equity buildup from paying down the debt over time is a factor.

- ✔ **Appreciation:** True wealth is created through *appreciation* (buying property and selling it years later for much more than you paid). Significant estates and generational wealth are created through appreciation.

The key to generating a profitable real estate portfolio is finding and purchasing properties that exhibit the potential for high occupancy and growth in income while keeping expenses and turnover reasonable. Success in real estate investing depends on purchasing a property for the right price so that you have the ability to use your management skills to increase the value over time. Don't base your investment decision on emotions. Falling in love with a property can lead to overpaying.

You also need to determine what work needs to be done to the property to correct any deferred maintenance or curable functional obsolescence. Even if you simply hold the property and look for cash flow and appreciation, you want to be able to evaluate the holding costs during your ownership period.

Then you need to determine the future value of the property to calculate the likely disposition price and determine your return on investment.

Figuring Net Operating Income

Knowledgeable real estate investors begin a serious analysis of a potential property acquisition by determining the projected *Net Operating Income,* commonly abbreviated as NOI. We find it surprising how many real estate investors don't make the effort to calculate the NOI before buying a property. Instead, the quick-and-easy nature of the benchmarks we cover in the previous chapter seduces unwitting investors into a false sense of security.

The calculation of Net Operating Income is simply

NOI = Gross Operating Income − Operating Expenses

NOI is the most critical factor in determining the potential for return on your investment in real estate. Determining the NOI of a property is one of the fundamental building blocks to analyzing real estate investments. Any decision — to buy, hold, or sell — should only be made after a careful analysis of the *actual current* and *projected future* NOI for a given real estate investment. Arriving at a reasonable estimate for future NOI is the key to determining the value parameters for your real estate investment. We recommend that you value a property based on the projected NOI for the next year, or preferably next few years.

The current NOI is fairly easy to obtain and is often provided by the seller (although in the rest of this section, we explain common problems with this seller-provided data). Deriving the projected NOI is a more time-consuming and in-depth process. The forecasting of a property's NOI is more of an art than a science. Many times, the estimation of NOI is based on a number of assumptions or projections about future events that are anything but certain. Will your tenants renew their leases (and at what rates)? Will the tenants make their rent payments and other contractual requirements as agreed in their leases? Will expenses stay within the expected range, or will there be significant world or local events that lead to a spike in costs (like the availability and cost of property insurance in the aftermath of the 9/11 terrorist attacks or a significant increase in the price of oil)?

Whether you receive current or projected NOI estimates from a seller, be careful to verify the numbers. Some sellers, and many real estate brokers and agents, prefer to provide a *pro forma NOI* (a *projection* of future financial performance of the property) that uses higher rents and lower expenses. These fictitious numbers are based on the hopeful theory that the new owner will raise the rents to market level and simultaneously lower the costs of operating the property. These assumptions are rarely valid. Unless the property has leases with built-in rent increases or that can be renewed at higher rates or below-market leases that are expiring while the demand is high, you seldom find a professionally managed property with below-market rents. If it were that easy to increase income, wouldn't the current owner do it? Expenses are also unlikely to decrease significantly unless you have an older property where a lighting or HVAC retrofit will decrease energy usage.

Some owners of rental properties with above-market leases coming up for renewal or some owners who know their expenses will increase dramatically will be tempted to sell their property using historical numbers. You need to consider historical numbers, but the most critical information to determine the value of the building to you as a potential new buyer is future income and expenses.

Have you ever seen a projection from a seller, her broker, or her sales agent that projects a lower NOI for an investment property on the market? They act as if the only way for NOI to go is up. Although you want to invest in properties where that is the likely result, the reality is that real estate is a cyclical business, and supply and demand factors have a major impact.

"Garbage in, garbage out" holds true for your projections of your future NOI. Therefore, make a careful and detailed analysis of the property you're considering. Real estate investing isn't something you should do by the seat of your pants. Develop your own operating pro forma prior to purchasing any property. And any evaluation or projection of the income stream for a property should begin with an analysis of each lease or rental agreement (which we cover in Chapter 11).

Evaluating income

To evaluate the income side of your budget, we advise that you painstakingly record and verify all income by using a zero-based budget concept. A *zero-based budget* is where you start with a blank piece of paper (or spreadsheet, if you enjoy computer software) and individually, tenant by tenant, create the projected rents and income stream for the property. (A similar zero-based budget concept is useful for determining your likely or expected expenses and is discussed in further detail later in the chapter.)

Sellers may provide or be asked to sign a certified rent roll or comparable document verifying the accuracy of the tenants and rents listed. Although this document may be a great exhibit in your lawsuit against the seller for fraud, we advise that you use this document cautiously. Conduct your own independent analysis of the current and future rent payments due under the terms of the existing leases. Don't just gather static data and numbers on your current tenants; you must be able to interpret the data. Evaluate the strength of each tenant. The lease may give you the legal right to future rent payments; however, a tenant who is unable or unwilling to meet his lease obligations won't be good for your rental collections.

You want a property that has tenants who not only have the current financial strength to meet their obligations under the lease but who will also enhance or increase your income in future years. For example, you may determine that one of your commercial office building tenants will be looking to expand and will probably replace a tenant that is barely surviving and unlikely to renew their lease.

It's truly amazing how little some commercial landlords know about the needs of their current tenants. Be sure to actually talk to your prospective tenants (in addition to getting the estoppel certificates discussed in Chapter 11). Tenants are the key to your future success, and you want to make sure that you can provide the proper environment so their businesses can grow and prosper while you benefit from their rental payments, which ultimately pay for the building you plan to own free-and-clear in the future.

But the income side of the equation involves more than just estimating rents. The typical income and expense statements for reporting in real estate include standard terminology that all real estate investors should know:

- ✔ **Gross potential income** or GPI is the maximum gross income that would be generated from the rent if the property were at 100 percent occupancy and all money owed were collected in full. (This is sometimes referred to as *gross possible income.*)

- ✔ **Effective gross income** or EGI is essentially the money that is actually collected. EGI is calculated by taking the GPI and then subtracting the vacancies, concessions, delinquencies, and collection losses and then adding the other income from late charges, returned checks, and all other secondary or non-rent sources.

In the sections that follow, we provide the details on what to subtract and add to work your way from GPI to EGI.

Accounting for vacancies

The real estate investment community seems to be locked on using 5 percent as the vacancy factor; brokers and even lenders typically use a 5 percent vacancy factor without any regard for the actual market conditions. This number may or may not be the right number to use; we advise that you carefully determine the most accurate estimate of future vacancy rather than use a standard figure such as 5 percent.

The issue of vacancies is particularly applicable to many new real estate investors who begin either by retaining their current homes as investment properties when they move up to larger homes or by purchasing rental properties as investments. Novice investors often simply compare the monthly rental rate that they plan on charging to the monthly costs for paying the mortgage and any other recurring expenses (property taxes, utilities, home-owner's dues, and so on). This practice can be dangerous if you don't have sufficient cash reserves for the unexpected — like being unable to find or retain tenants or having to evict a tenant who stops paying.

An eviction is particularly disruptive to your cash flow because you not only don't collect any income, but you also have the expenses of legal fees, court costs, and the costs of preparing the rental rate for the next tenant (plus vacancy) until the new tenant moves in and begins paying rent.

If you have a single-family rental home, the property is either occupied or vacant. With the average length of residential tenancies in many parts of the country at less than one year, using a 0 percent vacancy factor is unrealistic. Our suggestion for your pro forma for a single-family rental home is to antici-pate a loss of income equivalent to one month per every 12 months, which reflects an 8.3 percent vacancy rate. This rate may represent a vacancy, a delinquency, or a concession (see the following sections), but our experience indicates that, one way or another, you're likely to lose at least one month's rent/income on average per year, and you should allow for this prospect in preparing your pro forma to determine the potential income before making your investment decision.

Calculating concessions

A *concession* is any benefit or deal-sweetener offered by the landlord to entice the tenant to enter into a lease or rental agreement. Concessions can be anything of value that motivates the tenant, but most commonly include free or reduced rent or additional features (a ceiling fan, microwave, upgraded finishes, extra parking, and so on). In many areas, concessions are a significant factor in estimating future income. Remember that a concession of one month's free rent is essentially an 8.3 percent discount of the annual rent. A free month's rent for a simple residential tenancy with a monthly rent of $1,000 means that you'll only collect $11,000 in the first year, or an effec-tive rental rate of $916.66, or a concession rate of 8.3 percent. This reduction is a significant factor when added to your expected vacancy rate and allow-ance for collection loss (see the next section).

Deducting delinquencies and collection losses

The industry standard for *collection loss* (rent or other charges that the landlord must write off as uncollectible) is typically 0.5 percent of rental income. This is another number that seems to be acceptable as a general rule; however, savvy real estate investors make their own analyses of the actual collection loss they may experience based on the strength of the tenant, the strength and depth of the local job market, the average turnover of the area overall, the amount of security deposit they hold, and the nature of local tenant/landlord laws. For example, collection losses for residential properties in the Las Vegas area often exceed 2 to 4 percent, and the continued advent of pro-tenant legislation in California and other major metropolitan areas foretells increased losses to landlords because of the inability to evict nonpaying or disruptive tenants.

During a weak economic environment, collection loss can be even more significant, and prudent landlords take steps to make sure that they have financially sound tenants who can pay rent. The competition for these qualified tenants means that you may have to lower the rent or offer concessions, which are better options than trying to get top dollar from an unqualified tenant. Remember that the best qualified prospective tenants or applicants in a weak market will be in high demand from other rental property owners who are your competition.

Adding in additional income streams

In addition to rent, other types of payments are essential elements to your income stream. Other income items can consist of late charges, returned check charges, and various ancillary income items. The ancillary items depend on the type of investment property, but for residential properties, they can consist of laundry, parking, vending, Internet services, storage, concierge service, and so on. Examples for commercial properties can include sources similar to those for residential properties, plus items like common area maintenance charges (CAM), supplemental HVAC (heating, ventilation, and air conditioning) charges, special security requirements, and telecommunications.

Tallying operating expenses

Just as you did with your income, use a zero-based budget concept to forecast the projected operating expenses for your property. Although historical expenses are worth reviewing and sometimes can be quite accurate in forecasting future expenses, we recommend that you question every expense. Who knows, you may find that the current landscaper is actually willing to charge you less just to keep the account. Or maybe you have contractors and vendors you already use who will charge you less.

The income and expense information presented by most owners or their real estate agents doesn't accurately reflect the current financial results. Inevitably, they may claim that the rents are too low and they may show artificially lowered operating expenses in order to inflate NOI. As the potential purchaser of this property, you want to deal with reality, so be sure to require the seller to provide you with a copy of her federal tax return Schedule E for each year of her ownership — or at least the last several years. Rarely does the tax return overstate the income or understate the expenses of a rental property — and you want to base your decisions on fact, not fiction.

Utilities

Evaluate your utility costs as soon as you can, because this expense is typically one of the larger costs of operating your property and is also subject to significant increases. Determine the current and projected rates for the utilities by contacting the service providers for electricity, natural gas, water and sewer, telephone, cable, waste removal, and any other utilities that are provided at the property. Virtually all of these utilities are regulated locally or at the state level and must file future rates well in advance.

Thus, determining the future cost for utilities is relatively easy if your usage remains the same. But seriously consider any energy and resource efficiency improvements that you can make, such as lighting, low-flow toilets, automated sprinkler, or drip irrigation systems, and other ways to reduce the consumption and provide incentives for your tenants to conserve.

One sure way to get tenants to conserve is to make them responsible for paying for their own utility usage. This approach can dramatically improve your NOI, and it's often a win/win situation because many tenants make long-delayed energy-efficient changes to improve conservation practices. You can make these changes in a number of areas:

- ✓ **Electric usage:** Robert dramatically improved the NOI for one of his client's commercial office buildings by more than $100,000 per year simply by installing separate electric meters and requiring the tenant to pay for his own electricity. The significant improvement in NOI occurred even after the tenant was given a reduction in the rental rate based on the utility company's estimate of a reasonable monthly expense for electricity for that suite. The tenant was a food broker and had 12 large, inefficient freezers that helped to generate a monthly electric bill of more than $15,000 — paid by the landlord. Surprise, surprise — when the tenant began paying for its own electricity, it quickly cut the number of freezers in half and invested in new energy-efficient models.

- ✓ **Water usage:** Across the country, individual water meters are being retrofitted for each residential tenant. An EPA-sponsored three-year study recently concluded that billing residents for their water usage by direct metering can reduce annual water consumption by an average of 15 percent. In temperate climates, landscaping is the single largest consumer of water. Converting to drip irrigation or recycled water (if available) can dramatically reduce water consumption and thus your cost.

- ✓ **Waste collection and disposal:** This category is quickly becoming the next major cost item that landlords are passing on to tenants because these costs are rising rapidly in most areas of the country.

We recommend that you limit your investments to residential and commercial buildings with separate meters for water, sewer, and electricity (see the "Surveying Lease Options" section later in the chapter).

Management fees

A common mistake made by many investors is failing to incorporate the value of their time if they self-manage their property. Your estimate of operating costs should include a management fee even if you self-manage. Your time is worth something, and there is an *opportunity cost* (whatever other productive activity you could be doing with that time) as well. Also, you may decide in the future to hire a property manager so that you can focus on the acquisition, improvement, and disposition of your real estate holdings. Including a comparable management fee now saves your projections from taking a hit later. See Chapter 15 for more on hiring a property management firm.

Insurance

Like utilities, property-casualty insurance is another major operating expense for which you need to get a specific quote for future projections instead of relying on historical data provided by the seller. Insurance coverage and rates can vary widely from one insurance company to another and there are also many opportunities to benefit from package or volume purchases of insurance. See Chapter 16 for the scoop on risk management.

Other operating costs

Don't forget all of the other operating costs for your property, including your outside vendors that provide services. You may have landscaping, pest control, parking lot sweeping, painting, cleaning and janitorial, and other services. Contact each firm for pricing — and put these services out for competitive bids when you feel that the pricing and services offered aren't the best values.

Be sure to get current bids for all of the other expenses of owning and maintaining your property. For maintenance, you can look at historic numbers, but you want to keep the age and condition of the building in mind when setting your budget for upkeep.

Almost every real estate investor at some point considers purchasing a property that the seller claims has been fully renovated. The seller implies that because many of the building components are new, the required maintenance expenditures are nominal and your operating and capital expenses will be lower. Our experience is that even properties that have been recently renovated still have ongoing maintenance needs. Don't cut back on, or fail to allow sufficient funds for, ongoing maintenance and repairs when you crunch the numbers.

Calculating Cash Flow

As you begin to look at various properties that you may want to acquire, you discover that the real estate investment community always refers to the NOI of a given property and commonly uses that number to set the value or asking price of a property. The NOI is the number that tells you what you can afford to pay for the property. We show you the calculations in the "Figuring Net Operating Income" section earlier in this chapter.

However, don't confuse the NOI with *cash flow,* which is NOI minus debt service payments and capital expenditures (for example, new roof, appliances, floor coverings, and so on). In the example in Table 12-1, the Net Operating Income is $600,000, but the actual cash flow before taxes to the investor is $150,000.

Table 12-1	Sample Investment Commercial Property Cash Flow
Annual gross potential rental income (GPI)	$1,000,000
Plus other income	20,000
Plus CAM reimbursement	30,000
Minus vacancy and collection loss	(50,000)
Effective gross income (EGI)	1,000,000
Operating expenses	(400,000)
Annual Net Operating Income (NOI)	**$600,000**
Annual debt service	(400,000)
Capital improvements	(50,000)
Annual Before-Tax Cash Flow	**$150,000**

After you have your NOI, you can project your annual cash flow. The formula is straightforward:

NOI – Debt Service – Capital Improvements = Before-Tax Cash Flow

Servicing debt

The *broker information sheet* (or sales flyer) on an available property may provide proposed financing. However, make sure that the *debt service* projection in your income and expense pro forma relies on a firm financing commitment that you have received.

Although the annual debt-service payments are a direct result of the amount of the purchase price borrowed, for most conventionally financed properties, the debt service will be 80 to 90 percent of the NOI in the early years of your ownership of the property. If you have fixed-rate financing, the debt service is going to be an easy number to plug into your income and expense pro forma because the payment won't change. However, if you have an adjustable rate mortgage, you'll need to estimate future interest rates and debt service payments to calculate future cash flows.

Making capital improvements

In developing their estimates or pro formas of projected financial results for a proposed investment property, many investors neglect to account for, or seriously underestimate the need for, capital improvements to the property. *Capital improvements* are the replacement of major building components or systems such as the roof, driveways, HVAC, windows, appliances, elevators, and floor and window coverings. Real estate investing requires planning and the allocation of money to protect and preserve your property investment in the long run.

Often sellers indicate that the property had been fully renovated and imply that the purchaser won't need to make any capital improvements for many years to come. But buildings age and things wear and break — especially in rental properties. Just as homeowner's associations often are wise to put aside funds each year in a reserve account for capital improvements, you should allocate a portion of your income to reflect the fact that certain components of your property are deteriorating over time and will need to be replaced. Otherwise, you may find that your roof needs to be replaced and you don't have the funds to cover the expense.

Capital improvements are also an essential component of the repositioning or renovation plans that lead to improved financial performance for investment real estate. As an investor, always consider properties that owners have neglected to properly maintain and upgrade. This category is one of the best target markets for investing, and your pro forma income and expenses should contain a realistic capital improvement budget.

Your pre-purchase due diligence should include a detailed walk-through of the property by a qualified contractor who can identify health and safety issues that should be addressed immediately — either during escrow by the seller or by you as the new owner. A leasing broker or someone knowledge-able about the competitive properties in the market should then compile a prioritized list of needed work and cost-effective upgrades that will position your property to deliver above-market returns.

This important feedback should be documented with written summaries by suite or unit number, plus a detailed evaluation of all common areas to bring the property into consistency with your overall marketing plan. Then contact the appropriate suppliers and contractors to formulate a capital improvements budget by month or year.

Even with the most diligent walk-throughs and cost estimates, the reality of property renovation and repositioning is that the costs typically exceed your expectations and the timelines are rarely met.

The capital improvements or reserves for replacement vary based on the age, location, and condition of the property, as well as the tenant profile. The higher the turnover of tenants (and the less money the prior owner has invested in properly maintaining the property over the years), the higher the capital expenses. A location impacted by climatic conditions can also be a significant factor in the life span of building components. For example, properties located in a marine climate require more frequent painting and replacement of items affected by moisture and corrosion.

Capital expenses are subjective. Our advice is to be conservative and esti-mate toward the high side of a range. If you don't have to spend the funds, your real estate investment results are enhanced. But you don't want to plan on scrimping by not addressing needed repairs and replacements. Deferred maintenance is more costly to address in the future, plus it ultimately nega-tively impacts on your income if your property doesn't attract financially strong and stable tenants.

Surveying Lease Options

Leases for rental properties come in three basic forms:

- ✔ **Gross lease:** In a *gross lease,* the landlord pays for almost all of the oper-ating expenses of the property.

- ✔ **Modified gross lease:** *Modified gross leases* pass some of the expenses of owning and operating the building directly to the tenants. Examples of modified gross leases include leases where the landlord pays all operating expenses except for certain items such as utilities, parking, or janitorial expenses.

✔ **Net lease:** The term *net lease* can have an unlimited range of variables but typically provides for the tenant to pay for the majority of the costs of operating the building, including property taxes, insurance, and maintenance costs. Those leases in which the tenant pays virtually all costs associated with operating the building are called *triple net leases*.

You shouldn't include the cost of any tenant-paid services as an expense of the property. The leases for a commercial property can be gross leases, modified gross leases, or net leases, but residential properties are almost always leased on a gross basis, except utilities.

Comparing some of the options

There are different thoughts about which type of lease is best. Many investors believe that net leases reduce the owner's management of the property, but this assumption isn't necessarily true. The owner must still ensure that the property is properly maintained. One argument against net leases is that the tenant may skimp on the maintenance of the property, which is why you typically don't see net leases in residential properties. Can you imagine a residential tenant being responsible for all of the maintenance of his rental home?

We find that modified gross leases in which the tenant pays for expenses that she can control are a good balance for all types of properties. The following shows essentially how the relationship is structured in most apartment buildings:

✔ The landlord retains control of the property maintenance and makes the necessary repairs and upgrades inside and out to ensure the long-term integrity of the building instead of allowing it to be compromised by thrifty tenants. The landlord is also able to ensure that the assessed value is kept low and the property taxes are paid on time, plus make sure that proper insurance coverage is in place.

✔ However, the landlord doesn't control certain expenses that are better suited to be paid directly by the tenant. For example, tenants have a direct impact on the utility usage and are more careful to conserve if they pay that expense. This is why we recommend you limit your investments in residential property to those buildings with separate meters for water, sewer, natural gas/propane, and electricity. Likewise, some commercial tenants can live with weekly janitorial service rather than daily if they're paying the cost directly.

As the potential purchaser of a commercial property, carefully evaluate the leases and determine what operating expenses, if any, are paid by the tenants. You need to understand whether the property is using gross or net leases. Otherwise, you may be deceived regarding the actual NOI and cash flow that you will receive for the property.

Clearly, the rent charged for commercial properties with net leases, where the tenants are directly responsible for making the property tax and insurance payments and where they handle their own maintenance, will be lower than a similar property with a gross lease. But the end result may be similar because the higher rents received on the gross lease property will go toward those same expenses and costs that the tenant is paying at the net leased property.

Accounting for common area maintenance charges for commercial buildings

Costs in multitenant commercial buildings that are passed on to the tenant are called *common area maintenance (CAM) charges*. Paid proportionately by each tenant for the upkeep of areas designated for the use and benefit of all tenants, CAM charges include items such as parking lot maintenance, security, snow removal, and common area utilities. These charges are part of the tenant's rent and can be due in advance or paid in arrears; the lease establishes the terms. Some tenants negotiate that they don't have CAM charges. For accounting purposes, CAM charges are typically reflected in the cash flow as "CAM reimbursement" (see Table 12-1). Although they're indicated as an income item, they're essentially offsetting the corresponding expense items included in the operating expenses for the property.

The most common method is to use an estimated annual budget for the property as a basis for the collection of a monthly CAM charge. At the end of a previously agreed upon time period (usually annually), you calculate the actual expenses incurred for the common area items and reconciled against the amount actually paid by the tenants, billing the tenants for any shortfall or refunding any excess payments.

Handle the CAM reconciliation as soon as possible after the accounting is complete for the relevant time period in order to quickly collect any funds due, as well as to provide feedback in case the future estimates need modification.

The Three Basic Approaches to Value

Professional real estate appraisers traditionally use three basic valuation techniques to arrive at an accurate estimate of current value: the market data (or sales comparison) approach, the cost approach, and the income capitalization approach.

Typically, each valuation method arrives at a slightly to moderately different estimate of value, and the appraiser reconciles or weighs the different results based on the applicability or reliability in determining the final estimate of value. The appraiser's derived estimate of value may be greater or lower than the price a particular investor is willing to pay — the investment value. But lenders require appraisals to protect their position and show that the property has sufficient equity so that if they're suddenly forced to foreclose and sell, they're less likely to suffer a loss. In the following sections, we guide you through each process and then show you how to reconcile the different results.

Market data (sales comparison) approach

The *market data* or *sales comparison* approach takes the economic concept of substitution and applies it to real estate. In real estate, the *substitution principle* essentially states that the value of a given property should be approximately the same as a similar or comparable property that provides the same benefits. This method is very much like what you may do yourself when purchasing a major item for your home — you compare similar items at various stores to assist you in determining what price to pay. Likewise, you don't want to pay more for one property than a similar property would cost.

You've seen this concept at work in housing tracts in your area. When you see two similar homes built by the same builder at the same time on comparable lots, you expect them to sell for approximately the same price. (Of course, no two homes are identical, and adjustments in the price may need to be made for view, deferred maintenance, upgrades, terms of sale, and the specific supply and demand at the time of the proposed sale.)

The accuracy of the market data approach relies on a sufficient number of recent sales of comparable properties. This approach to valuation is primarily used for single-family homes, condos, and small apartment buildings because they're typically more plentiful and offer data from many recent sales.

If there is a shortage of completed sales, an appraiser may look at current listings and pending sales, but they typically discount such potential transactions because they're not finalized transactions, and many things can happen before the sale.

Typically, appraisers look for at least three comparable properties in close proximity to the subject property. Of course, the usage and type of real estate should be the same and a *good comp* is similar in age, size, features, amenities, and condition of the property. The timing of the sale is also important as well as the availability of seller financing.

Appraisers strive to find several comparable properties, but the reality is that every property is unique, and there are no *truly* identical sales or listings. So appraisers need to make either positive or negative adjustments to account for the differences. They then factor all of these variances into an adjustment to the price then calculate an indicated value for the subject property.

For example, you want to buy a duplex (that you can rent as an investment property) in your own neighborhood. You see one listed for $205,000 that is 2,500 square feet with two three-bedroom, two-bath units that are 1,250 square feet each. The property is about ten years old, in good condition, and has a great location on a corner lot. Using the market data approach, you contact a local broker and gather the recent sales data for comparable properties sold on the open market in your neighborhood. Table 12-2 contains the information you've collected for recent sales of duplexes in the same neighborhood.

Table 12-2		Market Data Summary		
Category	*Proposed Subject Property*	*Property A*	*Property B*	*Property C*
Price	$205,000	$170,000	$200,000	$220,000
Age	10 years	9 years	14 years	New
Location	Corner lot	Midblock	Corner lot	Midblock
Condition	Good	Fair	Good	Excellent
Features	Pool	N/A	N/A	Pool
Sale Date	On market	10 months ago	Last month	2 months ago

Because each property is different, you need to make some adjustments to formulate a price for the proposed property. The adjustments are made for items or features that typical buyers and sellers in that area feel have a material impact on value either positively or negatively. For example, in the Phoenix area, a rental home with a swimming pool is more desirable than one without, and property condition and corner lots tend to be important in all markets.

After researching the local market to figure out what factors are important to buyers and sellers, you determine that adjustments should be made for the subject property based on its age, location on a corner lot, its condition, and the fact that it offers a swimming pool (see Table 12-3).

✔ **Property A** is comparable in age to the subject property but is clearly inferior — it doesn't have the corner lot or the swimming pool and is only in fair condition. The property sold ten months ago, and your research shows that prices for comparable properties in the neighborhood have risen 5 to 6 percent over the last year. So overall, you expect that if this property was being sold today in good condition, and had the corner lot and the swimming pool, it would've sold for approximately $30,000 more than the actual sale ten months ago, or an adjusted sales price of $200,000. You made adjustments for the corner lot ($5,000), condition ($5,000), the swimming pool ($15,000), and market timing ($5,000) for a total of $30,000 in adjustments to bring the property in line for comparison to the subject property.

✔ **Property B** is a little older, but because it's been well-maintained and is in good condition, no adjustment is necessary for that factor. It's also on a corner lot and sold just last month, so no adjustments are necessary for these factors. However, it doesn't have a swimming pool, which you have determined is worth at least $15,000 in value. With the swimming pool, this property would have likely sold now for $215,000.

✔ **Property C** is brand new, has a swimming pool, and sold within the last two months. The only disadvantage when compared to your proposed investment is this property's location in the middle of the block. Overall, your research indicates that the price difference for brand-new properties is $15,000 higher than a ten-year old property like the subject property. But comparable properties located in the middle of the block sell for $5,000 less. Therefore, you need to adjust the Property C price lower by $15,000 for age and higher by $5,000 for the inferior location, which is a net downward adjustment of $10,000 and leads you to an adjusted value of $210,000.

After they're established, your adjustments are made to the actual historical sales prices of the comparable properties to account for differences between the comparable properties and the subject property. The result of your work is a set of adjusted comparable sales prices representing estimates of what the comparable properties would have sold for had they possessed all of the important features or characteristics of the subject property. These adjusted sales prices become value indicators for the subject property.

When using the sales comparison approach, you only make adjustments to a comparable sale price as it relates to the subject property. When a feature or characteristic of a comparable property is inferior to that of the subject property, the adjustment to the comparable sale price is positive (you add the adjustment amount to the comparable sale price). When a feature or characteristic of a comparable property is superior to that of the subject property, the adjustment to the comparable sale price is negative (you subtract the adjustment amount from the comparable sale price). Our example uses lump-sum dollar adjustments; another acceptable method is to apply percentage adjustments. In reviewing the results of your analysis and adjustments in Table 12-3, you feel that the asking price is right in line with (if not slightly below) the current market price for comparable properties in the neighborhood. You decide that you have a good investment if you can purchase the property for $205,000 or less.

Table 12-3	Adjusting Sales Price to Determine Value			
	Proposed Property	*Property A*	*Property B*	*Property C*
Price	$205,000	$170,000	$200,000	$220,000
Adjustment	0	30,000	15,000	(10,000)
Value	$205,000	$200,000	$215,000	$210,000

Cost approach

The *cost* approach to real estate valuation is a variation on the market data approach that's useful when you don't have a lot of comparable sales data. It's more commonly used, and even the preferred method, for proposed construction, brand-new properties, and unique properties that typically don't generate an income (including schools, hospitals, public buildings, or places of worship).

Real estate investors find that this method can be useful for establishing replacement cost. As we cover in Chapter 11, the replacement cost of a property can often be an indicator of barriers to entry that exist in the market. Owning superior location, well-maintained real estate in high demand with high barriers to entry for competing properties is one of the best ways to ensure the success of your real estate investments.

In determining valuation with the cost approach, evaluate each segment — the land and the improvements (buildings) — separately. Here are the steps an appraiser follows in applying the cost approach:

1. **Estimate the value of the land if vacant and being used in its highest and best use (see Chapter 11).**

   The appraiser looks for sales of comparable vacant land in the area.

2. **Estimate the current cost to reproduce the existing building as new, before depreciation.**

3. **Estimate all forms of accrued depreciation and deduct that amount from the calculation in Step 2 to arrive at the approximate cost to reproduce the building in its current condition.**

   Accrued depreciation can be caused by three sources:

   • **Physical deterioration:** Normal wear and tear that occurs from use over time. For example, a 12-year-old roof that can normally be expected to last 20 years. These conditions can almost always be corrected.

   • **Functional obsolescence:** Decline in the usefulness or desirability of a property due to changes in preferences by consumers. For example, a rental home with three bedrooms and only one bathroom. Functional obsolescence may be curable or incurable.

   • **Economic or external obsolescence:** Loss in value resulting from external forces. For example, the major employer in town closes down operations and the closest comparable jobs are in a city 25 miles away. You can't control it, which means you need to understand and correctly assess it because it will change over time and can greatly impact the future success of your rental property.

4. **Combine the value of the land and the value of the depreciated improvements to arrive at the total value of the property.**

Using the duplex example from the previous section, you determine that the cost of a comparable vacant lot would be $40,000. Checking with local builders in your market indicates that the cost to build a new property would be $80 per square foot; however, because the building is ten years old, there is some wear and tear. You therefore estimate that the cost to rebuild the property in its current condition is $70 per square foot (this isn't an exact science). The property is 2,500 square feet, so the total value of the depreciated improvements is $175,000.

Adding the land value of $40,000 to the $175,000 value for the depreciated improvements gives an overall value of the property of $215,000 under the cost method of valuation.

Income capitalization approach

This method of valuation is primarily used for larger income-producing properties but can be useful for small income properties as well. (It's not used for valuing owner-occupied properties or properties whose primary purpose isn't income producing.)

The *income capitalization* method is based on the principle that the greater the income generated, the more an investor is willing and able to pay for the property.

Our discussion of the income capitalization approach to valuation must start with the fundamental building block of determining value for this method — the *direct capitalization* or *IRV formula*. Here are the players in this formula:

- ✔ **Value (V):** With this method, you're looking to determine the value of a given property by examining the relationship between Net Operating Income (NOI) and the capitalization rate (R).

- ✔ **Net operating income (NOI):** Yes, it's back. Check out the "Figuring Net Operating Income" section earlier in this chapter to determine this piece of the puzzle.

- ✔ **Capitalization rate (R):** Also called the *cap rate* and *overall rate,* this number is based on the market or the buyer's objectives. It's the rate of return most investors seek for similar properties in a similar market at a given time.

Put it all into equation form and you get

$$V \text{ (value)} = \frac{\text{NOI (Net operating income)}}{\text{R (Capitalization rate)}}$$

To illustrate, take the example of the proposed acquisition of a duplex in your neighborhood. The seller provides you with financial information on the property for the past two years and after a careful analysis, using the techniques discussed earlier in this chapter, you determine that the projected NOI for this property in the next 12 months is $19,500 per year.

Based on discussions with real estate brokers and your local county assessor, an analysis of recent comparable sales indicates that conventional sales of similar properties in the same area have sold for a cap rate of 10 percent.

$$V = \frac{NOI}{R} = \frac{\$19,500}{.10} = \$195,000$$

Therefore, you calculate the as-is value of this property at $195,000.

The cap rate can be subjective, but it's a measure of the risk-adjusted return a particular investor would expect to receive if he purchased a similar property at a similar price. Real estate brokers and agents often have information on current cap rates in the local market. You can actually derive the cap rate yourself by examining recent sales prices for similar properties as long as you have reliable info on the Net Operating Income. The formula is simply

$$R \text{ (Capitalization rate)} = \frac{NOI \text{ (Net operating income)}}{V \text{ (value)}}$$

You can use this formula to determine the capitalization rate or investment performance based on a given NOI and a purchase price. If the property were available for $190,000, what would the rate be?

$$R = \frac{NOI}{V} = \frac{\$19,500}{\$190,000} = 10.26\%$$

You've increased your return by just over a quarter percent.

The direct capitalization method has some distinct advantages over the value benchmarks like the GRM or GIM (discussed in Chapter 11) because it includes operating expenses, but it still doesn't objectively consider potential appreciation, financial leverage, or the risk of the investment. It should, but often data you receive from recent comparable sales may not include your analysis of economic or external obsolescence, which is very important because it's out of your control. Each investor needs to consider these important variables or investment criteria and factor them into her cap rate calculations to determine the investment value of a given property. For example, properties with high appreciation potential, the ability to use positive leverage to increase overall return on invested capital, and low risk require a lower capitalization rate or expected rate of return.

Use future NOI projections in your income capitalization calculations because the historic numbers aren't relevant to your potential ownership except for financing. However, most lenders are sophisticated and discount unusually positive financial results or give you the benefit of a pro forma income-and-expense projection when determining the terms of your loan.

A *pro forma budget* is one in which the budget for next year or a given period of time is projected based on an analysis of the current data available for the building. For example, the historic operating reports for a commercial office building don't include the new lease with a major anchor tenant, but a pro forma operating budget does.

Reconciling the Three Results to Arrive at a Single Value

An appraiser takes the numbers derived from the market data approach, the cost approach, and the income capitalization approach and *reconciles* them to determine a single estimate of market value at a specific time. However, the appraiser doesn't simply take an average of the three estimates of value, because all three methods may not be equally valid or reliable for the subject property.

Rather, the reconciliation process takes into consideration the relative merits of each approach, with more weight given to the most applicable approach. For appraisals of income-producing real estate, appraisers and real estate investors generally rely most heavily on the income capitalization approach because the property is being acquired as an investment.

In the proposed investment in the example duplex, you've determined the following values:

- Market data: $205,000
- Cost: $215,000
- Income capitalization: $195,000

You're pursuing this property as a real estate investment rather than an owner-occupied property, so give the most weight to the value suggested by the income capitalization method. The next most relevant valuation method is the market data approach, which indicates a value of $205,000. Consider the value indicated by the cost approach, but don't give it that much empha-sis — the building is existing and isn't going to be rebuilt. Thus, by placing the most weight on the income capitalization indicated value of $195,000 and also factoring in the $205,000 from the market approach, you determine that $198,000 sounds about right for an offer.

You can then compare this value to the asking price for the property of $205,000. Although the seller may not be willing to accept an offer at $198,000, remember that you don't become wealthy in real estate by paying full retail price for properties. You're looking for a property that is available at a below-market price, such as a motivated seller may offer, or a property where you have the opportunity to add value.

Remember that the appraisal process isn't an exact science, but the prin-ciples of valuation are important for real estate investors and the concepts should be understood. You want to be able to estimate value so you don't overpay for a property. Your lender requires an appraisal to determine how much you can borrow. These same appraisal techniques can help you determine the appropriate asking price when you look to sell your real estate investment.

Putting It All Together: Deciding How Much to Pay

After you've done all of your research and calculations, the reality is that you still need to determine whether a proposed property is a good opportu-nity — and at what price? You don't want to pay retail, but the typical prop-erties you see are based on unrealistic representations by most sellers.

You want to buy when you project that the property has a strong likelihood of producing future increases in NOI and cash flow. So you should look for properties where your analysis shows that the income for the property can be increased or the expenses reduced.

In this chapter, we've covered NOI, cash flow, and the valuation techniques used by the professionals. Using those techniques can help you to determine the maximum price that you should pay for a property.

But sellers are also using similar techniques to set the maximum price they think they can squeeze out of the most generous buyer in the market. You need to understand how they may bend and twist the facts to present their property in the best light. The following examples demonstrate how being able to prop-erly value investment real estate before making a purchase offer is essential.

Examining the seller's rental rate and expense claims

Most sellers of investment properties claim that the rents are below market. Sellers may imply that instantly, and almost magically, upon purchasing the building the buyer will be able to enhance the value of her new investment property and improve her cash flow by merely (yet significantly) increasing rents.

Of course, you should be wondering: If I can make money by simply raising the rents, why doesn't the current owner increase the rents and then sell the building at a much higher price? After all, sellers know that buyers will base their offer on NOI. The answer is that they usually do raise rents before putting the property on the market. But sellers (and their real estate agents) still go ahead and claim that the buyer can raise the rents even more. And if a buyer hasn't done her homework and carefully evaluated the current rental market, she may well fall for the seller's tricks.

The same scenario is found with expenses. The seller typically cuts back on spending to show artificially low expenses, or claims that the buyer can cut expenses through an energy conservation program or some other seemingly sensible method. This mindset assumes that the current owner hasn't taken advantage of legitimate ways to cut down on expenses.

Of course, you can find exceptions where an owner has truly been too nice or lazy to keep the rents at market level or conduct an energy conversion to lower expenses. But we suggest that even if these claims are true, the buyer shouldn't pay an inflated price based on the assumption of being able to make these changes because she'll have to pony up to make the changes herself. Implementing these strategies to generate higher income and lower expenses also takes many months. For example, if you've ever given out a rent increase to full market value, you know that it's generally unpleasant and often can result in unwanted turnover and higher vacancy and operating expenses for several months, and *you* should be compensated for your efforts — not the seller (who lacked the fortitude to implement the rent increase).

Deciding which set of numbers to use

When you look at listings of properties for sale, you find that many sellers and their brokers or agents develop a pro forma, or future estimate, of the NOI. From this artificially high NOI, they then derive an above-market asking price for the property. They also use the unrealistic pro forma NOI to show all of the various value indicators such as GRM and cap rate. In reality, the NOI would even drop if you were to unexpectedly lose some of your key tenants or be faced with a major unanticipated expense. So remember that this pro forma is an *estimate* of future operations of the property. The future is uncertain, so none of the numbers are truly right or wrong. And you'll be amazed by how universally optimistic sellers are about how much more money you'll make than they did when you buy their property!

Although the IRV formula uses the future NOI and the value of the building is determined based on those numbers, we suggest that you find a seller who calculated his asking price based on actual historical operating income and expenses. You want to anticipate the future and pay for the present. You need to set your offering price based on your own calculations as to the NOI you truly expect to earn in the year after your purchase. (For more on IRV, see the "Income capitalization approach" section earlier in this chapter.)

The other key component to the IRV formula is the capitalization rate. We demonstrate that if you lower the capitalization rate or required return, you can dramatically increase the value of the property. A lower rate of return is required when the risk associated with the cash flow of a property is lower. The risk is lower when the property is competitive with or superior to other comparable properties, has minimal deferred maintenance, and has solid tenants with leases in place that are at market. Your goal is to find properties that lack these characteristics, but you can easily achieve with superior management — either yourself or with a professional property manager.

More sophisticated valuation techniques that real estate appraisers use

Although the traditional valuation methods used by appraisers are important for real estate investors to understand, additional investment analysis tools used by professional real estate brokers and investors analyze the cash flow generated by a property over several years to estimate the value. These methods don't take just a single year's net operating income (NOI) and estimate value based on an overall capitalization rate. Rather they use the following methods:

✔ **Discounted cash flow (DCF):** *The discounted cash flow* technique takes the annual projected cash flows for the proposed investment property and uses a discount rate to determine the present value. This method acknowledges the concept of *time value of money*, or that cash received in the future isn't necessarily as valuable as cash received today (for example, due to inflation)

(continued)

(continued)

✔ **Net present value (NPV):** *Net present value* is a commonly used measure of value that uses discounted cash flows to evaluate an investment considering the time value of money, plus the size and risk of an investment. Easily handled by software programs or a financial calculator, NPV is a calculation where each estimated future cash flow is discounted back to the present value by using the appropriate discount rate or target yield. This *discount rate* for individual investors is typically their opportunity cost, or the interest rate they can earn in a comparable investment that is similar in size, risk, and duration. Corporate investors generally use their cost of capital (the weighted sum of their cost of equity and their cost of debt).

The NPV can be a positive number, a negative number, or precisely zero. An NPV of zero means that the proposed investment exactly met the discount rate; a positive NPV indicates that if the investment performs as anticipated, the return will exceed the target yield. A positive NPV is also an indicator of how much more the investor can pay to acquire and improve the property, or it can be considered as a cushion or safety factor against shortfalls in future cash flows. Conversely, a negative NPV reflects that the property will fall short of the target yield by the amount of the NPV. The investor should lower her offer to purchase by the amount of the negative NPV, or she needs to increase the net projected cash flows or simply accept a lower than desired rate of return for this particular investment.

✔ **Internal rate of return (IRR):** The IRR is the most popular and widely quoted of the advanced valuation techniques for evaluating and comparing investment returns. The *IRR* is the percentage rate earned on all dollars invested for the specific periods each is invested. IRR doesn't measure the return of the equity dollars invested but only those additional dollars earned on the invested capital, so an IRR requires that the total dollars received exceed the dollars spent on the investment. The return on invested dollars is dependent on both the amount of the excess and when the excess is received. Bottom line: The IRR and NPV are related because the IRR is simply the interest rate at which the NPV for an investment is equal to zero (0). The IRR is useful to compare real estate opportunities with alternative investments such as money market accounts, mutual funds, stocks, bonds, and commodities.

Figuring the results for each of these methods has been simplified by the advent of software programs that can perform complicated calculations.

Thanks to the Institute of Real Estate Management (IREM), one of the best resources for real estate and property management education, many of these more sophisticated methods of valuing and analyzing the financial performance of proposed and existing real estate investments are available as an Excel spreadsheet template tool. This is exactly what Robert uses when he evaluates potential property acquisitions and you should learn to use it as well.

Refer to www.irem.org/REIFD for a helpful Excel spreadsheet template tool and guidebook provided by IREM (www.irem.org).

Chapter 13

Preparing and Making an Offer

....

....

*Y*ou and your real estate team log many hours in locating and valuing property. Then comes the moment when you must decide whether you want to try and buy a particular property or keep looking for a more attractive opportunity. In this chapter, we discuss how to negotiate a deal that meets your needs as well as the seller's. Finally, we cover the all-important details of real estate investment contracts.

Negotiating 101

You make money in real estate when you purchase your investment property. If you buy a well-located and physically sound property below market value and replacement cost, the property will provide you with excellent returns for many years. This is why smart negotiating is so important to being successful with your real estate investments.

Superior knowledge combined with superior negotiating leads to superior returns. This section explains how to be a champion negotiator.

Starting with the right approach

Although everyone approaches negotiating from their own perspective, we think that it's important to understand that the real estate community in most areas is actually a close-knit group of professionals who network. Thus, word of mouth referrals and a reputation for honesty and integrity are critical elements to your long-term success. Patience, vision, and perseverance are also great virtues when it comes to making the best real estate deals. Hard driving, one-sided transactions may make you some extra money in the short-run, but word travels fast.

A university study indicates that people who have a favorable experience share their positive feelings with an average of four others. However, those who've had a negative experience go out of their way to tell more than 20 people how they feel about you. Human nature also indicates that they likely embellish the story with each conversation.

Here's what we *don't* recommend:

- ✔ **A take-it-or-leave approach:** Even in a weak market with few buyers and many potential sellers, the my-way-or-the-highway style is a short-term, egocentric strategy. It may work if you plan to purchase only a single property in a geographic area, but we believe you need to be active in the same market for many years and build a positive reputation. And this bare-knuckles strategy doesn't always work even just once, because even the weakest sellers sometimes have alternatives and choices. They may decide life is better if they don't sell their property to an inflexible jerk.

- ✔ **A lowballing approach:** Making patently frivolous offers in an attempt to get lucky is another technique recommended by some real estate gurus. Our experience is that sellers aren't stupid, and they quickly eliminate further offers, even reasonable ones, from such greedy bottom-fishers.

The problem with many aggressive negotiating techniques is that you can get so wrapped up in just making the deal that you forget what you're doing. You can make some serious mistakes and buy properties that you should've eliminated during your pre-offer due diligence. Don't get emotionally involved in any potential property. You're buying investment real estate, not your dream home.

Building a solid foundation of knowledge

The most important negotiating tool in an investment property purchase is superior knowledge — if you're unwilling to do the homework necessary to justify the right price, you're almost guaranteed to overpay for real estate. Your goal as an investor is to set the maximum price that you can pay and still receive a solid return on your investment in light of the associated risks.

In order to achieve this goal, you need to know more about your proposed property acquisition than anyone else, especially the seller. You need to know about the property, neighboring properties, local and state laws, and all of the economic data we discuss in Chapter 10 that can help foretell which properties are in the path of progress versus those that have already seen their best days. Although an occasional seller dramatically underestimates the true market value of the real estate, the vast majority of properties you see offered for sale are overpriced. That is true regardless of where the real estate market pricing cycle is, including after a downturn in prices. You may encounter some sellers who enjoyed significant price appreciation over the preceding years but stubbornly refuse to accept that demand for their property has fallen and that prices must adjust to the current market reality. Of course, some of these sellers aren't really motivated and are just hoping to find an uninformed buyer. Don't let that be you!

Becoming intimately familiar with the local economy

We don't suggest that you mislead anyone, but an amazing number of current property owners just don't pay attention to even the most basic publicly available information. Nothing is immoral or illegal about having vision to upgrade and renovate a property to achieve its full value because your research with local agencies indicates that a major new employer is moving into the area, dramatically increasing demand for half-vacant and tired commercial properties — like the one you're considering for purchase.

You'll be extremely successful in negotiating great real estate deals if you not only know the right people and have a good real estate investment team but also know the important factors that affect supply and demand in the local market.

Maybe you're seeing local companies growing rapidly and hiring lots of new workers. You know that because of a local housing shortage, the many new families moving into the area will be unable to afford a new home and will need to rent instead. That's a good sign that rents will increase and the demand will be high for nice three- to four-bedroom rental homes located in quiet cul-de-sacs near the best schools. Clearly, you can use this information to properly negotiate the purchase of prime rental homes in such a market.

Or perhaps the final approval by the local transit district to extend a new light rail line into and through a rundown area of the community may really be a catalyst for positive change. So you do your homework and find an older couple who has lost interest in their commercial property in that area. You purchase and renovate this small retail strip center across from the new station because you know it's an attractive location for retail tenants targeting commuters.

Determine the current supply and demand in the marketplace so you know whether it's a buyer's or seller's market. That doesn't mean you can't still make some great real estate investments, but you need to be realistic. Buying in a seller's market at prices above replacement cost can be dangerous. Don't even consider it if your goal is a short-term hold on the property.

As the potential purchaser, discover as much as you can about the property and the owner before making an offer. How long has the property been on the market? What are its flaws? Why is the owner selling? The more you know about the property you want to buy and the seller's motivations, the better your ability to make an offer that meets everyone's needs.

Most real estate investors utilize the services of a real estate agent, who usually carries the burden of the negotiation process. Even if you delegate responsibility for negotiating to your agent, you still should have a plan and strategy in mind. Otherwise, you may overpay for real estate.

Figuring out the seller's motivations

Some listing agents love to talk and will tell you the life history of the seller. Encourage this free flow of information. The goal for you and your agent is to get the seller or his agent to reveal helpful information (without sharing any pertinent or strategic information about yourself). Always seek the answer to the most important question: "Why is the property owner selling?"

The more you know about the seller's needs and motivation, the better you can structure your offer to best meet the needs of the seller while still providing yourself with a great investment opportunity. You can also avoid wasting your time negotiating with a fake seller who isn't motivated to sell. Some sellers are really just testing the market or only willing to sell if they can get a price well over the market value.

Figure out how to spot these fake sellers early on. Look for the warning signs such as unexplained delays in responding to offers or questions, a reluctance to answer questions or give you access to the property, and a generally uncooperative attitude. If you see these signs, don't make an offer on the property.

Information is a two-way street. Don't give out any information about your motivations that gives the seller added negotiating leverage. The less you say about how much you like the property or your reasons for making the offer, the better. For example, many sellers are able to stick to their full price terms and as-is condition of the property if they know that the buyer is in a tax-deferred exchange (see Chapter 18) with its tight time restrictions. A buyer facing the possibility of paying significant capital gains taxes if she doesn't close the transaction within 180 days may suddenly be agreeable to almost any reasonable condition requested by a seller if she's down to her last week.

Bringing property-related data to the table

Information is the heart of negotiating. Bring facts to the bargaining table. Get comparable sales data to support your price. Too often, investors and their agents pick a number out of the air when they make an offer. If you were the seller, would you be persuaded to lower your asking price? Pointing to recent and comparable investment property sales to justify your offer price strengthens your case. Rarely do you find a seller of investment-grade real estate who doesn't have access to plenty of market data. But sellers often don't select the right comparable properties — preferring to creatively use just those comps that provide for the highest possible asking price.

If the property needs repairs, never rely on bids provided by the seller. You must independently verify the numbers with licensed professional contractors. You can also use these written proposals to support your position regarding the true cost to make needed repairs instead of just making verbal representations. Always leave yourself a little cushion or wiggle room. We have found that even with the most comprehensive bids from the top industry professionals, any significant renovation or remodeling project is likely to take longer and cost more than is estimated.

Assembling attractive and realistic offers

In this chapter, we cover and hopefully dispel many of the negotiating theories or fallacies of the get-rich-quick gurus. We don't want to just tell you what not to do, so here are some examples of realistic and creative ways to negotiate and structure a real estate offer that accurately reflects the value of the property but also provides you with a reasonable return on your investment.

Factoring in fix-up costs

Say you come across an opportunity to buy a great three-bedroom, two-bath house. You live close by, and you know the area is terrific. The house would be an ideal rental because it's two blocks from an excellent school. You estimate that the property will rent for $1,750 per month, and there's strong demand for rental homes. The seller is asking $200,000, which appears to be its market value — based on the home having no deferred maintenance. But you know that no rental property has *no* deferred maintenance, so you call your home inspection contractor. His report indicates that overall, the property is in decent condition, and the big-ticket items of appliances and flooring have recently been replaced. But he also has some bad news: The roof needs to be replaced before the next winter. You contact three reputable roofing contractors, and the best value bid for a roof replacement that'll last 20 years is $8,000. You also estimate that you'll need about $2,000 in minor repairs and upgrades to the landscaping and the irrigation system.

What should you pay? If you said $190,000, you aren't necessarily wrong, but you're not providing any room for unforeseen events — or any compensation or reimbursement for your time and the risk involved in overseeing and coordinating this work. We suggest that you take your actual conservative estimates for all repairs and add at least 50 percent. Cover those surprises that are likely to occur, plus compensate yourself for the time, effort, and risk associated with renovations. Contractors and other professionals always allow for contingencies, overhead, and profit when they present their bids, so why should a real estate investor who invests her sweat equity utilizing her own handyman or contracting skills not be equally compensated? This is one of the biggest (and most avoidable) mistakes that novice real estate investors make.

Creatively meeting the seller's price

Price is only one of several negotiable items, but it's the first item the seller reviews in a purchase offer. Because many sellers fixate on the price they receive for the property (perhaps they want to get at least what they paid for it themselves several years ago), you can offer the full price but seek other concessions in order to reduce the effective cost of buying the property. These creative offers allow you to pay what the property is worth, and the seller can feel satisfied that he held firm and received his full asking price:

- ✔ **Get the seller to pay for certain repairs or improvements.** The buyer should always look for the seller to correct all health and safety items and required pest control repairs before closing escrow. But other items can also be negotiated. For example, you can often entice the seller to provide a credit in escrow for the replacement of old worn-out carpeting, window coverings, or appliances. Likewise, rather than have the seller patch that 30-year-old roof that you'll be replacing anyway, have him take the cost of the repairs off the purchase price.

- ✔ **Seek attractive seller financing.** For example, you may find a small, well-maintained commercial property on the market for $200,000 that you believe is really worth no more than $195,000. But the seller is determined not to sell for less than his asking price. You can structure your offer at $200,000, with the seller agreeing to lend you some money at a below-market interest rate for ten years that essentially saves you much more than $5,000.

- ✔ **Have the seller pay all of the title, escrow, and closing costs.** Often, the seller and the buyer split the administrative expenses of a change of ownership. These costs are negotiable, and if the seller completely pays them, then the effective price paid by you, the buyer, is reduced.

The time that you need to close on your purchase is also a bargaining chip. Some sellers may need cash soon and concede other points if you can close quickly. And the real estate agent's commission may be negotiable too. Finally, try as best you can to leave your emotions out of any property purchase. This is easier said than done, but try not to fall in love with a property. Keep searching for other properties even when you make an offer — you may be negotiating with an unmotivated seller.

Infomercial negotiating strategies don't pan out

We hate to be the bearers of bad news, but those late-night TV infomercial gurus don't tell the full story when they and their testimonials say how easy it was for them to start with nothing and suddenly own vast real estate holdings that all seem to magically be worth millions and provide great cash flow. If it were really that easy, the gurus wouldn't be telling you about it — they would be busy making great deals just for themselves. (Only the multi-tasking and forever money-hungry Donald Trump seems to be able to make some of his own deals and sell you books and tapes at the same time!)

There *are* times when you buy just before the market takes off and you can't lose. But those infomercials claim that the buyers who follow their advice can leave the closing table with checks (you can buy a property with no money down and actually have the seller pay you at closing). They're not telling the full story that the funds are proceeds from a loan or other debt that was assumed or placed on the property. Or maybe the funds represent the seller's prorated share of the large property tax installment that you'll have the pleasure of paying in full next month!

Do you get excited and think you've found money when you withdraw cash from your bank account at an ATM? Of course not, and so you aren't fooled by receiving cash at a close of escrow if you're really just borrowing more against the property. Being able to borrow against real estate is one of its greatest benefits, but one that should never be confused with receiving free money!

The old adage "If it sounds too good to be true, it *is* too good to be true" applies to real estate and

particularly the thought that the best real estate is available to the average person at unbelievably favorable terms. There's so much capital available to owners of real estate that even truly desperate sellers have the ability to borrow against the value of the real estate. The interest rates and terms may be horrendous, but money is almost always available for any property that isn't a toxic waste dump, so there's no need for an owner to give his property away unless it has no equity. If the property has no equity, you may indeed be able to pay little or nothing down to the current owner, but that doesn't mean you're getting a great deal. Rather, you're simply stepping into the shoes of the seller and either assuming or placing new debt on the property for the full value without having any equity yourself. Remember, there's no free lunch — you usually get what you pay for.

The only way you can get these unbelievable terms as a buyer purchasing property dramatically below its market value is if the seller has a lot of equity and is overwhelmed, extremely motivated, and out of time. But if the seller has a lot of equity in a truly great property, he could simply borrow money against that equity, continue to own the property, and use its cash flow to pay off the loan. He wouldn't sell it to someone who listened to a CD in her car and made a ridiculously low offer.

Preparing to Make Your Offer: Understanding Contract Basics

The purchase and sale of real estate are always done in writing. The most critical document in any transaction is the sales contract, which is referred to as the *purchase agreement* in real estate transactions. After you have found a property that meets your investment goals, have your real estate agent prepare a real estate contract for presentation to the seller or her agent. Refer to www.dummies.com/extras/realestateinvesting for a sample purchase agreement.

A real estate contract is a legally binding written agreement between two or more persons regarding an exchange of some sort. These contracts are legally enforceable sets of promises that must be performed and that rely on the basics of contract law. (Contracts may also be oral, but as we discuss later in the section "Elements of a contract," oral contracts should be avoided.)

Bilateral versus unilateral contracts

Real estate contracts can be either bilateral or unilateral:

✔ **Bilateral:** Most real estate contracts are *bilateral,* meaning that each party to the contract promises to provide some *consideration* (something of value) and adhere to the terms of the contract. For example, the seller agrees to give the buyer title to the property in exchange for cash and/or a *promissory note* (a written document promising to pay the holder of the note a certain sum of money at some given time in the future).

✔ **Unilateral:** A unilateral contract is a one-sided agreement in which only one party promises to do something. An example is an *option agreement* in which the seller *(optionor)* gives a potential buyer *(optionee)* an unconditional purchase option for a certain period of time. The option is enforceable only by the optionee. If the option isn't properly exercised, the optionor's obligation and the optionee's rights expire.

Elements of a contract

A *legally binding* contract is valid because it contains all of the necessary elements that make it legally enforceable. In the following list, we outline the basic elements of a legally binding and enforceable real estate contract. The terms may sound a bit technical, but you need to be familiar with them.

✔ **Legally competent parties:** Every party to the transaction must have *legal capacity,* which is defined as being of legal age (18 in most states) and having the mental capacity to understand the consequences of its actions. Convicted criminals and certain mentally ill persons may not have legal capacity. Be careful when dealing with older persons if they seem to have any difficulty understanding or communicating. Politely inquire whether they have anyone who is acting on their behalf in a representative capacity. Most states have passed strict elder abuse laws, and you wouldn't want to find yourself in court defending allegations that you defrauded an elderly widow out of her home.

✔ **An offer:** An *offer* to purchase real estate is a written communication to the current owner of the buyer's willingness to purchase a specific property at the terms indicated. The seller can continue to market the property while considering the offer. Unless an expiration clause is included, an offer may be accepted by the seller at any time before it's rescinded by the buyer.

Virtually all offers have a specific expiration time. ("This offer is valid until Friday, January 19 at 5 p.m. EST only.") You want to allow the seller a reasonable time to receive, consider, and evaluate your offer, but enforce the expiration clause to minimize the seller from using the offer as a negotiating tool with other interested parties, shopping your offer around, or trying to entice another buyer to raise her offer. Also, if the offer is open-ended, the buyer has to affirmatively rescind the offer, which is more work and trouble than simply having the offer expire after some passage of time.

✔ **Acceptance:** *Acceptance* is a positive written response in a timely manner to the exact terms of an offer. Acceptance legally requires that the buyer must be given legal notice of the acceptance. Commonly, the seller doesn't accept the offer as presented but proposes changes in the terms or conditions — which is a *counteroffer.*

✔ **Counteroffer:** This is legally a new offer; the original offer is rejected and is void. Counteroffers can go back and forth until both buyer and seller have agreed and the final accepted offer becomes the binding agreement between the parties. Just like offers, counteroffers must be in writing and can also be rescinded at any time prior to acceptance.

✔ **Consideration:** Consideration is basically the exchange aspect of the deal: The buyer offers payment of money or something of value to the seller, who agrees to give over ownership of the property in return. A real estate contract isn't binding if each party doesn't offer at least some consideration to the other party.

✔ **Clearly and uniquely identified property:** This identification is required so there's no uncertainty about precisely which property is being sold and transferred to the buyer. Typically, a legal description of the property is used.

✔ **Legal purpose:** The real estate contract must be for a legal purpose and can't be for an illegal act or an act so immoral that it's against public policy. For example, a buyer purchasing a single-family home with the intent to run his property management company there would want to cancel the purchase if during the due diligence process he discovers that such use violates local prohibitions against operating a business in a residentially zoned area.

✔ **Written contract:** A written contract is required for all enforceable transfers of real estate. All terms and conditions of the purchase agreement or sales contract must be set forth in writing, even for minor items that may not seem consequential. Generally, the written contract helps ensure that there is no confusion about what is included in the sale. For example, if you want to make sure that the supplies in the maintenance shop for a commercial or apartment building are included and not taken before the sale, you must specify it in the contract. Remember that if something isn't in writing, it's not part of the contract.

Agreements for the sale of real estate must be in writing or they're unenforceable. *Never* make an oral agreement of any type regarding real estate no matter how convenient, expedient, or reasonable it may seem at the time. The Statute of Frauds is a legal concept that requires all transfers of real estate to be in writing to be enforceable in a court of law. Real estate–related contracts that must be in writing include sales contracts or purchase agreements, leases for more than one year, real estate loans secured by a mortgage or note, listing contracts and commission agreements with agents, and an employment agreement with an agent to locate property.

A failure to meet all of these essential elements can lead to the contract being declared void. A void contract has no legal force or effect and is unenforceable in a court of law. A *voidable real estate contract* is one that may be treated as legally unenforceable at the option of a party (usually the injured party) but remains enforceable until that party exercises her option. An example is a real estate contract with a minor that is voidable only by the minor.

Besides all the legal elements, real estate sales contracts specify the sale price and the terms and conditions as well as any contingencies (see the "Using contingencies effectively" section later in the chapter). The contract must be signed and include a standard statement that "time is of the essence," which ensures that all dates and times of day noted in the contract are important and can't be ignored by any of the parties without the written consent of the other party; otherwise, there is a breach of the contract. If the contract is breached, the other party may be entitled to monetary damages or can sue to force the seller to complete the sale.

Addressing Key Provisions in the Purchase Agreement

The purchase agreement is the legal document that outlines the details of the transaction for your proposed purchase of the subject property. Depending on where you live, there are other terms for a contract for the purchase of real estate, such as a *sales contract,* an *offer to purchase,* a *contract of purchase and sale,* an *earnest money agreement,* and a *deposit receipt.*

No matter what you call it, the purchase agreement is the most important document in the sale of real estate. It includes the basic info — the names of the sellers and buyers, a description of the property, and the proposed financing terms — and indicates how much you pay, when you pay, the terms and conditions that must be met to close the transaction, and the conditions under which the agreement can be canceled and the buyer's deposit returned.

Don't let a real estate agent tell you that your offer must be on a certain form, because although many purchase agreement forms are available, none are required. Which form you use is up to you — we recommend that you use a purchase agreement form that's easy to read and understand. The more complicated the language, the more likely it is that the parties get confused or disagree on the meaning of the terms of the offer.

To find forms to use in your real estate investment activities, look to local title and escrow companies and your local association of realtors. Although legally up-to-date and often very thorough and excellent, most of these firms and Realtor boards don't offer their proprietary forms to the public. Robert's good friend, the late California real estate attorney James B. McKenney developed plain-language forms used throughout the country by real estate investors and property managers. The sample purchase agreement in the appendix was provided by Cari Lynn Pace, the current owner of Professional Publishing, LLC; website: www.trueforms.com.

Go over the form in detail with your real estate broker or agent and carefully consider the terms that you want to offer in each paragraph. Don't leave any blank spaces, and have your attorney mark through any clauses that you feel aren't appropriate. Just because a certain clause is preprinted doesn't mean that you can't cross it out or modify the language to suit your needs. Make sure that you clearly initial any changes and require the other party to also initial every single change and the bottom of each page to ensure that you agreed on the specific terms.

Some of the terms are at your discretion, but your real estate agent can advise you as to the local custom and practice concerning issues such as the standard for earnest money deposits (see the next section) or the length of contingency periods for inspections of the property, books, and records. Your agent can also inform you about local standards for prorating the closing agent costs and the other miscellaneous costs of the transaction.

The following sections cover other key provisions you should carefully evaluate, because you must make many decisions about your offer before the purchase agreement is ready for your signature.

Showing intention with an earnest money deposit

Right after the purchase price, one of the most important terms that can set the emotional tone for further negotiations is the amount of the earnest money deposit you're willing to submit with your purchase offer. The *earnest money deposit* is usually fully refundable for a defined time period. Your deposit is held in trust by either the seller's agent or a title or escrow company. Never make an earnest money deposit payable directly to the seller.

The purpose of the deposit is to show good faith by the buyer and the intention to follow through with the terms of the purchase agreement. The amount of the deposit varies in different areas depending upon local custom or the specific needs of a particular transaction. Also, depending on state law, the earnest money deposit may or may not go into an interest-bearing account. If you can, always insist that your earnest money be placed in an insured trust account that bears interest and that the purchase agreement clearly spell out that you (the buyer) are credited with all interest earned.

Some psychology is involved because the size of the deposit has an effect on the desirability of the offer. An offer with no earnest money or a nominal amount may be interpreted by the seller as coming from a buyer who isn't serious about the transaction or lacks the cash to make a meaningful deposit. From the perspective of the seller, with occupied rental income properties, the tenants are often disrupted or inconvenienced with any potential sale of the rental property. The seller rightfully won't want to bother his tenants with a buyer and his due diligence unless he is confident that the buyer has every intention of going through with the transaction if the property checks out. The size of the earnest money deposit can often separate the sincere buyers from those buyers just looking.

A lousy recommendation suggested by some real estate investment gurus is for the buyer to offer a promissory note with her offer. That's a sure way for a seller to identify that you're not a serious buyer. Such no-money-down seminar graduates may be classified as bottom-feeders or opportunists who are really only interested in properties with desperate and uneducated sellers.

When determining the earnest money deposit, remember that if you don't live up to the agreement or don't cancel it within the allowed time frames, you forfeit the deposit to the seller. The forfeiture of the earnest money deposit for nonperformance is called *liquidated damages,* which is essentially the payment for any and all damages incurred by the seller as a result of you not completing the purchase as proposed. Under the terms of most purchase agreements, a seller who keeps the earnest money deposit can't sue for any further damages.

To avoid any expensive lessons about earnest money, follow this advice:

- As a buyer, make sure you know the exact date upon which your earnest money *goes hard,* which is the real estate industry term meaning it's nonrefundable and passes to the seller regardless of whether you complete the purchase of the property.

- Don't wait until the last few days to cancel your purchase agreement. If you're still unsure of your interest or ability to complete the transaction as proposed, send a written cancellation of the purchase agreement and then try to renegotiate additional time, while spelling out in detail exactly what your concerns are and why you need more time.

- Both buyer and seller must agree to any changes in writing. Never rely on any verbal representations as to any extensions or changes of terms or conditions.

Assigning your rights

Many purchase agreements specifically include a clause giving the buyer the ability to assign his interests to another party. *Assignment* is the transfer of the right or duties under a real estate contract by the buyer to a third party. This is an extremely important clause for buyers, and we strongly encourage you to include the right to assign the contract as a term of your purchase offer. In the contract, simply include the language "or assignee" after the name of the legal entity indicated as the purchaser. Of course, if the pre-printed purchase offer has a clause that prohibits assignment, you need to cross out that language and have both parties initial the change.

Leaving the buy-and-flip door open

Even though we're not ardent promoters of the buy-and-flip strategy, the ability to assign or transfer your purchase agreement to another real estate investor gives you the opportunity to realize a profit without ever having to close on the deal yourself. When the real estate market is appreciating rapidly, some real estate investors have found that the property has increased in value so significantly that they can sell their contractual position.

In the early- to mid-2000s in certain really hot housing markets, some real estate speculators went to new housing tracts and signed contracts with builders — up to a year or more before the property was built. Then, during the extended contract and escrow period, the value of the property being built went up, so the buyer was able to merely transfer their contractual rights to buy the property at the locked in price and terms to another buyer for a profit.

The reality is that profiting from speculating on new housing tracts isn't guaranteed or easy. Builders aren't naïve, and many don't allow the assignment of the purchase agreement — so the buyer must actually complete the sale and then resell the property to earn their profit, if they actually turn a profit after deducting the costs of two transactions. Also, many builders specify that they don't sell to buyers from out-of-state or who won't occupy the homes. Some simply require larger earnest money deposits for speculators, and others actually require the buyer to contractually agree to not sell the property for at least one year. If housing prices fall rather than rise (as they did in the late 2000s in Las Vegas, where it has been conservatively estimated that more than 40,000 homes were previously purchased in this manner), the buyer may have to complete the purchase or lose his earnest money deposit. These facts haven't stopped many of the late-night infomercial kings from promoting the idea that fantastic returns can be achieved by simply placing nominal deposits on homes to be constructed. We've even heard of some charlatans who hold seminars to attract investors willing to fund these speculative ventures or worse yet, use `www.craigslist.com` or cardboard roadside signs seeking "real estate apprentice" with the implication that easy money can be made. Often they're a form of scheme and should be avoided. Our advice is to never invest in real estate with partners that you just met at, or that invite you to attend, a nonaccredited real estate seminar!

Installing an emergency exit

The ability to assign your interests in a purchase agreement can be a lifesaver in another scenario. Many savvy investors have gotten into a real estate transaction in which the due diligence time frames have passed and their earnest money is at risk — and they're unable or unwilling to complete the transaction. This situation typically happens because the buyer has second thoughts, doesn't have enough money to close, finds a better deal, or doesn't have the capability to handle the problems with the property. In this scenario, an assignment would allow the buyer to potentially recover his earnest money deposit or even his due diligence costs from another interested buyer rather than walk away and let the seller take the earnest money (and then turn around and sell the property to another party). The buyer who has the property under contract controls the property and can make a deal with other parties.

Setting the closing date

An important term of your purchase offer is the proposed closing date for the transaction, which determines the anticipated escrow period (see Chapter 14 for escrow information). The length of the escrow period is a matter of negotiation between the buyer and seller, with consideration given to the length of time needed to obtain financing and the amount and complexity of due diligence necessary to complete the sale. A complicated financing transaction, a property in need of a zoning change, or possible environmental issues require a much longer escrow period than a simple transaction.

Of course, the seller is usually interested in selling the property as soon as possible and wants a short escrow period and a fixed closing date; the buyer generally wants as much time as the seller will allow, some flexibility on the closing date, and the unilateral right to close the transaction earlier if he's completed his work. But the lack of a specific time line can create problems for the seller, particularly if she's trying to buy another investment in a tax-deferred exchange (see Chapter 18) or has tenants in place who need to be vacated.

The more time for the buyer, the better opportunity he has to make sure he's not making a mistake — and the seller knows that. But, the seller also knows that many buyers aren't serious about purchasing the property or use an extended due diligence period to find problems with the property and try to wear down the seller into granting concessions or lowering the purchase price.

Some buyers also use a long escrow period to tie up the property, hoping to find another investor who will pay more for it. If they find one, they can then close escrow and immediately flip the property in a *double escrow,* which is actually two separate transactions done at the same time. The investor purchases the property from the original owner and simultaneously sells the property to a new buyer, usually at a profit, without really even taking possession of the property other than for possibly a matter of minutes between the recording of the two transactions.

Ultimately, what you agree on in the purchase agreement is legally binding, but it's really just an estimated closing date because so many different moving parts can affect when you close the sale. The closing date should be met unless both parties agree to an extension with a written addendum or escrow instruction (see "Ironing out straggling issues" later in the chapter).

Using contingencies effectively

A *contingency* in a real estate purchase agreement is simply a condition that must be fulfilled or an event that may or may not happen in the future before a contract becomes firm and binding. Contingencies can be for the benefit of either the seller or the buyer; if the contingencies aren't met, the deal doesn't go through. The seller of an estate property, for example, may require a contingency that the probate court approves the sale. Buyers often have contingencies for financing, physical inspections, the review of the current tenant leases and service contracts that will run with the property, and other items. Naturally, sellers attempt to eliminate unreasonable contingencies. For instance, most purchase agreements include contingencies that ask for 10 to 30 days to conduct the physical inspection and/or approve the books and records. If you request 60 days to conduct these items, the seller may reject your offer as unreasonable.

Contingencies are escape clauses that can protect the buyer from purchasing a property that doesn't meet his needs. Without contingencies, purchasing a property would be extremely risky because you'd have to be sure that you had all of the financing in place and that the property was in good condition, met your needs, and the terms and conditions were acceptable before you even made the offer. Few buyers would be willing to do this, or they'd do it but discount their offer to account for the additional risk.

Although legally different from an option, contingencies can have a similar effect by allowing a prospective buyer the exclusive opportunity to buy the property in a limited time frame but not obligating the buyer to complete the transaction.

The terms of most purchase agreements provide that by certain defined dates, all of the contingencies must be resolved one way or another by the *beneficiary,* or party that stands to gain from the contingency. After it's in place, a contingency has one of three outcomes:

- ✔ **Contingencies can be satisfied.** This means that the pending sale is no longer subject to cancellation or modification for that particular item. For example, the buyer can comply with the financing contingency upon receiving a written loan commitment at acceptable terms.

- ✔ **The beneficiary of the contingency can unilaterally agree to waive or remove the contingency.** For example, the seller may have asked for a contingency to identify a replacement property as part of an IRS section 1031 tax deferred exchange. If the seller decides not to do an exchange, then she may simply notify the buyer in writing that she's waiving that condition or contingency.

- ✔ **A contingency can be rejected or fail.** The beneficiary of the contingency is then no longer obligated to perform under the contract. For example, the buyer may receive a termite inspection report indicating that there's extensive damage and infestation and then decide that he's no longer interested in completing the purchase. Under this scenario, the buyer typically receives the return of his earnest money deposit (and is glad that he diligently conducted a physical inspection).

Although the list varies depending on the property type, size, and location, here are contingency clauses that we recommend:

- ✔ **Marketable title:** Obtain a preliminary title report with full and complete copies of each and every exception and have your attorney review these documents.

- ✔ **Financing:** Outline the specific terms (type of loan and maximum acceptable interest rate) of a new loan required in order to complete the purchase. Require copies of the current loan documents and the most recent loan statement, plus receiving the approval of the lender in writing, if you're attempting to take over existing financing.

✔ **Appraisal:** This condition demands that an independent professional appraisal of the property arrive at a value equal to or greater than the proposed purchase price. This requirement may be a necessary part of the financing or simply a safeguard to prevent you from overpaying for the property.

✔ **Physical inspection:** Most purchase agreements include an inspection clause mandating that you have unlimited access to the property for a certain amount of time to inspect the interior and exterior of the property. Hire qualified property inspectors, including specialists in key areas such as roofing, plumbing, and electrical systems, to conduct a thorough inspection of all rental units or suites. The results of the inspection can be used to negotiate with the seller by giving her the opportunity to make the necessary repairs, adjust the purchase price, or simply terminate the purchase agreement.

✔ **Books and records inspection:** If you're purchasing a large residential or commercial property, another important contingency is the opportunity to review and inspect the income and expense statements and the leases. Ask for a copy of the seller's Schedule E (filed with the IRS) to ensure that the income and expenses for the property are consistent with what the seller has been reporting. If the seller refuses to provide these tax documents, there is nothing you can do — but simply making the request sends a signal that he better not be misrepresenting the actual numbers. If litigation ever ensues, these documents can be subpoenaed and used as a basis to prove fraud and misrepresentation. A review of the leases should also include estoppel agreements (see Chapter 10).

✔ **ALTA property survey:** This survey shows the property boundaries or parcel map along with the site plan for all existing improvements, plus any easements and restrictions. It may be required by the lender, particularly if the loan is from an institution.

✔ **Contracts:** Make sure you receive copies of all service agreements and contracts currently in place at the property. Ideally, the seller should be required to cancel or terminate all nonessential contracts (unless they're especially attractive in the current market conditions) at the close of escrow so you have the option of bringing in your own preferred vendors.

Ironing out straggling issues

In addition to the contingency clauses, many buyers negotiate a separate clause giving them the unilateral right to extend the closing date under certain conditions. For instance, the lender may require an environmental report, which when received indicates that further investigation is necessary before it can make a loan commitment. Or you may need legal action to get access to a stubborn occupant's property. A well-written purchase agreement provides for an extension of the closing date under such circumstances. Be sure that all parties agree to any such extension in writing prior to the closing date indicated in the purchase agreement to avoid any potential disputes.

Be sure that your purchase agreement clearly indicates what personal property is included. The personal property can be a significant factor in large apartment buildings because it can include the appliances and window coverings, plus common area furnishings and fixtures, as well as parts, materials, and supplies for future maintenance and repairs.

Depending on your plans for the property, you may want the property transferred with or without tenants. If the tenants aren't on valid and enforceable long-term leases, and you can increase the property value by renovation and gaining new tenants, requiring the seller to deliver the property vacant and what's called *broom clean* (free of debris, dirt, personal property, furniture, and so on) at the close of escrow can be prudent. This is also true if you buy a seller-occupied property. Either include a clause requiring that they vacate prior to the close of escrow or negotiate a lease with them for continued tenancy at mutually agreeable terms.

Presenting the Purchase Agreement

After you and your agent are comfortable with the purchase agreement you've prepared, insist that the offer be presented by your agent in person. Although much business today is transacted electronically, the best negotiation is done eyeball-to-eyeball, and your agent can get a much better sense of the other party's personality and needs and wants through an in-person meeting.

Your offer should include a set time limit for response. Depending on the type of property and the size of the transaction, give the seller 24 to 72 hours from when you believe that he will actually first receive your offer to respond to the offer. The larger and more complicated the transaction, the more time the seller needs to evaluate your offer. The seller can accept your offer as presented, respond with a counteroffer, or even outright reject the offer or simply let it expire. After your offer for the property is accepted, you control the property and you have it *under contract*.

Chapter 14

Due Diligence, Property Inspections, and Closing

. . . .

In This Chapter

▶ Getting the ball rolling on escrow

▶ Taking care of your due diligence and property inspections

▶ Renegotiating the deal or seeking credits in escrow

▶ Considering various title-holding arrangements

▶ Finishing up the transaction

. . . .

*Y*our work as a buyer is just beginning when you have an accepted offer for your proposed acquisition, the property is under contract, and an escrow account has been opened. You control the property and can begin to determine whether the seller has accurately represented it.

In Chapters 11 and 12, we cover the pre-offer due diligence, which is essential in weeding out properties that clearly fail to meet your investment goals. Now the formal due diligence period begins. *Due diligence* is the pre-escrow process you (or your representatives) perform to investigate the property's physical and fiscal condition.

Only complete the transaction if the property physically and fiscally meets your needs and the financing is satisfactory. But the property may actually still be worth pursuing if the seller is willing to correct deficiencies or give you a monetary credit to cover your costs to complete the necessary work yourself.

In this chapter, we focus on some of the important issues in opening an escrow, conducting formal due diligence, performing property inspections, handling credits in escrow, the various methods of taking title, and ultimately closing the transaction and taking over your new property.

Opening Escrow

Escrow is a method of completing a real estate transaction in which a disinterested third party acts as the intermediary to coordinate the closing activities. The first step after the buyer and the seller sign the purchase agreement is for the *earnest money* funds (the money you give the seller upfront as partial payment and confirmation of your good faith and intent to close the deal) to be deposited with the escrow holder and put in an escrow account in the name of the buyer. (Check out www.dummies.com/extras/ realestateinvesting for a sample purchase agreement.)

A real estate transaction for even small investment properties can be complicated, because the buyer and seller have different interests that need to be fairly represented. The escrow holder acts as a neutral third party who handles the details of the transaction and often serves as the referee when disagreements develop between buyer and seller. In some parts of the country, the role of the escrow officer is much more limited. Your real estate agent can guide you as to the custom and practice in your area.

An escrow officer at an escrow company or a title company can handle escrow. Although escrow officers handle most escrows, in some areas of the country, attorneys act as the intermediary throughout the transaction. We refer to escrow officers, escrow agents, and real estate attorneys who handle the closing simply as *escrow officers* throughout this chapter.

Our good friend Ray Brown (and coauthor with Eric of *Home Buying For Dummies* [John Wiley & Sons, Inc.]) recommends that you remember that the escrow officer is a human being. Pick up the phone and introduce yourself. Ask if she has everything she needs for the transaction to go forward efficiently. Also let her know how she can reach you at various times of the day or week. Although the professional escrow officer remains an unbiased and fair intermediary, this personal touch never hurts and may make things easier if your escrow doesn't proceed smoothly.

Escrow instructions

The escrow officer prepares the escrow instructions that guide the transaction between the parties. The *escrow instructions* are derived from the specific terms found in the purchase agreement and in any other written documents mutually agreed upon by both the buyer and seller.

The escrow instructions are critical. To minimize surprises, carefully review the instructions before you sign them, because that's the document that the escrow holder relies upon exclusively to determine what to do in the event of a dispute. Unless allowed in the escrow instructions, the escrow officer can't make any changes or respond to any requests without a written agreement signed by all parties.

The escrow officer only performs items that are mutually agreed upon, in writing, by both the buyer and the seller. If the escrow officer receives conflicting information or requests, nothing happens until all parties reach an agreement or obtain a court order instructing the escrow officer. If something isn't allowed in the escrow instructions, both the seller and the buyer must present a fully executed change order to the escrow officer modifying the agreement. In other words, make sure that the escrow instructions meet your expectations before you sign them.

Preliminary title report

Soon after the escrow instructions have been signed, your title company should send you a copy of the preliminary title report (or *prelim*). Have this extremely important document reviewed by an attorney unless you have a lot of personal experience and the prelim contains relatively few indicated items.

The preliminary title report indicates the current legal owner of the property and any mortgage liens, unpaid income tax liens, property tax liens, judgment liens, or other recorded encumbrances against the property. It also shows any easements, restrictions, or third-party interests that limit your use of the property such as the Covenants, Conditions, and Restrictions (C, C, and Rs) commonly found with planned unit developments, community associations, or condominiums.

Obtain and review copies of the detailed backup materials for each item so that you know exactly what's encumbering the property. The approval of the preliminary title report by the buyer is one of the basic contingencies in most real estate transactions (see Chapter 13 for more on contingencies). You have the right (subject to certain time limitations) to cancel the purchase if the preliminary title report contains unacceptable items. Of course, you can also require the seller to have unacceptable items removed or renegotiate the price and terms in order to continue with the transaction.

The preliminary title report gives you a good idea as to whether the seller can provide you with marketable title to the property, but it isn't the same thing as title insurance, which we cover later in this chapter.

Removing contingencies

As we discuss in Chapter 13, the purchase agreement should contain a number of contingencies that allow the buyer and seller the opportunity to cancel the transaction if certain items aren't satisfactory. It's the escrow officer's job to track these contingencies and receive and follow the instructions from the buyer and seller. One of three things happens with contingencies:

- Contingencies can be approved or satisfied.
- The beneficiary of the contingency can unilaterally agree to waive or remove the contingency.
- A contingency can be rejected or fail.

Contingencies create a sort of option and are critical elements that can make or break a transaction. The purchase agreement and escrow instructions usually contain deadlines — the parties have certain rights pertaining to contingencies for a limited period of time. For example, the physical inspection contingency may provide only ten days to make the inspection; after that the contingency is considered approved (or satisfied) and the seller has the legal right to refuse access for a physical inspection.

The holder of the contingency option must notify the escrow officer at once if the contingency is rejected or fails. Also, it isn't the escrow officer's responsibility to attempt to negotiate or mediate a resolution of any rejected contingencies or other deal-threatening issues that arise during the escrow. It's up to the buyer and seller and their respective agents to come up with solutions and keep the deal alive.

Estimating the closing date

After all of the buyer's and seller's contingencies pertaining to items such as the financing, appraisal, books and records, and the physical inspection have been met or waived, the escrow officer advises the parties of the estimated closing date for the transaction.

Our experience is that when buying real estate, the process generally takes longer than planned. Therefore, if you're intent on keeping your efforts to purchase your investment property from going awry because of unanticipated delays, make provisions upfront that provide the additional time to properly close the transaction. These provisions typically take the form of closing extension options and may involve an additional payment to the seller (new money above and beyond the current agreed payments in the proposed purchase) to cover their continued costs of ownership or an increase in the amount of funds paid by the buyer to show good faith. Often you have an agreement to release some or all of the earnest money or down payment to the seller as a nonrefundable payment.

This suggestion doesn't mean that the escrow should be allowed to drag on for many months, but the more costly the property in escrow, the more likely you are to encounter unexpected challenges in satisfying or removing contingencies. Nonresidential property transactions tend to take longer to complete because the leases are more complicated to analyze and the buyer wants estoppel certificates from each tenant. (See Chapter 11 for more on estoppel certificates.) For example, lenders, with their layers of approvals and particular requirements, often cause unforeseen delays, including phase I reports (discussed later in the chapter) on potential environmental issues (particularly for non-residential properties). Also, when the real estate market is active, appraisers can be backlogged and your appraisal delayed; your loan application won't go far toward approval before the appraisal is complete.

No matter the size of your deal, negotiate the right to extend escrow. Some local Realtor boards have even developed a separate addendum that provides for extensions under certain conditions in order to enhance the likelihood of the transaction's completion. These extensions usually provide for an initial 14-day extension at no cost if the closing is delayed due to issues beyond the buyer's control. However, additional extensions are typically only allowed if the buyer compensates the seller for the equivalent of the seller's mortgage payment and/or her lost rental income if the property is vacant.

Conducting Formal Due Diligence

The formal *due diligence period* (the time period between the acceptance of an offer and the close of escrow or completion of the sale), is the time to ask those tough questions. Don't be shy. Talk to the tenants, the neighbors, any homeowner's or commercial association, governmental agencies, and the contractors or suppliers to the property, and be sure that you know what you're getting. Communicate regularly and work closely with the seller and his representatives, but only rely on information provided in writing. This time period may be your best or only opportunity to seek adjustments, if important issues have been represented inaccurately. After the property sale is completed, it's too late to ask the seller to fix the leaky roof unless she has engaged in an intentional effort to cover up the true condition of the property. Your remedies may only be in court, which can be costly and reserved only for the most serious or expensive issues.

Practical examples of due diligence include collecting economic data about the region and neighborhood, calling competitive properties for current market rental rates and concessions, verifying the accuracy of the financial information and leases presented by the seller, and conducting a thorough physical inspection of the property by a licensed general contractor or property inspector. Although you may have completed some of these items before presenting your initial offer (see Chapter 13), some of the information may have only become apparent from a review of the seller's actual books and records plus the unlimited access to the property that's generally only available during the formal due diligence.

Don't underestimate the importance of this step — this review of the books and records, along with the physical inspection, reveals the actual operations of the property and allows you to determine whether the property is suitable, fairly priced, and meets your financial goals. The due diligence period is your last chance to decide whether you should complete the transaction or cancel the escrow, get your money back, and search for a new possible acquisition.

Reviewing the books and records

Although savvy real estate investors conduct pre-offer due diligence and often receive a copy of a pro forma operating statement, you likely won't have an opportunity to review the actual books and records until you're formally under contract and in the due diligence period. Here are some things to make sure you have on hand *before* the deal is final:

- ✔ **Seller-verified income and expense statement for at least the past 12 months:** The actual income and expense history reveals any surprises that may not have been obvious from the pro forma statement you received from the seller. The best source of this information is the seller's Schedule E from her federal income tax return — you can be fairly sure that she's unlikely to overstate income or understate expenses to the IRS! After you have the most accurate numbers, you may find that the property has a serious problem with collections, or your anchor tenant's suite has several large refrigerator units tied to your common electric house meter. This statement also gives you a good idea of where to look for opportunities to improve on the financial performance of the property.

- ✔ **Seller-verified rent roll:** A *rent roll* is a list of all rental units with the tenant name, move-in date, lease expiration date, current and market rent, and the security deposit. Also, get a seller statement that no undisclosed verbal agreements, concessions, or side agreements have been made with any tenant regarding the rent, security deposits, payment of the utilities, or any other aspects of the financial terms of the lease or rental agreement.

- ✔ **Seller-verified list of all tenant security deposits on hand:** When acquiring a new rental property, follow state or local laws in properly handling the tenant's security deposit. Many state laws require the seller and/or purchaser of a rental property to advise the tenants in writing of the status of their deposit. The law usually gives the seller the right to either return the deposit to the tenant or transfer it to the new owner.

  If the seller refunds the security deposits, you have the challenge of collecting deposits from tenants already in possession of the rental unit or suite, which is never easy. For this reason, strongly urge the seller to provide you a credit for the full amount of the security deposits on hand in escrow and have each tenant agree in writing to the amount of the security deposit transferred during the sale. This strategy streamlines the process and prevents you from having to recollect security deposits from current tenants. To avoid problems at the time of move-out, send your tenant a letter confirming the security deposit amount.

✔ **Copies of the entire tenant file of each current tenant:** Make sure you have the rental application, current and past leases or rental agreements, all legal notices, maintenance work orders, and correspondence for every tenant. Also, insist that the seller advise you in writing about any pending legal action involving your tenant's occupancy.

✔ **Copies of every service agreement or contract:** Review all current contractors and service providers the current owner uses (maintenance, landscaping, pest control, boiler maintenance, and so on). If you plan to terminate the services of a contractor or service provider, the seller may be willing to send a written conditional notice of termination indicating that, if the property sells as planned, that contractor's services will no longer be needed as of the close of escrow. You can then find new contractors or maybe even renegotiate better terms with the current company.

✔ **Copies of all required governmental licenses and permits:** In many areas, rental property owners are now required to have business licenses, certificates, or permits. Contact the appropriate governmental office in writing and make sure that they're properly notified of the change in ownership and/or billing address. Often these governmental entities have stiff penalties if you fail to notify them of a change in ownership in a timely manner. And they'll eventually discover the change in ownership, because they usually monitor the local recording of deeds and receive notification of changes in billing responsibility from local utility companies. Make sure that you have current copies of all state and local rental laws and ordinances that affect your rental property.

✔ **Comprehensive list of all personal property included in the purchase:** This inventory may include appliances, equipment, and supplies owned by the current property owner. ***Remember:*** Don't assume anything is included in the sale unless you have it in writing.

✔ **Copies of the latest utility billing:** Get all of the account and payment information for every utility provider, which may include electricity, natural gas, water/sewer, trash collection, telephone, cable, and Internet access. Prior to the close of escrow, contact each company and arrange for the transfer of utilities or a change in the billing responsibility as of the estimated escrow closing date. If provided with sufficient advance notice, many utility companies can have the meters read and/or the billing cutoff coincide with the close of escrow, preventing the need to prorate any of the utility billings between the owners.

Also find out whether the seller has any deposits on hand with the utility company and whether you need to place a deposit for service. You may be able to simply handle the transfer of the deposit through escrow with a written deposit transfer acknowledgment from the utility.

If a review of the property expenses indicates that utility costs are unusually high, you may want to insist on reviewing copies of the actual historical bills in order to determine whether there was a one-time variance or whether the property may benefit from conservation efforts.

✓ **Copy of the seller's current insurance policy (if available) and the loss history:** One of the most important steps in the takeover of your new rental property is securing insurance coverage. Make sure that you have the proper insurance policy in place at the time that you legally become the new owner. Most lenders won't fund your loan until they have written evidence that the property is adequately insured. Although the seller's policy can't protect you, request a copy of her policy or declaration of coverage and the loss history, because this information can be helpful to your insurance broker or agent when analyzing the property to determine the proper coverage.

When you receive this information, verify the accuracy of all records. Most sellers are honest and don't intentionally withhold information or fail to disclose important facts; but the old adage "buyer beware" is particularly true in the purchase of rental real estate. Questions and issues that are resolved at this time can eliminate unpleasant and contentious disagreements with your tenants in the future. The takeover of your new rental property can be chaotic, but don't fall into the trap of just verbally verifying the facts. Verify all information in writing and set up a detailed filing system for your new property. Ultimately, the best proof of the expenses is to insist on receiving copies of last year's invoices to verify operating costs such as utilities.

With experience, you'll be able to evaluate a property with surprising accuracy just by looking at the actual income and expenses. Look for discrepancies between the pro forma operating statement given to you during pre-offer due diligence and the actual income and expense numbers provided by the seller during escrow due diligence. There are many tricks that sellers and their brokers try to get past the unwary buyer. For example, watch for property tax numbers that will significantly increase upon a sale of the property if such taxes are based on the market value of a property or sales price. Also, be careful if the rent roll lists vacant units at higher market-rent rates that exceed the actual rental rate for the occupied units.

Inspecting the property

The condition of a property directly affects its value. The prudent real estate investor always insists on a thorough physical inspection before purchasing an investment property even if the property is brand new.

A new investment property may look good on paper and your pre-offer due diligence may reveal no legal or financial issues or concerns. But your investment is only as good as the weakest link, and a physically troubled property is never a good investment (unless you're buying the property for the land and plan to demolish the current buildings).

You're probably making one of the biggest financial purchases and commitments of your life. Though real estate investors by nature tend to be frugal, never try to save money by foregoing a proper physical inspection by qualified experts. Unless you have extensive experience as a builder and contractor, you probably have no idea what you're getting into when it comes to evaluating the condition of most building systems. But even if you have experience, never rely on your own inspection entirely or try to save money by cutting corners. Even experienced and fully qualified real estate investors can find their judgment tainted by an emotional attachment to the property.

Our experience shows that an inspection usually pays for itself. Inevitably, you're going to find items that the seller needs to correct that are greater in value or cost to repair than the nominal sum you spend on the inspection. This value isn't just a marketing ploy by inspection firms, but it also isn't a game that you "win" if you can offset the inspection cost by finding enough items that the seller must correct or provide credit in escrow for — as some real estate gurus seem to believe. Instead, the inspection is a serious matter and not just a way to squeeze more from the seller.

The best result is if the inspection reveals no problems. Although you've spent money, it's a great relief to know that your property (at least at the time of the inspection) is in good condition. That doesn't mean there won't be repair or replacement items that need your attention in the future, possibly even the very near future. In Robert's early days in real estate investing, he worked for an apartment developer whose favorite saying was "To own is to maintain!"

Virtually all real estate purchase contracts provide that the transaction can be canceled without penalty or loss of the earnest money deposit if the buyer's physical inspection isn't satisfactory. But often, additional negotiations between the buyer and seller result. It's this competently prepared written inspection report that provides the information you need and serves as the basis to go back and ask the property seller to fix the problems or reduce the property's purchase price (see the "Negotiating Credits in Escrow" section later in the chapter).

Savvy real estate investors actually have a two-step inspection process with their initial pre-offer walk-through of the property as a prelude to even making the offer. If the offer is made and accepted, the professional inspection is to identify any deal-killer problems with the property or any items that warrant renegotiation. You're looking for two types of defects:

✔ **Patent defects:** Defects that are readily visible by simply looking at the property. Patent defects may be a broken window or a leaking faucet.

✔ **Latent defects:** Hidden and hard-to-see defects that require intrusive or even destructive testing. Examples include corroding copper pipes underneath the slab or ceiling or window leaks that the owner has cosmetically repaired through patching and painting to hide from potential buyers. That is why disclosures are so important.

Disclosure requirements

With purchases of a residential rental property with four or fewer units, many states have seller *disclosure requirements:* Sellers must provide the buyer with a written transfer disclosure statement that outlines all known structural and mechanical deficiencies. In many areas, sellers must also complete a comprehensive information questionnaire. The agents, if any, for both parties also complete a written disclosure indicating that they've made a reasonably diligent visual inspection of the interior and exterior of the property.

However, investors purchasing residential investment properties with five or more units or any type of commercial property typically don't have the same legislative protections. This discrepancy is based on the premise that these buyers and sellers and their respective agents are more sophisticated and don't need the mandatory protections of a formal written *transfer disclosure statement* (commonly abbreviated as *TDS form*).

Whether the transfer disclosure statement form is legally required or not, sellers in some states still have a legal duty to disclose any and all material facts that could impact the value or intended use of the property. For example, if the property had severe roof leaks last winter and the roof hasn't been competently repaired, the seller must disclose this fact. Even if the roof had major leaks and was professionally repaired, an ethical seller will disclose this fact and provide you with a copy of the invoice outlining the specific work done and the individual or firm that performed the repairs.

The as-is gambit

Some sellers attempt to avoid any disclosures by proposing that their property is being sold to you strictly on an as-is and where-is basis. The theory (which is supported by many late-night real estate gurus when they're the seller) is that an as-is sale means that the seller isn't required to correct any deficiencies in the property before the completion of the sale and they're not responsible for any issues that arise after the sale. They erroneously believe that such terms are legally enforceable under all conditions and act as a blanket disclaimer against claims of misrepresentation, fraud, or negligence. However, in most areas of the country, the as-is strategy only offers minimal protection to the seller.

Be extremely careful if considering the purchase of a property offered on an as-is basis. An as-is property is a major red flag; you should sincerely consider whether it's worth the increased risk. Although the seller may simply be following the ill-advised recommendations of their broker or seminar guru, some sellers are dishonest and hide significant issues that reduce the property's true value. A property offered on an as-is basis significantly below the expected market value is rarely a good deal.

Likewise, when you're selling your investment property, don't attempt to hide behind the as-is language. This technique isn't effective and hurts your reputation as a real estate investor. Our advice, regardless of any legal requirements, is to *disclose, disclose, disclose*. Fully document all disclosures in writing, with copies of any invoices or reports, because failure to disclose material facts that affect the value or use of the property is a serious issue and one that often finds its way to the courthouse for resolution.

You also want to be aware of some tactics that sellers may use to avoid inspections. Refer to www.dummies.com/extras/realestateinvesting.

Types of inspections

If you can get full access to the property, go ahead and conduct your own brief physical exterior and interior inspection before making your offer. This initial overview doesn't cost anything other than your time and keeps you from wasting further time on properties that have obvious major problems. But this walk-through is no substitute for a professional inspection.

Don't rush the inspection process. The seller must give you complete and unfettered access to the entire property. Don't agree to any unreasonable time or access limitations. We've seen sneaky sellers who unrealistically limit access to the property, particularly if it's occupied. Make sure that the tenants have been properly notified, as required by law and/or their lease agreements, with a liberal access time period so that you can thoroughly conduct all of your inspections without interference or interruptions.

There are generally three types of professional inspections performed during the due diligence period while your property is in escrow, and we cover them in the following sections.

Physical or structural inspection

Naturally, you as the buyer want to have all of the physical aspects of the structures on your property inspected. However, your lender may also require you to pay for a separate physical assessment or property inspection report by a firm of its choice. This stipulation is typical only for medium to large residential and commercial types of properties.

You can also have your architect inspect the property and determine any changes of use or modernization that will enhance the property. Because the key to success in real estate is in creating value, a professional architect can be an invaluable team member who can offer many suggestions. Of course, she can also quickly tell you that your plans aren't structurally or fiscally feasible, and you can move on to another potential property.

Areas that you want to hire people to help you inspect include

- ✔ Overall condition of property
- ✔ Structural integrity
- ✔ Foundation/slab, crawl space, basements, subflooring, and decks
- ✔ Roof and attic
- ✔ Plumbing systems, including fixtures, supply lines, drains, and water heating devices
- ✔ Electrical systems, including all service panels, generators, and ground-fault circuit-interrupters (GFCI)
- ✔ Life safety systems, including smoke detectors, carbon monoxide detectors, radon detectors, intrusion alarms, and fire alarms or fire panels
- ✔ Heating and air conditioning systems
- ✔ Landscaping, irrigation, and drainage
- ✔ Doorways, walls, and windows
- ✔ Moisture intrusion and insulation
- ✔ Seismic, land movement, or subsidence (sinking) and flood risk
- ✔ Illegal construction or additions and zoning violations

Some specific telltale signs indicate the property may have serious structural issues and require further investigation:

- ✔ **Cracks:** Look at the entire property, including foundation, floor coverings, walls, ceilings, window and door frames, chimney, and any retaining walls, for cracks. Don't let the seller or her agent tell you these cracks are merely settlement cracks; let your qualified property inspector or other qualified professional make that determination. A few isolated hairline cracks may be naturally occurring settlement of the structure over time, but if you can stick a screwdriver into the crack, something else is going on.

- ✔ **Unleveled or squishy floors:** As you walk through the property, pay attention to any slant or sloping of the floors (you can easily check by using a level). Also watch for any soft spots in the flooring on upper levels, including the ground floor if the property has a raised foundation with a crawl space or basement.

- ✔ **Misaligned structure:** Buy one of those handy laser levels and walk through the property looking for floors, walls, and ceilings that are uneven or out of plumb. Another sign of misalignment is when doors or windows stick and don't open or close easily (although that can also happen from being painted shut).

✔ **Soil issues:** Excess groundwater, poor drainage, or cracked/bulging retaining walls or concrete hardscape can be signs of soil issues such as slope failure or ground subsidence that requires inspection by a civil or soils engineer. Be sure that the property drains properly and that all drains are properly installed and maintained.

✔ **Moisture intrusion:** Look for current and historical indications of leaks such as discoloration and stains on ceilings, walls, and particularly around window and door frames. Musty odors or the smell of mold may be merely stale air or poor housekeeping, or they may indicate ongoing moisture issues. Sump pumps anywhere on the property are a red flag that should be explored in detail.

✔ **Plumbing leaks:** Have a qualified plumbing contractor or other expert check all possible sources of leaks or moisture — under sinks, supply lines for faucets, toilets, dishwashers, and washing machines, plus roofs, windows, sprinklers, and drainage away from the building.

Don't buy a property with the polybutylene domestic water supply systems (Qest was the most widely known brand and was manufactured from 1978 through 1995). The track record for these products hasn't been acceptable. Many properties experienced an extremely high rate of failure that resulted in class-action lawsuits and settlement funds for redoing these plumbing-affected properties. Unfortunately, the deadline for claims in the most prominent of these settlements was in 2008 and 2009 so don't let anyone tell you now that you can simply replumb such a property and make a claim for reimbursement.

Carefully inspect for any signs of water intrusion. Allegations of property damage and serious negative health effects from resulting environmental toxins and mold are a real problem for both residential and commercial rental property owners throughout the country.

And to minimize the chance of having to deal with unpleasant calls from tenants in the middle of the night, we strongly advise that you immediately install steel-braided supply lines on all water sources — including sinks, toilets, dishwashers, and washing machines. Also, make sure to check that sink and bathtub overflow drains aren't clogged and are properly connected.

Pest control and property damage

Pest control firms are the natural choice for this type of inspection, but what they inspect is actually more than just infestations by termites, bedbugs, carpenter ants, powder post beetles, and other wood-destroying insects. A thorough pest control and property damage inspection also looks at property damage caused by organisms that infect and incessantly break down and destroy wood and other building materials. These conditions are commonly referred to as *dry rot,* but ironically they're actually a fungus that requires moisture to flourish.

The report you receive from your pest control and property damage inspector usually includes a simple diagram of the property with notations as to the location of certain conditions noted. Some require attention immediately; others are simply areas to watch in the future:

- ✔ **Part I items:** The most serious problems are infestations or infections that must be dealt with at once to protect the structure from serious damage. These recommendations may also include the repair and replacement of compromised structural elements. Unless otherwise agreed, the seller is virtually always required to pay for this work. Your lender won't fund the property loan until a professional pest control firm and/or licensed contractor completes such required work.

- ✔ **Part II items:** These items are recommended but not required work; as a prudent real estate investor, you'll address them yourself right after the close of escrow or will require the seller to take care of them before completing the purchase. These items may not be a current structural deficiency that endangers the property or occupants, but if not corrected, they may cost substantially more to repair in the future. If not resolved now, these conditions will continue to fester and develop into required items that must be addressed when you sell the property later on.

Environmental issues

For commercial and residential rental investment properties with five or more units, a lender usually requires a *phase I environmental report,* which reviews the property records for the site, including all prior owners and uses of the property and aerial photographs and may include a site visit, but no testing.

Review the report prepared for the lender at your expense, and make sure that there are no surprises. Only purchase properties if they have a clear environmental report, regardless of the price. The downside of environmentally challenged properties is so significant that you should obtain the phase I environmental report even if you're purchasing the property for cash.

Most properties don't have problems, and the phase I report is all that is required. But Robert has had clients whose purchase came to a complete halt over something as simple as car engine crankcase oil in the dumpster area of an apartment building. Such a condition results in a negative phase I report, making further investigation and remediation necessary. Problems found in the phase I report can be ridiculously expensive and cause delays of several weeks or even months while additional testing and analysis takes place, a phase II environmental assessment report is prepared, and contractors complete the required work per the specifications outlined by the environmental engineers and consultants.

Also be extremely careful when purchasing commercial, retail, and industrial properties, particularly if they have certain types of tenants, such as dry cleaners, photographers, gas stations, auto repair, and any industrial tenants that use petroleum solvents. Watch out for any property, and especially vacant spaces, sporting the ubiquitous 55-gallon drums.

Have an environmental engineer check drains and pipes that connect to the storm drain system or sewer to ensure that toxic or hazardous materials haven't been disposed of through your proposed property. If the EPA or comparable state agency later determines that the source of the contaminants was your property, you could face a budget-busting cleanup bill. The governmental agencies don't care that these violations occurred under prior ownership.

Lenders are extremely concerned about making a loan on a property with the potential for environmental hazards. They know that many buyers would simply walk away from the property and leave them with the devastating cost of cleaning up the property. That's why most lenders now require buyers to remain personally responsible for environmental issues even if the loan is *nonrecourse* (the lender can only foreclose on the underlying property in the event of a default). This provision is commonly referred to as a *carve-out* and is designed to protect the lender from owners who may be tempted to bail out and leave the lender on the hook for a contaminated property.

Qualifying the inspectors

Just like selecting the closing agent, many real estate investors pick inspectors as an afterthought or simply take the recommendation of their real estate agent. But inspect the property inspectors before you hire one. As with other service professionals, interview a few inspectors before making your selection. You may find that they don't all share the same experience, qualifications, and ethical standards. For example, don't hire an inspector that hesitates or refuses to allow you to accompany her during the inspection.

The inspection is actually a unique opportunity for most property owners and, because you're paying, we strongly recommend that you join the inspector while he's assessing your proposed purchase. What you learn can be invaluable and may pay dividends throughout your entire ownership. When an unscrupulous contractor later tries to tell you that you need to completely replumb your property, you can tell him to get lost if your property inspection revealed only isolated problems that can be resolved inexpensively.

About half of the states now have a license or certification requirement whereas a few only have trade practice guidelines. This regulation is all relatively new because in 2000 virtually no governmental licensing or supervision of inspectors existed. Regardless of whether your state has strict licensing or certification requirements, every real estate investor needs to look out for her own interests and look for telltale signs of potential problems. Red flags include inspectors who are affiliated with a contractor, offer a special discount if you call whom they recommend, or credit their inspection fee toward work.

Only consider full-time, professional inspectors. Hire an inspector who performs at least 100 comprehensive inspections per year and carries errors and omissions insurance. Such coverage isn't cheap and is another key indicator that the person is working full-time in the field and is participating in ongoing continuing education.

Many inspectors are licensed general contractors, but not all home inspectors have designations or credentials specifically relating to inspecting real estate. One of the best certifying trade associations for professional property inspectors is the American Society of Home Inspectors (ASHI), which was founded in 1976. In addition to home inspections, many ASHI members are qualified and experienced enough to assist you with your due diligence physical or structural exterior and interior inspection of multifamily residential properties and all types of commercial properties. You can find certified inspectors and more info about the inspection process including tips and checklists at www.ashi.org.

Some individuals or companies adopt names that at first glance may indicate adherence to certain professional practices. For example, a fictitious but potentially misleading name is "Professional Property Inspection Association." Do some research to find the best state or regional association and one whose qualified members adopt a code of ethics. For example, in California, the California Real Estate Inspection Association (CREIA) is the group that offers education and designations for real estate inspectors.

Review a copy of inspectors' résumés to see what certifications and licenses they hold. A general contractor's license and certification as a property inspector are important, but also find out whether they've had any specialized training and whether they hold any specific sublicenses in areas such as roofing, electrical, or plumbing. These can be particularly important if your proposed property has evidence of potential problems in any of these areas. For example, if a property has a history of roofing or moisture intrusion problems, an inspector who's a general contractor and roofer is an extra plus.

The inspection report must be written, and to avoid surprises, request a sample of one of the recent inspection reports that have been prepared for a comparable property. This simple request may eliminate several potential inspectors but is essential so that you can see whether an inspector is qualified and how detailed a report he will prepare for you. Check out Figures 14-1 and 14-2 for a sample interior inspection checklist.

The advent of digital photography is a boon to property inspectors and makes their sometimes mundane and difficult-to-understand reports come to life. Select a technologically savvy inspector and require her to electronically send you her report, including digital photos documenting all of the

Unit Inspection Checklist

____ Mold   General condition of rental units   ___ Plastic Supply Lines

Tenant Name(s) _____   Unit Number _____   Date _____

Kitchen	Condition:					Appliances	Condition:				
Floors/floor covering	E	G	F	P	N/A	**Gas stove/oven**					
Walls & ceiling	E	G	F	P	N/A	Outside	E	G	F	P	N/A
Windows/locks/screens	E	G	F	P	N/A	Burners	E	G	F	P	N/A
Window coverings	E	G	F	P	N/A	Drip pans	E	G	F	P	N/A
Doors/knobs	E	G	F	P	N/A	Hood vent/microwave	E	G	F	P	N/A
Light fixtures/bulbs	E	G	F	P	N/A	Timer/controls	E	G	F	P	N/A
Cabinets/cupboards	E	G	F	P	N/A	Broiler pan	E	G	F	P	N/A
Drawers/countertops	E	G	F	P	N/A	Light	E	G	F	P	N/A
Shelves/drawers	E	G	F	P	N/A	Other _____	E	G	F	P	N/A
Sinks/stoppers/faucets	E	G	F	P	N/A	**Refrigerator (Size _____)**					
Drains/plumbing	E	G	F	P	N/A	Outside	E	G	F	P	N/A
Other _____	E	G	F	P	N/A	Inside	E	G	F	P	N/A
Dishwasher						Ice trays	E	G	F	P	N/A
Outside	E	G	F	P	N/A	Other _____	E	G	F	P	N/A
Rack	E	G	F	P	N/A	**Garbage disposal**	E	G	F	P	N/A
Other _____	E	G	F	P	N/A	**Angle stops/supply lines**	E	G	F	P	N/A

General comments, including specific notes for all health & safety issues: _____

_____

_____

Living Room						Dining Room					
Floors/floor covering	E	G	F	P	N/A	Floors/floor covering	E	G	F	P	N/A
Walls & ceiling	E	G	F	P	N/A	Walls & ceiling	E	G	F	P	N/A
Windows/locks/screens	E	G	F	P	N/A	Windows/locks/screens	E	G	F	P	N/A
Window coverings	E	G	F	P	N/A	Doors/locks	E	G	F	P	N/A
Doors/locks	E	G	F	P	N/A	Ceiling fans/bulbs	E	G	F	P	N/A
Light fixtures/bulbs	E	G	F	P	N/A	Closet/shelves	E	G	F	P	N/A
Closet/shelves	E	G	F	P	N/A	Other _____	E	G	F	P	N/A
Fireplace	E	G	F	P	N/A	Other _____	E	G	F	P	N/A

General comments, including specific notes for all health & safety issues: _____

_____

_____

Hall						Bedroom 1 (smallest)					
Floors/floor covering	E	G	F	P	N/A	Floors/floor covering	E	G	F	P	N/A
Walls & ceiling	E	G	F	P	N/A	Walls & ceiling	E	G	F	P	N/A
Windows/locks/screens	E	G	F	P	N/A	Windows/locks/screens	E	G	F	P	N/A
Window coverings	E	G	F	P	N/A	Window coverings	E	G	F	P	N/A
Doors/knobs/locks	E	G	F	P	N/A	Doors/knobs/locks	E	G	F	P	N/A
Light fixtures/bulbs	E	G	F	P	N/A	Light fixtures/bulbs	E	G	F	P	N/A
Closet/shelves	E	G	F	P	N/A	Closet/shelves	E	G	F	P	N/A
Doorbell	E	G	F	P	N/A	Other _____	E	G	F	P	N/A

Guest or 2nd Bedroom						Master Bedroom					
Floors/floor covering	E	G	F	P	N/A	Floors/floor covering	E	G	F	P	N/A
Walls & ceiling	E	G	F	P	N/A	Walls & ceiling	E	G	F	P	N/A
Windows/locks/screens	E	G	F	P	N/A	Windows/locks/screens	E	G	F	P	N/A
Window coverings	E	G	F	P	N/A	Window coverings	E	G	F	P	N/A
Doors/knobs/locks	E	G	F	P	N/A	Doors/knobs/locks	E	G	F	P	N/A
Closets/shelves	E	G	F	P	N/A	Closets/shelves	E	G	F	P	N/A
Light fixtures/bulbs	E	G	F	P	N/A	Light fixtures/bulbs	E	G	F	P	N/A
Other _____	E	G	F	P	N/A	Other _____	E	G	F	P	N/A

General comments, including specific notes for all health & safety issues: _____

_____

_____

Figure 14-1: Sample interior unit inspection checklist Robert uses for large multifamily apartment communities (page 1 of 2).

Unit Inspection Checklist (Side 2)
General condition of rental units

Condition:

Master Bath

Floors/floor covering	E	G	F	P	N/A
Walls/tile/grout/ceiling	E	G	F	P	N/A
Windows/locks/screens	E	G	F	P	N/A
Window coverings	E	G	F	P	N/A
Doors/knobs/locks	E	G	F	P	N/A
Light fixtures/bulbs	E	G	F	P	N/A
Exhaust fan/heater	E	G	F	P	N/A
Counters/shelves	E	G	F	P	N/A
Mirrors/cabinets	E	G	F	P	N/A
Sink/basin/faucets	E	G	F	P	N/A
Angle stops/supply lines	E	G	F	P	N/A
Drains/plumbing	E	G	F	P	N/A
Tub/shower/caulking	E	G	F	P	N/A
Shower head/tub faucet	E	G	F	P	N/A
Shower door/curtains	E	G	F	P	N/A
Shower tracks	E	G	F	P	N/A
Towel racks	E	G	F	P	N/A
Toilet bowl/seat	E	G	F	P	N/A
Toilet paper holder	E	G	F	P	N/A
Other _____	E	G	F	P	N/A

Condition:

Bathroom 2

Floors/floor covering	E	G	F	P	N/A
Walls/tile/grout/ceiling	E	G	F	P	N/A
Windows/locks/screens	E	G	F	P	N/A
Window coverings	E	G	F	P	N/A
Doors/knobs/locks	E	G	F	P	N/A
Light fixtures/bulbs	E	G	F	P	N/A
Exhaust fan/heater	E	G	F	P	N/A
Counters/shelves	E	G	F	P	N/A
Mirrors/cabinets	E	G	F	P	N/A
Sink/basin/faucets	E	G	F	P	N/A
Angle stops/supply lines	E	G	F	P	N/A
Drains/plumbing	E	G	F	P	N/A
Tub/shower/caulking	E	G	F	P	N/A
Shower head/tub faucet	E	G	F	P	N/A
Shower door/curtains	E	G	F	P	N/A
Shower tracks	E	G	F	P	N/A
Towel racks	E	G	F	P	N/A
Toilet bowl/seat	E	G	F	P	N/A
Toilet paper holder	E	G	F	P	N/A
Other _____	E	G	F	P	N/A

General comments, including specific notes for all health & safety issues: _____
_____
_____

Other Items

Gas hot water heater	E	G	F	P	N/A
Heating/thermostat	E	G	F	P	N/A
Heat pump; A/C	E	G	F	P	N/A
A/C filters & vents	E	G	F	P	N/A
Cable TV/antenna	E	G	F	P	N/A
Electrical system	E	G	F	P	N/A
Telephone	E	G	F	P	N/A
Other _____	E	G	F	P	N/A

Smoke Detectors

Date, if replaced

Hallway	OK	Inoperative	_____
1st bedroom	OK	Inoperative	_____
Guest or 2nd bedroom	OK	Inoperative	_____
Master bedroom	OK	Inoperative	_____

Laundry Equipment

Washer	E	G	F	P	N/A
Gas dryer	E	G	F	P	N/A

General comments, including specific notes for all health & safety issues: _____
_____
_____

Moisture Intrusion/Mold/Mildew (record location and detailed description, including possible source)
_____
_____

Tenant Profile

Health/Safety/Housekeeping issues: Y   N   Describe: _____
_____

Other potential lease violations: Y   N   Describe: _____

Pet?   Y   N   Type _____   Problems: _____
_____

Additional Items/Comments
_____
_____
_____
_____
_____

Figure 14-2:
Sample interior unit inspection checklist (page 2 of 2).

conditions noted. With the report in the electronic realm, it's a simple process to email this information as needed.

Although the cost of the inspection should be set and determined in advance, the price should be a secondary concern because inspection fees often pay for themselves. Just like many other professional services, there is a direct correlation between the pricing of your inspection and the amount of time the inspector takes to conduct the inspection and then prepare the report. If the inspector only spends a couple of hours at your new 20-unit apartment building, whatever you pay her is too much.

Finally, require the finalists to provide the names and phone numbers of at least ten people who used the company's services within the past six months. Randomly call and make sure that these clients were satisfied and that the inspector acted professionally and ethically.

Negotiating Credits in Escrow

Most purchase agreements require the seller to deliver the property in good physical condition with all basic systems in operational order unless otherwise indicated. But the inspection process often reveals deficiencies that need to be corrected. For example, the physical and structural inspection by the property inspector may indicate the need to repair a defective ground-fault circuit-interrupter (GFCI), or the pest control and property damage report may show evidence of drywood termites that need to be eradicated.

So with your inspection reports in hand, preferably with digital photos, you're prepared to contact the seller's representative(s) and arrange for the seller to correct the noted items at his expense. The seller may debate some of the items and claim that the property is being sold as-is even if he didn't previously indicate any such thing. Be prepared to refer him to the warranty of condition clause in your copy of the purchase agreement; hopefully he takes care of the problems without any further grumbling or delay.

Some sellers and buyers actually prefer to handle deficiencies through a monetary credit in escrow in favor of the buyer so that the buyer can make the needed repairs on his or her own. This route is particularly beneficial if you plan on making significant renovations to the property or the item is one of a personal nature — like the type and color of replacement carpet for a rental house. In that case, giving you a credit that you can use to pick the type, grade, and color of carpeting or even an entirely different type of floor covering that suits your needs is a sensible approach. The seller shouldn't be concerned as long as the amount is equal or less than his cost to do the work; plus, the seller doesn't have the hassle of coordinating the work or making payments.

Negotiating for repairs or monetary credits can be challenging, and knowing where to draw the line can be difficult. Requiring the seller to make needed repairs or give a credit in escrow is common in most transactions and fully accepted in the industry. But some buyers use the due diligence period to completely renegotiate the purchase agreement. They make a virtually full-price offer with long contingency time frames for the physical inspection so they can keep the property off the market for an extended period. Then they have their inspection team scour the property looking for every single item that's wrong so they can demand that the seller significantly lower the price. Because the buyer has the property tied up, the seller is unable to cancel escrow and move on to another, more reasonable buyer. This strategy may work once or twice but will quickly earn you a negative reputation among sellers and agents. You may soon find it difficult to buy additional properties.

A buyer who receives a credit in escrow is often anxious to get started on making improvements to get the property in rent-ready condition immediately upon the close of escrow. Although tempting, you should be wary of making significant renovation or repairs to the property before the close of escrow. If the sale of the property doesn't go through, you may have spent considerable sums to upgrade the seller's property without any recourse.

As a buyer, use the escrow time period to your advantage and obtain all of your bids and proposals so that you're ready to begin as soon as the escrow closes. We recommend that you formulate your renovations and marketing plan in advance, but only sign contracts that contain a contingency clause that the agreement is null and void if your transaction doesn't go through, and only begin the actual work after you legally have title to the property.

Determining How to Hold Title

You must bear many issues in mind when deciding how to take title to your new investment property. Maintaining your privacy, minimizing your tax burden, and protecting your assets from claims and creditors are critical elements to most real estate investors. Take the time to evaluate and decide the most opportune way to take title to your property.

Don't allow the form of ownership to be made as an afterthought! Many real estate investors don't take this decision seriously and by default take title on the advice of their real estate agent or the closing agent. Sometimes the first discussion about how title will be taken is when it's time to sign the documents and close escrow.

Of course, there's no one single right answer to the question of how to hold title, because each real estate investor or investment group has different perspectives and needs. The legal forms of ownership vary from state to state, so check your options with the assistance of legal, accounting, and tax advisors. To make the best decision, you need the assistance of your real estate team (see Chapter 6). Consult with your tax advisor and attorney to understand the current ramifications as well as consider the impact on your estate planning needs and goals.

After reviewing the options of taking title and deciding which one is best for your proposed real estate investment, make sure that you inform your escrow officer so that the deed is properly prepared for your signature just before closing your escrow.

In the following sections, we review some of the basics of each form of ownership — including privacy, taxation, and protection considerations — so you can build a working understanding of the pros and cons of each of the primary alternatives available.

Sole proprietorship

A *sole proprietorship* is certainly the easiest and cheapest form of ownership and requires no special prerequisites. Simply have title to the property vested in the name of an individual person on the deed, and you have a sole proprietorship. Other advantages include the following:

- ✔ **Exclusive rights of ownership:** You have complete control and discretion over the use of the property and the right to sell, bequeath, or encumber the property any way you see fit.

- ✔ **Minimal legal costs to establish:** You may need a business license or to register with your state as a DBA (doing business as), but generally there are no additional legal expenses to set up and maintain a sole proprietorship.

- ✔ **Simple record keeping:** It can be a negative if you aren't disciplined.

However, sole proprietorship also has its downsides, including the following:

- ✔ **Unlimited liabilities:** You have no legal protections against lawsuits or other claims (even if caused by an employee), and your name is easily obtained through public records. Other forms of ownership can create a barrier between you and claimants and creditors.

- ✔ **No real tax advantages:** Sole proprietorships offer no real advantages in the area of death and taxes! All income and expenses are reported directly on your personal tax return, and there is no preferential tax treatment or avoidance of the probate courts in the event of your death.

- ✔ **Possible marriage complications:** A sole proprietorship can become complicated if you're married or later get married and intend to keep your investment property as a separately held asset. Check with your tax advisor before making any significant changes in your marital status because you need to keep detailed accounting records to avoid any commingling of funds from community property that could create an interest for a spouse in the real property.

Joint tenancy

Joint tenancy is a way in which two or more individuals may hold title to a property together where they own equal shares of the property. Joint tenancy is only available to individuals (not legal corporate entities) because a unique feature of holding title in a joint tenancy is the *right of survivorship.* Upon the death of one of the joint tenants, the entire ownership automatically vests in equal shares to the surviving individual or individuals without going through the probate process.

In order to form a joint tenancy, there must be unity of time, title, interest, and possession. *Unity of time* means that all joint tenants must take title by the same deed at the same time. Another requirement is that each joint tenant own an equal interest or percentage of the property — so if you have two joint tenants, they each own 50 percent, whereas four joint tenants would each own 25 percent of the entire property. Any ownership of a property in disproportionate shares can't be a joint tenancy.

Each joint tenant is legally entitled to the right of possession and can't be excluded by the others. Some states specifically require the joint tenancy deed to include the wording "joint tenants with right of survivorship."

One concern is that joint tenants can sell, bequeath, or encumber their portion of the property without the consent of the other owners. It's possible for the joint tenancy to be terminated in the event of a judgment lien or bankruptcy. Likewise, a new joint tenant can only be added by executing a new deed. Income and expenses from operations of the property are reported on each individual's tax return.

Another unique advantage to joint tenancy, besides the right of survivorship, is that you get a stepped up basis on your deceased joint tenant's portion of the property. Receiving a *stepped-up basis* means that the taxable basis is increased for the portion of the property owned by the deceased joint tenant to the current market value at the time of death. This ability can be a tremendous benefit for the surviving joint tenants and allows them to sell the property with significantly lower taxes.

For example, suppose two joint tenants buy a property for $200,000. Many years later, one of the joint tenants dies, and the property is appraised at $300,000. The new adjusted basis for the surviving joint tenant is $250,000 representing the original basis of $100,000 plus $150,000 (one half of $300,000) for the deceased joint tenant's interest. This basis is important when calculating the gain or loss upon sale of the property, so having the basis increase can dramatically lower your taxable capital gain (see Chapter 18 for details).

Although marriage isn't a requirement to use this method of holding title, traditionally, joint tenancy has been the most common way for married couples to hold title to investment properties. One of the primary advantages of joint tenancy is that the death of one spouse can result in a complete step up in basis to the fair market value at the time of death rather than just a step up for the portion owned by the deceased joint tenant. Depending where you reside, states have additional options for married couples, such as community property or tenants by the entireties. Refer to www.dummies.com/extras/realestateinvesting for information about community property and tenancy by entireties.

Tenancy in common

One of the most common forms of co-ownership is *tenancy in common* (also known as *tenants in common* or TIC). A tenancy in common is the ownership of real property in which several owners each own a stated portion or share of the entire property. In most states, if the deed is silent as to the form of ownership, tenancy in common is the presumed method of holding title.

Unlike joint tenancy, in a tenancy in common, each owner can own a different percentage, can take title at any time, and can sell his interest at any time. Another distinguishing characteristic is that each owner has complete control over her portion of the property and can sell, bequeath, or mortgage her interest as she personally decides without any feedback from or recourse for the other owners. Further, upon her death, her share becomes part of her estate and can be willed as she sees fit.

Tenants in common products are now being aggressively touted by financial advisors as an investment product of choice for the owners of appreciated real estate who are looking for a more passive investment without the challenges of property management. These investments offer the investor a way to own fractionalized interests in real estate and can be structured as direct ownership of property with a deed for their interest, or many are actually security interests. The sponsored tenants in common products usually have a management agreement or governing document to address issues of control and avoid the problems discussed later in this chapter.

Tenancy in common is a popular way to hold title for real estate investors but can be a problem unless there are clear understandings, preferably in writing, as to the asset and property management decisions of operating the property. But even then, problems and challenges are possible:

- ✔ **Death of an owner:** You may find that a co-owner has left his interest in a property you partially own to someone that you don't get along with.

- ✔ **Sale by an owner:** Because each owner has equal rights of control over the property, serious conflicts may arise when one owner wants to sell or borrow against the property. Or an owner may decide to sell to an individual or entity, which disrupts the spirit of cooperation among the various owners.

✔ **Financial problems of an owner:** You're financially tied to your co-owners for better or worse even in their activities other than the jointly owned property. A judgment against one of the co-owners could lead to the creditor foreclosing on that co-owner's interest in the property to satisfy a monetary judgment. Or a bankruptcy by one co-owner could lead to the bankruptcy court ordering a forced sale of the property to satisfy the bankruptcy creditors unless the other co-owners were willing to pay off the creditors and buy out the financially challenged co-owner.

✔ **Different plans:** Each co-owner may have a different goals and strategy for the property or the way it should be managed. With tenancy in common ownership, absent a written governing document, there's no majority rule or simple way to arbitrate differences in opinions. Because a single owner can thwart the mutual plans of all the others, disagreements about whether to borrow money by using the property as collateral or whether to sell the property can result in a legal action. Robert has served as a court-appointed referee in several of these actions (called *partitions*), and they can be quite stressful for the parties — who can't seem to agree on anything!

Income and expenses from operations of the property are reported on the individual's tax return, but a problem with tenants in common is that new investors acquiring a TIC interest may not qualify for the tax-deferral benefits generally associated with a 1031 like-kind exchange. The promoters and sponsors of the TIC programs often portray these investments as the answer to all your needs, but in reality, they aren't giving folks the full story. *Buyer beware* — before making any move, consult your tax advisor about the tax ramifications of selling appreciated real estate and investing the proceeds into a tenants in common or fractionized interest. *Liquidity* (ability to sell your interest) is also a concern because there are currently no public secondary markets for tenants in common interests. See our comments in Chapter 4, and remember: If it seems too good to be true, it probably is!

Partnerships

A real estate *partnership* is a form of business enterprise in which two or more persons join together to pool their capital and talent to purchase, manage, and ultimately sell real estate. Investors in a real estate partnership don't have actual title or ownership interest directly in the property but actually own a partnership interest.

Although a partnership interest technically is transferable, a partner seeking to sell will find few, if any, ready buyers and will likely have to severely discount his asking price below its intrinsic value. The best option is to negotiate a buy/sell agreement prior to acquiring any properties in which the terms are thoroughly discussed and each partner has the ability to leave at any time based on predetermined criteria. Often, such agreements call for the other partners to purchase the outgoing partner's share.

A partnership isn't a corporation, and generally takes one of two forms:

- ✔ In a **general partnership,** each partner has the right to fully participate in the management and operations of the property and each partner is fully responsible for the debt, legal obligations, and any business losses incurred. General partnerships are easy to establish, but a serious concern is that each individual partner is able to contract on behalf of the partnership and all partners are then legally liable for these actions. Another disadvantage of a general partnership is that the death, bankruptcy, or withdrawal of one of the general partners may require the dissolution and complete reorganization of the general partnership.

- ✔ A **limited partnership** consists of one or more general partners along with one or more limited partners. The general partner (who can be an individual or a corporation) handles management and operations and has unlimited liabilities. The limited partners are restricted from participating in management and operations of the property and only have their actual cash investment at risk. Limited partnerships have been popular because they allow folks to invest relatively small amounts into larger real estate deals. Also, a limited partnership can continue on even if one of the partners dies, files bankruptcy, withdraws, or sells his partnership share.

Partnerships have been a common and successful way for individuals to work together to purchase larger real estate investment properties. Often, they bring together individuals with complementary resources and skills. For example, a good partnership may include a real estate broker, a property manager, a real estate financial analyst, and a real estate lender. The complementary skills of this partnership offer insight into each phase of the investment. In another common arrangement, one of the partners doesn't have any real estate expertise or acumen, but instead provides a significant portion of the investment capital.

The expertise of the general partner can be an advantage of real estate partnerships over TICs, where the TIC governing documents typically provide that each owner can vote their proportionate share and the majority makes the decisions. The problem is that a collective majority in a TIC may not have the real estate experience to make the best decision. In a real estate partnership, the owners of minority interests often find they have little input into the major decisions of the partnership (such as refinancing and selling or exchanging the property). But this hands-off approach can actually be beneficial and a lot less stressful if the general partner is competent and knows what she's doing.

From a taxation standpoint, real estate partnerships must prepare an IRS form 1065 tax return and pass through the respective share of all profits and losses and depreciation to each individual partner. Each partner then reports these numbers on her personal tax returns. At the time of death of a partner, there are several tax related issues concerning the handling of the partnership interest, so consult a tax advisor.

Refer to www.dummies.com/extras/realestateinvesting for additional information about private placement partnerships.

Limited Liability Company

Now available in all 50 states, the *limited liability company* (LLC) is a relatively new hybrid form of doing business that combines characteristics of a partnership and a corporation. This setup is an unbeatable combination for many real estate investors and a great way to hold title to real estate holdings. LLCs have essentially replaced corporations and partnerships as the most common way to hold title to real estate because they offer the advantages of allowing each member to have a say in the management while extending limited liability to all members, without the burden of *double taxation* that occurs with corporations. (Profits of corporations are first taxed at the corporate level, and then the profits distributed to individual shareholders are taxed again on their personal returns.)

An LLC is a separate entity like a corporation and therefore carries liability protection for all of its members, but it can be structured like a partnership so that the taxation flows through to each member individually. This feature simply requires the LLC to declare itself a joint venture with the IRS and indicate how it wants to allocate the taxation of income and expenses. Like a partnership, an LLC is required to prepare and file an IRS Form 1065, Partnership Tax Return, unless it makes the joint venture election.

Check with your own tax advisor, but many advisors recommend that their clients use a Limited Liability Company because it offers the best of both worlds — limited liability plus favorable and simplified tax treatment. Every state has its own requirements. Contact an attorney to have her prepare the articles of organization and an operating agreement (which are usually filed with the secretary of state).

The owners of an LLC are called *members* and can be virtually any entity, including individuals, partnerships, trusts, corporations, pension plans, or even other LLCs. Typically, LLCs have multiple members that can own different percentages; however, virtually all states permit single-member LLCs (but not without some potential issues with the IRS that you should discuss with your tax advisor in advance). Fortunately, a husband and wife are considered two members when forming an LLC.

Despite all these advantages, seek the counsel of an attorney who specializes in the formation of LLCs to give you help with the following issues:

- ✔ **IRS limitations:** IRS regulations have some limitations on the characteristics of the LLC. An attorney can advise you on the best structure to establish — one that emphasizes the importance of limited liability and centralized management while foregoing continuity of life and easy transferability of interests. In addition to filing a partnership tax return with the IRS, most states also require an annual report of activity along with filing fees, withholding, or even franchise fees; however, most states don't have any minimum charges.

- ✔ **Costs:** The costs can be much greater than for other forms of ownership. Be sure to consult with a local tax advisor for details on the typical costs for operating an LLC in your state. Currently, the highest base cost for an LLC is found in California: a minimum franchise tax fee of $800 per year plus additional taxes based on gross receipts.

For more information on forming and operating an LLC, please see *Limited Liability Companies for Dummies* by Jennifer Reuting (John Wiley & Sons).

Corporations

A partnership consists of people, but a *corporation* is a legal entity owned by one or more shareholders. The most well-known form that corporations take is that of public corporations like Google and Johnson & Johnson, which have shares traded on a stock exchange. Real estate investors can also create their own private or closely held corporations to own real estate.

A real estate investor can establish a corporation by filing articles of incorporation and bylaws with the appropriate state agency, usually the secretary of state's office. Corporate requirements vary from state to state, so consult your tax and legal advisors prior to implementing a corporate form of ownership for real estate assets. Nevada and Delaware are two of the more popular states in which to incorporate, but your legal and tax advisors can tell you if these states provide any advantages for your personal situation. Typically, you're best off to incorporate in your state of residence.

The appeal for real estate investors to form a corporation is that there is limited liability for shareholders. The owners of a corporation actually own stock, which is personal property. Thus, when corporations own real estate, the shareholders don't actually own the real estate. They own shares of stock in the entity that legally owns the property. Therefore, the most a shareholder can lose is her equity investment.

A disadvantage for many real estate investors is the initial expense to have an attorney draft the organizational documents. Then there are the costs to cover the rather extensive reporting requirements at both the state and federal level to maintain their corporate status. If the corporation isn't sufficiently capitalized or fails to meet all of the detailed organizational and reporting requirements, creditors or lien holders can pierce the corporate veil and seek personal liability for individual shareholders.

There are two types of corporations available:

- ✔ **C Corporation:** Although *C Corporations* (the most well-known and popular type of corporation) have the advantage of continuity of life in the event a shareholder dies, their downside is the double taxation of profits. Another negative is that if the corporation has losses, it has to carry them over to the next tax year because the shareholders can't use C Corporation losses on their personal returns.

- ✔ **S Corporation:** A primary benefit of this type of corporation is the ability to avoid double taxation by passing through the profits and losses directly to the individual shareholders. But *S Corporations* are rarely used in the ownership of real estate because their primary disadvantage is that a liquidation of the S Corporation is a taxable event. So even if the shareholders of the S Corporation can agree to an equitable distribution of the assets, the IRS deems the liquidation as taxable and the shareholders must pay capital gains taxes and possibly sell some of the assets. (Note that in a liquidation of an LLC, the assets may be distributed to the members without a taxable event occurring.) There is also difficulty for shareholders that aren't involved in the day-to-day operations. The IRS requires *material participation* (an IRS term that indicates whether an investor worked and was involved in a business activity on a regular basis) for the realization of tax benefits.

Only consider using a corporation to hold your real estate assets if you're willing to pay for the professional, legal, and accounting advice upfront and on a continuing basis to make sure that the protections of limited liability can't be violated. Although corporations have some inherent advantages, the drawback of double taxation and the ongoing technical requirements and expense to maintain the corporate status make utilizing the corporation entity unsuitable for the average real estate investor.

Closing the Transaction

The closing of escrow is the consummation of the real estate transaction and the goal of the buyer, the seller, the brokers, and all the other professionals who were part of the effort. It's the culmination of numerous individual acts and of often constant negotiation right up until the last moment. The closing of escrow occurs only when all conditions of the escrow instructions and purchase agreement are fulfilled, including any funding of the loan. Quite a few details must come together before the escrow officer can actually close the transaction and record the deed.

The actual process or formalities of closing the escrow are handled in different ways throughout the country. Some areas bring all the parties together; an attorney acts as the closing agent, and funds are transferred among the parties after all the documents have been signed and notarized. Your escrow officer is at the center of activity as the essential elements come together to make your goal of purchasing an investment property a reality. Your team of inspectors, appraisers, lenders, and attorneys all have roles in completing the due diligence required to ensure that there are no surprises with your potential new property acquisition.

However, there are still a few more fundamental items and details that need to be addressed as you wind down the escrow before you can call the property your own. Snags are still possible, so keep an eye out for the following:

✔ **Lender requests:** You need to make sure that you're in contact with your lender to avoid any last minute snafus. Lenders are notorious for needing just one more signature or asking questions at the last minute about the source of your down payment. These questions aren't as random as they may seem and are usually brought up by the loan committee or final person who must sign off on your loan.

✔ **Document errors:** Don't assume the documents are correct. They're prepared by people who may not be careful or who even cut and paste from documents used in prior escrows that have nothing to do with your transaction. Robert completed a large refinance loan of a commercial property, and while proofreading the lender-prepared documents, he noted that they contained several mistakes, including an incorrect loan amortization term.

✔ **Availability of parties and busy periods:** You need to be available to review and sign the loan documents, so let the lender or your mortgage broker know if you're planning any trips around closing time. But during certain times of the year, things just take a lot longer. The December holidays are the worst, but spring break and major three- or four-day weekends can also be times when your favorite property inspector, loan officer, or escrow officer may be planning to be out of the office.

Eleventh-hour issues are bound to arise, so don't leave important details to the last minute or you may struggle to make deadlines, particularly if there is a penalty clause to extend your escrow. You can almost guarantee lost documents and other unexplained communication breakdowns that occur any time you have so many moving parts. Anticipate logistical delays and allow time for anything and everything to take twice as long as it should.

Estimated closing statement

Several days before the projected date for the close of your escrow, both the buyer and the seller receive a copy of the estimated closing statement with the various charges. You may receive this statement at the time you sign some or all of the documents, or it may be sent to you separately. This is an extremely important document because this is the best time to raise any issues or concerns if you feel that an error has been made.

The estimated amounts can, and usually do, change slightly. Often the escrow officer or closing agent estimates these expenses a little on the high side because any shortage of funds prevents the escrow from closing, but any overage can easily be credited or refunded back to the buyer or seller.

The buyer should pay particular attention to the estimated closing statement because it indicates the funds expected to be received from the lender or credited from the seller if there's seller financing. It also indicates the amount of additional cash funds that the buyer needs to deposit in the form of a wire transfer, cashier's check, or other certified funds. The buyer must provide these *good funds* in plenty of time for the escrow to close — your personal check will take up to a week to clear and credit cards and PayPal aren't accepted! **Remember:** If you have a large sum of money deposited in escrow, arrange for the escrow company to place the funds in an interest-bearing account.

Title insurance

Title insurance has evolved to become a vital element in most real estate transactions. Title insurance companies track all recorded documents and transfers of interests in real estate so that they can issue *title insurance* — policies that assure the purchaser that the title to the property being transferred is legally valid and unblemished. This kind of title is commonly referred to as a *clean and marketable title*. Title insurance is like any form of insurance in that it defends and pays the claims made against the insured. There are two types of title insurance policies issued in most transactions:

✔ The seller provides one to the buyer to protect herself against claims that the purchase of the property wasn't a marketable title. For example, maybe the heir to a former owner may suddenly claim that there was a fraudulent transfer of the property years ago. If you bought title insurance when you purchased the property, the title company defends any legal action or compensates you in the event that the claim is valid and you lose the property.

✔ Mortgage lenders require title insurance to protect against someone else claiming legal title to your property. The lender provides funds toward the purchase of the property and wouldn't be protected if the property ownership were to change based on a claim of an improper transfer of title. There are many ways that a title can be transferred improperly — for instance, when a husband and wife split up and the one who remains in the home decides to sell and take off with the money. If the title lists both spouses as owners, the spouse who sells the property (possibly by forging the other's signature) has violated the law. The short-changed spouse can reclaim rights to the home even after it has been sold. In this event, both you and the lender can get stuck holding the bag in the absence of title insurance.

Most state insurance departments monitor and regulate title insurance companies because a company's ability to pay claims is always important. Although title insurers rarely fail, and most states do a good job shutting down financially unstable ones, check with your state's insurance department if you're concerned. Title insurance companies receive ratings from insurance-rating companies, so you can ask the insurer for copies of the latest report.

Don't simply use the company that your real estate agent or lender suggests — shop around. Because many title companies provide escrow services, you need to watch out for companies that quote very low prices on one service and make up for it by overcharging in other areas. When you call around for title insurance and escrow fee quotes, get a handle on all the charges; there may be miscellaneous or hidden administrative fees that can sneak up on you and become major items — document preparation, notary services, courier fees, and express mail. If you find a company with lower prices, consider asking for an itemization in writing so that you don't run into any surprises.

Check with your title insurance company for special *riders* (clauses) that save you money if you're buying a distressed investment property with the intention of quickly renovating and selling the property in less than 24 months. (That's two title insurance policies — you pay for a lender's title insurance policy as the buyer and then a seller's title insurance policy when you sell the property.) These special policies typically cost you 10 to 20 percent more upfront but can be a real bargain if you can avoid having to purchase a brand-new title policy for a short holding period.

Property insurance

You must have insurance, often one of the larger expenses for investment properties. Unless you purchase the property entirely for cash, you can't close the transaction and take over the property until you have a certificate of insurance in place. Your lender, or even the seller if he's providing any financing of your purchase, will prudently insist that you have adequate insurance coverage with policy limits that effectively protect your financer's collateral or financial interest in the property.

In accounting terms, property insurance is a *fixed expense* (like your property taxes), which means that although you may be able to turn off the natural gas (a *variable expense*) when your property is unoccupied, you must have insurance coverage — even if your property is vacant. In fact, insurance is likely more important if your property is vacant for an extended time frame.

In order to avoid surprises in your cash flow, determine the cost of insurance while you're still in your due diligence phase of the transaction. At this point, you retain the ability to cancel without penalty if you find that proper insurance coverage is either not available or priced way too high.

Another benefit of getting your insurance early in the due diligence process is that your insurance agent or an underwriter from the insurance company may even inspect the property before providing you with a quote. Of course, any inspection by the insurance company is limited in scope and is never a substitute for your own inspection or the detailed written inspections you need from your property inspector and other industry professionals or experts (see "Inspecting the property" earlier in the chapter). But it can be important to know whether the insurance company is going to require any upgrades or changes to the property as a condition of offering insurance.

For example, many companies no longer write policies for multifamily residential properties that have balcony- or pool-fence wrought-iron railings with pickets spaced greater than 4 inches apart, due to the potential hazards to small children. The cost to correct this condition can be expensive, and you would want to include such costs in your negotiations with the seller or at least include the amount in your capital budget. (We discuss the role of insurance in an effective risk management program in Chapter 16.)

You may trust your insurance broker or agent, but don't allow your escrow to close until you have written documentation confirming that your property insurance coverage is in force. It may seem improbable, but many properties have suffered a catastrophic loss or liability claim *in a matter of hours* after the property changed hands and the new owner's insurance coverage wasn't yet in place. Robert was an expert witness in a case where an owner thought his insurance agent had placed earthquake coverage on his new apartment purchase only to discover a few days after a devastating earthquake had substantially destroyed his building that the request for coverage was never sent in!

Final closing statement

Just before your transaction is complete and escrow is closed, you receive a closing statement from the escrow officer. Besides the actual purchase price, there are several expenses incurred in the process of purchasing real estate that must be worked out between the buyer and the seller. For example, the seller may have paid the property taxes for the balance of the year, and the buyer should reimburse him for the amount attributable to his ownership period after the close of escrow.

The buyer and seller need to pay some expenses, such as escrow and recording fees. Who pays what is usually outlined in the escrow instructions and is determined by a combination of the purchase agreement negotiations between the parties and custom and practice in the local real estate market. Table 14-1 contains a breakdown of the allocation of expenses that are typical in the purchase of investment properties.

Table 14-1 Typical Allocation of Expenses		
Item	*Paid by Seller*	*Paid by Buyer*
Broker's commission	X	
Escrow fees	Split 50-50	Split 50-50
Recording fees: Loan payoff	X	
Recording fees: Transfer		X
Transfer tax	X	
State or local revenue stamps	X	
Seller's title policy	X	
Lender's title policy		X
Loan origination fee		X
Loan commitment fee		X
Appraisal		X
Credit report		X
Loan prepayment penalty, if any	X	

In addition to the allocation of expenses between the buyer and seller, the final closing statement contains *credits* (items that accrue to the benefit of the party receiving the credit) and *debits* (items that are paid out of escrow on behalf of the party being debited). Table 14-2 has a breakdown of the usual accounting of the debits and credits on the closing or settlement statement.

Table 14-2	Usual Accounting on Closing Statement				
Item	*Buyer Credit*	*Buyer Debit*	*Seller Credit*	*Seller Debit*	*Prorated*
Selling price		X	X		
Buyer's loan principal	X				
Buyer's loan points/ fees		X			
Prepaid interest		X			
Property inspection fees/appraisal		X			
Payoff seller's loan				X	
Tenant's security deposits	X			X	
Buyer's earnest money deposit	X			X	
Additional cash down payment	X			X	
Unpaid bills (for example, utility charges)	X			X	X
Prepaid property taxes		X	X		X
Prepaid insurance		X	X		X
Prepaid expenses (for example, utility deposit)		X	X		X
Supplies left by seller for buyer's use		X	X		X

The day before you close on the property, take a brief walk-through to make sure that everything is still in the condition it was before and that all the fixtures, appliances, window coverings, and other items the contract lists are still there. Sometimes, sellers ignore or don't recall these things and consequently don't leave what they agreed to in the sales contract.

The importance of conducting a final property inspection prior to closing escrow is illustrated by one of Robert's expert witness cases. The buyers of a single-family home failed to close escrow as planned because they decided they didn't want to put the 20 percent down payment in cash but instead were negotiating with their mortgage broker to arrange a second loan that could be combined with their first trust deed to give them 100 percent financing. The seller had moved out on the original estimated closing date, and the home sat vacant for several weeks until the buyers were able to arrange and fund the second loan. With the transaction dragging on past the expected close of escrow, the anxious buyers failed to inspect the home that one last time before finally closing escrow. Unfortunately, sometime between when the seller moved out and the buyers first saw the property after they had closed escrow and taken title, the property experienced a severe water leak that completely flooded a good portion of the home and created a serious mold issue. The remediation cost was in the tens of thousands of dollars, and litigation ensued because the insurance companies for both the seller and buyer refused coverage on the basis that no one could determine precisely when the damage occurred. Ultimately, the buyers' insurance covered much of the out-of-pocket repair costs, but the matter wasn't resolved for over two years, and the buyers didn't have loss of rent coverage to make up for rent lost during that period.

The escrow officer or closing agent usually processes the mandatory reporting of the real estate transaction to the Internal Revenue Service and the state tax authorities, if required. If she doesn't file the required 1099-S form, the brokers or the buyer and seller may be required to handle the reporting, which includes the identity of the property transferred, the sales price, and the Social Security numbers of the buyer and seller.

Be sure to keep a copy of the closing statement, because this document establishes your initial cost basis when you go to sell the property and need to determine your capital gain. Also, some of the expenses paid at the close of escrow may be deductible on your tax return, such as prepaid interest or points on your loan and property taxes and insurance.

Deed recording and property takeover

Although the escrow officer may have all of the signed documents, and funds have been transferred to the proper accounts, you aren't the proud owner of your investment property until the deed is recorded. The procedure for recording the documents varies throughout the country but is becoming more standardized. Nearly every county utilizes a county recorder to record documents like real estate deeds, mortgages, deeds of trust, and other real estate documents as a public notice. Typically, there is an office of the county clerk and recorder, sometimes in the county courthouse in smaller jurisdictions.

Electronic document processing technology has made great strides in improving the efficiency in recording and retrieving documents at virtually all recorders' offices. Now documents can be retrieved by computers in a matter of seconds and are usually indexed by grantor and grantee.

After you receive word that the deed has been recorded, the transaction is finalized; you're the new owner, and you begin the property takeover process. There are several steps that you should take in the first few days of ownership, including

- ✔ Conducting a final walk-through and inspection of both the property's exterior and interior to make sure that the property hasn't been damaged prior to the close of escrow.

- ✔ Verifying that all items indicated on the personal property inventory list are present.

- ✔ Making sure that all keys were received (if the property is vacant, you should change the locks as an added precaution).

- ✔ Checking the utility meters to make sure that the utility company has switched the billing as of the close of escrow so you don't get billed for the former owner's usage.

- ✔ Meeting with tenants and assuring them that you're a responsive and concerned property owner who wants to cooperatively resolve issues.

Another issue to address right after the closing is the possession and control by the former owner. Because the escrow closing and recording can often happen during the day without any specific notice, it's best to wait until the following calendar day and personally verify that only the tenants that should be there are occupying the property. If the owner is still residing on the premises or is using some of the property for his own use, you need to immediately ask that he turn over full possession unless you've made other formal written arrangements in advance. To minimize this prospect, we suggest that you include significant daily monetary damages in the purchase contract for any unauthorized holdover usage by the seller.

Congratulations! You're now ready to begin managing your property and increasing its value as you build the foundation of your real estate portfolio.

Part IV

Operating the Property

Unit Inspection Checklist
General condition of rental units

_____ Mold   _____ Plastic Supply Lines

Tenant Name(s) _____ Unit Number _____ Date _____

Condition: **Condition:**

Kitchen

Floors/floor covering	E	G	F	P	N/A
Walls & ceiling	E	G	F	P	N/A
Windows/locks/screens	E	G	F	P	N/A
Window coverings	E	G	F	P	N/A
Doors/knobs	E	G	F	P	N/A
Light fixtures/bulbs	E	G	F	P	N/A
Cabinets/cupboards	E	G	F	P	N/A
Drawers/countertops	E	G	F	P	N/A
Shelves/drawers	E	G	F	P	N/A
Sinks/stoppers/faucets	E	G	F	P	N/A
Drains/plumbing	E	G	F	P	N/A
Other _____	E	G	F	P	N/A

Dishwasher

Outside	E	G	F	P	N/A
Rack	E	G	F	P	N/A
Other _____	E	G	F	P	N/A

Appliances

Gas stove/oven

Outside	E	G	F	P	N/A
Burners	E	G	F	P	N/A
Drip pans	E	G	F	P	N/A
Hood vent/microwave	E	G	F	P	N/A
Timer/controls	E	G	F	P	N/A
Broiler pan	E	G	F	P	N/A
Light	E	G	F	P	N/A
Other _____	E	G	F	P	N/A

Refrigerator (Size _____)

Outside	E	G	F	P	N/A
Inside	E	G	F	P	N/A
Ice trays	E	G	F	P	N/A
Other _____	E	G	F	P	N/A
Garbage disposal	E	G	F	P	N/A
Angle stops/supply lines	E	G	F	P	N/A

General comments, including specific notes for all health & safety issues: _____
_____

Living Room

Floors/floor covering	E	G	F	P	N/A
Walls & ceiling	E	G	F	P	N/A
Windows/locks/screens	E	G	F	P	N/A
Window coverings	E	G	F	P	N/A
Doors/locks	E	G	F	P	N/A
Light fixtures/bulbs	E	G	F	P	N/A
Closet/shelves	E	G	F	P	N/A
Fireplace	E	G	F	P	N/A

Dining Room

Floors/floor covering	E	G	F	P	N/A
Walls & ceiling	E	G	F	P	N/A
Windows/locks/screens	E	G	F	P	N/A
Doors/locks	E	G	F	P	N/A
Ceiling fans/bulbs	E	G	F	P	N/A
Closet/shelves	E	G	F	P	N/A
Other _____	E	G	F	P	N/A
Other _____	E	G	F	P	N/A

General comments, including specific notes for all health & safety issues: _____
_____

Hall

Floors/floor covering	E	G	F	P	N/A
Walls & ceiling	E	G	F	P	N/A
Windows/locks/screens	E	G	F	P	N/A
Window coverings	E	G	F	P	N/A
Doors/knobs/locks	E	G	F	P	N/A
Light fixtures/bulbs	E	G	F	P	N/A
Closet/shelves	E	G	F	P	N/A
Doorbell	E	G	F	P	N/A

Bedroom 1 (smallest)

Floors/floor covering	E	G	F	P	N/A
Walls & ceiling	E	G	F	P	N/A
Windows/locks/screens	E	G	F	P	N/A
Window coverings	E	G	F	P	N/A
Doors/knobs/locks	E	G	F	P	N/A
Light fixtures/bulbs	E	G	F	P	N/A
Closet/shelves	E	G	F	P	N/A
Other _____	E	G	F	P	N/A

Guest or 2nd Bedroom

Floors/floor covering	E	G	F	P	N/A
Walls & ceiling	E	G	F	P	N/A
Windows/locks/screens	E	G	F	P	N/A
Window coverings	E	G	F	P	N/A
Doors/knobs/locks	E	G	F	P	N/A
Closets/shelves	E	G	F	P	N/A
Light fixtures/bulbs	E	G	F	P	N/A
Other _____	E	G	F	P	N/A

Master Bedroom

Floors/floor covering	E	G	F	P	N/A
Walls & ceiling	E	G	F	P	N/A
Windows/locks/screens	E	G	F	P	N/A
Window coverings	E	G	F	P	N/A
Doors/knobs/locks	E	G	F	P	N/A
Closets/shelves	E	G	F	P	N/A
Light fixtures/bulbs	E	G	F	P	N/A
Other _____	E	G	F	P	N/A

General comments, including specific notes for all health & safety issues: _____
_____

Go to www.dummies.com/extras/realestateinvesting for some reminders that can assist you when making your real estate purchase.

In this part ...

✔ Comprehend that being a good landlord requires knowledge, training, and experience if you lease your property to tenants.

✔ Glean from the mistakes of the many landlords who have come before you when renting their property so you don't encounter the same issues.

✔ Know how to attract and retain good tenants, which can boost the value of your property, by following our time-tested strategies of property management.

✔ Be prepared for the unexpected or unfortunate if they should occur, by having the proper insurance and risk management plans in place.

✔ Account for all the income and expenses on your investment properties and know how to reduce your tax bill (legally, of course) when it comes time to sell.

Chapter 15

Landlording 101

In This Chapter

▶ Deciding between a property manager and managing yourself

▶ Making sense of discrimination and environmental laws and requirements

▶ Getting along with existing tenants while making desired changes

▶ Understanding the keys to filling vacancies

▶ Dealing with leases and other contracts and money collection like a pro

*A*t the moment that you close the deal on buying a rental property, you've probably already put in dozens, if not hundreds, of hours. Now, however, the real work begins. To maximize the value of your investment, you've got to attract and retain excellent tenants, stay on top of government regulations, keep your eyes open for ways to cost-effectively improve your property, and handle contracts and money flowing in and going out. This chapter shows you how to be the best landlord that you can be.

Hiring Management Help: Yes or No?

A *property manager* can be responsible for all operations of a property, including marketing, tenant selection, rent collection, tenant relations, maintenance, and accounting. Many beginning real estate investors do all the work themselves — painting, cleaning, making repairs, collecting rent, paying bills, advertising, and showing the rental units. However, after a while, most investors delegate jobs that they aren't suited for or don't enjoy. Some new owners, of course, do just fine managing their own rental units. But others discover firsthand that on-the-job property management training can backfire with some costly lessons.

Evaluating your situation and the possibility of self-management

If you have the right traits for managing property, have the time, and live close to your property, consider doing it yourself. Among the advantages of self-management are

- ✔ **You save the monthly property management fee.** Property managers' fees can be significant, so a potential advantage for the do-it-yourself approach is that you can save yourself a good deal of money. However, as we discuss in a moment, you must examine the bigger picture of the value of your time and realistically assess how much of your time property management takes up. You could also cost yourself a lot more than you save if you inadvertently make a serious mistake, such as violating a fair housing law.

- ✔ **You can save on maintenance costs.** By keeping direct control of the management, you decide who does the repair work and mows the lawn. If you're qualified and have the time, doing your own maintenance or yard work is usually a good idea; if you hire someone else to do it for you, the cost can devour your monthly cash flow in a hurry — especially in the early years of ownership when cash flow is often tight. Develop a list of reliable fix-it and landscape personnel who are licensed, do good work, and charge fair rates. However, a property management company may get volume pricing or discounts that an individual managing just a few rental units won't.

Some owners who self-manage can tell you exactly how much money they "saved" by not hiring a property manager, but the one factor that many real estate investors overlook is the value of their own time in dealing with management issues.

If you earn your living regularly from something other than managing rentals, managing your investment property may not be worth your valuable time. If you're a higher-income, full-time professional, getting frequent calls from prospective renters or getting a midday emergency call and rushing off on weekdays to handle some minor crisis at your rental unit isn't only impractical, it may be downright damaging to your career. Receiving emergency calls in the middle of the night can make you too tired to go to your job the next day. If your property isn't in the safest area of town, doing a repair or collecting rent in the evening may actually be dangerous.

As a jobholder, look at your annual income and figure out approximately what you earn per hour. Do the same for the cash savings you generate by managing your own property. Unless your management efforts produce significant cash savings compared to your job, you may be better off hiring a property manager for your rental units.

The same guidelines hold true even if you're an independent business owner or self-employed. Your schedule may be more flexible than that of a nine-to-five employee. But if you're earning $50 an hour, it doesn't make sense to devote hours of your productive work time to managing rental units, which may only amount to cash savings of $25 an hour.

Property management is truly a 24/7/365 commitment. Carving out time when you're completely free from the unexpected interruption can be difficult. Your rental prospects and paying tenants will expect an immediate response to even their most routine inquiries. Property managers can respond quickly in today's society and get the best tenants because they're the ones who appreciate a professional and responsive relationship with their landlord. If you aren't as responsive as residents expect, they could refuse to pay rent and defend your efforts at eviction by claiming that you breached the implied warranty of habitability.

Assessing your skills and interests

To fill the position, you have to possess the corresponding basic skills and interests. Use the following questions to examine your own personality and skills to see whether you're cut out to be your own property manager:

- ✔ **Are you a people person?** Serving as a landlord is a labor of love. You must enjoy people and solving problems — while often being unappreciated yourself.

- ✔ **Do you have the temperament to handle problems?** Responding to complaints and service requests in a positive and rational manner is key, even if the resident is angry and hostile.

- ✔ **Are you comfortable with numbers and basic accounting skills?** And are you meticulous, timely, and accurate with paperwork?

- ✔ **Do you have maintenance and repair abilities?** If you're handy and take on electrical or plumbing jobs, what if something goes wrong and the resident argues that the job should have been done by a professional? Do you have insurance to cover any property damage or personal injury that results from a mistake you make? Being able to work with your hands goes a long way, but if you're adept at finding and managing good contractors and vendors, you're still in the game.

- ✔ **Are you willing to work and take phone calls/emails/text messages in the evenings and on weekends?** Who needs a weekend, right?

✔ **Do you have sales and negotiation skills?** You need to sell the space, but know your competition so you can close the deal but not give away the store.

✔ **Are you willing to commit the time and effort?** Other important tasks, such as determining the right rent and becoming and staying familiar with property management laws that are constantly changing, will take even more time.

If you're shy or impatient, or prefer to avoid any conflict or are easily manipulated, you aren't suited to being a property manager. You need to convey a professional demeanor to your tenants. They must see you as someone who will take responsibility for the condition of the property and operational systems of the unit. You must also insist that tenants live up to their part of the bargain, pay their rent regularly, and refrain from causing unreasonable damage to your property.

A rental property manager must be fair, firm, and friendly to all rental prospects and tenants. You need to treat everyone impartially and remain patient and calm under stress. You must be determined and unemotional in enforcing rent collection and your policies and rules. And you must maintain a positive attitude through it all. Not as simple as it looks, is it?

When you manage a rental property, you don't just have to deal with your current tenants. You also have to interact with rental prospects, contractors, suppliers, neighbors, and government employees. People, not the property, generally create most rental management problems. Be prepared to be flexible and learn from your property management experiences. The really good property managers may have credentials, but they have also graduated from the school of hard knocks. Practice makes perfect.

Finding and Hiring Pros

Management companies accept the responsibility for all property. The right property manager can make a big difference in the cash flow your rental unit generates by finding good replacement tenants quickly and making sure that maintenance is done in a timely manner without breaking your budget. You need a property manager who is committed to helping you get the optimum results from your rentals. Try to find property managers familiar with your kind of investment property and knowledgeable about the local rental market. With a little research, you can find the right fit for your property.

A poor management company can cut into your profits, not only with their fees but also by providing improper maintenance and leasing to poor-quality tenants who may run your property into the ground. A bad property manager can leave you in worse shape than if you had managed the property yourself.

Doing the research

Visit the office of your management company and spend time interviewing the specific property manager that will have hands-on management of your rental property. Make a few extra phone calls to check references and don't sign a management contract until you feel confident that the company you hire has a sound track record. Checking with the property management company's chosen referrals isn't enough. Ask for a list of all their clients and contact the ones with rental properties similar in size and type to your own. Make sure the rental owners you contact have been with the property management company long enough to have a meaningful opinion.

You specifically want references for the property manager that will handle the day-to-day management of your property. Some companies have you meet initially with their most qualified and competent manager and then hand you off to a newbie who may not even know as much as you do about property management. Of course, having very experienced and credentialed senior property managers or owners can be a great resource, but you just need to make sure who exactly will be servicing your property.

Make sure that the firm you hire manages property exclusively, particularly when selecting a management company for a single-family home, condo, or small commercial, or residential rental property. Many real estate sales offices (as opposed to property management firms) offer property management services; however, this service is often more about obtaining the listing to sell the property later on. Many property managers in real estate sales offices don't have the same credentials, experience, and expertise that an employee of a property management firm has. The skills required to represent clients in *selling* property are quite different than the skills required to *manage* property. Go with the best property management company and then select the most competent sales agent when you look to buy or sell your income property.

Also, be sure to investigate these issues:

✔ **Licenses:** Most states require property managers to have either a real estate license or a property manager's license or both. Call or use the Internet to verify that the property manager and the management company have a current license in good standing. Specifically ask about any pending or recent complaints or audits and the outcome during your vetting process because licensing disciplinary actions can take many months or even years before they appear online.

✔ **Credentials:** Also examine the property manager's credentials. The Institute of Real Estate Management (IREM), an organization of professional property managers, provides professional designations, including the Certified Property Manager (CPM) and Accredited Residential Manager (ARM) designations. A select group of management firms have earned the Accredited Management Organization (AMO) designation. Check www.irem.org to see if your manager is currently IREM-approved because some sneaky individuals or companies earn credentials and claim to hold them, but actually fail to meet the minimum ongoing requirements to maintain the credential or stay current with an ever-changing real estate management industry.

✔ **Insurance:** The company should carry insurance for general liability, automobile liability, worker's compensation, and professional liability (errors and omissions). The management company is your agent and will be collecting your rents and security deposits, so they should also have a large fidelity bond to protect you in case an employee embezzles or mishandles your money. Remember that they have multiple clients so the amount of the fidelity bond needs to cover much more than the average funds in the trust account just for your properties.

✔ **Accounting:** Look for a management company that offers you a separate federally insured trust depository account along with the ability to provide separate accounting for each client or property managed rather than a master trust account where multiple clients' funds are commingled.

Talking money

In most management contracts, property management companies have the ability and right to perform emergency repairs without advance approval from the owner. Of course, this arrangement allows the property management company to take care of problems that occur unexpectedly. Most management contracts contain clauses that allow property managers to undertake repairs up to a specified dollar amount without the owner's advance approval. The limit should be commensurate with the type and size of the property. Commercial properties and larger residential properties may have a $2,500 limit, whereas a small duplex may have a limit of $250.

When you're in the early stages of working with a new management company, make sure you closely monitor their expenses. Even though they may have the legal right to use funds up to a certain amount, they should always keep you informed. Many management companies have in-house maintenance crews, and keeping these workers busy making repairs at properties they manage can be a lucrative profit center. They may offer low management fees knowing that they can make it up by markups on (often unnecessary) repairs. Although legal, if properly disclosed, some management firms routinely receive and keep discounts that they negotiate with contractors, vendors, and suppliers, and the disclosure is likely buried in the contract's fine print. Be sure to inquire specifically before you sign the management contract because this practice is becoming common and accounts for misleadingly low management fee quotes from some firms. Look for a property management firm that doesn't mark up materials, supplies, or maintenance labor.

Typically, management companies receive a percentage of the collected income for managing a property; some management firms offer a flat fee per month or a dollar amount per unit per month for the entire property. Try to find a company that has a management fee that is a percentage of the collected income; this kind of fee is a strong motivator to the management company to ensure that the rents are collected and kept at market rate. Generally, the larger the rental property, the lower the management fee percentage. Management fees for single-family homes, condos, and small rental properties typically run 9 to 10 percent; medium size properties 6 to 8 percent; and large residential properties of 200 or more units around 3 to 5 percent. Fees for commercial-type properties have a similar scale.

Additional fees for the leasing of vacant space are often justified, because the most time-intensive portion of property management is tenant turnover. When one tenant leaves, the rental unit or the commercial, industrial, or retail suite must be made rent-ready; then the property manager must show the property and screen the tenants. Leasing fees or charges for residential rentals can vary but are often either a flat fee of a few hundred dollars or a percentage of the rent, such as half of the monthly rental rate. Leasing commissions for commercial, industrial, or retail properties are almost always a percentage of the gross rent with a declining scale where the longer the lease, the lower the percentage in the later years.

Testing for Environmental Issues

Take precautions to ensure that your rentals are a safe and healthy environment. Although legal implications and substantial liability for failing to meet required state and federal disclosures are also motivators, most owners simply don't want to see their tenants get sick or injured. Check for the following issues:

- ✔ **Lead:** Some older buildings may still contain lead paint (which was banned in 1978). A lead test is the only way to verify the existence of lead. Often, the best solution is to manage the lead rather than remove it, because the removal processes can release large amounts of lead dust and can be costly. As a residential rental owner, know the dangers of lead and the federally required disclosures for residential properties only (providing a lead paint pamphlet at the beginning of the tenancy and a different pamphlet when certain repairs or modifications are done that you can get at www.epa.gov/lead). Most states have lead hazard reduction laws, some of which require testing and maintenance in addition to the federal disclosure requirements.

✔ **Asbestos:** Although there are currently no federal disclosure rules for asbestos in rental housing and no federal requirements to investigate or remove asbestos, check with local and state officials for possible disclosure requirements. Asbestos was added to a variety of products to provide strength, heat insulation, and fire resistance. In most products, asbestos is combined with a binding material so that it's not released into the air. As long as fibers aren't released, there are no known health risks. However, asbestos is dangerous if disturbed. Studies of people exposed to asbestos clearly show that breathing high levels of the fibers can lead to an increased risk of lung and other cancers. Don't test for asbestos on your own. Hire a professional environmental testing firm because the act of breaking open potentially asbestos-containing material to obtain samples can release asbestos into the air and create a dangerous situation. See www.epa.gov/asbestos for more information.

✔ **Radon:** Radon is an invisible, odorless, radioactive gas, and a known cancer-causing agent, found in soil and rock in all parts of the United States. Inside some buildings, high levels of radon gas have been found to cause lung cancer. But most radon found in buildings poses no direct threat because the concentration is generally within the safe level. No federal requirements to disclose or test for radon currently exist, but it's potentially a serious issue and one that's receiving more attention. Conduct tests, which are cheap and simple to do, to determine radon levels in your rentals, and check with local authorities for more information about the prevalence and precautions to take. Visit the EPA Web site at www.epa.gov/radon for more information.

✔ **Mold:** Mold has been around since biblical times and is found everywhere, but allegations that exposure to certain types can be hazardous are rather recent with several well-publicized lawsuits. If there's a claim of mold by your tenant, follow the EPA guidelines and protocol and consult with experts if the problem is severe and persistent. Although a common claim is respiratory illness by some individuals while in direct contact with elevated mold levels, there are still no conclusive scientific guidelines as to acceptable limits for exposure, but rental owners should take claims of mold exposure seriously. Minimize the possibility of mold in your building by identifying and quickly addressing moisture intrusion. Use qualified professionals and carefully document all communication to minimize the prospect of being sued by your tenants.

Deciding on Rental Policies

As a landlord, you have some important business decisions to make regarding the terms under which you rent to tenants. Among other items, you should give plenty of thought to the length of the lease term and the amount of the monthly rent and security deposit, as well as some other important policies, all of which we cover in this section.

Determining lease length

The *lease* or *rental agreement* is the legal document that specifies the terms and conditions of the agreement binding the property owner and the tenant. It's a contract between the owner of the property and the tenant for the possession and exclusive use of the property in exchange for the payment of rent. Residential rental property owners commonly use one of two types of agreements (for information on other aspects of leases, check out Chapter 11):

- **Month-to-month agreement:** More common with residential properties than with commercial, industrial, or retail rentals, a month-to-month rental agreement is automatically renewed each month unless the owner or tenant gives the other proper written notice (usually 30 days) to terminate the tenancy. Month-to-month agreements give you much more flexibility than leases, because you can increase the rent or change other terms of the tenancy on 30 days' notice.

  Some owners prefer the flexibility offered by a month-to-month rental agreement to a lease. Although the month-to-month rental agreement does allow your tenants the right to move at any time merely by giving a 30-day written notice, the reality is that most tenants don't like to move and often stay long-term. The majority of tenants only move because of a job transfer or another significant reason, or because the rental owner doesn't properly maintain the property.

- **Fixed-term lease:** Commercial, industrial, and retail investment property owners almost always use long-term leases exclusively. Fixed-term contracts obligate you and the tenant for a set period of time, and some owners like the commitment required from the tenant. The most common residential lease terms are for 6, 9, or 12 months and rarely exceed two years. With such a lease, you can't increase the rent or change other terms of the tenancy until the lease expires. You can't terminate or end the tenancy before the lease expires, unless the tenant doesn't pay his rent or violates another term of the lease. And in court, you have the *burden of proof,* which means you're the one who has to prove that the tenant didn't live up to his part of the contract.

Setting the rent

Establishing the rent is one of the most important yet difficult tasks for most investment property owners. If you set your rent too high, you'll have a vacant rental unit. And if you set your rent too low, your profits will suffer or, worse, you won't even cover your expenses. You can use two common methods for determining how much rent you should charge for your rental property — *return on investment* (which examines your costs) and *market analysis* (which looks at a comparable property's rent).

Examining the return on your investment

The first step in determining your rent based on the return on your investment is to calculate your costs of owning and operating your rental property. You need to estimate costs for your mortgage, property taxes, insurance, maintenance, leasing, management, and a profit on your invested funds (for the details on this topic, see Chapter 12).

Suppose that for a residential rental unit, your monthly mortgage, tax payments, and operating expenses come to $800, plus you want a $200 monthly return (10 percent per year on your original cash investment of $24,000 in this rental property). Thus, you need to generate a monthly rent of $1,000 ($800 + $200). (This simple calculation doesn't take appreciation, increasing equity, or tax advantages of real estate into account.)

Although you may have calculated that you need $1,000 per month for your rental unit, if the rental market is such that comparable units are readily available for $900, you may not be able to fully achieve your financial goals at this time. With most real estate investments, the initial returns may not match your original projections; in the long run, rents often increase at a greater rate than your expenses, your debt service remains constant, and your return on your initial investment improves.

Many new investment property owners make the mistake of overestimating the potential income from their rental property while allowing for no rental discounts or concessions, and anticipating virtually no vacancy or bad debt. When reality strikes, they can be faced with negative cash flow, and ultimately, they may even lose their rental property.

Setting the rent is particularly critical if you own single-family or condo rental units or other small residential or commercial rental properties, because the rent loss from an extended vacancy or one bad tenant can seriously jeopardize your investment. Be conservative in setting your rents (along with being cautious in tenant screening and aggressive in maintaining your properties) to attract good, long-term tenants who pay on time. To avoid surprises, use a conservative budget for your rental property that anticipates rental income at about 92 percent of the market rent for a comparable rental unit or suite, which is based on the assumption that you will have one month's vacancy or collection loss each year.

Surveying comparable rents

Knowing how much money you need to break even is important for evaluating the potential return on your real estate investment. And setting your rents properly is an independent decision based on current market conditions. Unfortunately, the realities of the rental market may put limits on what rent you can reasonably charge for your rental unit or suite, regardless of your costs of owning and maintaining the investment property.

Evaluating the rental rates being charged for similar rental units or suites in comparable locations is a great way to gather information before setting your own rent. Make minor adjustments in your rent because of variations in the location, age, size, and features of the properties you're comparing. For example, if you own a residential investment property and one of your competitors has an available rental unit that is nearly identical to yours, your rent should be slightly higher if you also have a swimming pool. Of course, be honest and make downward adjustments for aspects of your rental property that aren't as desirable as alternatives.

In order to determine the market rents in your area, do your homework and locate comparable rental properties, which are those properties that your tenants are most likely to also consider when looking for a rental unit or suite. They may be located right in the neighborhood or in other areas.

Deciding on security deposits

Rental property owners are permitted to collect a security deposit from tenants upon move-in and hold it until the tenant leaves. The *security deposit* provides financial protection for the property owner in the event that the tenant falls behind in his rental payments or damages his rental unit or suite.

For residential properties, state laws often limit the amount of the security deposit, require interest to be paid on the deposit, and detail what are lawful deductions. Check with the local affiliate of the National Apartment Association for your state's security deposit laws. (Certain rental owners may be exempt from the rules.)

In most rental markets, typical security deposits are well below the maximum allowed by law. We recommend that you collect as large of a security deposit as the market can bear (staying within the legal limits). Don't lower or waive the security deposit. If the required funds to move in are too high for a desired tenant, collect a reasonable portion of the deposit prior to move in and allow the tenant to pay the balance in installments.

Because the funds don't belong to you, several states require that residential security deposits be held in a separate trust bank account. Some states require that owners provide tenants with a written notice indicating the location of this bank trust account at the beginning of the tenancy. All of these requirements and more are covered in the recent version of Robert's book *Property Management Kit For Dummies* (John Wiley & Sons, Inc.).

Creating policies and guidelines

Many owners of small investment property don't worry about setting detailed policies and guidelines (often called *house rules*) because they think the lease or rental agreement covers it all. But setting up some basic rules in writing that can be modified as necessary upon proper written notice to the tenants is a good idea because it ensures that you and your tenants are on the same page and gives you flexibility as you manage your property. The rules you draft should be more informal and conversational in tone than your lease. Be clear, direct, and firm, yet not condescending. Make sure your policies and rules are reasonable and enforceable. They must not discriminate against anyone because of race, sex, national origin, religion, and so on. Be particularly careful to review your house rules to avoid any reference to children unless related to health and safety issues.

In addition to the lease, take care of these issues:

✔ Give your residential tenants a copy of the required environmental disclosure form and the EPA pamphlet for lead-based paint and lead-based paint hazards, which is required under federal law. Have them sign an acknowledgment of receipt.

✔ Inform your new tenant of the importance of smoke detectors. You may even want to create a separate smoke detector agreement to be sure your tenants fully understand the importance of this vital safety equipment and that they must take an active role in ensuring that the smoke detectors remain in place and operate properly.

✔ Have pet-owning residential tenants complete and sign an animal agreement, which outlines pet-specific policies and rules at your property. Retain control over the number, type, and size of the animals on your property. You can meet and photograph the animal so there's no doubt as to what you have approved. Remember that guide/assistance dogs for the disabled aren't pets, and thus not subject to pet restrictions or pet rules. Tenants still need to obtain permission to house the guide dogs, and property owners can reasonably be required to agree to reasonable rules of conduct (which are slightly different than pet rules) for assistive animals.

Working with Existing Tenants Upon Property Acquisition

If you're like most investment property owners, you're acquiring property that's already occupied. Tenants are typically full of apprehension when their rental unit ownership is changing, so it's extremely important to begin your relationship with your tenants on a positive note.

Meeting tenants and inspecting units

When you first acquire a residential rental property, contact your tenants and reassure them that you intend to treat them with respect and have a cordial yet businesslike relationship. Deal with tenants' questions honestly and directly. The most common concerns usually include the following:

- ✔ Potential for a rent increase
- ✔ Status of their security deposit
- ✔ Proper maintenance or condition of their rental unit
- ✔ Continuation of certain policies, such as allowing pets

Just as you're evaluating your tenant, your tenant is evaluating you during these initial contacts. Be open and honest. Failing to do so can result in a loss of credibility should you later implement changes that you didn't acknowledge up front. And don't make any promises that you won't keep. Unlike in politics, renters have plenty of choices and will move along if you lie to, deceive, or otherwise disappoint them.

If you're investing in commercial investment properties, you should also meet with your tenants and listen to their concerns about the property. Although they typically aren't as concerned about sudden rent increases (because they're likely on a long-term lease), they're interested in hearing about your plans to maintain and upgrade the property or make any other improvements that may increase their business. Also, it's never too soon to begin courting your commercial tenants for a lease renewal.

Provide your tenants with a letter of introduction during this brief in-person meeting. This letter provides your tenant with your contact information, explains your rent collection policies, the status of their security deposit, and the proper procedures for requesting maintenance.

Although you most likely had a brief chance to view the interior of the rental unit or suite during the due diligence period before escrow closed, walking through again with the tenant now that you're the owner can be helpful. Pay special attention to the proper use of the space, particularly for commercial tenants where illegal activities such as the use or storage of hazardous materials may be a serious liability issue.

Don't just knock on the door and expect to walk through your tenant's rental unit or suite. But if you're at your investment property delivering the letter of introduction, you can schedule a mutually convenient time to meet. Some tenants will be glad to meet with you right then, but others won't. Giving your tenants time to think about any issues that they want to discuss is beneficial for both of you. In most states, tenants don't have to let you enter their rental unit unless you have a legal reason and have given proper advance notice.

The former owner of the investment property may have had a policy of documenting the condition of the rental unit or suite at the time the tenant took possession. If so, compare the noted condition when you actually walk through the rental unit or suite. If proper documentation of the move-in condition wasn't made, consider preparing such information during your walk-through. This practice allows you to establish some sort of baseline for the condition of the unit to use upon the tenant's move-out, which can help you determine the amount of the security deposit to be returned to the tenant.

Entering into a new rental agreement

Although you may want to make some changes in the terms or policies, when you acquire an occupied rental property, your legal and business relationship is already established by whatever agreement the tenants had with the former owner. Therefore, you need to wait until the expiration of the lease to change the terms — or provide a month-to-month tenant with proper written notice of proposed changes as required by state or local law.

Most new owners convert existing tenants to their own lease or rental agreement as soon as possible.

- ✓ **Single-family home, condo, or a small residential rental property:** Implementing your own rental agreement as soon as legally allowed is relatively easy and can be done upon the lease's expiration or upon 30 days' written notice if the tenant is on a month-to-month rental agreement.

- ✔ **Larger residential rental properties:** You may want to gradually transition to a new agreement upon tenant turnover rather than require current tenants to sign a new lease. It's quite a significant project at a larger property to generate all the new leases and then meet with each tenant one-by-one to go over the new lease. If they sign a new lease voluntarily, you can enforce it. Otherwise, you'll need to wait until the current lease expires. Of course, if the tenancy is month-to-month, management can serve the appropriate notice of change of terms of tenancy along with the new month-to-month agreement.

- ✔ **Commercial properties:** Unless the parties agree to a voluntary change of lease terms, you really have no choice but to implement new leases upon tenant lease renewal or turnover as the existing leases are valid and binding until their expiration.

Consider the potential impact of making significant changes in the rental rates or policies immediately after you acquire the property. For example, although you may have strong feelings against allowing pets on your residential rental property, your new tenants may have pets already. Although you legally have the right to implement a no-pet policy upon lease renewal or upon giving proper legal notice, you're almost guaranteed a vacant rental unit if you do so. Impose your policies over a reasonable time frame, but be sure you're aware of the potential financial consequences in the short run.

For residential investment properties, the tenant information the seller provided you during escrow (see Chapter 14) may be outdated. One quick way to update your records is to have the tenants voluntarily complete your rental application form. In many states, you may not have a strong legal argument for requiring existing tenants to provide this information; however, many tenants may understand your reasoning and not mind. Other tenants may be reluctant to complete an entirely new rental application, in which case you may not require them to complete all sections of the form. However, even if you receive initial resistance, seek this updated information prior to renewing any lease. You need to assess the financial qualifications of your tenants, particularly if you anticipate future rent increases.

Increasing rents

When you acquire an investment property, part of your research is to establish the fair market rental value of your new property. If the tenant's current rent is below market value and he's on a month-to-month rental agreement, one of your toughest decisions as the new owner of a rental property is how to handle rent increases.

As the new owner, you likely have much higher mortgage payments and expenses to make necessary repairs and upgrades to the property than the last owner did. Some tenants will be upset and antagonistic about rent increases, however, and there is little you can to do to appease them.

The majority of tenants reluctantly accept a rent increase as long as the rent isn't raised beyond the current market rent for a comparable rental unit or suite in the area and you're willing to make needed repairs or upgrades to their rental units or suites. Providing the tenants with information on comparable rentals in your area should support the reason for your increased rent request.

Finding Stable, Trustworthy Tenants

Vacant rental units or suites don't generate rental income, so efficiently fill your vacancies with good, stable, rent-paying tenants. To ensure that you do so, follow some precautionary measures on your own before beginning to assess potential tenants.

Setting up a systematic screening process is particularly critical if you only own a single-family rental, rental condo, or a small, multiunit rental property. Deadbeat tenants who go from property to property causing damage and not paying rent are experienced and shrewd. They know that the novice property owner is more likely to be fooled and that the large, professionally managed properties have screening procedures to verify every single item on their rental applications.

Sometimes the mere mention of the tenant screening process is enough to make the rental prospect fidget and then shift into the classic "I'm just looking" mode. Don't rush or allow a prospect to hurry you through the tenant screening and selection process. The wrong decision can be financially devastating, particularly if you own just one or two rental units or a small commercial investment property.

More than 90 percent of your residential rental applicants will be good tenants, pay their rent on time, take good care of their homes, and treat you and their neighbors with respect. You just need to carefully guard against those few bad apples; don't hesitate to deny prospects who can't meet your standards. Verifying information on prospective tenants' rental applications takes a while, but it's time well spent. Relying on your instincts is inaccurate, arbitrary, and illegal.

Establishing tenant selection criteria

In order to increase your chances of finding a long-term, stable tenant —
and avoiding charges of discrimination — your tenant selection criteria and
screening process should be clear, systematic, and objective. Tenant selection criteria are *written* standards that you use to evaluate each prospective
tenant's qualifications as a tenant for your property. Determine your minimum qualifications and adhere to them, applying them *consistently* and *fairly*
to *all* rental applicants. Of course, your written criteria can't be discriminatory or violate any federal, state, or local fair housing laws.

In order to establish your selection criteria, review what you're looking for in
a tenant. At a minimum, we suggest that you seek tenants who are financially
responsible, pay their rent on time, and are likely to renew their leases, treat
rental property with care, and be good neighbors. With commercial properties, you're also looking for tenants with complementary businesses that
enhance rather than compete with your current tenants.

You aren't required to provide your rental prospects with a copy of your
written tenant selection criteria, but there are potential benefits to doing
so. Although you must offer all prospects a rental application and process
each one received, there is an advantage to prospects making their own
decision not to apply for your rental based on the criteria you've set up.
The key is to follow the criteria without exception and have the information
available if you're challenged. Decide when you're most comfortable discussing the criteria — from the first inquiry call, when you actually receive
the application, and so on — and once again, be consistent.

Always be thorough when you screen all applicants. You run the risk of a
charge of illegal discrimination if you deviate from your written standards
for certain applicants. There are many legally acceptable reasons to deny a
rental application. Be sure that your requirements are clearly understood
and followed.

The fact that you carefully prescreen all prospects is a positive factor not
only for you but also for your rental applicants, your current tenants, and
even the neighbors. In fact, you have a responsibility to your current tenants
to weed out the unqualified tenants with a track record of disrupting neighbors. The good rental prospects will appreciate the fact that their neighbors
had to meet your high standards, too.

If you're in the rental housing business for long, you hear about six-figure or
larger legal awards against rental property owners for violating fair housing
laws. Problems often arise when investment property owners are unaware
that their policies or practices are discriminatory. Families, children, and

folks with disabilities often suffer from this lack of knowledge. Federal and state laws prohibit discrimination, and these laws impact your advertising, tenant screening, and selection process.

The federal Fair Housing Act prohibits discrimination on the basis of race, color, religion, national origin, sex, familial status, and handicap (referred to as disability in many states). Check the state and local fair housing laws in your area; some additional state and local protected classes include age, sexual orientation, gender identity, occupation, source of income (government assistance, Section 8), educational status, medical status, and even physical body size.

Discrimination is a major issue for investment property owners and has serious legal consequences. If you don't know the law, you may be guilty of various forms of discrimination and not even realize it until you've been charged with discrimination. That's why knowing the law is so important.

With residential rental properties, another form of illegal discrimination is *steering* — guiding a rental applicant toward living where you think he should live based on race, color, religion, national origin, sex, familial status, handicap, or any other protected class. Not showing or renting certain living units to a person because of their protected class status is one form of steering; however, so is the assigning of any person to a particular section or floor of a building, because of any of those bases. Advertising or promotion that indicates or implies a preference is also discriminatory.

All commercial and residential rental applicants should receive information on the full range of vacant space or rental units available and be able to decide which suites or units they want to see.

Residential rental property owners often have good intentions when they suggest that a rental prospect with children see only rental units on the ground floor or near the playground. However, such practices are a violation of current federal fair housing laws as they restrict housing options and can be used by some unscrupulous landlords as an excuse or justification to cover up their intentional discriminatory actions.

Being fair to families and children

All residential rental properties must be offered to all applicants, including those with children, as federal and state legislation has virtually eliminated "adult only" residential housing. The only exception to equal opportunities for families is for those residential communities operated in strict accordance with the rules applicable to senior housing, either 55 and older or 62 and older. However, because there's less regulation of nonresidential properties, some commercial property owners may be within their legal rights to use their business judgment to refuse or discourage an applicant with plans to use the leased space as a daycare or other business that caters to children.

Some rental property owners are concerned about renting to families with children because of hazards on the property that may be dangerous for kids. For example, the property may not have any safe areas for the children to play. Although you may truly only have children's best interests in mind, it's the parent's right to decide whether the property is safe for their children. Of course, you do need to take reasonable steps to make your property safe.

Charging rental applicants with children higher rents or higher security deposits than applicants without children may be found to be discriminatory as is offering different rental terms, such as shorter lease terms, fewer unit amenities, or different payment options. The property facilities must also be fully available for all tenants, regardless of age, unless there is a clear safety issue involved. For example, some states have laws allowing a policy that an adult must accompany children under 14 when using the swimming pool.

As a rental property owner, you should welcome renters with children. Families tend to be more stable, and they look for safe, crime-free, and drug-free environments in which to raise their kids. Along with responsible pet owners, who also have difficulty finding suitable rental properties, families with children can be excellent, long-term renters. And typically, the longer your tenants stay, the better your cash flow. Give families an equal opportunity; however, don't show a preference toward them.

Dealing with tenants with disabilities

The federal fair housing regulations state that property owners must

- ✔ Make reasonable accommodations at the owner's expense for tenants with disabilities, so they can enjoy the rental property on an equal basis. A common example would be providing a wider and more convenient parking space when practical, or assigning a space to a resident with a disability when there are otherwise no assigned spaces.

- ✔ Make reasonable adjustments to their rules, procedures, or services upon request.

- ✔ Allow tenants with disabilities the right to modify their living space at their own expense, under the following conditions:

  - The modifications can only extend to what is necessary to make the space useful and comfortable based on disability-related need.

  - The modifications don't make the unit unacceptable to the next tenant, or if they do, the tenant agrees to return the rental unit to its original condition upon vacating the property.

- The tenant must obtain your prior approval and ensure that the work will be done in a workmanlike manner, including obtaining any necessary government approvals or permits.

- In some limited circumstances, the tenants must pay the funds necessary to perform the needed restoration into an interest-bearing escrow account to ensure that the work is actually completed and there will be no liens against the property.

Note: In housing projects that receive federal funding and are subject to section 504 of the Rehabilitation Act of 1973, landlords will be expected to do necessary physical modification of the premises to the extent that doing so isn't an undue financial or administrative burden.

Discrimination against people with disabilities in residential housing is covered in the federal Fair Housing Act. However, in July 1990, Congress passed the Americans with Disabilities Act (ADA), which has far-reaching impact on most commercial and retail real estate. The ADA has limited requirements for many rental property owners, because it applies only to the public areas and not the private or common areas of residential properties.

Under the ADA, all areas of a property to which the public is invited must be accessible by individuals with disabilities. For example, a rental property with an on-site office, model units (and other amenities if they're allowed to be used by the public, like a clubhouse used for a polling place, or a pool used for YMCA swim meets) must be accessible to persons with disabilities. The removal of existing physical barriers at the rental property owner's expense is required whenever it's "readily achievable and technically feasible." The ADA also establishes parking requirements if the residential property provides public parking, such as prospective resident spaces.

The ADA applies to all commercial properties and to the public part (if any) of a residential property. The ADA rather than fair housing law controls any parking for prospective residents or an on-site office. If the public uses other parts of the property (versus the common areas used only by residents and their guests), those areas are always subject to the ADA. The ADA doesn't include a grandfather clause. Owners are required to remove barriers to accessibility, but they aren't required to make changes if they aren't reasonably achievable or technically feasible. Professional complainants seek out ADA violations in both residential and commercial rental properties, so know what accessibility requirements apply to your property.

Many local municipalities work closely with HUD to investigate ADA complaints and handle enforcement. Also, local jurisdictions oversee and enforce handicapped parking requirements for multiunit rental properties. Check with your local building and code enforcement office for details.

Residential properties built for first occupancy on or after March 13, 1991, also must have been built in compliance with fair housing construction accessibility guidelines. Those guidelines apply to the common areas and the dwelling units. Older properties that were built in compliance with the building codes at that time of construction need not make those areas accessible unless as part of a renovation project. If changes need to be made to allow residents accessibility, fair housing law requires that landlords allow the individual disabled resident to modify the property as needed.

If you have a no pets policy, keep in mind that fair housing law requires rental property owners to make reasonable accommodations in the form of exceptions to their pet rules if necessary. One specific common accommodation is not having any limitations or not discouraging occupancy by tenants who need a *support animal.* Companion or service animals that assist tenants with daily life activities aren't pets; they're exempt animals and must be allowed in all rental properties, regardless of any "no pet" policies. Fair housing laws also prohibit you from requiring an animal or pet deposit, or increasing the tenant's security deposit because he has a support animal. Further, you can't make any rules limiting the types or breeds of animals (for example, allowing German shepherds only) or an unreasonable size restriction. You can, however, establish reasonable rules of conduct for the animals and should note that the tenant is still responsible for any damages done by the animal. Some tenants seek the accommodation of a companion animal based on their need for comfort or companionship, and federal law requires owners and managers to grant the request if the tenant's claim is verified and reasonable.

Advertising for tenants

Advertising is how you let people know that you have a vacant rental property available. Money intelligently spent on advertising is money extremely well spent. But when it's done poorly, advertising can be another black hole for your precious resources.

Determine the most desirable features of your rental property for your target market by asking your current renters what they like about where they live or work. You can also ask people who look at your property — whether or not they agree to rent — what aspects of your property they found of interest. Incorporate these selling points into your marketing efforts.

The best advertisement for your rental property is curb appeal — the exterior appearance. Properties that have well-kept grounds with green grass, trimmed shrubs, beautiful flowers, and fresh paint are much more appealing to your rental prospects. A well-maintained property often attracts a tenant who will pay more rent and treat your rental property with care.

Creating interest in your rental property used to be as simple as putting up a sign or placing an ad in the local newspaper. Although these tried-and-true methods of informing potential renters still often work, other options are available for you to consider. The target market for your rental property has a lot to do with which method of advertising works best for your rental unit. Referrals and property signs often give you good exposure to renters in your local area, whereas newspaper ads and real estate agents may let people or businesses relocating to your area know about your rental property as well. The Internet has become a powerful tool in reaching all segments of your target market.

Showing your rental

One of the most time-consuming aspects of owning and managing rental property is the time spent filling vacancies. Real estate investors with commercial properties often use professional leasing brokers, and owners of large residential properties have onsite managers and leasing agents. But residential rental property owners with small properties usually take this on individually, and it can be a huge time trap.

Efficiently scheduling showings

The most efficient approach to showing your small residential rental is to hold an open house — which enables you to show your property to several interested rental prospects within a couple of hours. Select a two to three hour period for your open house that is convenient for you and most working people (preferably during daylight hours). Combining a weekday early evening open house with one on the weekend enables virtually all prospects to fit the rental showing into their busy schedules.

Another benefit of an open house is that many folks feel more comfortable touring a rental property when other prospects are around. They don't have to be concerned about meeting someone they don't know in a vacant rental property. This approach also aids your own personal safety.

A newspaper ad simply indicating the time of your open house isn't a good idea, because you may end up with many unqualified renters walking through your property. But an open house where you invite all qualified prospects whom you have spoken with in response to your advertising is a good way to create a sense of urgency and competition, which often generates multiple applicants for your rental.

In a depressed rental market, or if you find that you need to fill a vacancy during the holidays, you may not be able to generate enough interest for an open house for multiple prospects. If you have to schedule individual appointments, keep these points in mind:

- ✔ Be prepared to show your rental units in the evenings and on weekends, when most of your prospects are available.

- ✔ Try to consolidate your appointments to a certain time frame, but don't push this too far. Asking prospects to conform to your schedule may turn them off.

- ✔ Call each person to verify the rental showing before making a special trip to the property. By calling, you're also reassuring the prospect that you'll be there and aren't going to be delayed. Exchanging cell phone numbers can be helpful here.

Showing vacant versus occupied rentals

When showing a vacant residential rental, be a tour guide but don't be too controlling. Allow the prospects to view the rental in the manner that suits them. Some prospects go right to a certain room, which gives you a clue about the importance that they place on that aspect of your property. If the prospects hesitate or are reluctant to tour on their own, casually guide them through the rental property.

As you begin to show the interior of your residential rental, avoid making obvious statements such as "This is the living room" or "Here's the bathroom!" Instead, listen and observe the body language and expressions of your prospects as they walk through the property. Don't oversell if they seem pleased, but feel free to point out the benefits of your rental.

Commercial properties are typically shown vacant after the prior tenant has vacated, although you may be able to obtain the cooperation of the vacating tenant to show prospects through the suite while occupied. Because commercial tenants almost always require some specialized tenant improvements, it can be more useful to work off of drawings of the space — rather than conduct a physical tour — and have a space planner show the prospect how the space will meet their needs. If you do show an occupied commercial space, just be sure not to disrupt the tenant's business activities.

In most states, if the current residential tenants are at the end of their lease or have given a notice to vacate, the owner is specifically allowed to enter the unit to show it to a prospective tenant. Of course, you must comply with state laws that require you to give tenants advance written notice of entry prior to showing the rental unit. Your tenant may agree to waive this requirement, but make sure that you have that agreement in writing.

Cooperate with the current tenants when scheduling mutually convenient times to show the rental — and respect their privacy by avoiding excessive intrusions. Although the current tenant may legally be required to allow you and your prospects to enter the rental unit for a showing, he doesn't have to make any efforts to ensure that the property is clean and neat.

Showing a vacant rental unit is generally much easier, but touring your prospect through an occupied rental property does have some advantages. Your current tenants can be a real asset if they're friendly and cooperative and take care of the property. The rental prospects may want to ask the current tenant questions about their living experience at your property.

If you can, get copies of recent utility bills from your current tenant, in case your prospective renters have any questions about utility costs. Utility expenses for electric, natural gas, water and sewer, and trash are becoming significant items in the budgets of many renters. You don't want your tenants to be unable to financially handle the typical monthly utility costs, because that may impact their ability to pay your rent. Plus, you may also be able to use low utility costs as a marketing tool.

If your current residential tenant is being evicted, isn't leaving on good terms, or has an antagonistic attitude for any reason, don't show the rental unit until the property is vacated. Also consider this strategy if your current tenants haven't taken care of the rental property or if their lifestyle or furnishings may be objectionable to some rental prospects.

Selling prospects

After you've qualified your residential rental prospect (see the "Establishing tenant selection criteria" section earlier in the chapter), persuade him that you have the best rental unit available. People want more than just a place to live. Tenants want to feel they can communicate with you if a problem arises. They also appreciate it when someone shows an interest in their lives. By showing an interest, you set yourself apart from other property managers. Some prospects will take a rental unit that isn't exactly what they're looking for if they have a positive feeling about the rental property owner.

No matter how closely your rental unit meets the stated needs and wants of your prospects, they often hesitate and doubt their own judgment. Don't be pushy, but convince the prospects that your property is right for them. After you succeed in this regard, you have to close the sale. This is one area where many rental property owners and managers suddenly get cold feet. They may do a great job handling the initial telephone rental inquiry, the preparation and showing of the rental property, and even objections, but become shy to ask the prospect to sign and commit money.

Your goal at the end of the showing is to receive a commitment from the prospect to rent by having him complete your rental application and pay the credit screening fee, first month's rent, and security deposit. But don't forget that you still need to thoroughly screen the prospect and confirm that he meets your rental criteria before you sign a lease or rental agreement.

If, despite your best efforts, the prospect is still undecided, make sure that he gives you a holding deposit. Remind him that you may make a deal with the next prospect and he'll be out of luck. If you have a lot of demand for your rental units or suites, you should develop a waiting list. (***Note:*** Receiving a large number of applicants may be an indication that you set your rent too low.)

Accepting applications and deposits

You must offer every interested prospect (age 18 and older) the opportunity to complete a written rental application. You want to avoid having a prospect accuse you of discriminating against him by not permitting him to fill out the rental application. And information provided on the application enables you to begin the screening process and select the best tenant for your rental property, using objective criteria and your rental requirements.

Rental property owners are legally allowed to choose among rental applicants as long as their decisions comply with all fair-housing laws and are based on legitimate business criteria. However, if you screen applications in the order that you receive them and approve the first application that meets your qualifications, you avoid any argument about preference.

Prior to accepting the rental application, carefully review the entire form to make sure that each prospective tenant has legibly provided all requested information. Pay particular attention to all names and addresses, source of income information, photo identification numbers, and emergency contacts. Make sure that the prospect has signed the rental application authorizing you to verify the provided information and to run a credit report. Finally, ask each prospective tenant to show you her current driver's license or other government-issued photo identification so that you can confirm that she provided you with her correct name and current address.

If you go over the application with the prospect, only ask questions that are part of the form. Don't ask the rental applicant about his birthplace, religion, marital status, children, or about a physical or mental condition — such questions may lead to accusations of discrimination. You can ask him if he has ever been convicted of a crime and whether he's at least 18 years old or an emancipated minor. Not all criminal convictions may justify denial of an applicant. For more details on the details of how to run and properly use criminal background checks, consult *Landlord's Legal Kit For Dummies* by Robert and attorney Laurence Harmon (John Wiley & Sons, Inc.).

After you approve the rental prospect, you should have him sign the rental agreement. If the prospect still insists he needs additional time, he should agree to pay the daily rental rate or you should refund his holding deposit and continue your leasing efforts.

If you use a holding deposit, you must have a written agreement or you're likely to encounter a misunderstanding or even legal action. State laws regarding holding deposits vary throughout the country, yet they're almost uniformly vague and can easily lead to disputes.

Verifying rental applications

Keep copies of all rental applications and corresponding verification forms, credit reports, and all other documents for both accepted and rejected applicants for at least three years. That way, if anyone ever makes a claim that you discriminated against him, your best defense will be your own records, which will clearly indicate that you consistently applied legal rental criteria. Here are the key items to review on renters' applications.

Adults' identity

Require each prospective adult tenant to show you his or her current driver's license or other similar (and official) photo ID so that you can confirm that the applicant is providing you with his correct name and current address. Advise each rental applicant that if his application is approved, you'll need a photocopy of his ID to be kept in his tenant file.

Ask about any discrepancies between the application and the ID provided. Even if the explanation seems reasonable, be sure to write down the new information. Maybe an old address appears on the photo ID, which you can check out further through a credit-reporting agency. Having a photocopy of the ID for each adult tenant is vital if a dispute about the tenant's identity arises in the future. In these situations, you need to be able to clearly show that you positively identified the tenant at move-in.

Rental history

When you first contact the rental applicant's current landlord, listen to his initial reaction and let him tell you about the applicant. Some landlords welcome the opportunity to tell you all about your rental applicant, but some current and prior landlords may be

✔ **Dishonest:** A landlord may be upset with the tenant for leaving his property or unwilling to say anything bad about a problem tenant so that he can get the tenant out of his property and into yours.

✔ **Unforthcoming:** Some landlords are concerned that they may have liability if they provide any negative or subjective information. Pose the questions in writing and ask for a written response. Then you'll have documentary proof of what was said and what wasn't.

When a current or prior landlord isn't overly cooperative, try to gain his confidence by providing him with some information about yourself and your rental property. If you're still unable to build rapport, try to get him to at least answer the most important question of all: "Would you rent to this applicant again?" He can simply give you a yes or a no without any details. Even better, we suggest that you ask specific fact-based questions that can be answered honestly, such as "Did you have an noise complaints or police calls to the unit?" or "Did they pay the full rent on-time each month?" Of course, silence can also tell you everything that you need to know.

Some applicants provide you with letters of reference from their prior landlords or even copies of their credit reports. Verify the authenticity of any documents provided by the rental applicant. Another useful screening tool is to request all tenants to provide copies of their water and utility bills for the past year. These documents can verify the tenant's prior address and also give you an idea whether they pay their bills on time.

Employment and income

Independently verify the company information and phone number the applicant puts on her application if you have any doubts about the authenticity of it. You also need to be careful that you confirm the sensitive compensation and stability of employment questions only with an appropriate representative of the employer. Be prepared to send letters requesting the pertinent information and include a self-addressed, stamped envelope. Be sure to tell your rental prospect that you may have a delay in providing her with the results of your tenant screening process.

In addition to the results of your verification calls, the applicant should provide you with proof of her employment income such as recent pay stubs. But no matter how strong the information is, verify it directly with the employer. Also verify other sources of income. For prospective commercial tenants, a copy of the most recent tax return is your best method of verifying income.

Credit history

Obtain a credit report on each applicant. A credit report shows all current and previous credit cards and loans, timeliness of making payments when due, plus all public record entries such as bankruptcy and judgment. You can figure out whether an applicant has been late or delinquent in paying his rent or other living expenses. The three major credit reporting agencies are Experian (www.experian.com; 888-397-3742), Equifax (www.equifax.com; 800-997-2493), and TransUnion (www.transunion.com; 800-888-4213). Credit information for commercial tenants can be found in the D&B database (www.dnb.com; 800-234-3867).

Carefully compare the addresses contained on the credit report to the information provided on the rental application. If there is an inconsistency, ask the rental prospect for an explanation. Maybe the person was temporarily staying with a family member or simply forgot about one of her residences. Of course, be sure to contact prior landlords and ask all the questions on the rental application verification form just to make sure that the applicant didn't neglect to tell you about that residence for a reason.

Information obtained in credit reports must be kept strictly confidential and can't be given to any third parties. In some states, the rental applicant is entitled to a copy of his own credit report upon request, and federal law allows anyone denied credit or housing on the basis of his credit report to obtain a free copy of the report.

Make sure that you're reviewing the credit report of your actual applicant. People with poor credit or tenant histories have been known to steal the identity of others — particularly their own children — by using the child's Social Security number. Many landlords no longer even ask for Social Security numbers, but if you do, one solution is to make sure that your credit reporting service provides a Social Security search, which clearly indicates whether there are any inconsistencies in the use of the number provided. You may not always be able to verify a Social Security number, and you don't want to be accused of discriminatory effect based on national origin, so talk to your applicant screening service about having an alternative screening method in these situations.

All personal references

You will occasionally find someone who tells you that the rental applicant is her best friend but goes on to candidly tell you she would never loan the applicant money or let him borrow her car. Plus, if you call the references given and find that the information is bogus, you can use this information as part of your overall screening and rejection of the applicant.

Dealing with rental cosigners

If your rental prospect doesn't meet the criteria outlined in your statement of rental policy, you may consider approving his application if he provides a cosigner or *guarantor*. A guarantor must be financially qualified and screened or the guarantee is worthless.

Require your guarantor to complete a rental application, pay the application fee, and go through the credit screening process (previous rental history isn't relevant for a co-signer because it's with the applicant). Keep in mind that the guarantor won't actually be occupying the commercial suite or living at your rental unit and thus will have his own housing costs. To ensure that the guarantor can meet all of his own obligations and cover your tenant's rent in case of a default, deduct the guarantor's cost of housing from his income before comparing it to your income requirements.

Although a lease guarantor can be very important and can give you the extra resources in the event of a rent default by your tenant, out-of-state lease guarantors aren't as valuable as in-state ones. Enforcing the lease guarantee against an out-of-state party can be difficult or even financially unfeasible.

Notifying applicants of your decision

Regardless of whether your rental applicant is accepted or rejected, be sure to notify the applicant promptly when the decision is made. If you have approved the applicant, contact him and arrange for a meeting and a walk-through of the rental unit prior to the move-in date.

Don't notify the other qualified applicants that you have already rented the rental property until all legal documents have been signed and all funds due upon move-in have been collected in full.

One of the most difficult tasks for the rental property owner is informing a rental applicant that you've denied his application. You obviously want to avoid an argument over the rejection, but even more importantly, you want to avoid a fair-housing complaint based on the applicant's misunderstanding about the reasons for the denial.

Notify your denied rental applicant in writing, and keep a copy of all rejection letters for at least three years. If you notify the applicant only by phone, you may have difficulty giving all of the details and required disclosures. The written notice-of-denial-to-rent form avoids a situation in which the applicant may form the opinion that you're denying his application in a discriminatory manner, in which case he may file a complaint with HUD or a state or local fair-housing agency.

Using a notice-of-denial-to-rent form to inform the applicant in writing of your decision as well as outline the valid reasons is an excellent idea. This form helps you to document the various legal reasons for your rejection of the applicant. It's a simple checklist that also allows you to provide the applicant with the required information per the federal Fair Credit Reporting Act.

If you reject an applicant based on his credit report, you're required by the federal Fair Credit Reporting Act to notify the applicant of his rights. Provide the denied applicant with a letter containing the mandatory disclosures so that you have proof that you complied with the law. You must also provide this information even if you have approved the applicant but have required him to pay a higher security deposit, higher rent, or provide a cosigner.

If your denial is based on something other than credit, then a written notice isn't required, but it's still advisable to send a letter or at least tell the applicant that he can send you a written request asking for a reason.

Reviewing and signing documents

Tenants and property owners alike are usually aware of all the legal paperwork involved in renting a property. And although sifting through all that legalese isn't fun for anyone, it's important. Rental property owners and tenants each have specific legal rights and responsibilities that are outlined in these documents, and being aware of what you're agreeing to — and being sure that your tenants know what they're agreeing to — is crucial.

After you approve the rental prospect, you should have her sign the rental agreement. If the prospect still insists she needs additional time, she should agree to pay the daily rental rate or you should refund her holding deposit and continue your leasing efforts.

Be sure that your tenant understands that when he signs your rental agreement, he's entering into a business contract that has significant rights and responsibilities for both parties. Be sure to have all adult occupants review and sign *all documents* — including any lease or rental agreement addenda — before taking possession of the rental unit. After the tenant has been given the keys and taken possession of the rental property, getting him to sign your required legal documents can be difficult, and regaining possession of your rental unit can be a long and expensive process. (Even if the tenant failed to sign the lease or rental agreement, an oral tenant/landlord relationship is established when you give the tenant the keys, but oral agreements often foster *dis*agreements, so avoid the situation altogether.)

Collecting the money

In your meeting prior to move-in, be sure to collect the first month's rent and the security deposit *before* you give the tenants the keys to the rental unit. Payment may be in the form of cash, a cashier's check, or a money order. But don't accept a personal check (because you have no way of knowing whether the check will clear). Provide a receipt for the payments.

Accept cash for the move-in or the monthly rent payment only when absolutely necessary and when you're sure that it's legal, because some states don't allow you to require cash. Regularly collecting cash for your rents can make you a crime target. Most convenience stores offer money orders for a nominal cost and are open at all hours, so let your tenant take the risk of carrying the cash to the bank or convenience store to get a money order. Tell your new tenant that your policy is to accept only a bank cashier's check or money order upon move-in. Also, let him know whether your rent collection policy allows him to pay his future monthly rent payments with a personal check.

Prior to giving the keys to your new tenant and allowing him to take possession, insist on having the payment in hand through *good funds* (as opposed to *insufficient funds,* where a person writes a check and doesn't have the money to cover it). Most owners do this by requiring cash, a bank cashier's check, or a money order. But many rental owners aren't aware that both bank cashier's checks and money orders can be stopped because they can be lost or stolen. However, the bank cashier's check and money orders are superior to personal checks because they do represent good funds and at least won't be returned to you because there was no money to cover them.

If, despite our strong advice, you accept a personal check, at least don't give the tenant access to the property until you've called and verified with the tenant's bank that the check will be honored. Your best bet is to physically take the check to the tenant's bank and cash it or at least have it certified. If the bank certifies the check, it's guaranteeing that there are sufficient funds available and that it will actually put a hold on the funds. Of course, cashing the check is the only sure way to collect your funds, because a devious tenant can always stop payment on even a certified personal check.

Inspecting the property with your tenant

The number one source of residential tenant/landlord disputes is the disposition of the tenant's security deposit. Many of these potential problems can be resolved with proper procedures before the tenant takes possession of the rental unit by using a move-in/move-out inspection checklist.

When properly completed, the inspection form clearly documents the condition of the rental property upon move-in by the tenants and serves as a baseline for the entire tenancy. If the tenant withholds rent or tries to break the lease claiming the unit needs substantial repairs, you may need to be able to prove the condition of the rental unit upon move-in. When the tenants move out, you'll be able to clearly note the items that they damaged or left unclean.

Complete the inspection form *with the tenants* prior to or at the time of move-in. Walk through the premises with the tenants and agree that all items are clean and undamaged *before* they move in their stuff. Note the condition of the carpets and floor coverings — one of the most common areas of dispute upon move-out. Although tenants shouldn't be charged for ordinary wear and tear, if they destroy the carpet, they should pay for the damage. Indicate the age of the carpet and whether it has been professionally cleaned as part of your rental turnover process. You can also take photos or videotape the unit before the tenant moves in for additional material to refresh the tenant's memory or show the court if the matter ends up there.

Renovating and Upgrading to Add Value

For residential properties, almost every rental unit has the potential for renovation or upgrades. Often this area is where the real value can be created in rental units: When you have a rental unit that is dated, you can renovate it and increase the rent. Pay particular attention to those items that would be quick, easy, and inexpensive to replace but that can really improve the overall look of your rental unit.

If you have an older investment property, renovating or making tenant improvements may be more difficult due to some of the hazardous materials used in your building's original construction. Asbestos and lead-based paint were commonly used in construction of many older properties, and these materials can be quite costly to remove. Often, you're better off just leaving them in place as long as they haven't been disturbed. Consult with experts in these issues before doing any work. Also, check with your local building, code enforcement, or health department for its requirements regarding the proper handling and disposal of hazardous materials.

Again, if your chosen investment properties are residential, keep in mind what features and strengths your prospective renters can find in competitive rental units. For example, if most of your competition offers dishwashers but your unit doesn't have one, you may want to install a dishwasher so that you remain competitive. Another simple upgrade is to replace your old electrical switches and outlets to create a more modern look.

Enhancing external appearances

Make sure that your rental prospects' first impression of your residential or commercial rental property is a positive one, because if it isn't, they'll most likely never take the time to see the interior. Start at the street and carefully critique your property as if you were entering a contest for the best-looking property in your area.

To attract tenants who will treat your property well and stay for a long time, be sure that your grounds and exterior areas are sparkling clean and the landscaping is well maintained. Renovating the grounds by removing trash, junk, and weeds is an inexpensive task. A nice green lawn, healthy shrubs, and shade trees enhance any investment property. Make sure that the building structure is presentable and inviting. Some specific exterior improvements to consider are ground level or hanging planters, brass or brushed nickel address numbers, awnings, fresh paint, landscaping, and cleanup.

First impressions are critical and one of the key areas seen by all prospective tenants is the front entry. Ensure the entryway is clean, well kept, and well lighted. The entry door should be cleaned or freshly painted or stained. Buy a new welcome mat. Remove or replace a broken screen door.

Improving what's inside

The most qualified renters always have choices. You're in competition for these excellent tenants, and you need to ensure that your rental stands out from the rest. The positive first impression of your rental property's exterior won't matter if the rental unit's interior is poorly maintained.

Don't show your rental until it's completely rent-ready. Although you may lose a couple of potential showing days by taking the time to get the unit ready, you benefit in the long run with a more conscientious tenant. Here's a list of things to check:

- ✔ All plumbing and appliances are operating properly.
- ✔ Locks have been changed and are operational. Pay attention to all latches and catches, doorknobs and pulls, doorstops, and sliding doors.
- ✔ Windows, window locks, screens, and window coverings should be clean, unbroken, secure, and operating properly.
- ✔ Paint and/or wall coverings should provide proper coverage, without holes, cuts, scratches, nails, or bad seams.
- ✔ Floor coverings should be clean and in good condition.
- ✔ Thoroughly clean the toilet, tub, shower, sink, mirrors, and cabinets.
- ✔ Check all closets and storage areas. Rods, closet dowels, hooks, shelves, lights, floors, and walls should be clean.

✔ Counters, cabinets, doors, molding, thresholds, and metal strips should be clean and fully operational, presenting no hazards.

✔ Check smoke, radon, and carbon monoxide detectors, all lighting, and electrical outlets, including ground-fault circuit-interrupters (GFCI) and circuit breakers for proper operation.

✔ Patios, balconies, and entryways should be clean and the railings secure.

✔ Check the heating and air-conditioning for proper operation. Be sure the thermostat, filters, vents, and registers are all in working order.

Using contractors

Particular maintenance and improvements are best handled by outside contractors. Use outside contractors for those trades that require specialized licensing or training. For example, it would be unwise for you to act as an exterminator or a contractor dealing with environmental hazards, or to attempt to recharge the coolant in an air-conditioning unit. Specific regulations are in place and unique knowledge is required in these areas.

Your skill level, time constraints, and opportunity cost may help determine whether you do some chores yourself or hire a pro. For example, cleaning, painting, and light maintenance may be items that you feel qualified to handle and can complete promptly.

Every day your residential rental unit sits vacant is costing you rental income that you can never recover. If you decide to paint your own rental unit, it may take you six days working in the evenings and on weekends to completely paint a single-family rental home. If the rental market is strong and the daily rental rate is $50 per day, you're actually losing money if you could have had the rental home professionally painted in one day for $200.

Regardless of how much work you choose to handle yourself, have on hand a list of competent and competitively priced service companies and suppliers for those times when you need a quick response. Your local affiliate of the National Apartment Association (NAA), the Institute of Real Estate Management (IREM), or the Building and Owners Managers Association (BOMA) can often provide names of service companies. Carefully check the references and the status of any bonds or licenses with the appropriate governmental agency, and ensure that they have the proper insurance in place before you allow them to commence any work on your property.

Chapter 16

Protecting Your Investment: Insurance and Risk Management

In This Chapter

▶ Creating your risk management plan

▶ Looking into insurance options

*A*fter years of accumulating resources, every investment property owner needs to be concerned about protecting her assets through insurance and risk management programs. After working and sacrificing to build your wealth through real estate, don't be careless and lose it.

The concept of risk management includes much more than simply having an insurance policy. You need to take care to practice proper maintenance and record-keeping and require that others provide you with coverage for their activities. That's what this chapter is all about.

Developing a Risk Management Plan

Many people get into the world of rental real estate without knowing how much risk they're exposed to just by owning real estate. You may read stories in the newspaper about lawsuits against deep-pocket defendants without much personal concern, but it's a reality shock when you're suddenly considered to be the one with those deep pockets.

Real estate investment property owners need a plan to minimize risks because they're frequent targets of those who suffer a personal injury or whose property is damaged. Many studies have shown that real estate rental property owners are sued more than any other single type of business entity.

But you can take steps to reduce and control your risk. Consider the following suggestions as preventive actions to minimize the potential of being named in a lawsuit:

- ✓ **Regularly inspect the property as part of a thorough maintenance program.** One of the easiest ways to minimize the potential of being named in a lawsuit is to routinely inspect your property and correct any noted deficiencies, such as health or safety problems. Be sure to comply with all advance notice of entry requirements and access limitation laws before going into the rental unit or going onto the tenants' exclusive exterior areas. Make and retain copies of your inspections and document that all items were promptly and professionally addressed.

- ✓ **Listen to and address tenant complaints.** Be open and responsive to feedback from your tenants and others expressing concerns. A track record of quick response to complaints is the best defense if you find yourself defending a claim or lawsuit alleging an injury or property damage due to your negligence.

- ✓ **Transfer the risk to others.** Transferring risk from the owner and property manager to the vendor or supplier is sound policy for managing and minimizing risk. You can do this contractually by only using licensed and qualified contractors and suppliers who provide their own insurance coverage. Require that they provide written evidence that they have proper insurance coverage in place naming you individually and the legal entity that actually holds title to your investment property as an additional insured prior to performing work or providing materials.

  If you use a management company to handle the property management for you, make sure that they require insurance declaration forms from all vendors and suppliers documenting $1 million minimum coverage limits prior to doing any work or even making deliveries to your property.

- ✓ **Remove certain risks or never allow them in the first place.** For example, many owners and managers of residential properties have removed diving boards and pool slides. Commercial property owners have restricted access to the roofs of their buildings with emergency door hardware.

Although you can minimize your risks by taking some of these steps, you can't eliminate all risks completely, and that's why you need proper insurance coverage. Insurance is a vital element in a risk-management program.

Getting the Insurance You Need

As the owner of investment real estate, insurance coverage is one of your best protections and an essential risk management technique to ensure that you hold on to the wealth that you create.

If you've ever sat down with a sharp and assertive insurance agent, you may know that some insurance companies sell you coverage against any possible danger or loss in the world. Experienced insurance agents seem to have mastered the art of describing all sorts of horrible problems that may befall your investment property. But you need to sift through the sales pitch, do further research, and decide which coverage is right for you — and make sure you're covered at a reasonable cost.

Your goal is to pay only for coverage for events and losses that can occur at your property. The right insurance coverage is worth a lot, but use resources wisely — hurricane insurance in Minnesota isn't worthy of your precious insurance dollars.

You need to be concerned about lawsuits and having the proper insurance coverage to defend yourself and protect your assets. Insurance not only provides protection against actual losses but also provides a legal defense against the claims made against you as the owner of real estate. The expense of retaining competent legal counsel is what makes the threat of a lawsuit so devastating to many real estate investors.

Don't assume that all potential losses are covered by your insurance coverage. Your best defense against losses is to properly manage your rentals and assertively eliminate, transfer, or control the inherent risks of owning and managing rental property.

Understanding insurance options

The proper insurance coverage can protect you from losses caused by many dangers, including fire, storms, burglary, and vandalism. A comprehensive policy also includes *liability insurance,* covering injuries or losses suffered by others as the result of defective or dangerous conditions on the property. Liability insurance also covers the legal costs of defending personal injury lawsuits — a valuable feature because the legal defense costs of these cases are commonly much greater than the ultimate award of damages, if any.

Common coverages

The following list describes the three levels of coverage available for *primary policies,* all of which include liability coverage. Many insurance companies offer competitive insurance packages especially designed to meet the needs of rental property owners, so remember to shop around.

- ✔ **Basic coverage:** Most companies offer a basic coverage package that insures your investment rental property against loss from fire, lightning, explosion, windstorm or hail, smoke, aircraft or vehicles, riot or civil commotion, vandalism, sprinkler leakage, and even volcanic eruptions.

  This coverage often doesn't include certain contents, such as boilers, equipment, and machinery unless specifically added as an endorsement. Based on the type of property you have, you may need to consult with your insurance agent about additional coverage that may be beneficial.

  But just because you own a small retail strip center with a couple of plate glass windows doesn't mean you need to have the special coverage that's offered. Insurance companies often have minimum policy premiums, so certain insurable items and acts aren't worth insuring because the potential for a claim is minimal and the costs are high.

- ✔ **Broad-form coverage:** You get the basic package, plus protection against losses of glass breakage, falling objects, weight of snow or ice, water damage associated with plumbing problems, and collapse from certain specific causes.

- ✔ **Special form:** This coverage is the broadest available and covers your property against all losses, except those specifically excluded from the policy. It offers the highest level of protection and may not be much more expensive, but is often a good value. Additional coverages included with special form that are helpful to landlords include vandalism, malicious mischief, and theft — for that occasion when your tenant under eviction decides to vandalize and damage your rental property as they skip out in the middle of the night!

An insurance company can pay owners for losses in two ways:

- ✔ **Actual cash value:** The coverage pays the cost of replacing property less physical depreciation. The standard policies most insurance companies offer provide for actual cash value coverage only.

- ✔ **Replacement cost:** This coverage pays the cost of replacing the property without subtracting for physical depreciation. You must specifically have an endorsement and pay extra for replacement cost coverage. However, we do encourage you to purchase it.

As with homeowners' insurance policies, the location, age, type, and quality of construction of your property are significant factors in determining your insurance premiums. Be sure to get an insurance estimate before you buy your property to avoid unpleasant surprises (older properties with wood shake shingles located away from fire protection may not even be insurable, for example) and realize the benefits of lower risk properties. For example, newer commercial buildings, and even some residential properties, were constructed with fire sprinklers and alarms that reduce your insurance premiums — so do hard-wired, permanently installed, and actively monitored intrusion alarms).

Some insurance companies have a *coinsurance clause* that requires rental property owners to carry a minimum amount of coverage. If you carry less than the minimum amount of coverage, the insurance company imposes a coinsurance penalty that reduces the payment on the loss by the same percentage of the insurance shortfall. For example, if you carry only $1 million in coverage when you should have $2 million, you're only carrying 50 percent of the minimum required insured value. If the building suffers a loss, the insurance company pays only 50 percent of the loss.

Many rental property owners first become investors by renting out their former personal residences when they buy new homes. They may not realize they should immediately contact their insurance agent and have their homeowners policy converted to a landlord's policy, which contains special coverage riders that aren't in the typical homeowner's policy. Because of the increased liability risk for rental properties, some insurance companies may not even offer this coverage, whereas others specialize in this business. Either way, obtain proper landlord's coverage for your rental property, or you may face the possibility of having your claim denied.

If you own multiple investment or rental properties, consider

- ✔ **A single insurance policy that covers all locations:** Rather than have separate policies for each rental property, you can get better coverage with a single policy. For example, if you currently have three properties each with a $1 million policy, you could get a single policy with a $3 million limit at a more competitive cost.

- ✔ **An aggregate deductible:** An aggregate deductible is the portion of your loss that you essentially self-insure, because the losses at any of your three properties can go toward meeting the aggregate deductible.

Excess liability (umbrella) coverage

Excess liability (umbrella) coverage can be a cost-effective way to dramatically increase your liability protection and is designed to supplement your main or basic policies. An umbrella policy provides both additional and broader coverage beyond the limits of the basic commercial general liability insurance and other liability coverage and this coverage is only available after the primary policy limits have been exhausted.

Your primary policy may have liability limits of $500,000 or $1 million, but an umbrella policy can provide an additional $1 million in vital coverage at a cost of $2,500 to $5,000 per year. Depending on the value of your property and the value of the assets you're seeking to protect, buying an umbrella liability policy with higher limits may make sense. Umbrella policies are available in increments of $1 million with even lower rates per dollar of coverage as the limits go higher. The most common umbrella coverage amount for the owners of large investment properties now is $5 million at an annual cost of approximately $5,000 to $8,000.

Purchase your umbrella policy from the same company that handles your underlying primary liability insurance package. The reason: If you have two different insurers rather than just one, the companies may have different agendas if legal problems arise.

Additional insurance options

A variety of other insurance coverages also make sense for most rental property owners:

- ✔ **Loss-of-rents (or business interruption) coverage** provides income (enabling you to make mortgage and other payments) if your property is severely damaged by fire or another calamity.

- ✔ **Workers' compensation** insurance pays employees and covers their medical expenses if they're injured or become ill as a result of their job. There are workers' compensation laws in all states; be sure to fully comply with them. This insurance coverage is often available through a government agency, whereas private insurance companies also offer coverage in other areas.

  Although some states may not require you to carry this coverage unless you have a minimum number of employees, we advise carrying workers' compensation coverage even if you don't have *any* employees. For example, any contractor you hire to perform work on your rental property should have his own workers' compensation insurance policy to cover all of his employees. However, if someone gets hurt and the contractor has limited or even no coverage, his injured employee may target you for compensation. Don't take chances; this coverage can often be added to your standard insurance policy for little cost.

✔ **Non-owned auto liability coverage** protects you from liability for accidents and injuries caused by your employees while working and using their own vehicle. Also, require them to provide proof of a valid driver's license (with a clean driving record) and proof that they currently have their own auto and liability coverage with reasonable limits.

✔ **Fidelity bonds** provide reimbursement if you have a dishonest employee who steals your rents.

✔ **Endorsement for money and securities** covers losses caused by dishonest acts of nonemployees.

✔ **Building ordinance insurance** covers the costs of demolition and cleanup, plus the increased costs to rebuild if your rental property is partially or fully destroyed and the property needs to meet new or stricter building code requirements. This coverage is extremely important if your property is built at a *higher density* (more units or square footage or beyond height limits) than current zoning allows; it compensates you for the lost property value if you can't rebuild the same size building.

Mold: The heir-apparent to asbestos

One coverage that's becoming much more difficult to obtain is a type of *environmental* insurance that specifically covers mold, fungus, and related issues. The number and magnitude of mold claims by tenants of both residential and commercial type properties have become a real challenge to the insurance industry, with some highly publicized lawsuits claiming huge property damage and severe personal injury claims. Although certain insurance companies still offer limited coverage for mold and related causes, specifically inquire as to the exact protection included in your policy. Some policies don't cover actual damages for property and personal injury but do offer a legal defense.

The best way to avoid claims of property damage and personal injury from mold is to properly maintain your property and only turn over possession of the rental unit or suite in good condition that's documented in writing. The challenge with most mold claims is that water intrusion and the subsequent concerns about mold typically occur within the tenant's space in areas where the owner has no access or control. Or the tenant can even be the cause of the source of moisture through negligence or inadequate cleaning.

Thus, the rental property owner must rely on the tenant to minimize the likelihood of mold as well as report any concerns immediately. Many owners now use a lease addendum advising tenants of their responsibilities in this area. (See Robert's *Property Management Kit For Dummies* [John Wiley & Sons, Inc.] for the latest on mold claims and more than 200 forms to use when managing your rental properties.) Rental property owners should respond to all tenant concerns promptly and professionally while routinely inspecting accessible areas.

> ✔ **Flood, hurricane, and earthquake insurance** are examples of coverage available for a separate cost. This coverage can be critical in the event of a natural disaster. However, these policies often are expensive with extremely high deductibles, making them unattractive for the average small rental property owner. Get quotes nonetheless, and see whether it's something you think you can afford.

Determining the right deductible

The *deductible* is the amount of money that you must pay out-of-pocket before your insurance coverage kicks in and is a form of *self-insurance* (covering the potential loss yourself). Typically, deductibles for small rental property owners range from $500 to $1,000; larger real estate portfolios have much higher deductibles of $5,000 to $10,000. The higher the deductible, the lower is your insurance premium. As your financial ability to self-insure grows, evaluate the possibility of having a higher deductible and using your savings to purchase other important coverage.

Selecting potential insurers

The coverage you can get as a rental property owner varies among insurers, with some firms specializing in real estate. Be sure to interview and select a qualified insurance broker or agent who understands your unique needs. The insurance professional can then provide you with information on the kinds of coverage worth considering. *Insurance professionals* are either independent brokers or exclusive agents who just write policies for one company.

As with any competitive product or service, speak with multiple independent insurance brokers and a couple of exclusive company agents to ensure that you receive the best value on desired insurance coverage. Keep in mind that the lowest premium is often not the best policy or value for your specific needs.

In addition to the price of a policy and the insurer's reputation and track record for paying claims, an insurer's financial health is an important consideration when you choose a company. Insurers can go belly up. Major rating agencies that research and evaluate the financial health of insurance companies include A. M. Best, Moody's, Standard & Poor's, Fitch, and Weiss. Each rating agency uses a different letter-grade system. Some companies use AAA as their highest rating, and then AA, A, BBB, BB, and so on. Others use A, A–, B+, B, B–, and so on.

During the financial crisis of 2008, as well as during other times, you may have heard about some insurers getting into trouble despite prior high ratings. That happens, but don't worry about an insurer going belly up and not paying claims. Insurers are regulated and overseen at the state (and federal) level and troubled insurers are merged into stronger ones.

Just as it's a good idea to get more than one medical opinion, two or three financial ratings can give you a better sense of the safety of an insurance company. Stick with companies that are in the top two — or, at worst, three — levels on the different rating scales. You can obtain current rating information about insurance companies by asking your agent for a listing of the current ratings.

After you've made your decision as to which policies and insurers you want to do business with, be sure that you pay the premium, and insist on evidence that the insurance company has provided coverage. Typically, you receive a written binder as soon as you have coverage; however, your best proof of coverage is a formal certificate of insurance. The certificate of insurance is essential — prudent real estate owners never rely on verbal representations that they're covered.

Talking with tenants about renter's insurance

Renter's insurance is secured by and paid for by your tenants and covers losses to the tenant's personal or business property as a result of fire, theft, water damage, or other loss. As a rental property owner, you want to encourage your tenants to have this coverage. They pay the premium and you benefit from renter's insurance because it covers any claims in the event that the tenant or her guest starts a fire or flood. This coverage also can help you avoid a claim in case a tenant's guest was injured inside her rental unit or caused damage to the rental property.

One of the benefits of renter's insurance is that when your tenant has a renter's insurance policy to handle her claims, she is less likely to sue you or threaten you with a lawsuit. Also, if the tenant makes claims against her own policy, then the tenant's premiums go up rather than yours.

Most commercial tenants have this coverage, but residential tenants often think they don't need renter's insurance because they have few valuables. But renter's insurance covers much more than just their personal possessions; it also protects against liability claims made by injured guests or visitors. The insurance also offers supplemental living expenses if the rental unit becomes uninhabitable due to fire or smoke damage. And it protects the tenant in the event that the tenant causes damage to another tenant's property. Robert has seen several such lawsuits resulting from the negligence of one tenant who caused an overflowing toilet, bathtub, or sink in her rental unit to become a waterfall into the downstairs unit or common area. You can suggest or even require that your tenants carry renter's insurance, but be aware that in some areas your competitors may not follow your lead and you may find that you'd have trouble keeping your rentals occupied if you insisted that your tenants carry renter's insurance.

Dealing with claims

Record all the facts as soon as an incident occurs on your rental property, particularly if it involves injury. Because one of the primary issues in contention is the property condition at the time of the incident, a digital camera is extremely helpful to document facts and minimize extensive disagreements or discussions at a later date or during litigation. You can also use a recording device if you have obtained permission in advance from those involved (preferably the acknowledgment should be in writing).

Be sure to immediately contact your insurance company or your insurance agent. Follow up with a written letter to ensure they were notified and have the information on file.

Put a reliable filing system in place to keep documents handy because litigation may not occur until years after the incident. For example, if a young child is hurt on your property, the statute of limitations doesn't begin until the child has reached 18 years of age. In these cases, the tenancy records and maintenance records may be subpoenaed and be critical to defending your actions of up to 20 years ago.

Chapter 17

Recordkeeping and Accounting

. . . .

In This Chapter

▶ Putting your property records and files in order

▶ Tracking the income and expenses for your rental activities

. . . .

Recordkeeping and accounting may not be the most exciting aspects of real estate investment property ownership, but they're among the most rewarding. Every real estate owner should be interested in knowing how much money she's making on her properties and how much she's spending. She should also know how she can potentially reduce her taxes.

Traditionally, the least favored aspect of owning real estate is keeping all of the required paperwork and doing the accounting. More property managers have gained clients because of these essential but tedious requirements than any other reason. But recordkeeping has roles in maintaining your assets as well as documenting performance. And the accounting is the report card or feedback that tells you just how well you're doing.

Now, we can't turn you into an accountant in the course of one chapter. Whole books are written on the subject. But what we can do is provide you with practical and useful information that you can use to organize your recordkeeping and accounting practices, and we can provide you with additional sources of information.

Organizing Your Records

If you have an aversion to details and keeping track of things, managing your own investment rental properties may not be for you. If you own rental property, you need to prepare many important written records and keep them ready for prompt retrieval. Scanning and storing documents electronically is easier today than ever, so you may opt to keep many of these files and copies of all important documents on your computer.

Keeping records up-to-date and accurate

Maintaining complete and accurate records of all transactions is extremely important in the world of property management. Having your records squared away is necessary on four fronts:

- ✔ **Taxation:** You have to report your income and expenses for each rental property on IRS Form 1040 Schedule E to determine your taxable profit (or loss). The IRS requires rental property owners to substantiate all income and expenses by maintaining proper records, including detailed receipts of all transactions to support the accuracy of your tax returns.

- ✔ **Financial management:** If you don't accurately document all the income streams coming in and the expense payments going out, you won't be a real estate investor for long. Check out the "Knowing What to Account For" section later in the chapter for tips and information on this key aspect of your rental property. Financial management is also an excellent barometer on the success of your rental property toward providing you with cash flow, equity build-up, and appreciation.

- ✔ **Litigation:** Courts typically take the stance that residential tenants (and even small commercial tenants) are merely consumers, so the burden is primarily on the owner to provide any documents outlining the relationship or understanding between the parties. If the owner can't provide the required records, the tenant almost always prevails.

- ✔ **Future refinancing or sale:** Having accurate and detailed accounting records is important when you look to refinance or sell your property because the amount you can borrow or the sales price you can achieve will likely be based on the Net Operating Income (NOI) that you report. Both a future lender and a buyer will look for stable and predictable income as well as reasonable operating and capital expenses that support the fact that you competently managed, operated, and maintained the property.

Here are a few documentation tips (check out the "Filing made easy" section later in the chapter for ideas on how to store this info):

- ✔ **Document your income on income journals:** Income journals are also called *cash receipt journals* and consist of the master rental income data collection sheet and ledgers for each individual rental unit or suite.

- ✔ **Keep all bank deposit slips:** Although your bank may or may not require a deposit slip with your transaction, make a listing of all items deposited to keep for your records in case there's a discrepancy between your recordkeeping and the bank's records.

✔ **Get a written receipt for all expenses:** Rental property expenses, even if you write a business check or make an electronic payment, must have a written receipt to fully document the expenditure. The IRS may not accept a check as proof of a deductible property expense unless you have a detailed receipt as well. Many home improvement suppliers and vendors now provide detailed receipts with specific descriptions of the purchased items, making this much easier than in the past.

If you have multiple rental properties, develop and assign a one- or two-character code for each property and mark each receipt accordingly. (Indicate the unit or suite number, if appropriate.) When you have information for multiple properties on a single receipt, make photocopies and store the receipts in the folders you've set up for your respective properties. This way, you can provide evidence of the expense for each property instead of having to wade through all your folders looking for the information you need.

If you use your vehicle for your rental property activities, be sure to keep a detailed written log of all your mileage. Your mileage is a deductible business expense as long as it's directly related to your rental property and you have accurate records to document the mileage. Some apps are available that record business expenses. Regardless of your system, make sure that this simple log indicates the date, destination, purpose, and total number of miles traveled. You may be surprised at the number of miles you travel each year for your rental activities — the deductible expense can be substantial.

Here's a general guide of how long to retain your records:

✔ Keep all records pertaining to your rental property for a minimum of three to five years. (For property managers managing properties for others, the time period depends on the legal requirements of the state regulatory commission or department of real estate where the property is located.)

✔ For tax purposes, records regarding the purchase and capital improvements made during your ownership need to be maintained for as long as you own the property.

✔ Certain property records such as those concerning injuries to minors should be maintained essentially forever. Although even the IRS has a statute of limitations (except in the case of fraud), the statute of limitations for injuries to minors typically doesn't begin to run until the minor reaches the age of majority (usually 18).

Filing made easy

Every rental property owner should have a basic filing system with separate records kept for each rental property. You may opt to keep many of the accounting records and files on your computer, including the recent ability to scan and store most documents, but for owners of one to several rental units, a manual system works just fine. Your filing system can be a simple accordion filing box with dividers, which you can find at any office supply store. If you own more properties and outgrow the accordion filing box, use a lockable fireproof filing cabinet.

Organize your records at the property level and the unit level. You'll have some documentation overlap, but the benefit of having complete, easily retrievable records at your fingertips greatly outweighs the effort involved in making some photocopies. Start at the property level, and construct the following:

- ✔ **Ownership file:** From the moment you take your first steps toward purchasing an investment property, begin storing hard copies of your paperwork in a property ownership file. Keep all the important documents of this transaction, including purchase offers and contracts, the closing statement, appraisals, loan documents, insurance policies, due diligence inspection and pest control reports, and correspondence. You may be tempted to go paperless by scanning and storing everything electronically, but these documents are critical, and you must always keep hard copies because electronic files can be lost. Also keep a photocopy of your deed in the property file, and place the original in a fireproof safe or bank safety-deposit box.

- ✔ **Income and expense files:** Each of your rental properties should have its own file section with separate folders for income reports like rent rolls, as well as a separate folder for each of the major property expense categories. Keep copies of all receipts in the expense folders, so that when tax time rolls around, you can easily locate the information you need. Start a new file for each tax year.

- ✔ **Master maintenance file:** We recommend keeping a master property maintenance file for the records and receipts for all maintenance and capital improvements for each rental unit or suite and the common areas. This one-stop source gives you the records you need for all repairs and maintenance during your ownership and can be helpful for your accountant in calculating your basis in the property when you ultimately sell or exchange the property.

Moving on to the unit level, put these files together:

- ✔ **Tenant file:** Create a separate file for each tenant that contains all the important documents for each tenant, including her rental application, lease agreement, the tenant ledger showing all charges and payments, all legal notices, tenant maintenance requests, and correspondence. Although you can scan and store backup copies of these documents, always keep the original of each document and provide the tenant with a photocopy. You'll need the signed originals of all pertinent documents should legal action ever become necessary. Individual tenant files are closed out and a new tenant file established upon turnover of a rental unit to a new tenant.

When your tenants vacate, attach a copy of any paperwork from the termination of their tenancy and bind the entire tenant file together. Transfer it to a separate file for all former tenants, filed alphabetically by rental property.

✔ **Unit maintenance file:** We recommend keeping a separate maintenance file for each individual rental unit or suite with the records and receipts for all maintenance and capital improvements. This system gives you a history of the physical condition of each rental unit or suite throughout your ownership. This file remains open even when the tenants change.

Use a system for recording all significant tenant complaints and maintenance requests. This will provide a valuable paper trail if a dispute ever arises regarding your conduct as an owner in properly maintaining the premises. Failing to have good records may well hurt your case should a dispute escalate and end up in court.

Knowing What to Account For

The financial management aspects of accounting for all the funds you receive and expend are critical elements of running your real estate rental property activities. After all, the ownership and management of even a single rental property is a business, and the government expects you to have proper financial records in order to prepare your tax returns.

But proper financial management isn't just for the benefit of the government. With accurate and timely information, you can manage your rental investment more efficiently and effectively. And when you decide to sell or exchange your rental property, your property will often generate a higher price if you have complete and accurate records, because buyers feel more comfortable knowing exactly what they're purchasing. If you don't have these records, the potential purchaser may err on the side of overestimating your expenses, which will reduce his proforma calculation of the NOI that he will earn so he will decrease the price that he is willing to pay you accordingly.

New technology in banking is particularly helpful to the rental housing industry and is simplifying and expediting the rental collection and reporting procedures.

✔ Some rental property owners now offer their residential and especially their commercial tenants the ability to make rent and other payments by automatic draft (automated clearing house, or ACH), or increasingly by electronic fund transfers to the property owner's account on a predetermined date. Credit cards are another option for owners with many rental units (or small owners that use a property management company) although banking fees cut into your collected rents.

✔ Even the traditional payment by check is enhanced with the advent of *electronic check truncation,* where smart phones or check readers or data entry software at larger residential properties can capture the salient information from the tenant's check and immediately debit their account. This electronic processing shortens the collection time and eliminates checks or money orders being returned for nonpayment.

✔ Online banking can also provide rental property owners the ability to make their own payments to vendors and suppliers electronically. Additionally, online banking provides access to records that immediately reflect all receipts and disbursements and minimizes the chance of fraud by employees handling cash by making the tracking of daily activity easier.

Documenting income and expenses

If your tenants pay by check, you can always let the cancelled check serve as the tenant's receipt, but the best policy is to provide a receipt whenever possible, regardless of the method of payment. Likewise, track your expenses by using checks or credit accounts rather than making cash purchases for which you receive generic receipts, because the legitimacy of generic receipts can be challenged.

Keep your rental property activities separate from your personal transactions. Although the IRS doesn't require you to keep a separate checking account for each rental property that you own, you need to be able to track the income and expenses for each property individually.

As you add rental units or commercial properties, the accounting becomes much more complex and the recordkeeping more critical. That's when you must seriously consider hiring a property manager with good recordkeeping and accounting procedures who will create detailed monthly reporting that can be given to your accountant for tax planning and reporting.

Hiring a good tax advisor is a wise investment for even small rental property owners because tax rules are various and complex. For example, certain expenses can be classified as operating expenses and deducted in the current year to reduce your taxable income, but some expenses are considered capital items and must be depreciated or amortized over the estimated useful life of the improvement.

> ✔ One of the advantages to owning real estate is that you can deduct all operating expenses from your rental income. These operating expenses include payroll, maintenance and repair costs, management fees, utilities, advertising costs, tenant screening fees, insurance, property taxes, and interest paid on mortgage debt. You also benefit from *depreciation,* which is a noncash deduction that reduces your taxable income in the current year but is recaptured in the future. Depreciation is discussed in more detail in Chapter 18.

> ✔ Capital items typically include your building equipment or components that extend the useful life of the building and have a longer life span or are brand new, rather than routine maintenance or a repair. Your accountant is usually instrumental in providing guidance as to which items can be expensed versus the items that must be capitalized.

> Rental property expenditures for capital items must be accounted for separately and are capitalized when their cost basis is depreciated or amortized over multiple years rather than deducted as an operating expense in the current year. This means that you aren't able to reduce your taxable income by the full cost incurred but by a prorated amount over several years. Your accountant will generate depreciation or cost recovery schedules indicating the amount that can be deducted each year. Also, your accountant can keep you informed about changes in the federal tax code that affect depreciation deductions of certain capital expense items.

> ✔ Some costs of financing, such as loan fees or points paid at the time of the loan, can't be taken as an operating expense and must be amortized (taken incrementally) over the life of the loan. However, if you refinance or sell the property and pay off the loan, then you can take a full deduction of remaining unamortized loan fees in that tax year.

Be sure you accurately record the payment of a tenant's security deposit. These funds aren't typically considered income; instead, they're considered a future liability that is owed back to the tenant if the tenant honors the terms of the rental agreement. The security deposit may become income at a later date if you apply any portion of it to cover delinquent rent, cleaning, repairs, damages beyond normal wear and tear, or other charges.

Creating a budget and managing your cash flow

Every rental property should have a *budget,* which is simply a detailed estimate of the future income and expenses of a property for a certain time period, usually one year. A budget allows you to anticipate and track the expected income and expenses for your rental property.

Many rental owners neglect to allocate and hold back enough money for projected expenses, so when it comes time to make a repair, for example, they don't have the money set aside to cover it. If you set up a budget, you're better able to anticipate your expenses.

Although the budget for a single-family or rental condo is fairly simple, a proper budget for a newly acquired multiunit apartment or commercial building can require some careful planning. That planning includes a thorough review of past expenses and the current condition of the property. Trends in expenses, such as utilities, can also be important when estimating the future cash flow of a rental property, so be sure you don't overlook them. Check out the income and expense categories we cover in Chapter 12 — the process is essentially the same whether you're formulating a prepurchase income/expense pro forma or the annual budget for ongoing operation of the property.

Many owners rely on cash flow from their rental properties not only to cover their expenses but also to supplement their personal income. But particularly if you're a small rental property owner, you need to have a built-in reserve fund set aside before you start taking out any rental income funds for personal reasons. Maintain a reserve balance large enough to pay your mortgage and all the basic property expenses for at least two to three months without relying on any rental income. When you don't have long term leases with stable tenants or the local rental market has low demand for your type of rental property, it may make sense to increase your cash reserves to an amount that allows you to sleep at night. Also, remember to allocate funds to cover semiannual and annual expenses such as your property taxes (if not impounded by your lender) and potential income tax due on your rental property net income.

Set up a bank account where you set aside money for anticipated major capital improvements. For example, you may own a rental property that will need a new roof in the next five years. Rather than see your cash flow wiped out for several months when it comes time to pay for that new roof, you can begin setting aside small amounts of money into a capital reserve account over several years. Lenders on large residential and commercial type properties often require the monthly funding of a capital item reserve and replacement account. For large apartment projects, this expense can be from $150 to $400 per unit per year. The owner can periodically submit requests (with copies of paid invoices) for reimbursement of qualified expenditures such as appliances, floor coverings, roofing, exterior painting, and other capital items.

Doing Your Accounting Manually

Most rental property owners begin their real estate investing with a single rental home or condo. At this level, the accounting is extremely simple and can be done manually with pencil and paper in a simple spiral notebook or an accountant's columnar pad. But when you expand to multiple rental units or commercial properties, you need to look for better and more efficient systems that are geared to the specific needs of rental property accounting.

The classic manual accounting system for rental properties is a peg board set up for a one-write system (each transaction is entered once, using stacked carbon documents). A single entry records information needed for a consecutively numbered rental receipt, the tenant's individual ledger card, a bank deposit ticket, and the daily cash receipt journal that provides a master record of all transactions. This popular rental accounting system is still used by some rental property owners and managers and is available from Peachtree Business Products (800-241-4623 or www.pbp1.com).

Using Software

When you own several properties, consider using a computer with a spreadsheet or general accounting software program. Spreadsheet programs, such as *Microsoft Excel,* can handle a few rental properties. Somewhat better are the general business accounting packages, such as the entry-level *Quicken,* and the more advanced *QuickBooks* or *Sage 50 Accounting.* These programs can handle and streamline all the basic accounting requirements of managing a handful of rental properties.

Recognizing the value of professional accounting software

However, as good as these programs are, they lack the specific rental property features and reporting that are invaluable to effective property management. If you have more than five rental properties, we strongly recommend purchasing a professional rental accounting software program. These programs typically offer the following:

- ✔ Complete accounting (general ledger, accounts receivable, accounts payable with check writing, budgeting, and financial reporting)

- ✔ Tenant and lease management, including many standard rental management forms

- ✔ Tenant service requests, maintenance scheduling, and reminder notes

- ✔ Additional services such as electronic payments, tenant screening, payroll, and utility billing

Another advantage to using the computerized rental property accounting software packages is the ability to have your mortgage and other bills deducted electronically. Or you can work with these software packages to pay your bills online. If your tenants pay their rent electronically as well, you can decrease the time you spend handling rent collection and accounting.

Many property management accounting packages are available for a nominal investment, but don't be penny-wise and pound-foolish. Many of the less expensive systems may work in the short run, but if something goes wrong, you may be left stranded without technical support or help. If a software firm has only a few systems in place, you're in for a much higher risk of program errors or incorrect results. The software may not even be updated or supported years down the road. Your financial investment, and all the timesaving and other significant benefits of computerized accounting, may be lost if the software package isn't backed by a solid company.

When you use a management company, you typically receive several important accounting reports within a couple of weeks after the end of each accounting month. If you review these reports regularly, they can provide you with a good understanding of your rental investments and give you the opportunity to inquire about or suggest changes in the operations. But if you manage your own property and do your own accounting, it's important to actually review and analyze the financial reports in the same manner as you would if you had entrusted your investment to a property manager. You may think that you know everything you need to know about your rental property, and setting aside those monthly reports until tax time may seem harmless, but they're great tools for improving your management results if you use them properly.

You can customize the financial reporting offered by software programs to meet your needs. Monthly reports often contain income and expense information compared to the monthly budget as well as year-to-date numbers.

Identifying some of the better programs

Each of the many program types available has its own strengths and weaknesses. Following are a few programs that we highly recommend:

✔ **Quicken Rental Property Manager (RPM):** If you have a modest real estate empire of fewer than ten separate properties, you'll find that this software package is affordable and acceptable option that's superior to manual systems or user-customized computer spreadsheet software. Unlike prior versions, the more recent editions of *RPM* don't require you to have the basic *Quicken* software to cover everything you need to prepare your own reports. These days, *RPM* is essentially an upgraded or specialized software built on the foundation of *Quicken Home & Business* and is fully integrated. You can even prepare your federal 1040 Schedule E to hand to your accountant or import directly into *TurboTax* if you prepare your own tax return.

On the downside, *RPM* is still primarily an accounting program that has been modified to handle some basic rental housing needs. It lets you write checks and even uses accrual (rather than cash basis) accounting, but it doesn't include work orders, assist in preparing tenant notices, or have any of the other important features that can simplify your life as a property manager — features that are found in the more robust software packages that we recommend.

Additionally, *RPM* users report that even though the program has improved significantly in the past few years, it still has many blind spots when it comes to partial rent payments, coded expenses among various categories, and some of the other day-to-day issues faced by landlords. We suggest that you carefully follow the user reviews as subsequent versions are released and see whether the concerns about the product are issues that you find troubling. Clearly, if you own only a couple of single-family or condo units, you won't have any problems. But if you have more units, if your income sources are complicated (such as miscellaneous income or if you accept rent from multiple roommates), or if detailed breakdowns of your expenses are important, then this entry-level product will frustrate you.

One aspect of *RPM* that we particularly like is that parent company Intuit seems to have made a commitment to this product and is introducing frequent updates that allow users to easily decide when the new features are worth the investment in the latest edition. But if you decide that changes aren't really that important, the company continues to support its *Quicken* family of products for several years. For information on *RPM* and other *Quicken* products, go to `http://quicken.intuit.com`.

✔ **Rent Manager:** One of the most popular software programs for landlords with small- to medium-sized portfolios who've outgrown RPM
or simply need a more comprehensive software package than RPM is
Rent Manager by London Computer Systems (LCS). LCS offers a Small
Business Edition of *Rent Manager* that's perfect for owners and managers with up to 175 units.

Rent Manager has everything you need, starting with a strong financial accounting package that includes a general ledger with accounts
receivable and accounts payable, budget management payroll import,
and financial reporting. The property management tools include rent
collection (even preparing the bank deposit slips), tenant lease management, contact management and word processing (for correspondence
and all types of notices), as well as a work-order module. We really like
the built-in marketing features that allow you to monitor the results of
your advertising, track your prospects, and even quickly post ads on
Craigslist or to your own website.

Rent Manager is offered in an online version and a stand-alone version.
We recommend the online version because you get automatic updates
and LCS handles all data backup and technical support. Visit www.
rentmanager.com for more details.

✔ **Yardi Voyager:** For rental property owners or property management
companies with portfolios of 250 or more rental units, we recommend
the *Yardi Voyager* asset and property management software suite.
Robert's property management company uses this industry-leading,
browser-based software, and he has been impressed with its ability
to provide real-time daily and weekly reporting to effectively manage
properties. *Yardi Voyager* also offers detailed monthly financial reports,
which allow his company to provide a greater level of service to clients
and outperform the competition. (See their full product line at www.
yardi.com.)

✔ **Yardi Genesis:** For smaller property owners and managers, Yardi
Systems also offers a fully integrated, Windows-based product called
Yardi Genesis that has much of the same basic functionality as *Yardi
Voyager* but with less sophisticated reporting capabilities and fewer features and configuration options. *Yardi Voyager* is accessible anywhere
via the Internet, whereas *Yardi Genesis* is accessible only through a local
network. Like *Yardi Voyager, Yardi Genesis* includes all the basic features
of prospect and tenant management, fully integrated accounts receivable and accounts payable, a general ledger, and cash management. It
also allows ready access to information, elimination of duplicate entries,
and spontaneous delivery of reporting.

✔ **Point2 Property Manager (P2PM):** *P2PM*, another Yardi Systems creation, is geared specifically toward the small multifamily manager and is an easy-to-use property management and accounting software-as-a-service option. *P2PM* is easy to implement as well. Simply go to the *P2PM* website at `www.point2propertymanager.com`, sign up for a monthly or annual option, and begin using.

Yardi has a variety of pricing and hosting options for its software available on either a monthly or annual basis that can be based either on total program users or units. A variety of optional modules are available to enhance internal operations, streamline processes, and increase service level to residents and clients.

When evaluating different software packages, gather as much info as possible. Be sure to talk to actual product users, preferably people in your area with comparable rental properties and similar accounting needs. Determine what features a program offers, how easy it is to operate, its computer hardware requirements, the availability and cost of technical support, and the strength and reputation of the company backing the product. Obtain a demo or trial version of the software that you can use before you buy, just to make sure it's truly what you want.

Just like with any technology product, another factor to keep in mind is not just whether the product meets the current standards but whether it incorporates or has the ability to upgrade and include the latest trends. The current trends in the rental housing industry software that you should look for include web-based Software as a Service (SaaS), subscription-based software, automatic posting of vacancies on Craigslist and other sites, integrated hosting and management of websites, electronic maintenance work order requests, electronic rent collection and bill payment, and integrated credit checks and applicant screening.

Chapter 18

Looking at Tax Considerations and Exit Strategies

*R*eal estate is a great investment that offers you the opportunity to leverage a small cash investment to own and control large holdings that generate cash flow and can appreciate significantly over time. But cash flow, leverage, and appreciation aren't the only advantages of real estate. Utilizing current real estate tax laws has always been a key benefit for real estate investors.

Applying tax strategies properly allows rental real estate investors the ability to shelter income and even to eliminate — or at least defer — capital gains. Success in real estate, like all investments, is generally determined by how much money you keep on an *after*-tax basis. Real estate offers the potential to minimize taxation, so real estate investors need a thorough understanding of the best techniques to optimize their financial positions.

We discuss tax advantages in this chapter, but don't let tax considerations drive your decisions. Purchasing real estate should always be an economic decision. Only when a deal makes economic sense (both at the time of purchase and after the sale) should you consider the tax aspects. Also, real estate taxation is a constantly changing, complicated area. Although this chapter covers the key concepts, it isn't a substitute for professional tax advice. Every real estate investor needs a competent accountant or tax advisor (who specializes in real estate) on her investment team. We recommend that you meet with your tax advisors regularly throughout the year, rather than only just before the tax filing due date.

Because the subject is so entwined in tax considerations, we also cover real estate sales — also known as *exit strategies*. The tax implications of various exit strategies are important to understand so that the real estate investor can select the best one for each sale and minimize the tax consequences of selling real estate holdings.

Understanding the Tax Angles

The tax laws regarding investment real estate are unique and far more complex than those regarding homeownership. For example, a homeowner can't deduct his costs of operating and the repairs and maintenance of his home — but as the owner of a rental property, you can deduct such costs. Also, the benefits of depreciation apply only to rental real estate and aren't available for property held as a personal residence.

Tax laws change frequently, so check with your tax advisor before taking any action. Use a tax attorney, certified public accountant (CPA), an enrolled agent (EA), or a tax specialist to prepare your tax returns if you have investment real estate. In the sections that follow, we discuss some important rental real estate tax concepts that you should understand if you want to make the most of your property investments.

Sheltering income with depreciation

Depreciation is an accounting concept that allows you to claim a deduction for a certain portion of the acquisition value of a rental property because the building wears out over time. Depreciation is an expense, but it doesn't actually take cash out of your bank account. Instead, you treat the depreciation amount as an expense or deduction when tallying your income on your tax return, which decreases your taxable income and allows you to shelter positive cash flow from taxation. Depreciation lowers your income taxes in the current year by essentially providing a government interest-free loan until the property is sold.

The use of depreciation by real estate investors can be used to defer, but not permanently eliminate, income taxes. The annual deduction for depreciation is a reduction in the *basis* (calculated as your original cost in the property plus capital improvements) of the rental property, which is *recaptured* (added to your taxable profit) in full and taxed upon sale. Currently, all deductions taken for cost recovery are recaptured and taxed at 25 percent when you sell the property.

Depreciation is only allowed for the acquisition value of the buildings and other improvements, because the underlying land isn't depreciable. The theory is that the buildings and other improvements ultimately wear out over time but the land will always be there. Because the amount of your depreciation deduction depends on the highest portion of the overall property value being attributable to the buildings, it's advantageous to allocate the highest fair market value of your rental property value to the improvements to increase your potential deduction for depreciation.

To determine the appropriate basis for calculating depreciation, many real estate investors have traditionally used the property tax assessor's allocation between the value of the buildings and land. But the IRS doesn't allow the assessor's allocation. It does accept an appraisal, which can be quite expensive unless you have a recent one available. But a more cost-effective method that the IRS accepts is the Comparative Market Analysis (CMA) that most brokers offer at a nominal charge or even for free.

Before 1993, depreciation could be accelerated in the early years of rental property ownership. This option led to poor decision making on real estate deals that were motivated by the significant tax shelter offered by real estate, with only a secondary concern about return on investment or appreciation.

But under current tax laws, recently acquired rental properties can only use straight-line depreciation. *Straight-line depreciation* reduces the value of the rental property by set equal amounts each year over its established depreciable life. The period of time during which depreciation is taken is called the *recovery period.* For properties placed in service or purchased on or after May 13, 1993, the IRS requires straight-line depreciation with the following recovery periods:

- ✔ **Residential rental property:** The recovery period is 27.5 years (or a cost recovery factor of 3.636 percent each year). A property qualifies as residential if the tenants stay a minimum of 30 days or more and no substantial services are provided, such as medical or health care.

- ✔ **Commercial properties:** The recovery period is 39 years (or an annual cost recovery of 2.564 percent). Mixed-use properties are classified as commercial unless the income from the residential portion is 80 percent or more of the gross rental income.

The cost recovery deductions for both the year of acquisition and the year of sale must use the *midmonth convention requirement,* which means that regardless of the actual day of sale, the transaction is presumed to have been completed on the 15th of the month. Thus, the depreciation deduction is prorated based on the number of full months of ownership plus ½ month for the month of purchase or sale.

Commercial property owners typically modify vacant spaces to get potential tenants to sign a lease. The IRS requires that the cost of those improvements be depreciated over 39 years even though the lease and the actual useful life of the improvements are much shorter. This topic is a constant source of lobbying by commercial real estate interests seeking depreciation schedules that more closely coincide with the actual length of lease. The tax laws were changed temporarily to a 15-year cost recovery from 2004 through 2013. You can take a deduction in the current year for the full remaining undepreciated portion of the tenant improvements that were torn out as a result of one tenant vacating and new tenant improvements being installed for the next tenant. For example, if you replace carpet that hasn't been fully depreciated, you can deduct the remaining unamortized value in that tax year.

Minimizing income taxes

Taxpayers generally have two types of income:

- **Ordinary income:** This category includes wages, bonuses and commissions, rents, and interest and is taxed at the federal level at various rates up to 39.6 percent. The taxable income you receive from your rental property is subject to taxation as ordinary income.

- **Capital gains:** These are generated when investments (such as real estate and stock) are sold for a profit. The income you realize upon the sale of your investment property is subject to taxation as a capital gain. Capital gains are classified as short-term and long-term:

  - **Short-term:** For property held for 12 months or less, capital gains are taxed at the same rate as ordinary income.

  - **Long-term:** For property held for longer than 12 months, gains are taxed at lower rates than ordinary income with a current rate of 0, 15, or 20 percent, depending on your overall tax bracket.

But you can't pay taxes until you figure out exactly what part of your income will be taxed. To do that, you need to perform a *cash-flow analysis.* The cash flow from a property — positive or negative — is determined by deducting all operating expenses, debt service interest, capital improvement expenses, damages, theft, and depreciation from rental income.

Calculating the cash flow of a property follows the format shown in Table 18-1. We provide the details for most of these items in Chapter 12. Here, we provide a quick summary and then factor in the taxman.

1. **Start with the *Gross Potential Rental Income* (GPI) for the property.**

   This figure is the hypothetical maximum rent collections if the property were 100 percent occupied at market rents and all rents were collected.

2. **Subtract the *loss to lease* (which is the amount the contract rent is less than the market rent) and the rent that isn't collected due to**

vacancy and collection loss (the failure of tenants to pay) to arrive at the Net Rent Revenue (NRR).

3. **Add the other income (laundry, parking, money collected from former tenants, income from the rental of a cellphone tower on the roof, and so on) to the NRR to establish the Effective Gross Income (EGI).**

4. **Subtract the operating expenses from the EGI to calculate the Net Operating Income (NOI).**

   As we discuss in Chapter 12, the NOI is the essential number used in the income capitalization method of determining the value of the property.

5. **Subtract the capital improvements and interest paid on the debt service from the NOI to arrive at the before-tax cash flow (BTCF).**

6. **Subtract the *straight-line depreciation* (which is merely a noncash accounting deduction that reduces your tax liability without requiring an actual cash expenditure) from the before-tax cash flow.**

   The result is the *taxable income.*

7. **Multiply this year's taxable income or reportable loss by your ordinary marginal income rate to determine your tax liability or savings.**

8. **Deduct the tax liability (or savings, if the taxable income is negative and the loss can be used in the current tax year) and the annual debt service principal payments from the net taxable income, and then add the noncash deduction for the straight-line cost recovery.**

   You now have the after-tax cash flow (ATCF).

Table 18-1	Calculating After-Tax Cash Flow
Gross potential rental income	$100,000
Subtract loss to lease	(2,000)
Minus vacancy and collection losses	(2,500)
Net Rent Revenue (NRR)	95,500
Plus other income	2,500
Plus Common area maintenance (CAM) reimbursement (if any)	2,000
Effective Gross Income (EGI)	100,000
Minus operating expenses	(40,000)
Net operating income (NOI)	60,000
Minus capital improvements	(5,000)
Minus annual debt service interest	(35,000)

(continued)

Table 18-1 *(continued)*

Before-tax cash flow (BTCF) without principal payments	20,000
Minus the straight-line cost recovery	(12,000)
Net taxable income	8,000
Minus tax liability (or savings)*	(5,148)
Minus annual debt service principal payments	(4,000)
Plus the cost recovery	12,000
After-tax cash flow (ATCF)	**10,852**

*Calculation of Tax Liability

Net operating income	**$60,000**
Minus annual debt service interest	($35,000)
Minus the straight-line cost recovery	($12,000)
Net taxable income	**13,000**
Times investor's tax rate	39.6%
Tax liability	**$5,148**

Understanding passive and active activity

In 1986, Congress enacted passive income and loss provisions to eliminate the use of real estate tax shelters that were structured primarily to provide considerable tax benefits for investors.

Rental owners often start out with their real estate activities serving as second incomes. The majority of their income often comes from professions and sources totally unrelated to real estate. The taxation rules that apply to these part-time real estate investors are different from the ones that apply to real estate professionals. Unless you qualify as a real estate professional (discussed later in this chapter), the IRS classifies all real estate activities as *passive* and sets limits on your ability to claim real estate loss deductions.

A special IRS relief provision exclusively for rental real estate activities may permit a moderate-income real estate investor to offset other income with up to $25,000 in excess losses from rental real estate. The potential deduction is limited to a maximum of $25,000 per tax year for all real estate investment properties combined. Real estate investors can take a rental property loss deduction of up to $25,000 against other income in the current tax year as long as their adjusted gross income doesn't exceed $100,000. If the adjusted gross income exceeds $100,000, the real estate investor will be denied 50¢ of the loss allowance for every dollar over $100,000, so that the entire $25,000 loss allowance disappears at an adjusted gross income of $150,000. In order to be able to take this deduction, the following four requirements must be met:

- ✔ **The properties must qualify.** Certain types of properties don't qualify, including net leased properties and vacation homes in a rental pool.

- ✔ **The taxpayer must own a minimum of 10 percent of the property based on value.** Interestingly, the IRS allows a taxpayer to include the interests held by his or her spouse even if they don't file a joint return.

- ✔ **The taxpayer must actively participate in the management.** This rule doesn't mean the real estate investor can't utilize a management firm. A real estate investor can meet the active participation requirement by simply communicating with his management company about the approval of new tenants, determining the rental terms, approving repairs or capital improvements, or making other similar owner decisions with the management company handling the day-to-day issues.

- ✔ **The taxpayer must file her tax return as an individual.** Corporations, certain trusts, and other forms of ownership aren't allowed to take this special deduction.

Any losses disallowed in one year are called *suspended losses* and can be saved and applied to reduce rental or other passive income in future years. If the suspended losses can't be used in this manner, the real estate investor will be able to use them when she sells the rental property to effectively reduce the taxable gain. Thus, the losses ultimately benefit the investor, but the time value of money concept (which shows that money becomes worth less over time due to inflation) indicates that the ability to use the losses now is worth more than some time in the future.

Qualifying as a real estate professional

The IRS passive loss rule states that all real estate rental activities must be treated as passive income with only two possible exceptions:

- ✔ The maximum of up to a $25,000 deduction for some taxpayers as discussed in the "Understanding passive and active activity" section earlier in the chapter

- ✔ The relatively small number of individuals who can meet the IRS requirements to be classified as real estate professionals

For a taxpayer meeting the eligibility requirements relating to his real estate activities, the rental real estate activities in which he participates aren't subject to the $25,000 limitation. Real estate investors who can be classified as real estate professionals are permitted to deduct all of their rental real estate losses from their ordinary income, such as current employment income (wages, commissions), interest, short-term capital gains, and nonqualified dividends.

The IRS has defined a *real estate professional* as an individual who materially participates in rental real estate activities and meets *both* of the following requirements:

- ✔ More than 50 percent of her personal services or employment were performed in a real property business or rental real estate activities, including acquisition, operation, leasing, management, development or redevelopment, construction or reconstruction, and brokerage.

- ✔ These activities represented at least 750 hours per tax year. (Work hours as an employee don't qualify unless the taxpayer is at least a 5 percent owner of the employer.)

These individuals are considered *active investors* and are allowed to claim all their real estate loss deductions in the year incurred, to offset positive taxable income or offset gains at the time of sale. But the IRS considers each interest of the taxpayer in rental real estate to be a separate activity, unless you choose to treat all rental real estate interests as one activity. This choice is an important step. Consult with a tax advisor to determine whether aggregating your rental real estate activities is advantageous and, if so, to make sure you properly make the required election when filing your tax return.

But qualifying as an active investor is complicated. The IRS now allows the taxpayer to qualify as a real estate professional by combining hours spent on rental and nonrental real estate activities. For example, even a part-time real estate broker or property manager may be able to demonstrate over 1,000 hours in a typical year in qualified real estate activities such as listing and selling, leasing and managing rentals, and renovation or construction. So meeting the 750 hours isn't a problem, but the 50 percent test requires that the 1,000 real estate activity hours be more than 50 percent of all work hours in a year. This threshold can be a problem if you have other extensive nonqualified work activities, and a new calculation must be made each year. If you do qualify, carefully document your activities and the hours spent in each through appointment books, calendars, or narrative summaries.

A potentially useful real estate investment strategy for some married couples is to have a stay-at-home spouse become an active real estate agent or property manager and accumulate at least 50 percent of his or her employment or business time with a minimum of 750 hours per year selling and managing the family rentals. With the real estate professional qualification met, their rental activities are now active, and they can deduct all of their rental real estate losses. However, lawyers can't get a break, because the IRS has specifically ruled that real estate attorneys can't qualify.

Material participation, which requires the real estate investor to be involved "in a regular, continuous, and substantial manner," shouldn't be confused with active participation (which we define in the "Understanding passive and active activity" section earlier in the chapter).

Considering Exit Strategies

A successful investment strategy doesn't simply involve buying and operating properties. The *disposition* or *exit strategy* has a significant impact on overall success.

Begin your exit-strategy planning while you're acquiring property. That is, develop a game plan to work towards before you buy the asset. You can always change or modify your plans, but knowing your exit strategy prior to acquisition is good practice.

You do your homework, buy the right property at the right price, and add value by maintaining and improving the property and obtaining good tenants. So, why undo your good work by selling the property for less than it's worth or paying too much in taxes because you failed to explore ways to defer your capital gains (which can keep more of your money working to keep your portfolio growing)?

When you're looking to buy rental real estate with appreciation potential, seek those properties that have deferred maintenance and cosmetic problems that allow you to buy them at a good price. When you go to sell your property, you want to get full value, so before you begin to list or show your available property, scrutinize the curb appeal and physical condition, looking for those items that need attention. Don't rely on your own eye; ask a trained, professional real estate agent or property manager who isn't familiar with the property to give you some feedback. Some individuals and companies offer services called *staging* (placing temporary furniture and other items in the dwelling to make it more appealing) to reduce the required marketing time and maximize the value of the property being sold.

We thoroughly cover the purchase agreement and other issues involved in a real estate transaction in Chapter 13. Because we firmly believe that the proper and ethical way to conduct business in real estate is to use standardized forms and practices, there's no need to present new forms or tactics that are slanted to favor your position as the seller. In the long run, you benefit by treating people fairly in your real estate transactions.

If you build a reputation for being ethical, you receive many more opportunities than if you use one-sided methods designed to take advantage of others.

When it's time to sell the property, you have several options, but not all of them have the same tax consequences.

Selling outright

One exit strategy is to simply sell the property and report the sale to the IRS. As long as capital gains tax rates are low, this strategy may work for taxpayers who are nearing the end of their prime real estate investing years and are looking to slow down and simplify their lives.

In an *outright* or *all-cash sale,* you simply sell the property, report the sale to the IRS, and determine whether you have a taxable gain or loss. If it's a gain, taxes are due; if you've held the property for at least 12 months, the low capital gains tax rates of 0 percent or 15 or 20 percent apply. (Seller financing isn't considered an all-cash sale, nor is an installment sale, which we cover later.) Don't forget the 25 percent tax rate on cost recovery deduction that's triggered on the sale.

Although an outright or all-cash sale is fairly straightforward, real estate investors are often interested in postponing the recognition of their gain on sale so that they can postpone the payment of taxes due. This situation is where an installment sale or an exchange (discussed later) can be useful.

Although the sale of a property can make sense, remember that refinancing an investment property with substantial equity is another great way to free up additional cash for real estate acquisitions, other investments or purposes.

Calculating gain or loss on a sale

Preparing and retaining accurate records from the initial purchase of your rental property and throughout the ownership is extremely important because the sale of a real estate investment property must be reported to the IRS.

Several factors go into the required calculation to determine whether there's a gain or loss on the sale that can either increase or reduce the overall income:

✔ The sales price is a major factor.

✔ Any capital improvements made to the property should be included.

✔ Accumulated depreciation taken during the holding period increases your taxes when it's recaptured.

✔ Also, if the property had operating losses that couldn't be taken in prior tax years, those suspended losses increase the adjusted basis and lower the potential taxable gain (or increase the loss available to shelter other income).

Table 18-2 outlines the following gain (or loss) on sale calculation.

Table 18-2	Calculating Total Gain or Loss on Sale
Gross sales price	**$1,500,000**
Minus selling expenses	(50,000)
Net sales proceeds	**1,450,000**
Minus adjusted basis (see Table 18-3)	(700,000)
Total gain (or loss) on sale	**$750,000**

Step 1: Determine the net sales proceeds

The *net sales proceeds* are the gross sales price minus the selling expenses. The *selling expenses* are all costs incurred to complete the sales transaction such as real estate commissions, attorney and accountant fees, settlement and escrow fees, title insurance, and other closing costs.

Step 2: Determine the adjusted basis for the property

When the property is just acquired, the *basis* is simply the original cost of the property (the equity down payment plus the total debt incurred to finance the property plus closing costs, appraisal, and environmental reports). If the owner didn't purchase the property, the basis is one of the following:

✔ The fair market value at the time of transfer for property received as an inheritance

✔ The carry-over basis if the property is received as a gift

✔ The substituted basis if the property was acquired in a tax-deferred exchange.

However, the basis isn't static — it changes during the ownership period. To adjust the original basis, take three factors into account (see Table 18-3 for the sample calculations):

Table 18-3	Adjusted Basis Calculation
Original acquisition cost or basis	$750,000
Plus capital improvements	50,000
Minus accumulated cost recovery	(100,000)
Minus any casualty losses taken	0
Adjusted basis	$700,000

✔ **Capital improvements:** During the holding period, owners often make some capital improvements or additions to the property. *Capital improvements* are money spent to improve the existing property or construct new property. These capital improvements are added to the original acquisition cost to determine the adjusted basis.

Routine and normal repairs required to keep the property in good working order over its useful life are deductible expenses during the tax year in which they're incurred. They're not capital improvements for the purpose of the adjusted basis calculation. For example, replacing a few shingles or even re-roofing a portion of the property is a repair, but completely replacing the roof is a capital improvement. A newly constructed addition that increases the rentable square footage of the rental property is a capital improvement. The capital improvement includes all costs incurred such as contractor payments, architect fees, building permits, construction materials, and labor costs.

✔ **Depreciation:** At the same time, the straight-line depreciation taken each tax year is accumulated and reduces the adjusted basis of the property. Note that the total accumulated depreciation is included in the overall calculation of the gain or loss upon sale as part of the adjusted basis but is reported separately and is taxed at a different rate on the taxpayer's tax return.

✔ **Casualty losses taken by the taxpayer:** Casualty losses can result from the destruction of or damage to your property from any sort of sudden, unexpected, or unusual event such as a flood, hurricane, tornado, fire, earthquake, or even volcanic eruption.

Step 3: Determine the total gain or loss on the sale

The total gain or loss is determined by taking the net sales price and subtracting the adjusted basis (see Table 18-2).

Step 4: Factoring in accumulated cost recovery and suspended losses

If you have suspended losses reported on the taxpayer's tax returns during the ownership period, deduct them from the net sales proceeds (see Table 18-4). The *suspended losses* are those losses that the taxpayer couldn't use in prior tax years because he didn't meet the strict IRS requirements. See the "Understanding passive and active activity" section earlier in the chapter for more info. That figure is the *capital gain from appreciation.*

Table 18-4	Capital Gain from Appreciation
Total gain on sale (from Table 18-2)	$750,000
Minus straight-line cost recovery	(100,000)
Minus suspended losses	(75,000)
Capital gain from appreciation	$575,000

Step 5: Determine total tax liability

The net gain on sale is taxed as ordinary income unless the property was held for more than 12 months. Fortunately, most real estate investors do hold the property for more than 12 months and can qualify for the lower long-term capital gains tax rates. In fact, if the property has been held less than 12 months, all depreciation that has been taken is recaptured as ordinary income.

For tax purposes, the net gain on sale must be allocated between the capital gain from appreciation and the recapture of the accumulated depreciation. The seller doesn't automatically get the benefits of the lower flat 0 or 15 percent maximum capital gains tax and may even have to pay the maximum depreciation recapture tax rate of 25 percent if she's in a higher income tax bracket as is the investor in our example. (The depreciation recapture rate is based on your ordinary income tax bracket but won't exceed 25 percent.)

In Table 18-4, the total gain on sale of $750,000 is reduced by $100,000 in accumulated depreciation and suspended losses of $75,000 for a gain from appreciation of $575,000. In Table 18-5, we break the taxation of the capital gain down between capital gain from appreciation and depreciation recapture. The accumulated depreciation is recaptured at 25 percent, resulting in a tax liability of $25,000. The gain from appreciation was taxed at the maximum capital gains flat rate of 20 percent, resulting in a tax liability of $115,000. So, the total tax liability is $140,000.

Table 18-5	Total Tax Liability Calculation
Straight-line cost recovery	$100,000
Times tax rate on recapture	25%
Total tax due for recapture	$25,000
Capital gain from appreciation	$575,000
Times tax rate on capital gain	20%
Total tax due on capital gain	$115,000
Total tax liability	**$140,000**

If the sale of the property results in a net loss, the loss must first be applied to offset net passive-activity income or gains. If there are none, or after they're exhausted, the net loss can be applied to reduce the income or gains from nonpassive activities such as earned income or wages.

Selling now, reaping profits later: Installment sale

An *installment sale* is the disposition of a property in which the seller receives any portion of the sale proceeds in a tax year following the tax year in which she sells the property. The time value of money indicates that it's generally better to have the use of money today than in the future. Knowledgeable real estate investors seek ways to minimize or defer the taxes that they need to pay. One way to accomplish this goal is by using the *installment sale method* — within specified IRS limits, the sellers of real estate can report their receipt of funds as actually received over time rather than as a lump sum at the time of the sale.

A taxpayer who sells his property on the installment method is able to report only the *pro rata* (proportionate) part of the proceeds actually received in that tax year. The advantage is that the taxable gain is spread over several years and can be reported in years in which the taxpayer may have a lower tax bracket. This technique is ideal for property sellers who don't need to take their equity at the time of sale because they have other sources of income or want to minimize taxes or both.

This scenario includes transactions in which the seller provides the financing and received payments over time. When financing is difficult for buyers to obtain, sellers may offer to take a mortgage note from the buyer for some (or even all) of their equity in the property. As discussed in Chapter 5, having the seller take a note for equity is a common no-money-down strategy.

An installment sale can be an effective way for a seller to assist the buyer in making the purchase as well as to defer the recognition of income and thereby reduce the capital gains tax.

Here's how it works: A real estate investor sells a property for $1.5 million that has an adjusted basis of $700,000. The buyer makes a down payment of $250,000, assumes the current loan balance of $500,000, and accepts seller financing of $750,000. The terms of the installment sale require the buyer to pay the principal balance of $750,000 owed to the seller at $250,000 each year over the following three years, plus interest. The buyer reports the gain according to the timing of the principal payments.

The amount of the gain that must be reported in a given tax year is equal to the total principal payment multiplied by the profit ratio. The profit ratio is calculated as follows:

Profit Ratio = Gross Profit ÷ Contract Price

The *gross profit* is the sale price minus the selling costs and adjusted basis.

Sale price	$1.5 million
Minus costs	$50,000
Minus adjusted basis	$700,000
Gross profit	$750,000

The *contract price* is the sale price minus the current loan balance.

Sale price	$1.5 million
Minus loan balance	$500,000
Contract price	$1 million

Therefore, in this example, you figure the profit ratio as follows:

Profit Ratio = Gross Profit ÷ Contract Price

Profit Ratio = $750,000 ÷ $1 million

Profit Ratio = 75 percent

With the profit ratio, you can compute the gain that must be reported each year.

Year of sale: $250,000 × 75% = $187,500
Year two: $250,000 × 75% = $187,500
Year three: $250,000 × 75% = $187,500
Year four: $250,000 × 75% = $187,500

Thus, the seller reports $187,500 as the gain in the year of sale, plus $187,500 for each of the next three years. The seller reports the interest paid by the buyer to the seller on the deferred principal payments as ordinary interest income.

If this example were an outright sale, the seller would report the entire $750,000 gain in the year of sale, but the installment sale allows her to report the gain as the principal payments of $187,500 are received each year for four consecutive years. There's no difference in the total gain, simply the timing of the reporting of the gain.

Although there are many proponents of the buying-and-flipping real estate investment strategy, they often overlook the fact that flipping properties for a quick profit can have significant and expensive tax implications. If the IRS sees that you routinely buy and flip properties, it classifies you as a *dealer* — a taxpayer who buys property (called *inventory* in this case) with the intention of selling it in the short run — as opposed to an *investor,* a person who purchases properties seeking appreciation and income from long-term ownership. It's possible for real estate investors to simultaneously hold some properties for long-term investment and other properties the IRS classifies as inventory, making the owner a dealer. The dealer label comes with two drawbacks:

- ✔ Dealers aren't allowed to use the installment sales method to spread the recognition of their gain over multiple tax years. The entire profit must be reported and fully taxed in the year of the property sale.

- ✔ Profit from the sale of a property is considered earned income and is taxed as ordinary income at your personal income tax rate — even if you hold the property for longer than 12 months. (If you hold a property for longer than 12 months, it's typically eligible for the long-term capital gains tax rate, and a dealer would thus lose this benefit.)

Transferring equity to defer taxes

The concept behind a *tax-deferred exchange* is that an investor can transfer the built-up equity in one property to a new property and maintain, essentially, the same investment except that the physical asset is different. The IRS considers a qualified tax-deferred exchange to be one continuous investment and thus no tax is due on the profit from the sale of the relinquished asset as long as the investor invests all proceeds into the replacement property.

Tax-deferred exchanges are often referred to as *1031 exchanges* — the name comes from Section 1031 of the IRS Code that covers them. And there are actually three different types of tax-deferred exchanges:

- ✔ A straight exchange in which two parties trade properties of approximate or equal value.

- ✔ A three-party or multiparty exchange, which involves three or more parties buying, selling, or exchanging properties. This situation happens when one party in an exchange doesn't want a property owned by the other party but prefers the property currently owned by a third party. These transactions can actually involve any number of owners and can be quite complex. They should only be done with the ongoing advice and consultation of an experienced tax professional.

- ✔ A *delayed exchange* — sometimes also referred to as a *Starker exchange* — which allows the sale of the relinquished property and the purchase of the replacement property to occur at different times as long as strict rules are followed. This exchange is by far the most used 1031 exchange. (*Reverse Starker exchanges* can also be completed when an accommodator, on behalf of the taxpayer, acquires a replacement property first and then sells the relinquished property at a later date.)

The capital gains tax is deferred, not eliminated. If you sell your property during your lifetime and don't qualify for a tax-deferred exchange, you pay tax on both the capital gain and the recapture of the total depreciation taken since the original investment.

Meeting your goals

A tax-deferred exchange is an important tool if you're looking to increase the size of your real estate holdings. Tax-deferred exchanges can be effective tools to postpone the recognition of a gain on real estate investments. They allow the investor to transfer equity to a larger property without paying taxes. Plus, there's no limit to how often or how many times that a taxpayer can use an exchange. Therefore, you can keep exchanging upward in value, adding to your assets over your lifetime without ever having to pay any capital gains tax.

The tax-deferred exchange is particularly useful for real estate investors who specialize in buying and renovating properties and want to reinvest their profits into a larger property rather than sell the property and run the risk of being classified by the IRS as a dealer. A tax-deferred exchange can also help you achieve other goals such as

✔ Trading for a property in a better location.

✔ Acquiring a property with better cash flow.

✔ Making better use of the significant equity that can exist in properties held for many years. Plus, those properties have typically exhausted their depreciable basis, and an exchange can enhance that.

Following the rules

As with any transaction that involves those three letters — IRS — you must play by the rules for the 1031 exchange:

✔ **The relinquished property and the replacement property must both be investment real estate properties located in the United States.** Actually, the majority of all tax-deferred exchanges involve properties domestically, but the IRS does allow a tax-deferred exchange of a foreign property for another foreign property. The key is that both properties must be domestic or foreign — no mixing and matching is allowed!

✔ **You must trade only like kind real estate.** *Like kind real estate* means property held for business, trade, or investment purposes. The broad definition of *like kind* doesn't mean *same kind*. It allows real estate investors to use a 1031 exchange, for example, to defer taxes when they sell an apartment building and buy raw land, or vice versa; exchange a single-family rental home for a small office building; and so on. But neither your personal primary residence nor property held as inventory where the investor is defined as a dealer (see the "Selling now, reaping profits later: Installment sale" section earlier in the chapter) qualifies.

✔ **An exchange must be equal to or greater in both value and equity.** Any cash or debt relief received is considered to be *boot* (any receipt of money, property, or reduction in liability owed) and is taxable. For example, if you want to complete a tax-deferred exchange and the property you relinquish is valued at $1 million with a loan balance of $500,000, you must purchase the replacement property for more than $1 million, and its equity has to be equal to or greater than $500,000.

✔ **A neutral third party should be involved:** This neutral third party, called a *facilitator, exchanger,* or *accommodator,* should be appointed prior to the closing of any escrow. An exchange agreement must be signed, and the neutral third party must hold the proceeds unless the properties close simultaneously.

✔ **The potential replacement property must be clearly and unambiguously identified in writing within 45 days from the close of the relinquished property.** The IRS has limitations on how many replacement properties may be designated, or taxpayers would simply identify a long list of potential replacement properties. There are three specific tests to meet this requirement; they can get quite technical, but the most-commonly used is the *three property rule*. Under this rule, you can designate a maximum of three replacement properties of any fair market value, and you must purchase one or more of those properties.

✔ **The closing of the replacement property must occur within 180 days of the close of the relinquished property.** Meeting this requirement isn't as easy as it may sound, as we detail in the next section.

Refer to www.dummies.com/extras/realestateinvesting for information about not using commingled 1031 accounts.

Counting (and countering) complications and risks

The tax-deferred exchange has some complications and risks. Our experience is that the identification of the replacement property within 45 days can be a real challenge, especially because only a limited number (usually three) of properties can be identified. In a tight or competitive real estate market, the real estate investor can quickly find himself unable to actually complete the purchase of the replacement property within the 180-day limit, in which case the sale becomes a taxable event.

Real estate owners looking for a replacement property (commonly called an *upleg*) are often tempted to chase a property and overpay. They rationalize that the capital gains deferral is so valuable that they can justify overpaying for the property because they'd otherwise have to pay taxes of the recognized gain. But such investors should realize that this isn't a tax-*free* exchange, only a deferral of a gain that may be taxable in the future.

In 2000, the IRS issued new guidelines that clarify the proper use of the *reverse 1031 exchange*. A reverse 1031 exchange can be complicated and should only be done with the guidance of an experienced tax advisor. Essentially, it allows real estate investors to have an accommodator purchase and hold their new investment properties while they then follow the 1031 guidelines to sell the relinquished property. The advantage is that the real estate investor is sure to have the replacement property in hand; one of the major challenges to a 1031 exchange is the risk involved in having to identify the replacement property within 45 days and complete the acquisition within the 180-day limitation. You should have a written exchange agreement, and title to the replacement property must be taken in the name of the accommodator until your relinquished property is sold.

Calculating the substituted basis

The calculation of the basis of the new property can be quite complicated if anything other than the property is exchanged. In an exchange, the tax is deferred and the potential gain is carried forward by calculating the substitute basis for the new replacement property. An example of a substitute basis calculation without any boot is shown in Table 18-6. This substitute basis would be used in the event you sell the property during your lifetime without doing a tax-deferred exchange and have a taxable transaction. See your tax specialist to deal with any additional variables in the transaction.

Table 18-6	Substituted Basis Calculation in an Exchange
Value of property exchanged	$1,500,000
Minus basis of property exchanged	700,000
Gain on property exchanged	$800,000
Value of property acquired	$3,000,000
Minus gain on property exchanged	$800,000
Substituted basis on property acquired	**$2,200,000**

Using the capital gains exclusion to earn a tax-free gain

Another great tax benefit available for homeowners and real estate investors alike is the capital gains exclusion under Internal Revenue Code 121. Many investors have found that the principal residence capital gains exclusion can be the core of a profitable (and tax-free) investment strategy known as *serial home selling.* (For more information on this topic, see Chapter 2.) Simply buy and move into a property that can be renovated and sell it after a minimum of two years, and you can earn a tax-free gain of up to $500,000.

The gain on the sale of a principal residence is tax free up to $250,000 for individual taxpayers and up to $500,000 for married taxpayers who file jointly if they meet some simple requirements:

- ✔ You must own and have occupied or used the home as your principal residence for a total of 730 days (24 months) in the last 60 months — ending on the date of sale or exchange. The occupancy doesn't have to be continuous, and the home doesn't need to be your principal residence at the time of the sale or exchange. Only one spouse needs to legally hold title, but both must meet the use test.

The factors considered by the IRS to determine whether a property meets the principal residence use test include

- Is the residence used as the address of record for driver's license, tax returns, utilities, credit card bills and other billed items, and employment purposes?

- Is this residence where you actually reside and where you keep your furniture, furnishings, and clothes?

✔ Generally, the seller can only use the exclusion once every two years. Vacations and short absences count as usage for the two-year use test.

The IRS provides partial principal residence exemptions for sellers who don't qualify for the full exemption. The partial exemption is based on the number of actual months the seller qualified divided by 24 months. A partial exemption is allowed for

✔ **Work reasons:** For instance, a change in employment where the home seller's new job location is at least 50 miles farther away from the old principal residence than the former job location.

✔ **Health reasons:** For instance, the need to move to care for a family member or a broad range of health-related reasons. Consult with your tax advisor, because you can meet this requirement in many ways — particularly if a physician recommended the move.

✔ **Unforeseen circumstances:** Examples run the gamut and include a divorce or legal separation, engagement break-up, death, incarceration, multiple births, large increase in assessment dues, lost job or demotion, becoming ineligible for unemployment compensation, and so on. Many circumstances can qualify as unforeseen circumstances, so see your tax advisor for more information about your specific situation.

The taxation of real estate is complicated and constantly changing, so we have just covered the tip of the proverbial iceberg here. If you want in-depth details and advanced real estate tax strategies, we strongly recommend Vernon Hoven's *The Real Estate Investor's Tax Guide* (Dearborn Financial Publishing). Vern has a master's degree in taxation and teaches accounting and tax professionals all the new laws at his popular seminars (www.hoven.com). This excellent book has more than 400 pages dedicated to explaining all the ins and outs of real estate taxation with many examples that bring the material down to an understandable level.

Selling as a lease-to-own purchase

The typical *lease option* combines a standard lease with a separate contract giving the tenant a unilateral option to purchase the rental property during a limited period of time for a mutually agreed upon purchase price. The tenant isn't required to exercise the option. (For more on lease options, see Chapter 3.)

Investors can use the lease option to increase cash flow and also sell their properties without paying the usual brokerage commissions. A lease option is really a real estate rental transaction combined with a potential sales transaction and financing technique. The seller can generate additional cash flow because a lease option generally consists of a monthly rental payment that's higher than the market rent, with a portion of the additional payment being applied to the option purchase price. Both parties can realize a savings on the brokerage commission because the transaction is usually completed without the full services of real estate brokers. But it's a good idea to have either an experienced broker or real estate attorney review the transaction documents, which is a minor (but worthwhile) expense.

Working through an example

Each lease option is unique, but here's an example of how a deal may be structured: An investor owns a rental home with a current market rent of $1,000 per month and a current market value of $120,000. Real estate forecasts indicate that appreciation will be 4 percent, or approximately $5,000, in the next 12 months.

The tenant signs a 12-month standard lease and agrees to pay $1,200 per month with $1,000 in rent and $200 as a nonrefundable option fee that applies to the down payment. The investor and tenant also enter into an option-to-purchase agreement that offers the tenant the right to buy the property within 12 months of the lease for $125,000 (the agreed upon estimated fair market value of the property by the end of the option period).

The investor receives an additional cash flow of $200 per month. If the tenant exercises the option, the tenant receives a credit toward the down payment of $200 per month for each month that he paid the option fee. If the investor has used her standard lease form and the lease option documents are drafted properly, she still has the right to evict the tenant for nonpayment of rent or any other material lease default.

In most cases, tenants don't exercise the purchase option because they haven't accumulated the money required for the down payment and their share of the closing costs. In the meantime, you've increased your monthly rental income by $200 and had a good tenant. At the end of the option, the tenant is aware that he has paid an additional $2,400 in rent that would've been applied to the down payment or purchase price if he'd exercised his option. You can either renegotiate an extension of the purchase option with the tenant or you can negotiate a new lease without the purchase option.

Proceeding with caution

Avoid long-term lease options. Real estate appreciation can be unpredictable. Don't provide a set option purchase price for any longer than one or two years, or include a clause that the purchase price will increase by an amount equal to the increase in the average median home price in your local area.

If you're interested in using a lease option, have a real estate attorney with extensive experience in lease options review the lease and option contract in advance. Lease options can have serious business and even ethical problems if not properly drafted. If poorly structured, your lease option may be considered a sale with the following negative consequences:

- ✔ A lease option may trigger the due-on-sale clause with your lender, who may force you to pay off the entire outstanding loan balance.

- ✔ If the property is deemed a sale by the IRS, you can no longer use your tax benefits of depreciation and deductible expenses.

- ✔ Your property may be reassessed for property taxes. In many parts of the country, reassessment is based on a change in ownership. An aggressive tax assessor can use the lease option to increase the assessed value. Investigate local reassessment policies in advance.

- ✔ You may be liable for failure to comply with seller disclosure laws. There are severe penalties if you don't make the legally required disclosures, including those found on the transfer disclosure statement (TDS) discussed in Chapter 14.

- ✔ You may not be able to evict the tenant even if he defaults on the lease. The courts may consider that the tenant is really a buyer and that a traditional eviction action doesn't apply because the lease option is essentially a contract to purchase real estate. This situation may require expensive and lengthy court proceedings.

Ethically, keep the nonrefundable option fee reasonable, so if the value of the property declines or your tenant doesn't exercise her option for any reason, you can feel comfortable that the tenant has been treated fairly. Or you may want to renegotiate or consider offering an extension.

Transferring your property through a gift or bequest

A property given as a gift carries the same tax basis from the seller to the new owner. For example, if the tax basis of the property is $100,000, even though the fair market value at the time of the gift is $500,000, the recipient's tax basis remains $100,000. If the recipient were to immediately sell the property, he would have a taxable gain of $400,000. Thus, gifting property to heirs during your lifetime may not be the best strategy.

But death provides a tax-free transfer of real estate. Some investors are determined to avoid paying tax completely and have adopted a strategy of buy and hold for life. They use the tax-deferred exchange for years to rollover their gains into larger and larger properties and then completely avoid paying tax by never selling. Real estate transferred to your heirs upon death receives a full step up in basis. So in the example above, the party inheriting the real estate with a fair market value of $500,000 now has a tax basis of $500,000 and will only owe taxes on any future gain. So, if you want to make your real estate wealth creation strategy span multiple generations, consider taking advantage of these tax benefits!

Part V
The Part of Tens

Go to www.dummies.com/extras/realestateinvesting for a list of ten misperceptions that real estate investors often have and what you can do to avoid making these mistakes.

In this part ...

- ✔ Enhance the value of your property with proven ways, such as raising the rent, reducing turnover, and cutting back on operating expenses.

- ✔ Understand how refinancing any rental property that you have to a lower interest rate can help build equity more rapidly.

- ✔ Consider purchasing real estate property that falls in the fixer-upper category and buy it at the best price possible to build your wealth.

- ✔ Renovate the fixer-uppers that you purchase the right way by focusing on renovations or upgrades that increase the desirability of the property to your target market.

Chapter 19

Ten Ways to Increase a Property's Value

As we cover in Chapter 12, you can receive a return on your real estate investments basically in four ways — cash flow, *equity* build-up from loan paydown, tax benefits, and property appreciation. A great aspect of real estate is that you can buy properties according to your particular financial and personal needs. Different properties are geared more toward achieving one of these types of return than another. For example, an investor with significant earned income may focus on properties with tax benefits and not worry as much about cash flow. Investors nearing retirement prefer properties with cash flow. And all investors who have financed their rental property acquisition benefit from equity build-up while looking forward to appreciation.

Successful real estate investors continually ask themselves, "How can I improve the returns on my real estate investment in each category?" In this chapter, we highlight more than ten of the best ways that you can enhance your return on investment with rental properties.

Raise Rents

Although most rental properties have other sources of income, the largest source is almost always the rents. Real estate investors wisely begin with an understanding that rent increases lead to greater cash flow.

However, setting the proper rent and maintaining the optimum market level rents upon turnover of tenants is one of the most common challenges faced by property owners. Many rental property owners are reluctant to raise rents because they're concerned that their good tenants may leave. This is a valid concern, but it shouldn't prevent you from getting rents to market level — one of the fastest and simplest ways to improve your cash flow. Of course, you should always look for cost-effective ways to improve the property and make sure that your rents are competitive and a fair value.

We recommend raising the rental rate modestly each year rather than waiting for two or three years and then hitting your tenants with a major increase all at once. Tenants are less likely to move as a result of this consistent and predictable, but lower increase strategy; they understand that the costs of operation are rising slightly each year. Most commercial leases contain annual rent adjustments tied to a consumer price index or set rental rate increases. Use this effective strategy for all types of rental property.

If your rents are already at market levels, look to make upgrades to the property to justify higher rents. Maybe adding a combination microwave/exhaust vent unit above the stove, providing storage lockers, or installing a deck or awning can provide an improvement that justifies higher rent. Any improvements that enhance the quality of living or bring the property to a level similar to higher priced properties in the area can lead to increased market rents.

Reduce Turnover

The single most important factor in determining the expenses of most rental properties is turnover. In both residential and commercial properties, tenant turnover is simply bad for the bottom line. A tenant moving out almost certainly means a loss in rental income, plus you're hit with the increased expenses (marketing, tenant screening, maintenance and repairs, and often capital improvements) to make the rental unit or suite available to show prospective tenants. Signing long-term leases with qualified tenants, continually maintaining the property in top condition, and being responsive to the tenants can help reduce tenant turnover, which directly improves the Net Operating Income and cash flow. Doing so also increases the value of your building, which is your goal if you refinance, decide to sell, or use the 1031 tax-deferred exchange to upgrade your investment to a larger income property.

Another effective tool to reduce the loss of rent during tenant turnover is to prelease the rental unit or tenant suite. If you can prelease the rental to a new tenant only a few days or weeks after the current tenant vacates, you dramatically reduce your lost rent and increase your cash flow. After you receive a tenant's notice to vacate, immediately seek permission to enter and determine what you need to do to make the property ready for the next tenant. Also begin advertising for a new tenant and gain the cooperation of the departing tenant to show the property. Preleasing is one of the simplest ways to increase your net income, but it requires some planning and a cooperative departing tenant that you should have if you have been a diligent and conscientious landlord and have been responsive to your tenant's needs.

Consider Lease Options

A *lease option* is an agreement that allows the tenant the right to purchase the leased property at a predetermined price for a certain period of time. Sellers typically use lease options in slow real estate markets to create additional interest in the property — even a potential buyer currently without a down payment has the opportunity to eventually become a homeowner.

There are many other benefits to the rental property owner willing to offer a lease with an option to purchase the property. You can often sell the property for a value above the current market, and the lease option usually requires a one-time option fee that you can keep if the buyer doesn't exercise the option. Also, the renter/buyer typically pays a higher monthly rental payment with a lease option because a portion of the payment is applied to the ultimate purchase price. The higher monthly payments can be beneficial to you if the cash flows for the property are currently negative. Check out Chapter 3 for more on lease options.

Develop a Market Niche

Rental properties catering to seniors have always been popular, and the demographics clearly support continued attention to this dynamically growing market niche. Some senior properties are targeting those in need of special care and food services, and that is difficult for many landlords. But there is a growing need for properties with activities and social programs that appeal to active seniors and don't require specialized skills or significant capital investments.

Robert has had success in Las Vegas (of all places!) with smoke-free apartments. After a long day at work in a smoke-filled environment, a health-conscious nonsmoking resident doesn't need to have smoke wafting into her rental unit from her neighbor's. Although there are additional costs upfront in thoroughly cleaning, completely repainting, and installing all new flooring and window coverings, the demand (and thus the occupancy) for these units is high. This trend is catching on, and some states are even contemplating laws that require landlords to offer smoke-free housing, so you may as well be ahead of the trend. You may even qualify for lower casualty and fire insurance rates.

According to a study by the National Multi Housing Council (NMHC), student housing is also a great opportunity, with Generation Y (those born between 1982 and 2001) coming of age and going to college in record numbers. Some real estate investors find the market ripe for renovating rental units; college students nowadays would rather have a private rental unit with their own bathroom facilities and a high-speed Internet connection than a traditional dorm. Figuring out how to handle the seasonality of student rentals can be a challenge, but this market will continue to offer more opportunities.

Maintain and Renovate

The curb appeal or first impression that your property gives is critical to your overall success. Far and away the easiest way to increase cash flow and value is to simply clean up and address the deferred maintenance found in most properties. One of the fundamental rules of real estate is basic supply and demand. If your property really stands out and looks much better than comparable properties, you generate high demand; your rental will stay occupied at top market rents. That's what cash flow is all about.

Besides curing the simple deferred maintenance, another great way to increase cash flow (and value) is to renovate the property. The key here is to spend money only on items that enhance the property and provide a quick payback. Examples include submetering utilities, upgrading appliances, or adding new features that tenants desire.

For residential rentals, the best return on investment inside the units is found in updating the baths and kitchens. Adding systems to limit access of non-residents for parking and building entry can also be a positive enhancement in urban areas, because crime is a concern for many tenants. For commercial properties, upgrading dated interior common areas, including elevators and restrooms with higher-quality materials and fixtures generally offers the greatest return.

One of the most cost-effective ways to increase the aesthetics and curb appeal of any type of property is through landscaping improvements. Often you can simply replace declining or dead plantings. If you want to do more, have your landscaping maintenance firm make suggestions or contact a landscape architect. With water becoming more expensive every day, be sure to look into the installation of an automated, water-conserving, drip irrigation system, or even recycled water if it's available in your area. Robert has recently installed the first and only recycled water landscape irrigation system for a residential property in California and has been enjoying tremendous savings over the ever-increasing cost of potable water.

Cut Back Operating Expenses

One of the first steps to take after you purchase a rental property is to evaluate current operating expenses. See whether there's room for improvement, particularly without negatively impacting your tenants.

Asking the local utility companies to perform an energy audit can pinpoint ways for you to reduce expenses. New technology is making the use of LED lighting, solar energy, and hydronics heating systems extremely attractive. The rapidly increasing costs for water and sewer services in many areas of the country have made the installation of individual submeters cost effective for allocating and recouping the cost from each tenant based on her actual usage. Separate water meters for landscape areas only will eliminate your sewer charges if your local water utility offers them. The best way to achieve conservation of resources at your properties is to make your tenants directly responsible for their resource usage. This lets the tenants control their own costs and saves you money.

For larger residential and commercial properties, ask each of the current contractors and service providers to present a proposal or bid. Find other comparable firms and ultimately give your business to those firms that are insured and offer the most for your dollar. As your real estate empire grows, you'll know who are the best value providers, and you may find that contractors and service providers offer discounts based on volume.

Another great way to reduce your operating costs without any reduction in types and extent of coverage and policy limits is to combine your various rental properties under one insurance policy. Contact your insurance broker for details.

Scrutinize Property Tax Assessments

A review of the expenses for most rental properties indicates that the property tax expense is often one of the largest costs in owning real estate. In many parts of the country, property taxes are tied to the value of the real estate. If that's true for your area and real estate values decline, contact your local assessor and inquire about getting a reassessment. A lower assessment leads to a direct reduction in your property tax bill and a corresponding increase in your cash flow.

You may feel helpless against the bureaucracy, but remember that tax assessors have been known to make clerical errors or to fail to take all factors into account when valuing rental property. Some assessors don't carefully determine the proper value of your property but seek to assess the property at the highest possible level that won't trigger a request for reassessment. If there are no limitations, they may even raise the assessed value each year until you react. After all, the higher your property's assessed value, the higher your property taxes and the more money for local governmental spending. Remember no one is going to look out for your best interests but you.

If you feel that your assessment is too high, contact your assessor. She may be willing to make an adjustment if you back up your opinion with careful research and a good presentation. Or you may need to make a formal property tax protest. Protests are often first heard within the assessor's office or a local board of appeal. If a dispute continues, appeals may be taken to court in many states and that is when you're likely to want to retain a professional to present your case and support it with relevant data from the local market.

Refinance and Build Equity Quicker

Although you may have little control over interest rates and are at the mercy of your lender unless you have a fixed-rate loan, don't forget that refinancing to a lower rate can have a tremendous impact on your cash flow. Of course, going with an interest-only loan or a 40-year mortgage can also reduce your debt service payment and increase your cash flow, but these options are extremely risky and not advised.

You can enhance your equity build-up through refinancing to a shorter-term loan. When you first purchase a rental property, your rental income to make your mortgage payments is typically very tight, and you need to use financing with 20-year or even 30-year amortization terms. But after you've owned the property for several years, you may find that the cash flow has improved to the point that the property can handle a higher mortgage payment. That is when you refinance your long-term mortgage to a shorter-term mortgage, so that the amount of principal reduction paid with each payment dramatically increases.

Another way to achieve similar results is to arrange to make additional payments designated as principal reduction. This strategy can significantly reduce the total amount of interest paid over the remaining life of the loan and bring the loan payoff date much closer because the interest paid on the loan is a function of the outstanding principal balance. Robert routinely applies this strategy when refinancing properties that have improved fundamentals — increase in value and increased cash flow — so that he can go from a 20- or 30-year loan to a 15-year loan. If the interest rates have fallen, the monthly playment may not even have much of an increase.

Before refinancing or making additional principal payments, make sure that your loan doesn't have a prepayment penalty. Lenders count on a certain investment or financial rate of return on their money, and the early payoff of a loan results in additional costs, so they may include a penalty in the first few years of the loan. Also, some lenders waive prepayment penalties if they handle your refinance.

Take Advantage of Tax Benefits

The tax benefits received from real estate vary from investor to investor, but most rental property owners find tax benefits to be a boost to their return.

Even novice real estate investors can take advantage of the generous tax savings with the capital gains exclusion for their principal residences. This exclusion allows sellers to completely eliminate any income tax on their capital gain of up to $500,000 if they meet the simple requirements outlined in Chapter 18. For investors willing to live in the property during renovation, the serial homeselling investment strategy can be used every couple of years to produce tax-free profits.

Real estate investors in large residential and commercial properties routinely use a simultaneous or tax-deferred exchange (see Chapter 18), which allows them to keep their money working rather than paying taxes. The more money you have invested in real estate, the better your cash flow and your accumulation of wealth.

As we cover in Chapter 18, depreciation or cost recovery allows the owner to take a noncash deduction that reduces the taxable income from the property. Land isn't depreciable, so the amount of depreciation is determined by the value of the buildings. One way to maximize real estate's potential tax shelter is to be aggressive in allocating much of the acquisition cost of the property to the buildings to generate a larger deduction for depreciation.

Depreciation deductions are a noncash item, so they often result in a taxable loss even though the actual cash flow for the property is positive. Ask your CPA or tax advisor about *cost segregation* (determing separate and often accelerated depreciation schedules for various building components) to maximize your depreciation write-offs. Even if you can't immediately use a taxable loss to offset other earned income, you can use it in years that you have passive income such as a profitable taxable sale of another rental investment property.

Be Prepared to Move On

When most people think about real estate, they correctly determine that appreciation is where the real money is made. Over time, real estate has proven to be an investment that retains and increases in value. Even an average annual rate of appreciation of 5 percent dramatically increases your net worth over time.

However, appreciation can be heavily influenced by outside forces, such as the condition of the neighborhood and the local economy. That is why real estate investors need to perform a thorough due diligence review as discussed in Chapter 14. But even after you buy a property, you can't simply sit back and let the investment ride. If the neighborhood you're in starts to take a downward turn, be prepared to sell and reinvest in a more dynamic area that offers more upside potential.

Improve Management

Management is the one aspect of owning real estate that offers owners an advantage over other types of investments. You can't call the CEO of a large company and tell him to change his company's product or pricing, but superior management of your own rental properties can and will have a direct impact on your results.

The ability to control and immediately implement different management strategies can lead to more satisfied tenants and longer-term tenancies. Some owners are very hands-on with their properties, and others prefer to let a professional handle the day-to-day challenges, but a savvy investor knows that the best returns on investment go to owners that have top management.

Chapter 20

Ten Steps to Real Estate Investing Success

● ●

In This Chapter

▶ Reviewing the traditional approaches to real estate investing

▶ Understanding the get-rich-right strategy of real estate investing

● ●

*M*any real estate infomercial and seminar gurus make it sound really easy for anyone to make a fortune in real estate overnight. Buying foreclosures or properties with no money down can provide handsome returns, and there's no doubt that the acquisition of real estate below its intrinsic value enhances your chances of financial success.

This is simply the traditional sage advice (buy low, sell high) applied to real estate. And if you can do it routinely and without problems with title, devastating physical problems, or the negative tax consequences of being declared a dealer by the IRS, this strategy can be quite fruitful.

However, finding well-located, physically sound properties that are available at below-market prices isn't simple. Our experience is that most sellers know property values and don't simply give away their property. We often think that the old saying "You get what you pay for" was coined by a real estate investor who just bought a foreclosure only to find it has a large unrecorded tax lien, a large commercial tenant that filed bankruptcy and can void their lease, or a cracked slab.

In our experience, successful real estate investors tend to be savvy, hard working, conscientious individuals who enthusiastically perform comprehensive due diligence before buying a property. They don't reinvent the wheel with each deal, because they know their market niche, personal skills, and available resources. They have a vision and use their tried-and-true game plan for each property. If you develop these talents, you can uncover unique properties with value-added potential that are often missed by your competitors.

Robert refers to this method of real estate investing as the "Get-Rich-Right" strategy. The best news of all for new real estate investors is that this plan can be undertaken anywhere and initially can be done part-time. In this chapter, we give you ten methods to achieve a real estate fortune by using the "Get-Rich-Right" method.

Build up Savings and Clean up Credit

We disagree with some who imply that you can begin your real estate investment career without any cash. Our experience is that the best opportunities and the most options are available to the real estate investors who have both cash and good credit. So don't procrastinate — begin working on this step right now.

Sellers aren't likely to provide financing to a buyer with a poor credit history; because the purchase of real estate virtually always necessitates the borrowing of funds, make sure that your credit report is as accurate and as favorable as possible. Your credit score is a key element not only in qualifying for real estate loans, but also in getting the best terms to maximize your use of borrowed capital.

Get a copy of your credit report and correct any errors — pronto! At the very least, ask the credit-reporting firm to place a letter in your file with your version of any disputes. If legitimate delinquent balances appear, formulate payment plans and send the credit reporting firm updates showing the balance was paid or otherwise satisfactorily resolved.

The new real estate investor should also develop additional sources of income while holding or preferably even cutting current expenses; even if you can find properties where the seller provides all the financing, you can't escape certain out-of-pocket expenses or the opportunity cost of lost income as you expend your time and energy tracking down properties and performing the due diligence. We have yet to find a top-notch real estate inspector or escrow company that works for free.

Most people generate wealth and achieve a higher standard of living through sacrifice and living below their means in the short term or some even do so after they have substantial real estate cash flows. For ideas on how to track and reduce your expenses, pick up a copy of the latest edition of Eric's *Personal Finance For Dummies* (John Wiley & Sons, Inc.).

Buy Property in the Path of Progress

Locate properties that are in the *path of progress* — areas that will continue to improve through new investment and economic activity (see Chapter 10). You can't realistically physically relocate your property, so your analysis of the location and its future potential is critical. After you locate the best cities or neighborhoods, there are commonly two types of underachieving real estate assets to look for:

- Those income properties that are tired and worn and have extensive deferred maintenance
- Those that are physically sound but poorly managed

Your preference will depend on your specific talents and resources. Robert favors well-located, physically sound properties that simply have underperformed due to poor management. He's able to use his skills and expertise as a property manager to upgrade the properties, bring in new tenants, and increase the rents. Particularly attractive properties are those where the current owner or manager hasn't kept rents at the market level or that haven't been properly maintained cosmetically.

Buy the Right Property at the Best Price Possible

Always buy property for the best possible price. This strategy is simple and makes a lot of sense, but may be easier said than done. We suggest following certain guidelines. As a general rule, most of your real estate acquisitions should be in the fixer-upper category and priced accordingly. You want to buy those properties that offer specific challenges that match your personal talents so you can use your skills to upgrade and enhance the value of the property and increase the Net Operating Income over time.

A real estate investor using the "Get-Rich-Right" method doesn't buy a new or fully renovated property, unless it's in the path of progress or a prime location, because the value-added or appreciation to date has already been taken by the current owner. These properties may be solid investments, but you're limited to the market increases in rent and value only.

However, in some special situations, buying a new or fully renovated property *is* a good investment alternative. For example, buying a residential rental property in the first phase of an oceanfront community or another unique location that's difficult to replicate may be a great investment in the long run. The pricing in *first phases* of new developments is often very favorable because the developer must presell a certain number of the units before his permanent loan kicks in.

Two important characteristics of successful real estate investors are discipline and the ability to predetermine the maximum price they'll pay for a property to ensure plenty of room for appreciation potential. You don't want to simply lower your purchase price by the cost of the repairs, because the value you add to the property should be significantly higher than your out-of-pocket expenses including the time and risk you take in handling this work yourself. See Chapter 12 for advice on property valuation.

Renovate Property the Right Way

The "Get-Rich-Right" strategy depends on finding properties that are well located in the path of progress and then renovating them to increase cash flow and value. But don't overspend on physical improvements. You only want to make those renovations or upgrades that increase the desirability of the property to your target market. Your property is a rental unit, not your own home. You may want to put premium countertops and appliances in your home, but you can't get a good return on your investment if you overimprove your rental property. Pride of ownership is important, but you're running a business and overspending on one property will limit your ability to save up the next down payment and build your portfolio and achieve wealth.

Improvements should allow you to increase the rent or add to the property value so that you receive a return of $2 for every $1 spent on the improvements. The best fixer-upper properties for most novice real estate investors are those with simple fixes: Painting, landscaping, and minor repairs generally offer excellent results for only minor costs. These simple repairs are also within the skill set of most real estate investors, who may have developed and perfected their talents by maintaining and upgrading their own homes.

Although doing the work yourself is typically cheaper, don't forget to look at the time factor. It makes no sense to have a rental property off the market for three weeks while you spend evenings and weekends painting in a misguided attempt to save the $1,000 that a contractor would charge for painting that would take two days and allow you to rent it this weekend.

If you use contractors, get three comparable bids from licensed, competent professionals. However, if you already know you have a competitive bid, you can expedite the process by asking the contractor whether she can lower the price by 10 percent — then you don't have to go out and get additional bids. Of course, with your most commonly used contractors you can find that they'll know your routine and will overprice their bid by 10 percent or more. So with time you can establish a good understanding of what is a fair bid for all types of work that you routinely bid out.

Whether you do the work yourself or hire a contractor, make sure to obtain all required permits and meet the applicable building and occupancy codes for all improvements. The cost of the required permits and inspections will be yours, but make sure that your contract or agreement states clearly exactly who is responsible for obtaining the permits and arranging for all required inspections.

Keep Abreast of Market Rents

One of the biggest challenges for most rental property owners is determining the proper rent to charge tenants for newly renovated rental units. This aspect of property ownership and management simply requires some homework and research. Every property is unique, but your best indications of the market value of your renovated property can be found through a market survey of comparable properties.

After you've acquired and upgraded your new rental property, immediately test the new rental rate structure by offering your vacant rental units or space at the higher market rates you determined in your rental survey. The response you receive from prospects will let you know whether you're asking too much or whether you still have some room to give on your rents. After you install new tenants paying the higher rents, you can then make similar improvements for existing tenants and increase their rents to similar levels.

We recommend that you keep the rent level slightly below the full market rent for existing long-term tenants to show your appreciation for their long-term tenancy and to encourage them to stay. The cost of losing a tenant is high — a vacancy results in rent loss that you'll never get back, plus the added expense of advertising and preparing the rental property for the next tenant. For more on this topic, check out the latest edition of Robert's *Property Management Kit For Dummies* (John Wiley & Sons, Inc.).

Recover Renovation Dollars through Refinancing

One of the key elements of the "Get-Rich-Right" strategy is to keep your capital working and use leverage reasonably while maintaining sufficient equity to weather the ups and downs of real estate cycles and local economic challenges. Acquiring and renovating your rental property required cash, but you also have increased the income, which has created additional value. You can now use this increased value to refinance the property to cover your initial costs of acquisition and renovation.

Although we're always quick to advise against borrowing too much and over-leveraging your real estate investments, you also don't want to be too conservative and underestimate your cash needs. The cost of refinancing is such that you don't want to refinance the property more than once every several years, and if you suddenly need cash to overcome some unanticipated problems, the costs of short-term funds can be high. Borrow extra money or have an untapped line of credit available (which some lenders offer at no carrying cost to their best customers) to allow for reserves.

It can be extremely tempting in a strong real estate market to leverage over-aggressively, but don't get carried away. Don't borrow all of the equity in your own personal residence to go out and buy investment real estate. These individuals are really real estate speculators (people who gamble on real estate) and not to be confused with real estate investors.

You should always own your own home and have (and always maintain) a good cushion of equity before looking to acquire investment real estate. As has been evident in the late 2000s, the lessons of a falling real estate market are difficult for all investors but are totally devastating to those few investors who borrow too much against their own homes.

Remember that real estate markets have and will continue to have cycles, and you don't want to be too aggressive and find that your real estate empire collapses to the point that you yourself can't even afford to rent one of the apartments you used to own!

Reposition Property with Better Tenants

One of the best ways to increase the income and value of your newly renovated real estate investment is to reposition the property with new, more financially qualified tenants. So look to upgrade your tenants by marketing to a new target tenant profile and re-leasing the property.

Often your renovation efforts displace your current tenant anyway, but you probably don't want to renew the current tenants' leases even if you're able to work around them. The current tenants may be the reason that the previous owner sold the property (and that it's in need of a complete renovation)! Such tenants aren't likely to suddenly change their ways and will continue to use and abuse the property without any regard for your investment.

Robert advises not to renew the lease of an irresponsible tenant with a pet that destroyed the current flooring. You're better off bringing in a new tenant if you're going to have to invest in new carpeting in a rental unit. Likewise, you don't want to continue the tenancy of a tenant who won't be able to comfortably pay the higher rent that your fully renovated property is now worth.

This is often one of the toughest challenges for rental property owners — having to stand up to the current marginal tenant and not renew his lease. Although you may occasionally find that the current tenants are financially qualified and will treat the property as their own, the harsh reality is that most repositioned properties should start with a clean slate of tenants. At a minimum, require the current tenants to complete a rental application. Go over the lease renewal exactly as you would for a new tenant and use the same financial criteria.

Another way to improve the stability of your cash flow and minimize the chance of problems with your tenants is to increase the security deposit as long as you stay within the legal maximum. However, remember that market conditions usually restrict the amount you can charge for the security deposit. (Robert co-authored *Landlord's Legal Kit For Dummies* with Laurence Harmon [John Wiley & Sons, Inc.], which can help you with finding and retaining great tenants.)

Become or Hire a Superior Property Manager

Superior management makes the difference between average and excellent returns in the long run. After you renovate and reposition a property with new tenants at higher rents, you need to retain the tenants and minimize turnover. You can also further enhance net operating income by effectively and efficiently controlling expenses.

Even if you have just acquired your new rental property, you need to consistently work your long-term investment strategy by operating and managing the property effectively to achieve maximum value as if you were going to refinance or were preparing the property for sale.

Your target buyer is going to be someone that wants to buy a *turnkey property* (one that's operating optimally and doesn't require renovation or a change in tenants) for personal use or as a prime rental unit or *coupon clipping* investment (steady, highly predictable stream of income like bond investors receive). Real estate appraisers will determine a higher value for properties with a strong track record of solid Net Operating Income. Remember that to achieve maximum value, you need to have consistent income with rents at market rates, stable tenancy, and reasonable expenses. But don't go for lower expenses at the risk of decreasing curb appeal due to deferred maintenance.

Refinance or Sell and Defer Again

Notwithstanding the decline in property values in most areas in the late 2000s, many rental property owners find that they have a considerable amount of equity tied up in their property because of the appreciation that has occurred over the decades throughout much of the country. Having some equity in the property is good and keeps you from faltering should the local real estate economics take a hit, but too much equity just sitting in a property lowers your overall returns.

Our "Get-Rich-Right" strategy recommends that you use the equity in your current properties to expand your real estate holdings by investing in additional properties with a view toward diversifying to reduce your overall risk. You can access that equity to generate the cash you need in one of two ways: Either conservatively refinance your rental property or look to sell the real estate investment in a tax-deferred exchange.

The best option depends on market conditions. We suggest that you take advantage of favorable financing terms when available to refinance your stabilized long-term properties. You can use the proceeds to restock your capital account in order to invest in additional rental real estate or even make other investments. The best news of all is that you can pull the cash equity from your properties tax-free. Borrowing isn't dangerous if done in moderation.

Or you can sell the property and use the 1031 tax-deferred exchange to keep your equity working. Besides excess or *lazy* equity, some owners prefer the tax-deferred exchange option because they can enhance their use of depreciation to shelter their real estate income. A competent accountant or tax advisor can assist you in making the right choice between refinancing and a tax-deferred exchange. See Chapter 18 for more on tax-deferred exchanges.

Consolidate Holdings into Larger Properties

Fortunately, many real estate investors are able to master the concepts of buying and renovating rental real estate. However, they often become so successful that their real estate empire begins to control their lives.

Although owning a diversified portfolio of rental properties has some inherent advantages, the day will come when your extensive real estate holdings create management burdens. Most long-term real estate investors find that they reach the point where their management responsibilities and duties no longer conform to the lifestyle that they can afford. They often decide to simplify their lives and hire professional property managers so that a property manager can deal with the 4 Ts: tenants, turnover, toilets, and trash.

But finding and paying for a qualified property manager for a diversified portfolio of small rental properties isn't easy or cost-effective. Instead, look to the tax-deferred exchange and consolidate your real estate holdings into one or a handful of larger properties that can be professionally managed. You will still enjoy the benefits of real estate ownership without having to deal with the day-to-day challenges of management.

Index

• C •

• Q •

• R •

About the Authors

Eric Tyson, MBA, is a best-selling author and syndicated columnist. Through his counseling, writing, and teaching, he equips people to manage their personal finances better and successfully direct their investments. Eric is a former management consultant to Fortune 500 financial service firms and has successfully invested in real estate for more than two decades.

Eric earned his bachelor's degree in economics at Yale and an MBA at the Stanford Graduate School of Business. Despite these handicaps to clear thinking, he had the good sense to start his own company, which took an innovative approach to teaching people of all economic means about investing and money.

An accomplished freelance personal finance writer, Eric is the author of the national bestsellers *Personal Finance For Dummies* and *Investing For Dummies,* and coauthor of *Home Buying For Dummies* and was an award-winning columnist for the *San Francisco Examiner.* His work has been featured and quoted in hundreds of national and local publications, including *Newsweek,* the *Wall Street Journal, Forbes, Kiplinger's Personal Finance Magazine,* the *Los Angeles Times,* and *Bottom Line/Personal.* He also has appeared on FOX, NBC's *Today Show,* ABC, CNBC, PBS's *Nightly Business Report,* CNN, CBS national radio, Bloomberg Business Radio, and Business Radio Network. He's also been a featured speaker at a White House conference on retirement planning.

Despite his "wealth" of financial knowledge, Eric is one of the rest of us. He maintains a large inventory of bumblebee-colored computer books on his desk for those frequent times when his computer makes the (decreasing amount of) hair on his head fall out. He's online at www.erictyson.com.

Robert S. Griswold, MBA, MSBA, is a successful real estate investor and active, hands-on property manager with a large portfolio of residential and commercial rental properties who uses print and broadcast journalism to bring his many years of experience to his readers, listeners, and viewers.

He is the author of *Property Management For Dummies and Property Management Kit for Dummies,* and co-author of the *Landlord's Legal Kit For Dummies.* He has been the real estate expert for NBC San Diego, with a regular on-air live-caller segment since 1995. Robert was the host of a live weekly radio talk show, *Real Estate Today!,* for nearly 15 years, and was also the columnist for the syndicated "Rental Roundtable" and "Rental Forum" columns. These popular features have been published in dozens of major newspapers throughout the country, and Robert has been recognized twice as the No. 1 real estate broadcast journalist in the nation by the National Association of Real Estate Editors.

Robert's educational background includes having earned a bachelor's degree and two master's degrees in finance and business economics, real estate finance, international finance, real estate and urban land economics, and real estate development, all from the Marshall School of Business at the University of Southern California. His real estate investing and managing professional designations include the CRE® (Counselor of Real Estate), the CPM® (Certified Property Manager), ARM® (Accredited Residential Manager), the CCIM® (Certified Commercial Investment Member), the GRI® (Graduate, Realtor Institute®), the PCAM® (Professional Community Association Manager), and CCAM® (Certified Community Association Manager).

Robert has been retained on more than 2,000 legal matters as an expert in the standard of care and custom and practice for all aspects of real estate ownership, management, maintenance, and operations in both state and federal cases throughout the country. He's is the president of Griswold Real Estate Management, Inc., managing residential, commercial, retail, and industrial properties throughout Southern California and Nevada.

On a personal level, Robert enjoys travel (particularly cruises), sports, and family activities. He truly enjoys real estate and tries to keep life in perspective through humor!

Dedication

Eric: To my wife, Judy; my family — especially my parents, Charles and Paulina; my friends; and to my counseling clients and students of my courses for teaching me how to teach them about managing their finances.

Robert: First, I want to praise and thank God for the wonderful gifts and incredible opportunities He has given me. I dedicate this book to my four tremendous children — Sheri, Stephen, Kimberly, and Michael. My wife, Carol, deserves most of the credit for their good looks, incredible talents, and wonderful personalities. I am sure they get something from me too, maybe persistence and a great sense of humor! Oh, and humbleness! Naturally, I am eternally grateful to my parents, my father Wes (who passed away in 2008) and my mom Carol, for their unconditional love and infinite encouragement.

Authors' Acknowledgments

Writing a book from scratch is an enormous undertaking, and we couldn't have done it without some invaluable contributions from others. We'd like to thank Stacy Kennedy who kept us on track and added value to our chapters. We also appreciate the efforts of Chad Sievers, who did a masterful job as editor. And Mike Baker deserves special praise for believing in us and making this project happen.

We also would like to thank our technical reviewer Randall Bell, PhD, MBA, MAI, for his insightful review and comments.

Robert is indebted to Anna Leitzke for her countless hours of assistance in background research for our first edition.

Publisher's Acknowledgments

Acquisitions Editor: Stacy Kennedy
(Previous Edition: Mike Baker)
Project Editor: Chad R. Sievers
(Previous Edition: Kristin Demint)
Copy Editor: Chad R. Sievers
(Previous Edition: Megan Knoll)
Technical Editor: Randall Bell, PhD
Art Coordinator: Alicia B. South

Project Coordinator: Melissa Cossell
Cover Photos: ©iStock.com/Media Mates Oy

pple & Mac

ad For Dummies,
h Edition
78-1-118-72306-7

hone For Dummies,
h Edition
78-1-118-69083-3

acs All-in-One
or Dummies, 4th Edition
78-1-118-82210-4

S X Mavericks
or Dummies
78-1-118-69188-5

logging & Social Media

acebook For Dummies,
h Edition
78-1-118-63312-0

ocial Media Engagement
or Dummies
78-1-118-53019-1

VordPress For Dummies,
h Edition
78-1-118-79161-5

usiness

tock Investing
or Dummies, 4th Edition
78-1-118-37678-2

vesting For Dummies,
h Edition
78-0-470-90545-6

Personal Finance
For Dummies, 7th Edition
978-1-118-11785-9

QuickBooks 2014
For Dummies
978-1-118-72005-9

Small Business Marketing
Kit For Dummies,
3rd Edition
978-1-118-31183-7

Careers

Job Interviews
For Dummies, 4th Edition
978-1-118-11290-8

Job Searching with Social
Media For Dummies,
2nd Edition
978-1-118-67856-5

Personal Branding
For Dummies
978-1-118-11792-7

Resumes For Dummies,
6th Edition
978-0-470-87361-8

Starting an Etsy Business
For Dummies, 2nd Edition
978-1-118-59024-9

Diet & Nutrition

Belly Fat Diet For Dummies
978-1-118-34585-6

Mediterranean Diet
For Dummies
978-1-118-71525-3

Nutrition For Dummies,
5th Edition
978-0-470-93231-5

Digital Photography

Digital SLR Photography
All-in-One For Dummies,
2nd Edition
978-1-118-59082-9

Digital SLR Video &
Filmmaking For Dummies
978-1-118-36598-4

Photoshop Elements 12
For Dummies
978-1-118-72714-0

Gardening

Herb Gardening
For Dummies, 2nd Edition
978-0-470-61778-6

Gardening with Free-Range
Chickens For Dummies
978-1-118-54754-0

Health

Boosting Your Immunity
For Dummies
978-1-118-40200-9

Diabetes For Dummies,
4th Edition
978-1-118-29447-5

Living Paleo For Dummies
978-1-118-29405-5

Big Data

Big Data For Dummies
978-1-118-50422-2

Data Visualization
For Dummies
978-1-118-50289-1

Hadoop For Dummies
978-1-118-60755-8

Language &
Foreign Language

500 Spanish Verbs
For Dummies
978-1-118-02382-2

English Grammar
For Dummies, 2nd Edition
978-0-470-54664-2

French All-in-One
For Dummies
978-1-118-22815-9

German Essentials
For Dummies
978-1-118-18422-6

Italian For Dummies,
2nd Edition
978-1-118-00465-4

Available in print and e-book formats.

Available wherever books are sold. **For more information or to order direct visit www.dummies.com**

Math & Science

Algebra I For Dummies,
2nd Edition
978-0-470-55964-2

Anatomy and Physiology
For Dummies, 2nd Edition
978-0-470-92326-9

Astronomy For Dummies,
3rd Edition
978-1-118-37697-3

Biology For Dummies,
2nd Edition
978-0-470-59875-7

Chemistry For Dummies,
2nd Edition
978-1-118-00730-3

1001 Algebra II Practice
Problems For Dummies
978-1-118-44662-1

Microsoft Office

Excel 2013 For Dummies
978-1-118-51012-4

Office 2013 All-in-One
For Dummies
978-1-118-51636-2

PowerPoint 2013
For Dummies
978-1-118-50253-2

Word 2013 For Dummies
978-1-118-49123-2

Music

Blues Harmonica
For Dummies
978-1-118-25269-7

Guitar For Dummies,
3rd Edition
978-1-118-11554-1

iPod & iTunes
For Dummies, 10th Edition
978-1-118-50864-0

Programming

Beginning Programming
with C For Dummies
978-1-118-73763-7

Excel VBA Programming
For Dummies, 3rd Edition
978-1-118-49037-2

Java For Dummies,
6th Edition
978-1-118-40780-6

Religion & Inspiration

The Bible For Dummies
978-0-7645-5296-0

Buddhism For Dummies,
2nd Edition
978-1-118-02379-2

Catholicism For Dummies,
2nd Edition
978-1-118-07778-8

Self-Help & Relationships

Beating Sugar Addiction
For Dummies
978-1-118-54645-1

Meditation For Dummies,
3rd Edition
978-1-118-29144-3

Seniors

Laptops For Seniors
For Dummies, 3rd Edition
978-1-118-71105-7

Computers For Seniors
For Dummies, 3rd Edition
978-1-118-11553-4

iPad For Seniors
For Dummies, 6th Edition
978-1-118-72826-0

Social Security
For Dummies
978-1-118-20573-0

Smartphones & Tablets

Android Phones
For Dummies, 2nd Edition
978-1-118-72030-1

Nexus Tablets
For Dummies
978-1-118-77243-0

Samsung Galaxy S 4
For Dummies
978-1-118-64222-1

Samsung Galaxy Tabs
For Dummies
978-1-118-77294-2

Test Prep

ACT For Dummies,
5th Edition
978-1-118-01259-8

ASVAB For Dummies,
3rd Edition
978-0-470-63760-9

GRE For Dummies,
7th Edition
978-0-470-88921-3

Officer Candidate Tests
For Dummies
978-0-470-59876-4

Physician's Assistant Exam
For Dummies
978-1-118-11556-5

Series 7 Exam For Dummies
978-0-470-09932-2

Windows 8

Windows 8.1 All-in-One
For Dummies
978-1-118-82087-2

Windows 8.1 For Dummies
978-1-118-82121-3

Windows 8.1 For Dummies
Book + DVD Bundle
978-1-118-82107-7

Available in print and e-book formats.

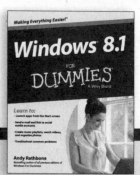

Available wherever books are sold. **For more information or to order direct visit www.dummies.com**